Blackstone in America
Selected Essays of Kathryn Preyer

D1594684

Blackstone in America explores the creative process of transplantation – the way in which American legislators and judges refashioned the English common-law inheritance to fit the republican political culture of the new nation. With current scholarship returning to focus on the transformation of Anglo-American law to "American" law, Professor Kathryn Preyer's lifelong study of the constitutional and legal culture of the early American republic has acquired new relevance and a wider audience.

All nine of Professor Preyer's important and award-winning essays are easily accessible in this volume, with new introductions by three leading scholars of early American law. The collection includes Preyer's work on criminal law, the early national judiciary, and the history of the book.

Mary Sarah Bilder is a professor of law at Boston College Law School and the Michael and Helen Lee Distinguished Scholar. She is the author of *The Transatlantic Constitution: Colonial Legal Culture and Empire*, which won the Littleton-Griswold Prize in American Law and Society, awarded by the American Historical Association. She also serves on the editorial boards of *Law and History Review, Journal of Legal Education*, and *New England Quarterly*.

Maeva Marcus is Director of the Institute for Constitutional Studies and a Research Professor of Law at George Washington University Law School. She is the author of *Truman and the Steel Seizure Case*; an editor of *The Documentary History of the Supreme Court of the United States, 1789–1800* (8 volumes); an editor of and contributor to *Origins of the Federal Judiciary: Essays on the Judiciary Act of 1789*; and a former member of the Permanent Committee for the Oliver Wendell Holmes Devise.

R. Kent Newmyer is a professor of law and history at the University of Connecticut School of Law and a Distinguished Alumni Professor Emeritus at the University of Connecticut. He is the author of *Justice Joseph Story: Statesman of the Old Republic* (1985), which won both the Littleton-Griswold Prize in American Law and Society, awarded by the American Historical Association, and the Silver Gavel Award, awarded by the American Bar Association. He is also the author of *John Marshall and the Heroic Age of the Supreme Court* (2001), which received the Francis Landry Award from Louisiana State University Press and an award from the State Library of Virginia for the best non-fiction book of the year.

Blackstone in America

Selected Essays of Kathryn Preyer

Edited by

MARY SARAH BILDER
Boston College Law School

MAEVA MARCUS
George Washington University Law School

R. KENT NEWMYER
University of Connecticut School of Law

CAMBRIDGE
UNIVERSITY PRESS

CAMBRIDGE
UNIVERSITY PRESS

32 Avenue of the Americas, New York NY 10013-2473, USA

Cambridge University Press is part of the University of Cambridge.

It furthers the University's mission by disseminating knowledge in the pursuit of
education, learning and research at the highest international levels of excellence.

www.cambridge.org
Information on this title: www.cambridge.org/9781107666627

First published 2009
First paperback edition 2014

A catalogue record for this publication is available from the British Library

Library of Congress Cataloguing in Publication data

Bilder, Mary Sarah.
Blackstone in America : selected essays of Kathryn Preyer / Mary Sarah Bilder,
Maeva Marcus, R. Kent Newmyer.
   p.   cm.
Includes bibliographical references and index.
ISBN 978-0-521-49087-0 (hardback)
1. Preyer, Kathryn (Kathryn Turner)   2. a Common law – United States – History.
3. Judicial review – United States – History.   4. Federal government –
United States – History.   5. Justice, Administration of – United States – History.
I. Marcus, Maeva, 1941–   II. Newmyer, R. Kent.   III. Title.
KF394.B455   2009
340.5'70973 – dc22   2008055957

ISBN 978-0-521-49087-0 Hardback
ISBN 978-1-107-66662-7 Paperback

Contents

Preface

Blackstone in America explores the creative process of transplantation – the way in which American legislators and judges refashioned the English common-law inheritance to fit the republican political culture of the new nation. With current scholarship returning to focus on the transformation of Anglo-American law to "American" law, Professor Kathryn Preyer's lifelong study of the constitutional and legal culture of the early American republic has acquired new relevance and a wider audience.

Professor Preyer's nine essays do justice to the complexity of the story of transformation. English law and legal institutions, imperfectly understood to start with, and themselves in transition, were refracted through colonial and state experience and then adjusted to the needs of the new nation, which itself was in the throes of radical transformation – from republicanism to democracy; from an agrarian economy to a commercial manufacturing economy; and already in the 1790s, from slavery to freedom. When these divergent forces and competing interests coalesced into political divisions, as they did in the 1790s, the stage was set for the creation of distinctively American legal institutions.

The political conflict over law and legal institutions focused on Constitutional interpretation and pitted those who championed nationalism (represented by the Washington and Adams Federalists) against a tenacious state and local legal culture (championed by the Democratic Republican party of Jefferson and Madison). In Kathryn Preyer's words, "The struggle to establish harmony between nationalism and localism, the whole and its parts, is the single greatest link between the past and present in this country's traditions."

"Harmony" was not established, however, as Preyer's scholarship makes clear. Rather, the competing parties, operating simultaneously at the state and national level, fashioned a legal institutional framework that struck an uneasy balance between nationalism and localism, between inherited ideas and creative improvisation. Traditional accounts of this period focus on the results; Preyer concentrates on the process itself – on the interplay of idealism and self-interest; the role of accident and contingency; and the indeterminacy of the final compromise. In short, Preyer's pioneering scholarship captures American legal institutions in the making.

During her lifetime, Preyer contemplated a collection of her essays, which she planned to entitle *Blackstone in America*. The essays, while conceptually of a single piece, were intended to be free-standing. The organization of this book follows her outline.

Part I deals primarily with developments at the national level, focusing on the Judiciary Acts of 1789 and 1801, and on the conflict between state and federal authority (the subject of her essay on the Callender trial). These essays draw on Preyer's important Ph.D. dissertation, "The Judiciary Act of 1801," completed in 1959 at the University of Wisconsin under the direction of Merrill Jensen and Merle Curti.

The subject of criminal law, broached in the Callender essay, is the main theme of Part II. Preyer's essay, "Crime, the Criminal Law and Reform in Post-Revolutionary Virginia," on this subject won the Surrency Prize awarded by the American Society for Legal History.

Criminal law is also the focus of the essays in Part III, dealing with the trans-Atlantic exchange of ideas between American and continental reformers.

In all of these essays, Kathryn Preyer's deep learning is manifest, as is her distinctive voice. The collection includes Preyer's major essays. She also wrote numerous book reviews (most of which are now available electronically) that reveal her extensive knowledge and critical insight. Her early work to the mid-1960s appears under the names Kathryn Conway Turner or Kathryn Turner. Minor changes have been made to the essays for clarity and grammatical correctness. In a few instances where minor errors have come to the editors' attention, they have been silently corrected.

The editors would like to thank the many friends of Kathryn Preyer who contributed to and participated in programs in her honor at the American Society for Legal History's Annual Meeting in November 2005 and at Wellesley College in September 2005. Thanks also to Professor

Christine Desan of Harvard Law School, who assembled much of Preyer's written scholarship, and John D. Gordan III. Senior Editor Lew Bateman of Cambridge University Press was enthusiastic about the collection from the outset, and the editors appreciate his efforts and those of the Press in publishing this volume. We gratefully acknowledge the administrative work of Emily Spangler at the Press. The editors also thank Ronald Cohen for his careful editing of the manuscript and his concern for the integrity of the original. Kathryn Preyer would have loved to have had him as her editor.

Above all, the editors are deeply grateful to Robert Preyer. His support and encouragement have been invaluable.

Editors' Note

In order to maintain the historical integrity of the original articles, we have retained Kathryn Preyer's style, citation format, and typing conventions throughout. The first three chapters were written under the name Kathryn Turner.

Acknowledgments

The editors of *Blackstone in America* thank the following for kindly granting them permission to use Kathryn Preyer's previously published essays in this collection:

Chapter 1. The Omohundro Institute of Early American History and Culture. "Federalist Policy and the Judiciary Act of 1801," *William and Mary Quarterly*, 3rd Series, XXII, 3–32 (January 1965). Copyright © 1965 *William and Mary Quarterly*. Used with permission.

Chapter 2. The Omohundro Institute of Early American History and Culture. "The Appointment of Chief Justice Marshall," *William and Mary Quarterly*, 3rd Series, XVII, 143–163 (April 1960). Copyright © 1960 *William and Mary Quarterly*. Used with permission.

Chapter 3. *The University of Pennsylvania Law Review*. "The Midnight Judges," *The University of Pennsylvania Law Review*, 109: 494–523 (February 1961). Copyright © 1961 *The University of Pennsylvania Law Review*. Used with permission.

Chapter 4. Oxford University Press, Inc. "*United States v. Callender*: Judge and Jury in a Republican Society," in *Origins of the Federal Judiciary: Essays on the Judiciary Act of 1789*, ed. Maeva Marcus (New York: Oxford University Press, 1992), 173–195. Copyright © 1992 Oxford University Press. Reprinted by permission of Oxford University Press.

Chapter 5. *American Journal of Legal History*. "Penal Measures in the American Colonies: An Overview," *American Journal of Legal History*,

XXVI, 326–353 (October 1982). Copyright © 1982 *American Journal of Legal History*. Used with permission.

Chapter 6. *Law and History Review*, University of Illinois Press, and the *American Society for Legal History*. "Crime, the Criminal Law, and Reform in Post-Revolutionary Virginia," *Law and History Review*, 1: 53–85 (Spring 1983). Copyright © 1983 American Society for Legal History. Used with permission.

Chapter 7. *Law and History Review*, University of Illinois Press, and the American Society for Legal History. "Jurisdiction to Punish: Federal Authority, Federalism, and the Common Law of Crimes in the Early Republic," *Law and History Review*, IV, 223–265 (Fall 1986). Copyright © 1986 American Society for Legal History. Used with permission.

Chapter 8. The Edward Mellen Press. "Cesare Beccaria and the Founding Fathers," in *The American Constitution: Symbol and Reality for Italy* (Lewiston, New York: The Edward Mellen Press, 1989). Copyright © 1989 Emiliana P. Noether. Used with permission.

Chapter 9. Professor Floriana Colao and Professor Luigi Berlanguer, University of Siena. "Two Enlightened Reformers of the Criminal Law: Thomas Jefferson of Virginia and Peter Leopold, Grand Duke of Tuscany," in "*La Leopoldina,*" *Criminalità e Giustizia Criminale Nelle Riforme del Settecento Europeo* (Milan, 1989) V: 657–687, eds. Luigi Berlinguer and Floriana Colao. Copyright © 1989 Floriana Colao and Luigi Berlanger. Used with permission.

Blackstone in America

Selected Essays of Kathryn Preyer

General Introduction

Stanley N. Katz

Kathryn Turner Preyer – Kitty to her friends – was one of the most admired legal historians of my generation, and surely the least well-known eminent scholar in the cohort. She was highly regarded by the legal history community not only for the series of stunningly original research essays she produced but because of her extraordinary capacity to befriend and nurture younger scholars in the field. But she never published a monograph, and historians tend to judge their peers by their books. This volume is our effort to put together the culminating volume she planned to write. The editors hope that this volume will introduce Preyer to the broad readership she deserved.

I was a latecomer to Preyer's specific academic field, early American legal history, having been trained as a colonial political historian. But it was my great good fortune to be selected as a Fellow of the Charles Warren Center at Harvard in its first year, and to meet Kitty Preyer, another Fellow. That was the year I was beginning to work in legal history, and Preyer took me under her wing. It is a wing I sheltered under for thirty-eight years. Only someone who worked with Preyer as a fellow scholar would know the distinctive way in which she brought the rest of us along. She was always patient, for of course she knew everything and we did not, but she was impatient when we made stupid mistakes. She let us know so in the bluntest of terms, and she knew how to ask the tough questions about what we were doing. She also expected us to engage ourselves in what she was doing, and she was not satisfied with simple-minded pieties – she wanted to know where we thought she had gone wrong. At the Warren Center, we talked about many things, and I have discussed a variety of topics (especially politics) with Kitty and Bob

Preyer over the years. But, above all, Preyer loved historical shop talk. She was a pro, and she taught me what it meant to be a pro.

After her death, Bob sent me the most up to date *curriculum vitae* he could find. She was not interested in self-promotion, so it is not surprising that the document dates from 1989. It is actually quite a lousy document of its type – her degrees (Goucher B.A. and Wisconsin Ph.D.) and teaching jobs (easy, since apart from a single year as an Instructor at Rockford College, she spent her entire career at Wellesley); five lines on various administrative assignments for the College over the years; four lines on fellowships; a page of major paper presentations; and two detailed pages of publications (none with a precise enough bibliographical reference that would have made it easy for a novice to find the article in the library!). As a professional, Preyer was concerned with teaching and scholarship.

What a fine and distinctive scholar she was. In Isaiah Berlin's terms, Preyer was a *hedgehog*. You will remember Berlin's definition:

There is a line among the fragments of the Greek poet Archilochus which says: 'The fox knows many things, but the hedgehog knows one big thing'.... For there exists a great chasm between those, on one side, who relate everything to a single central vision, one system less or more coherent or articulate, in terms of which they understand, think and feel – a single, universal, organizing principle in terms of which alone all that they are and say has significance – and, on the other side, those who pursue many ends...[1]

Preyer's "one big thing" was the role of law in the creation of the American republic, and especially the role of judges in articulating that law. Everything she wrote over her long and productive career addressed that problem, and of course the choice of that problem resulted from her "single central vision" – that the rule of law, supervised by a competent judiciary, is the key to the success of democratic society. Her related sub-theme concerned the democratization of the criminal law in a constitutional regime. She sometimes personified the problem by analyzing judicial appointments, especially in her fine article on the selection of John Marshall as Chief Justice of the Supreme Court (Chapter 2 of this volume).

Preyer was of course a historian, not a lawyer, though she spent a year (1962–63) as a Carnegie Fellow at the Harvard Law School, which became very much a home away from home for her. A student of Merrill Jensen and Merle Curti's at the University of Wisconsin, she was particularly influenced by Merrill's devotion to the rigorous analysis of source

---

[1] Sir Isaiah Berlin, *The Hedgehog and the Fox* (1953).

materials and by both his and Merle's profoundly progressive understanding of the origins of our national state. Her dissertation – a work of
scholarship that has never been replaced or surpassed in nearly fifty years –
was a study of the Judiciary Act of 1801, a piece of legislation that is still
one of the cornerstones of the federal judicial framework. In it, and in
her later work, she displayed a dual competence in history and law, one
of the first historically trained legal historians to do so. And, as she once
said about Morton Horwitz:

> Considerable effort has been made to make the history of technical areas of law
> understandable to the nonlegally trained scholar, and to treat the law as one of
> the dynamics of historical change, while retaining, as the center of gravity, the
> internal technical life of legal doctrine.[2]

Merle and Merrill taught Preyer that style was related to content, and
she never forgot. Hers was a style that I would call quietly magisterial –
Hemingway meets Oliver Wendell Holmes.

Preyer was a political historian of the law who understood fully that
law resides in a social and political system. Her earliest published essay,
on John Adams's appointment of the "midnight judges," shows how
skilled she was in contextualizing legal events:

> As a whole, the group of midnight judges reflected the relatively moderate political
> positions of the men who had selected them. They were not facsimiles of the
> fanaticism which had led the Federalists to prosecute the Whiskey Rebels and
> John Fries for treason and to enforce the Sedition Act with such vigor. One might
> have expected that some Republicans would even have sighed relief that Samuel
> Chase, Associate Justice of the Supreme Court, would ride the circuit no more![3]

Another of my favorite examples of Preyer's flair for context comes in
one of her brilliant articles on the emergence of a distinctively American
approach to criminal law. Consider these three Gibbonian sentences:

> Neither certainty nor proportionality characterized penal measures in the late
> eighteenth century to those who made the laws and administered them. At the
> same time as the European world, but particularly fuelled with the ideology
> of the beneficent potentialities of a newly independent American republic, some,
> although not all, former colonies joined other nations in the conviction that a more
> rational criminal code which made punishment certain but genuinely humane
> would not only increase enforcement of the law but could also reform the offender
> and in so doing actually reduce the number of criminal offenses. It was easy in

---

[2] Review of *The Transformation of American Law, 1780–1860, Journal of American History*, 1978, p. 1099.
[3] *Penn Law Review*, 1960-1, p. 522.

America to identify reason and humanity, the watchwords of the Enlightenment, with the successful republicanism of the new nation and to find in imprisonment the ideal embodiment of these new goals.[4]

Alas, Preyer's faithfulness to documentary evidence (a commitment she brought to her long advisory support of Maeva Marcus's *Documentary History of the Supreme Court of the United States* [Columbia University Press, 1986–2007]), and her reluctance to publish until she had her ideas and text "just right," meant that she put into print tragically little of the groundbreaking research that she had undertaken.

The deeper point is that Preyer's relatively modest publication record, in part the result of her dedication to her role as undergraduate liberal arts teacher, belies the huge influence she has had on our understanding of the primary role of law in American history. Reading over her list of publications, one realizes that she reviewed every significant book in early American legal history published since 1958 for one or another of the major scholarly journals. These reviews are a remarkable tribute to the breadth of her knowledge, the depth of her historical insight, and her uncanny ability to criticize without hurting. Would that the last quality were in greater supply.

Preyer was among the leading legal historians of the last half century. Her gem-like essays will always be monuments to her unique amalgam of intelligence, originality, breadth of vision, historical sensitivity, and deeply humane vision. That her scholarship on the early nineteenth century remains so germane to today's conflicts of law and politics is a testament to the enduring worth of what she wrote.

---

[4] "Penal Measures," *Journal of American History*, 1982, p. 353.

PART I

LAW AND POLITICS IN THE EARLY REPUBLIC

Introduction

Maeva Marcus

The four essays in this section – three of which are Kathryn Preyer's earliest publications – exemplify her engagement with what Stan Katz has called "Kitty's 'one big thing'... the role of law in the creation of the American republic, and especially the role of judges in articulating that law." The first three derive from Preyer's dissertation, "The Judiciary Act of 1801," and contain a thorough and perceptive examination of judicial affairs in the nation's first eleven years under the Constitution. The fourth, her last published article, deals with the trial of James Thompson Callender for seditious libel, but continues Preyer's lifelong search for the larger meaning of particular legal events for the nation's history. As she wrote, some scholars treat *United States v. Callender* "as a way station to a discussion of Justice Samuel Chase's impeachment. Yet some of the most important issues arising under the Judiciary Act of 1789 are to be discovered in the case: the relationship of federal and state authority, the relationship of judge to jury, the power of the judge at trial, the role of the jury, and the place of federal judicial authority."

A review of Preyer's dissertation and the four essays in this section reveals her unerring scholarly judgment and historical sense. Preyer's insights and intuitions, broached in a tentative voice when she does not have enough documentary evidence to support them, hold up well today. Her study of the Judiciary Act of 1801 demonstrates that the act was not a power grab by Federalists dismayed by their loss of the presidency and Congress. Rather, by starting with the Judiciary Act of 1789 – much praised but clearly deficient in several respects – she shows that members of the judicial and legislative branches had been intent on judicial reform well before the political troubles of the Federalists began. Looking not

7

only at the progress of legislation dealing with changes in the judicial system, but also at the political and economic history of the republic during its initial years, she concludes that what propelled the 1801 Act was a burgeoning desire "to extend the *scope* of federal *jurisdiction*" in order to support Federalist policies, joined with the need for a new organization of the third branch. The end of Federalist Party hegemony encouraged speedy consideration of the judiciary bill, she writes, but that bill had been bouncing around Congress long before the election of 1800, and the reforms contained in it were the product of years of trials and tribulations under the 1789 act. The purpose of the 1801 Act was inextricably linked to "the totality of major Federalist party policy."[1]

Preyer points out the error of looking at the history of the federal judiciary's first decade through the prism of the debates surrounding the Repeal Act of 1802 and the events leading to the *Marbury* decision, though she understands fully why historians tend to do this: no documentary record of sustained discussion about the judiciary existed before 1802. Her commonsense explanation for the fact that during the first five congresses, Congress had paid relatively little attention to the need for revisions in the federal judiciary is an obvious one: "In comparison to the domestic and foreign problems confronting Congress during the early years of the national history, the problems of the judiciary did not loom very large." Congressional records and newspapers of this period indicated that the federal judiciary rarely gained public attention. Other historians had noticed this and largely ignored the judiciary in their work. But Preyer did not make that mistake: the fact that the judiciary was considered relatively unimportant in the first decade did not mean that it actually *was* unimportant in building the new nation. Despite the lack of published court records, which would make research easier, Preyer delved into the events of the 1790s in order to point out the connections between economics, politics, and the judicial system that led to the passage of the Judiciary Act of 1801 and its subsequent repeal. As she noted at the end of her article on that Act: "At the center of the political maelstrom in 1801, the role of the federal judiciary had become one of the most concrete manifestations of the division between the proponents and opponents of the extension of federal power."

The conclusion of the final essay in this section, "*United States v. Callender*: Judge and Jury in a Republican Society," shows Preyer still

---

[1] Kathryn Conway Turner, "The Judiciary Act of 1801," Ph.D. dissertation, University of Wisconsin, 1959, pp. 309 and 302.

grappling with the large themes that occupied her entire scholarly life. Having demonstrated in the body of the essays how what happened at the trial logically flowed from a decade of conflict between the federal judiciary and the states, Preyer notes the absence by 1800 of any strong national institutions. She credits the Judiciary Act of 1789 with trying to deal with the complicated federal structure imposed by the Constitution, thus allowing an embryonic federal law and national legal culture to grow. The effort to define the relationship between nation and state that underlay many of the judiciary's problems is, in Preyer's words, "the single greatest link between past and present in this country's traditions." And it is what makes Preyer's scholarship important and relevant today.

I

Federalist Policy and the Judiciary Act of 1801

Kathryn Turner

In analyses of the Federalist decade, the organization of the government under the Constitution, fiscal and revenue programs, neutrality and foreign affairs, and the Alien and Sedition Acts all receive proper emphasis as identification marks of the Federalist party in power. Only passing reference, if that, is made to the Judiciary Act of 1801, enacted in the lame duck session of the last Federalist Congress. Indeed, awareness of the Act seems to have been kept alive chiefly because it must be summoned to serve as the cause of its own repeal in March 1802. The creation of sixteen new circuit court judgeships, followed by the appointment of Federalist partisans to judicial offices, has often been advanced to justify its repeal by outraged Republicans; by inference, the Act itself has come to be regarded as evidence of the political perversity of the Federalists in defeat. However, the timing of the passage of this Judiciary Act easily obscures the timing of its birth, and emphasis on organizational changes and partisan appointments easily obscures the significance of the jurisdictional revisions provided by the legislation.[1] Only when attention is given

Kathryn Turner is a member of the Department of History, Wellesllley College.
[1] Legal scholars who have commented on jurisdiction have not adequately placed the story in historical context. See, for examples of this, William W. Crosskey, *Politics and the Constitution in the History of the United States* (Chicago, 1953), I, 610–611, II, 759–764; Felix Frankfurter and James M. Landis, *The Business of the Supreme Court: A Study in the Federal Judicial System* (New York, 1928), 24–29; Erwin C. Surrency, "The Judiciary Act of 1801," *American Journal of Legal History*, II (1958), 53–65. Historians focusing on organization have failed to examine jurisdiction – e.g., Max Farrand, "The Judiciary Act of 1801," *American Historical Review*, V (1899–1900), 682–686. Recent studies of the Federalist period give virtually no attention to the legislation.

to the latter can the Judiciary Act of 1801 be seen as an integral part of Federalist policy; the Act was clearly not occasioned by the Republican victory in 1800.

The question of what authority should be conferred upon the federal courts always represented one important element in the struggle between advocates of centralization and the advocates of state power. The establishment of a system of inferior federal courts was among the issues sharply disputed at the Constitutional Convention;[2] evident within some of the state ratifying conventions were currents of fear over the potential challenge to the states represented by the authorization of the lower federal courts in Article III of the proposed Constitution.[3] In the first Congress, the contest between those who wished to confine the federal power within narrow limits and those who wished to vest in the federal courts the full judicial power that the Constitution authorized, resulted in a compromise measure, the Judiciary Act of 1789.[4]

The organization of the lower federal judiciary into two tiers of trial courts, district courts and circuit courts, is familiar. The three circuit courts, composed of two Supreme Court justices and a district judge, were also given authority to review certain decisions of the district courts.[5] The jurisdictional provisions of the Judiciary Act of 1789 reveal the extent to which Congress refrained from placing the full judicial power authorized by the Constitution within the exclusive jurisdiction of the federal courts. With the exception of admiralty and criminal jurisdiction,[6] significant areas of jurisdiction at both district and circuit levels were designed on a basis of concurrency with the state courts, and the powers of the Supreme Court were limited.[7] The federal courts had only concurrent jurisdiction over much civil litigation and then only on carefully defined terms.

---

[2] Max Farrand, ed., *The Records of the Federal Convention of 1787* (New Haven, 1911), I, 21, 124, 125, 127, 244–245, 292, 317, 341; II, 45–46, 136, 433.

[3] Jonathan Elliot, ed., *The Debates in the Several State Conventions on the Adoption of the Federal Constitution...*, 2d ed. (Philadelphia, 1863), II, 109–110, 112–114, 469, 480, 486–494, 517, 518; III, 57, 66–67, 443, 446, 468, 517, 521–562, 570–572; IV, 136–138, 140–147, 150–159, 162–169, 170–172, 257–258, 260, 265–266, 294–295, 306–308. See also the remarks of Luther Martin before the Maryland House of Delegates in Farrand, ed., *Records*, III, 152, 156, 204, 220–222, 273, 287.

[4] Charles Warren, "New Light on the History of the Federal Judiciary Act of 1789," *Harvard Law Review*, XXXVII (1923–24), 49–132, especially 49–65.

[5] Richard Peters, ed., *The Public Statutes at Large of the United States of America...* (Boston, 1845 –), I, 73 (Sept. 24, 1789), sec. 2, 3, 4, 21, 22.

[6] *Ibid.*, sec. 9, 11.

[7] *Ibid.*, sec. 13, 25.

Original jurisdiction of the circuit courts in cases where diversity of citizenship existed was concurrent with the state courts was specifically limited to controversies "between a citizen of the State where suit is brought, and a citizen of another State," and was confined to cases in which the amount in dispute exceeded five hundred dollars. Concurrent also was jurisdiction over civil suits in which an alien was a party or in which the United States was the plaintiff. Here, the same jurisdictional amount applied. A further restriction on the federal courts was the "assignee clause." To prevent collusive assignment to create federal jurisdiction, the federal courts were expressly denied authority over suits to recover the contents of promissory notes given assignees unless the suit might have been prosecuted in such a court had no assignment been made.[8] Interestingly enough, in the sphere of private civil litigation, no use was made of the Constitutional grant of judicial power over cases arising under the Constitution, laws, or treaties of the United States. The Act authorized removal to the circuit courts *before* trial of limited classes of suits begun in the state courts, subject again to the required five hundred dollars.[9]

Certain deficiencies of the Judiciary Act became apparent immediately after President Washington signed it in September 1789. For a decade, there were continuing protests by justices of the Supreme Court against a system that required them to ride circuit and to decide at the appellate level the same cases which they themselves had determined on circuit. Invited by President Washington to offer comments upon the operation of the new judicial system, the Supreme Court justices were quick to respond with a strong recommendation that the judges of the Supreme and circuit courts be separated.[10] The report presented to the House of

---

[8] *Ibid.*, sec. 9, II. In the assignee clause, an exception was made for foreign bills of exchange.

[9] *Ibid.*, sec. 12. Removals were limited to the following parties: 1) to a defendant who was an alien, 2) to a defendant who was a citizen of another state when sued by a plaintiff of the state where suit was brought, 3) to either party (if citizens of the same state) where title to land was in dispute, if one claimed under a grant of the state in which the suit was brought and the other claimed under a grant from another state. Note that the Act did not vest original jurisdiction over the latter class of suits with the circuit courts.

[10] George Washington to John Jay and the Associate Justices of the Supreme Court, Apr. 3, 1790, and Washington to Jay, Nov. 19, 1790, both in Henry P. Johnston, ed., *The Correspondence and Public Papers of John Jay*, III (New York, 1891), 396, 409; Jay to James Iredell, Sept. 15, 1790, in Griffith J. McRee, *Life and Correspondence of James Iredell* ..., II (New York, 1858), 292–296; Walter Lowrie and Walter S. Franklin, eds., *American State Papers: Documents, Legislative and Executive, of the Congress of the United States. Class X. Miscellaneous*, I (Washington, 1834), 51–52, 77–78.

Representatives in 1790 by Attorney General Edmund Randolph analyzing in detail the problems devolving from the dual obligations of the
Supreme Court justices recommended emphatically that the judges of the
highest court cease to be judges of the circuit courts.[11] A revised judiciary
bill, prepared and presented by Randolph at this time, attempted correction by composing the circuit bench from the judges of the district courts
within each of the circuits and leaving the Supreme Court at the seat of
government.[12] But Congress did nothing. In 1792, the members of the
Supreme Court again sought remedy for a system "appointing the same
men finally to correct in one capacity the errors which they themselves
may have committed in another," and the President again recommended
legislative attention to a revision of the judiciary system.[13] In 1793, the
Congress approved a bill stipulating that the attendance of only one of
the justices of the Supreme Court be required (together with the district
judge) at the circuit court.[14] Henceforth, circuits were assigned on a rota-
ting basis; but Supreme Court justices continued to review their decisions
made on circuit and the two-judge court created the problem of split
decisions at the circuit level. As Congress neglected pleas for more thor-
oughgoing reform, the judges resorted to their own ingenuity to fulfill
their duties while avoiding as much personal inconvenience as possible.[15]
When the justices of the Supreme Court in 1794 again asked the Congress
for remedy,[16] other than minor legislation altering the time and place of
certain district court meetings and procedural arrangements, no revisions
were attempted.

Despite their expressions of the need for reform, neither Chief Justice
John Jay nor Attorney General Randolph vigorously pushed the matter.
Jay's comments in a letter to a friend suggest the explanation for this lack
of aggressiveness. "The federal Courts have Enemies in all who fear their
Influence on State objects," the Chief Justice wrote. "It is to be wished
that their Defects should be corrected quietly. If these Defects were all

---

[11] *Amer. State Papers, Miscellaneous*, I, 23–24.
[12] *Ibid.*, 29.
[13] *Ibid.*, 51–52; Washington to both Houses of Congress, Nov. 6, 1792, in Jared Sparks,
The Writings of Washington . . . (Boston, 1834–37), XII, 31.
[14] *U.S. Stat.*, I, 333–334, sec. 1 (Mar. 2, 1793).
[15] The justices made informal arrangements to switch their assigned circuits in order to ease
the hardship of the judicial excursions following the biannual trip to Philadelphia for
the sessions of the Supreme Court. William Cushing to William Paterson, Mar. 5, 1793,
July 20, 1794; Paterson to Cushing, Aug. 9, 1794; and Samuel Chase to Cushing, Mar.
10, 1796, all in Robert Treat Paine Papers, Massachusetts Historical Society, Boston.
[16] *Amer. State Papers, Miscellaneous*, I, 77–78.

exposed to public view in striking colors, more Enemies would arise and the Difficulty of mending them encreased."[17]

Under such wavering leadership, small progress had been made toward revisions in the federal judicial organization by the time John Adams came to the presidency in March 1797. The relative indifference of Congress to judicial reform during these years reveals little that common sense does not explain. In comparison with the domestic and foreign problems confronting Congress during the early years of the national history, the problems of the judiciary did not loom very large. Only once, in 1793, over the Supreme Court decision in Chisholm *v.* Georgia, did Congress become strenuously exercised over a judicial question.[18] Lacking the overt impact of other party issues, the operation of the federal judicial system was abandoned to lawyers and judges. Not until the desire of leading Federalists to extend federal jurisdiction converged with professional dissatisfaction was change seriously contemplated. During the Adams administration, the cumulative force of pressures derivative from the shifting political scene and from national economic developments was to generate impetus in powerful quarters for judicial renovation.

Such Federalist policies of Adams's administration as an increased army and navy, the attendant increased revenue program, and the Alien and Sedition Acts – all, in essence, were made possible and rendered plausible by the threat of war with France. Within the nation at large, these policies aroused stormy opposition. Simultaneously, Republican distrust of the federal courts, which had mounted during the first decade of the national history,[19] reached a peak with the prosecution of their

[17] Jay to Rufus King, Dec. 22, 1793, in Charles R. King, ed., *The Life and Correspondence of Rufus King* ... (New York, 1894–1900), I, 509. The Chief Justice wrote the President that, much as the judiciary needed revision, "to convey necessary *information*, and to suggest useful *hints*, on the one hand, and, on the other, *so* to do both as to cause as few questions or divisions as possible in framing the addresses in answer, seems to be all that can be requisite." Jay to Washington, Sept. 23, 1791, in Sparks, ed., *Writings of Washington*, X, 501. Randolph counseled that judicial subjects be "rendered as mild as possible." Randolph to Washington, Aug. 5, 1792, *ibid.*, 513–514.

[18] 2 Dallas 419 (1793). The Court held that its jurisdiction extended to suits against a state by citizens of another state. See Charles Warren, *The Supreme Court in United States History* (Boston, 1924), I, 93–102. The result of the decision was the Eleventh Amendment prohibiting such suits, which was agreed to by Congress in 1794 and ratified in 1798.

[19] The distrust seemed to mount in direct proportion to decisions in those courts countering doctrines that constituted aspects of the policy nucleus of the opposition party. Hamilton *v.* Eaton, 2 Martin (N.C.) 1 (1792); U.S. *v.* Smith et al., 6 Danes's Abridgment 718

partisans, first under the common law of seditious libel and then under the Sedition Act.[20] Federalist leaders worriedly watched the growth of Republican strength,[21] and by early 1799 began to turn their attention to the federal judiciary. Real momentum for strengthening the judiciary begins in that year while the army bill still lingered before Congress, progressing, according to one Federalist, "like a wounded snake."[22] Party interests would prove more successful in generating pressure for judicial reform than pleas of Supreme Court justices.

As early as March 1798, a Senate committee had introduced a bill[23] to create five new districts in the federal court system and relieve the Supreme Court justices of all circuit riding by associating the district judges for circuit duty.[24] The next month, another committee recommended that there be four rather than three circuits, that two justices be added to the Supreme Court, and that two Supreme Court justices be assigned to each circuit.[25] Although the record is far from clear, the latter bill seems to have passed the Senate on May 25, 1798.[26] But no action was taken in the house before it adjourned, nor was anything further done in the third session.

(1792); Henfield's Case (1793), in Francis Wharton, *State Trials of the United States during the Administrations of Washington and Adams*... (Philadelphia, 1849), 49; U.S. *v.* Ravara, 2 Dallas 300*n* (1794); Ware *v.* Hylton, 3 Dallas 199 (1796); Hylton *v.* U.S., 3 Dallas 171 (1796); U.S. *v.* Isaac Williams (1797), in Wharton, *State Trials*, 652, 2 Cranch 82*n*; U.S. *v.* Worrall, 2 Dallas 384 (1798). Certain state judges had directly challenged the authority of the federal judiciary, refusing to allow defendants to remove cases from the state courts to the circuit courts. John Sitgreaves to Iredell, Aug. 2, 1791, in McRee, *Correspondence of Iredell*, II, 334; Respublica *v.* Cobbett, 3 Dallas (Pa.) 467 (1798); Rush *v.* Cobbett, 2 Yeates (Pa.) 275 (1798). Chief Justice Thomas McKean of Pennsylvania refused also to allow a bill of exceptions against his refusal to remove the action in another suit. Carey *v.* Cobbett, 2 Yeates (Pa.) 277 (1798).

20 See James Morton Smith, Freedom's Fetters: The Alien and Sedition Laws and *American Civil Liberties* (Ithaca, 1956).

21 Theodore Sedgwick to King, Nov. 15, 1799, in King, ed., *Correspondence of King*, III, 146.

22 Robert Troup to King, Apr. 19, 1799, *ibid.*, II, 597.

23 Mar. 21, 1798, in Joseph Gales, comp., *The Debates and Proceedings in the Congress of the United States*... (Washington, 1834–56), VII, 527; hereafter cited as *Annals of Congress*.

24 The provisions of this bill are not reported in the *Annals of Congress*. The only description I have located is in a letter from Chief Justice Oliver Ellsworth to Cushing, Apr. 15, 1798, in Robert Treat Paine Papers. Since no record of debate has been located, it is impossible to know the reaction to this proposal.

25 Apr. 20, 26, and May 8, 1798, in *Annals of Congress*, VII, 544–545, 549–550, 556.

26 May 8, 14, 15, 16, 22, 25, 1798, *ibid.*, 556, 558, 559, 561, 564.

Early in February 1799, Alexander Hamilton, concerned over what he was convinced was a rising tide of rebellion in Virginia and Kentucky, recommended a prudential legislative program to Theodore Sedgwick, a member of the Senate committee concerned with judicial revision. The heart of this was the recruitment of a large army.[27] Shortly afterward, Hamilton recommended to Speaker of the House Jonathan Dayton a more elaborate program in which Hamilton combined extension of the federal judicial system with his proposal for a permanent army and an extensive road-building program: "The safety and the duty of the supporters of the government call upon them to adopt vigorous measures.... Possessing, as they now do, all the constitutional powers, it will be an unpardonable mistake on their part if they do not exert them to surround the Constitution with more ramparts and to disconcert the schemes of its enemies."[28] At about the same time, Secretary of the Treasury Oliver Wolcott was urging upon the President as "indespensible" a revision of the judiciary system.[29] In November 1799, Sedgwick (who would become Speaker the following month) predicted that the Federalist opposition to the second mission to France would profit the Republicans unless his party exerted itself quickly. "If the real federal majority can act together much may and ought to be done to give efficiency to the government, and to repress the efforts of the Jacobins against it. We ought to spread out the judicial so as to render the justice of the nation acceptable to the people, to aid the national economy, to overawe the licentious, and to punish the guilty."[30] And on December 3, 1799, the President's opening message to the Sixth Congress recommended judicial revision in language that repeated almost verbatim the suggestions offered him by Wolcott in February.[31]

[27] Alexander Hamilton to Sedgwick, Feb. 2, 1799, in Henry Cabot Lodge, ed., *The Works of Alexander Hamilton* (New York, 1904), X, 340–342.

[28] Hamilton to Jonathan Dayton, 1799, *ibid.*, 329–336.

[29] Oliver Wolcott to John Adams, Nov. 15, 1799, in George Gibbs, *Memoirs of the Administrations of Washington and John Adams, Edited from the Papers of Oliver Wolcott, Secretary of the Treasury* (New York, 1846), II, 299. At this time, Wolcott opposed Hamilton on the army issue, managing to stay in his favor nonetheless. Stephen G. Kurtz, *The Presidency of John Adams: The Collapse of Federalism, 1795–1800* (Philadelphia, 1957), 323. Perhaps this explains why he urged upon the President a more vigorous judicial system.

[30] Sedgwick to King, Nov. 15, 1799, in King, ed., *Correspondence of King*, III, 146–147. Sedgwick represented Massachusetts in the Senate until March 1799. Elected in that year to the U.S. House of Representatives, he was elected Speaker when the Sixth Congress convened in December 1799.

[31] John Adams, Message to the Sixth Congress, Dec. 3, 1799, in *Annals of Congress*, X, 188–189.

   Almost immediately, both Houses of Congress appointed all-Federalist committees to report revisions of the judiciary system: Uriah Tracy of Connecticut, John Laurance of New York, Jacob Read of South Carolina, Samuel Dexter of Massachusetts, and James Ross of Pennsylvania, in the Senate; Robert Goodloe Harper of South Carolina, James Bayard of Delaware, Samuel Sewall of Massachusetts, Chauncey Goodrich of Connecticut, and John Marshall of Virginia, in the House.[32] The membership of the committee in the House was identical to that simultaneously preparing the first national bankruptcy act.[33] Wolcott reported: "The steady men in Congress will attempt to extend the judicial department and I hope that their measures will be very decided. It is impossible, in this country, to render an army of an engine of government, and there is no way to combat the state opposition but by an efficient and extended organization of judges, magistrates, and other civil officers."[34] Sewall wrote that the House committee would adopt a plan that discharged the Supreme Court justices from circuit duty, appointed new circuit judges to circuits, and extended the jurisdiction of civil causes in the circuit courts to all cases where the value in dispute exceeded one hundred dollars and in cases respecting titles to land.[35] Clearly, both radical reorganization and more extensive authority for the circuit system were being planned. When Robert Goodloe Harper introduced the bill in the House on March 11,[36] William Duane, the Republican editor of the *Aurora*, immediately sounded an alarm, warning of "that system of *consolidation* and concentration of authority what is called *Federal power*, that was foretold in convention and has been soberly progressing in a thousand forms ever since."[37]

---

[32] Dec. 12 and 9, 1799, *ibid.*, 15, 197.

[33] The simultaneous formation of these two committees with identical membership may not have been accidental. "It [bankruptcy bill] will be of public benefit.... It will give to the government an efficiency by submiting to it all the relations of creditor and Debtor, and the active agency of commercial interests and passions. It will also aid the government in another way, – it will render it absolutely necessary to spread out the national judicial by a creation of new districts and Judges, and instituting the offices of justice or something similar to it." Sedgwick to Henry van Schaak, Jan. 15, 1800, Sedgwick Papers, III, Mass. Hist. Soc.; also see Sedgwick to King, Feb. 6, 1800, in King, ed., *Correspondence of King*, III, 189–190. A Republican Congressman described the judiciary bill as "the eldest child of the bankrupt system." John Dawson to James Madison, Mar. 30, 1800, in Madison Papers, Library of Congress, Washington.

[34] Wolcott to Fisher Ames, Dec. 29, 1799, in Gibbs, *Memoirs*, II, 316.

[35] Samuel Sewall to Cushing, Feb. 25, 1800, in Cushing Papers, Mass. Hist. Soc.

[36] *Annals of Congress*, X, 623.

[37] *Aurora* (Philadelphia), Mar. 18, 1800.

The judiciary bill[38] contained two major innovations. The first dealt with organization. It reduced the number of Supreme Court justices from six to five[39] and abolished the district courts in favor of courts exercising only admiralty jurisdiction.[40] It divided the nation into twenty-nine districts organized into nine circuits. Each district was to have a circuit judge (with the exceptions of the districts of Champlain, Ohio, and Cumberland) and in each circuit, a federal circuit court was to be composed of the circuit judges of the several districts within the circuit.[41] The circuit courts were to be the sole trial courts in law and equity in the federal system.[42] The committee also proposed a considerable extension of jurisdiction. In a startling abandonment of the concept of sovereign immunity, it gave the Supreme Court jurisdiction over suits in tort or contract against the United States by "any state, body politic or corporate, company or person."[43] It extended the jurisdiction of the circuit courts to include "all actions or suits, matters or things, cognizable by the judicial authority of the United States," thus giving these courts, for the first time, the federal question jurisdiction they had not been given in 1789. The amount necessary to give jurisdiction was reduced from five hundred to one hundred dollars, and jurisdiction over cases involving title or bounds of land was specifically unrestricted by the value of the lands in question. The limitation as to venue that the Act of 1789 placed on the parties in diversity suits was abandoned, and no "assignee clause" was included. Jurisdictional amount for removals was reduced to one hundred dollars,

---

[38] The provisions of this bill are not given in the *Annals of Congress* but as a Bill to Provide for the Better Establishment & Regulation of the Courts of the United States 11th March, 1800, published by order of the House. A copy of this is at the Lib. Cong. No records of the committee exist.

[39] A Bill to Provide for . . . the Courts of the United States 11th March, 1800, sec. 3.

[40] *Ibid.*, sec. 27, 28, 32. The bill provided that the present district judges should be judges of admiralty until their deaths or resignations, when judges of admiralty should be appointed.

[41] *Ibid.*, sec. 10, 11. In the excepted districts, the present district judges of Vermont, Kentucky, and Tennessee would act as circuit judges.

[42] With the exception, of course, of the limited instances in which the Supreme Court exercised such jurisdiction according to the provisions of the Constitution.

[43] *Ibid.*, sec. 5. The bill authorized the jurisdiction when such plaintiffs "shall have any demand against the United States, for, or on account of any debt, contract, or damages whatsoever; or shall claim the right of soil in, of, or to any land held or possessed by the United States." Whether Congress had the power to confer upon the Supreme Court original jurisdiction in cases other than those described in the Constitution raised, of course, a significant constitutional question which would later be determined in Marbury *v.* Madison, 1 Cranch 137 (1803). It is interesting to consider John Marshall's opinion in that case in the light of his support for this proposal in 1800.

and here too suits involving land titles were exempt from the qualification. Furthermore, removal *after* trial was authorized when judgment had been given in a state court for a sum exceeding one hundred dollars against a defendant (in the specified classes of suits) who had not been personally served with process or who had not appeared.[44] And finally, the proposed legislation empowered the circuit courts to issue writs of prohibition, supersedeas, mandamus, or certiorari to the state courts to compel removal whenever the latter should refuse to permit it.[45] The Supreme Court became the only appellate court in the federal system; the avenue to review at this level widened through a reduction of jurisdictional amount to five hundred dollars instead of the two thousand formerly required.[46]

A Republican motion to postpone consideration of the bill was defeated, but Albert Gallatin was successful in his effort to strike the provision granting the Supreme Court jurisdiction over suits against the United States.[47] Debate then focused on the heart of the bill, the redivision of the nation into twenty-nine judicial districts. On a motion of John Nicholas of Virginia that the entire section be removed, fifty members voted in the affirmative:[48] the key provision of the bill was lost. Harper, making no effort to hide his disappointment, moved successfully to recommit the bill after the Republicans were defeated on a motion to postpone its consideration until the second session of the Sixth Congress.[49] A revealing Federalist argument against postponement was "that the close of the present Executive's authority was at hand, and from his experience, he was more capable to choose suitable persons to fill the offices than another."[50] The presidential election would not be held until November,

---

[44] *Ibid.*, sec. 16, 17, 18. The latter section also exempted from jurisdictional amount suits in which citizens of the same state claimed title under grants from different states.

[45] *Ibid.*, sec. 19. This provision may have been prompted by such refusals of state judges as noted in n. 19; there is, however, no direct evidence on the point.

[46] *Ibid.*, sec. 44, 45.

[47] Mar. 25 and 26, 1800, in *Annals of Congress*, X, 643–646.

[48] Mar. 27, 1800, *ibid.*, 646. Robert Goodloe Harper defended the proposal; so, in a "lengthy defense," did Marshall. The content of the debate is not recorded in the *Annals of Congress* nor in a variety of newspapers examined, nor has any account of Marshall's defense been located. Beveridge, in his biography of Marshall, fails to mention that Marshall was a member of the judiciary committee or that he made this speech. The vote is reported simply as Ayes 50. There were 106 members of the House in the first session, of whom 63 were Federalists and 43 Republicans. Manning J. Dauer, *The Adams Federalists* (Baltimore, 1953), 321.

[49] Mar. 28, 1800, in *Annals of Congress*, X, 647–649.

[50] *Ibid.*, 648.

but the partisan purposes to which the new act might be put were never so clearly and so publicly expressed. The *Aurora* shrilled: "Look at the measures agitating in the Congress – the Bankrupt Bill gives a patronage of nearly 250 offices great and small – the *Judiciary Bill* gives the nomination of 25 *new Judges* besides Marshall, Clerks, etc. to the amount of 100 offices in all! Why are these measures pushed forward now? Is it for the public good or for *party purposes*?"[51]

The narrow defeat in the House of the key section dividing the nation into twenty-nine districts forced the committee to amend its initial proposal. The amended bill, presented on March 31,[52] reduced the number of districts to nineteen and the number of circuits to six, and dropped the provision authorizing the issuance of writs to compel removals.[53] It left blank the jurisdictional amount. But using virtually the language of the Constitution, it granted jurisdiction over all cases in law and equity arising under the Constitution, laws, and treaties of the United States, and exempted these suits from jurisdictional amount. Removal privileges were extended to defendants in such federal question cases without regard to either jurisdictional amount or citizenship of the parties.[54] When the amended bill was called up, after debate (reported only as "warm and lengthy"), a Republican motion to postpone carried by two votes.[55] There the matter rested until the next session.[56]

Before Congress adjourned in May 1800, Hamilton had predicted that "the dread of unpopularity" would paralyze action and "prevent

---

[51] *Aurora*, Mar. 29, 1800. The paper also warned against the bill as a system for the consolidation of federal power. Mar. 18, 1800. Jefferson complained of the increased expense the proposed bill would entail. Jefferson to Madison, Mar. 25, 1800, in Paul Leicester Ford, ed., *The Writings of Thomas Jefferson*, VII (New York, 1896), 438.

[52] Mar. 31, 1800, in *Annals of Congress*, X, 650.

[53] A Bill to Provide for the More Convenient Organization of the Courts of the United States. 31 March 1800. Published by order of the House of Representatives. Lib. Cong., sec. 7.

[54] *Ibid.*, sec. 13, 14.

[55] Apr. 14, 1800, in *Annals of Congress*, X, 666. The vote was 48–46 with Federalists Alston of N.C, Dent of Md., Gray of Va., Hartley of Pa., Jones and Taliaferro of Ga., Davenport of Conn., Dwight Foster of Mass., and Jonathan Freeman of N. H. joining the Republicans. Thomas Adams wrote, "Consolidation of the States, is the bug bear so much dreaded," to John Quincy Adams, Apr. 1, 1800, Letters Received, Adams Papers, Mass. Hist Soc. Permission to quote from this and subsequent references to the Adams Papers has been granted by the Adams Manuscript Trust at the Mass. Hist. Soc. Also see Sewall to John Lowell, May 9, 1800, Lowell Papers, Mass. Hist. Soc.

[56] There was little doubt that the Federalists would bring the bill forward at the next session. Harper to his Constituents, May 15, 1800, in Elizabeth Donnan, ed., *Papers of James A. Bayard, 1796–1815* (Washington, 1915), 103.

the erection of additional buttresses to the Constitution."[57] With the judiciary bill postponed through the alliance of a handful of Federalists with the Republicans, the Speaker concluded that the legislation of the past session was "hardly worth the parchment."[58] As legislators of both parties turned their energies to the serious business of that summer – preparations for the election of 1800 – bitterness between the parties and between the factions of the Federalist party reached new heights. Taking no active part in the political campaign, the President remained at Quincy, and late in September requested the advice of his new Secretary of State in regard to the address to be delivered to Congress after it convened in November.[59] Marshall wrote the entire speech, which the chief executive delivered with only minor changes of wording, a speech that stressed the necessity of judicial revision in tones stronger than used the year before.[60]

The new judiciary committee of the House in this lame duck session included Federalists Roger Griswold of Connecticut, John Wilkes Kittera of Pennsylvania, and Archibald Henderson of North Carolina, together with two Republicans, John Nicholas of Virginia and Joseph Hopper Nicholson of Maryland.[61] By mid-December, just when it became apparent that the Federalists had been defeated at the polls, Adams received the resignation of Oliver Ellsworth as Chief Justice.[62] On December 19, the same day the Senate approved the nomination of John Jay to this office, Roger Griswold presented the Judiciary bill to the House of

---

[57] Hamilton to King, Jan. 5, 1800, in John C. Hamilton, ed., *The Works of Alexander Hamilton* . . . , VI (New York, 1851), 416.

[58] Sedgwick to King, May 11, 1800, in King, ed., *Correspondence of King*, III, 236–237. Some Federalists had also opposed their party on the proposed embargo against France, the release of volunteers for the additional army, and the Bankruptcy Act. Kurtz, *Presidency of John Adams*, 396.

[59] John Adams to Marshall, Sept 27, 1800, in Charles Francis Adams, ed., *The Works of John Adams* . . . , IX (Boston, 1854), 85.

[60] Speech to both Houses of Congress, Nov. 22, 1800, *ibid.*, 144. Marshall wrote two speeches, the originals of which are in the Adams Papers.

[61] Nov. 28, 1800, in *Annals of Congress*, X, 795. Marshall had resigned in May 1800 to become Secretary of State; Sewall had also resigned. The inclusion of the Republicans clearly must have been a maneuver to work out a compromise in committee, if possible. One can only speculate why the three Federalists who remained in Congress were not reappointed to the committee. That the Speaker regarded Roger Griswold more highly than he did Harper is plain. Sedgwick to —, Feb. 4, 1800; to Henry van Schaak, Feb. 9, 1800, in Sedgwick Papers, III.

[62] Ellsworth's letter is endorsed at the head of the text by Adams, "Rcd. Dec. 15, 1800." Letters Received, Adams Papers.

Representatives.[63] At this time, the House restored the original district
courts and established six circuit courts to be composed of three resident judges except in the Sixth Circuit, where only one judge was to be
appointed.[64] But it left intact the enlarged scope of jurisdiction from the
1800 bill and added to this cognizance, together with the district courts,
over all cases arising under the new Bankruptcy Act, which had passed in
April.[65] Although the bill was read twice and referred to the committee of
the whole, the main attention of Congress was concentrated on the Burr–
Jefferson contest. Jefferson's inital conviction that Congress would take
no action during the lame duck session[66] had turned to worry when he
reported to Madison the forwarding of the bill to commitment.[67] Bayard,
for his part, was confident of success.[68]

The reading of the bill advanced tranquilly to the section that divided
Virginia into two districts. Virginia Republicans then immediately moved
to retain one court only. Griswold retorted that the division was necessary
to make access to the federal courts more readily available for diversity
suits because the state courts could not "so well insure perfect justice as
the courts of the United States." Harper added that the national government ought not to leave the execution of its laws to the state governments
perhaps "possessing a disposition hostile to the laws they are called upon
to execute." Nor was Bayard disposed "to leave too much power in the
hands of men not immediately under the control of the government, nor
liable to impeachment in case of misuse of that power."[69] Defeated on
this motion, the Republicans went after the section defining the jurisdictional amount, left blank in the committee's bill. The lower the amount,

[63] U.S. Congress, Senate, *Journal of the Executive Proceedings of the Senate...*, I (Washington, 1828), 360; *Annals of Congress*, X, 837.
[64] Jan. 8, 1801, in *Annals of Congress*, X, 899–900; *U.S. Stat.*, II, 90–91, sec. 6, 7. In the
Sixth Circuit, the new court would be held by one circuit judge and the district judges
of Tennessee and Kentucky.
[65] *U.S. Stat.*, II, 92–94, sec. 11, 12, 13, 14.
[66] Jefferson to Caesar Rodney, Dec. 21, 1800, Jefferson Papers, Lib. Cong.; Jefferson to
Madison, Dec. 19, 1800, in Ford, ed., *Writings of Jefferson*, VII, 471.
[67] Jefferson to Madison, Dec. 26, 1800, in Andrew A. Lipscomb and Albert Ellery Bergh,
eds., *The Writings of Thomas Jefferson*, X (Washington, 1903), 187.
[68] James A. Bayard to Caesar [Rodney?], Jan. 5, 1801, in Donnan, ed., *Papers of Bayard*,
118.
[69] Jan. 5 and 7, 1801, in *Annals of Congress*, X, 878–880; *The Federal Gazette and
Baltimore Daily Advertiser*, Jan. 8, 1801. Federalists disputed among themselves whether
the Constitution made it *mandatory* that jurisdiction over federal questions be exercised
by the federal courts *exclusive* of the state judiciaries. After Harper stated his confidence
of the constitutionality of Congressional delegation of this authority, the motion was
withdrawn. *Annals of Congress*, X, 891–892, 895–896.

the greater the opportunity for suits to be tried in the federal courts with, potentially, a corresponding diminution of civil litigation heard before the state courts. The Federalist aim had been made clear in the bill proposed on March 11, 1801, which had set the jurisdictional amount at only one hundred dollars.

Nicholas was on his feet to propose that the blank be filled with the amount of five hundred dollars. His argument in support of his proposal is illuminating: "That the estate of Lord Fairfax, with the quit rents due thereon, had been confiscated during the Revolution by the State of Virginia; notwithstanding the confiscation, the heirs of Lord Fairfax had sold all their rights (which the assignees contended remained unimpaired). It might be their wish to prosecute in a Federal court, expecting to gain advantages in it which could not be had from the courts of Virginia. His object was to defeat the purpose by limiting the jurisdiction of the circuit courts to sums beyond the amount of quit rents, alleged to be due to any individual."[70] The vote on Nicholas's motion was a tie, 37–37, and the motion was defeated only through the casting vote of the South Carolina Federalist John Rutledge, Jr., who was chairman of the committee of the whole that day.[71] The blank subsequently was filled with the sum of four hundred dollars.[72] Nicholas's next move was to call for the restoration of the "assignee clause" lest a great mass of suits be transferred from the state courts to the federal system by collusive assignment. The Republicans maintained that the proposed extension of diversity jurisdiction would enable the creditor, who nominally assigned his claim to a citizen of another state or to a foreigner, to force his debtor into federal court. This court, it was charged, would be far removed from the debtor's home where the debt had probably been contracted, where witnesses would be found, and where a jury acquainted with his general character could be selected. It was further protested that in Virginia, all bonds were assignable and a great mass of the debts contracted were in bonds and promissory notes. North Carolina's particular interest in restoring the "assignee clause" arose from the fact that there the paper currency, which circulated at 25 percent below par, was legal tender in the state courts; it was asserted that judgments given in the federal courts were for specie only. Consequently, a creditor, enabled to commence his

---

[70] Jan. 7, 1801, in *Annals of Congress*, X, 897.
[71] *Ibid.*; *Independent Chronicle* (Boston), Jan. 15–19, 1801; *Federal Gazette*, Jan. 9, 1801.
[72] No information on the selection of this compromise figure has been located. Clearly, sponsors of the bill had to settle for what was possible.

suit in the federal courts, so it was argued, might obtain on a federal judgment 25 percent more than was really due him on a North Carolina contract.

Federalist proponents of the change retorted that those who received debts by endorsement were as legitimately creditors as the original holder of the obligation, and that this was one of the precise cases for which the Constitution provided. They attacked Nicholas's attempt so to limit federal jurisdiction over diversity suits as "another evidence of that invariable and unabating disposition to defeat the most important provisions of the Constitution, to destroy its energy, and to withdraw from it the respect of the citizens. . . ."[73] When the vote was taken, Nicholas's amendment to restore the "assignee clause" was carried 42–27.[74] Harper himself then moved to strike the section creating the separate admiralty courts, promising an amendment to provide additional district courts with admiralty jurisdiction in maritime locations.[75] Bayard continued confident of the ultimate passage of the bill,[76] and Rutledge wrote Hamilton optimistically of how "We shall profit of our short-lived majority."[77] The Federalist *Columbian Centinel* spoke for many of the Federalist proponents of the bill when it wrote in support of the measure in the following terms: "If free governments can ever be maintained without a *standing army* it can only be effected by a firm, independent, and extensive Judiciary . . . it has been the constant endeavor of the Federalists, to extend the protecting power of the Judiciary to every part of the Union, and to every case provided in the Constitution. Unhappily a mistaken timidity, and a disposition too prevalent, during the first years of the existence of our government, to conciliate the opposition, induced the First Congress not to invest the Federal Judiciary with the powers which the constitution authorized them to bestow. The error has been deeply felt and sincerely lamented."[78]

Throughout the week of January 12, the judiciary issue continued before the House. Following wrangles over the location of the courts

[73] Advocates of the bill styled the assignee amendment "unconstitutional" since it prevented a citizen of one state from suing another in the federal court. Except where the creditor dreaded "the undue influence of sinister feelings," they claimed he would likely prefer the state courts. Jan. 8, 1801, in *Annals of Congress*, X, 897–899.

[74] *Ibid.*, 899.

[75] *Ibid.*, 899–900.

[76] Bayard to Rodney, Jan. 9, 1801, in Donnan, ed., *Papers of Bayard*, 120.

[77] John Rutledge to Hamilton, Jan. 10, 1801, in Hamilton, ed., *Works of Hamilton*, VI, 510–511.

[78] *Columbian Centinel* (Boston), Jan. 14, 1801. Compare this with *Aurora*, Jan. 10, 1801.

and the number of circuit judges, a final effort to postpone consideration of the bill was defeated.[79] Also during the week, Jay's refusal to return to the Supreme Court was received by President Adams.[80] Federalist Congressmen, acutely aware that an immediate appointment to the Court was essential, enlisted Secretary of the Navy Benjamin Stoddert to tell the President that the judiciary bill would be brought to a vote in the House on January 20. Prevented by bad weather from paying a personal visit with the news, Stoddert dispatched a note to Adams on January 19: "As the bill proposes a reduction of the Judges to five – and as there are already five Judges in commission, it is suggested that there might be more difficulty in appointing a chief Justice without taking him from the present Judges, after the passage of this bill even by one Branch of the Legislature, than before."[81] Adams acted at once. On January 20, the Senate received the nomination of John Marshall as Chief Justice of the United States;[82] on the same day by a vote of 51 to 43, the new Judiciary Act was passed by the House of Representatives.[83] After a week's delay, the nomination of Marshall was approved,[84] and shortly afterward the judiciary bill was brought to the floor of the Senate.[85] Only a month remained to the Federalist administration.

The Senate had taken no action toward judicial revision before it received the bill from the House. Even though so little time remained, a few Federalists hoped for more thoughtful consideration of the bill,[86] but Senator William Bingham of Pennsylvania vividly described the situation confronting his party: "Such is the critical state of the Votes in the House, arising from the accession of Several Members, who are adverse to the Bill, that it is Supposed it will be in imminent danger, if it Should return to the House and be placed within their Power – The Committee therefore to whom it was referred, altho desirous of introducing Several

---

[79] *Federal Gazette*, Jan. 21, 1801.

[80] *National Intelligencer* (Washington), Jan. 14, 1801.

[81] Benjamin Stoddert to John Adams, Jan. 19, 1801, Letters Received, Adams Papers.

[82] *Senate Executive Journal*, I, 371. For further details regarding the impromptu appointment of Marshall, see my article, "The Appointment of Chief Justice Marshall," *William and Mary Quarterly*, 3d Ser., XVII (1960), 143–163.

[83] *Annals of Congress*, X, 915. Federalists Taliaferro of Ga., Dent of Md., Alston of N. C., and Gray of Va. voted with the Republicans. No Republicans supported the bill.

[84] *Senate Executive Journal*, I, 374.

[85] Feb. 4, 1801, in *Annals of Congress*, X, 738.

[86] Dwight Foster to Timothy Pickering, Feb. 4, 1801, Pickering Papers, Mass. Hist. Soc.; Samuel Bayard to Theodore Foster, Jan. 22, 1801, Richard Peters to John Adams, Feb. 6, 1801, both in Letters Received, Adams Papers.

Modifications, have reported the Bill without Amendment, and I am inclined to believe that we shall be compelled to take it, – for better and for worse – or totally reject it... the federal Party wish the appointments to be made under the present administration... the Importance of filling these Seats with federal characters, must be obvious."[87] Nothing was allowed to slow the momentum with which the bill was being propelled through the Senate. Not a single amendment was tolerated. The Republicans failed in their effort to prevent a third and final reading of the bill and were defeated in the attempt to introduce other minor alterations concerning the location of Kentucky courts. The judiciary bill was passed by the Senate 16 to 11 on February 7, 1801,[88] and signed with visible displeasure by its presiding officer, Thomas Jefferson.[89]

The Republicans, of course, had only bitter words for the Act. "The ground work laid for the future efforts of the Party – under a formidable and extended Judiciary wholly devoted to them – promises no peace," one Republican complained to Madison.[90] "You may judge of the character of this bill, when Harper boasts that it is as good to the party as an election, and Harry Lee that it is the only resource which the government would have to secure strength since the standing army could not be retained."[91] Already the Republicans were talking of repeal.[92] Robert Goodloe Harper attributed the opposition to the bill to those whose main object was to

[87] William Bingham to Peters, Feb. 1, 1801, Peters Papers, Historical Society of Pennsylvania, Philadelphia. See also James Gunn to Hamilton, Dec. 13, 1800, in Hamilton, ed., *Works of Hamilton*, VI, 483; Dwight Foster to Pickering, Feb. 4, 1801, Pickering Papers; John Adams to Richard Stockton, Jan. 27, 1801, in Adams, ed., *Works of Adams*, IX, 94; Marshall to William Paterson, Feb. 2, 1801, Paterson Papers, Transcripts, New York Public Library, New York.
[88] *Annals of Congress*, X, 741–742.
[89] Thomas Truxton to Hamilton, Mar. 26, 1802, in Hamilton, ed., *Works of Hamilton*, VI, 535.
[90] John Mercer to Madison, Feb. 8, 1801, Madison Papers, Lib. Cong. See also Stevens Thomson Mason to John Breckinridge, Feb. 12, 1801, Breckinridge Papers, Lib. Cong.
[91] *Aurora*, Feb. 23, 1801. For castigation by Republican press: *Aurora*, Jan. 10, Feb. 3, 23, 1801; *The Examiner* (Richmond), Feb. 6, 1801; *Independent Chronicle*, Feb. 23, 1801. The Federalist press, in its support of the measure, attacked the present power of state legislatures and state courts. *Columbian Centinel*, Feb. 7, 1801, declared: "*One sells land, receives the value stipulated – then annuls the sale – reclaims the land – and burns its records!* – Other Legislatures, *after receiving the amount of their notes and contracts, declare it inexpedient to pay the one or fulfill the other!* – the Constitution, as it is now mutilated, provides no redress in these extreme cases." See also *Washington Federalist* (Georgetown), Jan. 26, 28, 30, 1801; *New-England Palladium* (Boston), Feb. 6, 1801; *Boston Gazette*, Feb. 16, 1801; *Gazette of the United States* (Philadelphia), Feb. 6, 1801.
[92] *National Intelligencer*, Feb. 20, 1801; *Aurora*, Feb. 28, Mar. 3, 1801.

keep the federal government dependent on the state governments for the execution of its laws.[93] Gouverneur Morris, "heartily and cordially" approving of the bill, benignly observed that the Federalists "are about to experience a heavy gale of adverse wind; can they be blamed for casting many anchors to hold their ship through the storm?"[94] An Act to provide for the more convenient organization of the Courts of the United States became law on February 13, 1801.[95]

In its final form, certain salutary organizational reforms, long desired, were instituted. The sole duty of the Supreme Court Justices would be to hold two sessions of the Supreme Court annually.[96] After the next vacancy, the membership of that Court would consist of five judges only.[97] In place of the former circuit courts, held by the local district judge and the peripatetic Justices of the Supreme Court, six new circuits were established, each to consist of three resident circuit judges, except in the Sixth Circuit. Here, for the present, the new court would be composed of one circuit judge and the district judges of Tennessee and Kentucky.[98] Therefore, the Act provided for a total increase of sixteen federal judges; no provision was made to increase the number of district court judges, although additional district courts were provided in New Jersey, Maryland, North Carolina, and Virginia.[99]

The district courts were restored, their trial jurisdiction presumably continued from the Act of 1789. In cases arising under the Constitution, laws, and treaties of the United States, the circuit courts were given jurisdiction without regard to jurisdictional amount; in all other cases to which the judicial power of the United States applied, except where original jurisdiction was granted by the Constitution to the Supreme Court or by law to the district courts, jurisdiction was confined to amounts above four hundred dollars. Jurisdiction over cases involving title or bounds of land, however, was unrestricted by amount. Criminal jurisdiction was expanded beyond the Act of 1789 to cover offenses on the high seas. Jurisdiction over all penalties and forfeitures made under the laws of the

---

[93] Harper to his Constituents, Feb. 26, 1801, in Donnan, ed., *Papers of Bayard*, 140.
[94] Gouverneur Morris to Robert R. Livingston, Feb. 20, 1801, in Jared Sparks, ed., *The Life of Gouverneur Morris...*, III (Boston, 1832), 153–154.
[95] *U.S. Stat.*, II, 89.
[96] *Ibid.*, sec. 1.
[97] *Ibid.*, sec. 3. No debate on this change is recorded but Republicans charged that it was to prevent the appointment of a Republican to the Court. *Richmond Examiner*, Feb. 6, 1801.
[98] *U.S. Stat.*, II, sec. 7.
[99] *Ibid.*, sec. 21.

United States where the offense was committed within fifty miles of the circuit courts was made *exclusive* of the state courts.[100] In addition, the circuit courts were given cognizance, concurrently with the district courts, over all cases arising under the new Bankruptcy Act.[101]

The Act of 1801 also widened the privilege to remove litigation from the state courts to the circuit courts well beyond the Act of 1789, although less broadly than the bill rejected in 1800. To match the new grant of original jurisdiction, cases arising under the Constitution, laws, and treaties, commenced in state courts, were made removable without regard to jurisdictional amount or citizenship of parties. The jurisdictional amount, necessary in diversity cases, was reduced to four hundred dollars but was abandoned when these suits involved land titles[102] as well as in suits where citizens of the same state claimed land under grants from different states.[103] In suits against aliens or in diversity suits where process had not been served or where the defendant had not appeared, if judgment of the state court was given for more than four hundred dollars, the defendant could remove after trial to the circuit court.[104] Appellate procedures of the final Act followed the pattern established in 1789 – the jurisdictional amount was again set at two thousand dollars.[105]

The legislative history of the Act clearly shows that the Federalists embarked on a program of judicial innovation almost a year before the

[100] *Ibid.*, sec. 11.
[101] *Ibid.*, sec. 12.
[102] *Ibid.*, sec. 13. It should be remembered that the grant of original jurisdiction in cases of diverse citizenship under the Act of 1789 was restricted to controversies "between a citizen of the State where the suit is brought and a citizen of another state," a restriction which was duplicated in the removal section. The Act of 1801 made no such restriction in the original jurisdiction, thereby extending the jurisdiction over diversity suits, in both federal and state courts, quite literally, to "suits between citizens of different states" as the Constitution had authorized. It did, however, retain the restriction of 1789 for purposes of removal of diversity suits. Subject only, then, to the jurisdictional amount (which was waived for land suits), any suit between citizens of different states was triable in the first instance in any circuit court but was restricted as to removals if brought to a state court in the first instance. All cases, including those between citizens of the same state, that touched federal questions, could not only be tried in the first instance in the circuit courts, but could also be removed there before trial if the cause had been instituted in a state court.
[103] *Ibid.*, sec. 14. Under the Act of 1789, this class of suits had been removable to the circuit courts, but there was no original jurisdiction over them. Under the Act of 1801, since such suits fell under the judicial authority of the United States, they would come within the original jurisdiction of the circuit courts.
[104] *Ibid.*, sec. 13.
[105] *Ibid.*, sec. 33, 34.

election of 1800. If political defeat were not the precipitant, what explanations can be suggested for these fundamental changes in the judicial system?

The history of this period vibrates with persistent conflicts between various economic groups and conflicts between those who wished the national government strengthened and those who wished it decentralized. However, the way in which the *substance* of these conflicts poured through the funnel of the dual judicial system has not been studied directly so much as obliquely observed in later decisions of the Supreme Court. Yet the great cases through which the Marshall court asserted national supremacy and protected contractual rights are so emphasized in their constitutional significance that the historical significance of the issues that brought these cases to litigation in the first place is neglected.

During the 1790s, many local questions illuminate the contest over state policies; few were more charged with political emotion than those involving the ownership of land. Although land speculation was big business at the time the Constitution was adopted,[106] its days of litigation lay in the future. During the Federalist decade, momentous controversies involving land titles built within state courts and/or the lower federal judiciary. Consider some familiar decisions of the Marshall Court, handed down long *after* 1801, in which a dispute over land titles arising long *before* 1801 was the issue that initiated litigation and caused its entanglement in the net of federal-state relations. One thinks of Fletcher *v.* Peck, 6 Cranch 87 (1810), and the Yazoo lands; Green *v.* Biddle, 8 Wheaton 1 (1821), and the Kentucky lands; Huidekoper's Lessee *v.* Douglass, 3 Cranch 1 (1805), and the lands of the Holland Company; Fairfax's Devisee *v.* Hunter's Lessee, 7 Cranch 603 (1813), the determination of title to the Fairfax lands directly occasioning that cornerstone of federal supremacy, the great case of Martin *v.* Hunter's Lessee, 1 Wheaton 304 (1816). In considering these cases as a group, two facts stand out: first, state action was central to the controversy and, second, the issues involved in each were very much alive prior to 1801, some already in litigation. By bearing in mind these general considerations, some insight may be gained into the relationship between disputes over land titles and the motivation behind the Federalist drive for judicial revision.

---

[106] Forrest McDonald, *We the People: The Economic Origins of the Constitution* (Chicago, 1958), 396–397. John P. Frank, "Historical Bases of the Federal Judicial System," *Indiana Law Journal*, XXIII (1947–48), 267.

Early in the 1790s, the Holland Land Company purchased several million acres of New York and Pennsylvania land, including half a million
acres from Associate Justice James Wilson in the northwest of Pennsylvania, a section opened to occupation by a Pennsylvania statute of 1792
and subject to its provisions for settlement. Because of the ambiguities
of the legislation, which attempted to satisfy both settler and speculator,
the Holland Land Company found itself almost immediately confronted
with potentially serious legal difficulties in Pennsylvania. Composed of
representatives both of speculative interests and of settlers, the legislature
passed various acts in an effort to bring some order out of the confusion resulting as settlers moved in to take title to lands. In 1797, the
Board of Property clarified the terms on which it would issue patents
on lands warranted in 1792 or 1793. These provisions were operated
easily to the benefit of the Company while the Federalists controlled the
state. However, after political control passed to the Republicans in 1799,
the new Board of Property reversed the rulings of its predecessor and
the Company, or purchasers of its lands, was confronted with countless counter-claimants to tracts of lands patented under the 1797 ruling.
The Holland Land Company faced the almost certain prospect of losing
title to hundreds of thousands of acres for failure to comply fully with
state legislation. With the future of the northwestern lands dependent on
the interpretation of the legislation by the courts of the state, a lawsuit
became a symbol of speculator against settler and a test of opposing party
policies. The case, Commonwealth v. Tench Coxe, 4 Dallas 170, came
on for argument in the Supreme Court of Pennsylvania in March 1800;
the decision went against the interests of the Company.[107]

In Georgia, original titles to the Yazoo lands had been redistributed
by legislative action in 1796. Secondary bona fide purchasers of lands

[107] See Paul Demund Evans, *The Holland Land Company* (Buffalo, 1924), 23–26, 31–
33, 107–126; Shaw Livermore, *Early American Land Companies: Their Influence on
Corporate Development* (New York, 1939), 205–209; Crosskey, *Politics and the Con-
stitution*, II, 719–753; Sanford W. Higginbotham, *The Keystone in the Democratic
Arch: Pennsylvania Politics, 1800–1816* (Harrisburg, 1952), 118, 128–129, 189–190;
Harry Marlin Tinkcom, *The Republicans and Federalists in Pennsylvania, 1790–1801:
A Study in National Stimulus and Local Response* (Harrisburg, 1950), 215–241. Petitions from settlers flowed to the legislature requesting action. 4 Dallas 205n. In 1803
James Ross, counsel for the Company, advised alien members to bring suit in the fed-
eral courts. Amid intense sentiment in Pennsylvania against federal jurisdiction over
the issue, this was done and the Supreme Court upheld the interests of the Company
in 1805. Huidekoper's Lessee *v.* Douglass, 3 Cranch 1. See Evans, *Holland Land
Company*, 144–155.

patented under the revoked act of 1795 wished for a means of establishing their titles but the Eleventh Amendment prevented them from suing Georgia; and, by the rescinding act, the state barred from its own courts suits based on the original grants. The Judiciary Act of 1789 provided no trial jurisdiction over federal question cases. To be sure, a Yazoo suit in diversity had come to the federal circuit court for Connecticut in 1797, but no decision had been rendered.[108] In 1800, Congress authorized commissioners to report on claims of individuals in the territory, many of them claiming on the basis of the grants of 1795, but whether remedy would come by this means was not known.[109]

Like the Yazoo affair in Georgia, the question of title to the Fairfax lands in Virginia was far from settled in 1800, and remained an important ingredient in state politics. This complex tangle involved titles to tracts of that immense grant, overlapping boundaries, Virginia sequestration laws, and two treaties between the United States and Great Britain. Under authority of a Virginia statute of 1785, part of the confiscated Fairfax lands had been sold or granted by the state to numerous settlers in the Northern Neck. In 1793, a syndicate including John and James Marshall contracted to purchase the main part of the Fairfax estate. Two important suits derived from these circumstances. After decisions in 1794 in the lower court of the state and in 1795 in the federal circuit court for Virginia had been given in favor of the Fairfax heir,[110] many settlers holding land under authority of state legislation petitioned the legislature for remedy to quiet their titles.[111] The legislature enacted a compromise

---

[108] Bishop and Bishop *v.* Nightingale and Miller, Circuit Court Records, Chancery, I (1790–1812), Federal Records Center Annex, Boston. In 1799, the Supreme Judicial Court of Massachusetts held the Georgia repealing statute void under the contract clause of the Constitution. Derby *v.* Blake, 226 Mass. 619.

[109] See Charles H. Haskins, "The Yazoo Land Companies," in American Historical Association, *Papers*, V (New York, 1891), 395–437; Livermore, *Land Companies*, 146–162; Albert J. Beveridge, *The Life of John Marshall* (Boston, 1916–19), III, 546–547; A. M. Sakolski, *The Great American Land Bubble*...(New York, 1932); Milton S. Heath, "Laissez Faire in Georgia, 1732–1860," *Journal of Economic History*, III (1943), Supplement, 78–84. In 1803, claimants sought a judicial determination of the question in the federal courts in the famous case Fletcher *v.* Peck, 6 Cranch 87. In 1810, the Supreme Court held the repeal act unconstitutional on the grounds that it impaired the obligation of contract.

[110] Hunter *v.* Fairfax's Devisee, 1 Munford (Va.), 218 at 222–223; 3 Dallas 305 (1796); and Supreme Court Appellate Records, Dockets, National Archives, Washington.

[111] Petition of the Inhabitants of the Counties of Hardy, Hampshire, and Shenandoah, Hardy County Legislative Petitions, 1786–1819, Box 1, photostat from original in Virginia State Library, Richmond.

in 1796[112] but by 1800 there had been no judicial determination of the issues by either the highest court of the state or the highest court of the nation.[113]

The chaotic condition of Kentucky land titles at the turn of the century arose from the terms of the Ordinance of Separation from Virginia[114] as well as from the fact that settlement outran the speed with which entries recorded at the land office could be properly surveyed. Some claims were grounded on Virginia law; others rested on Kentucky law after the new state began to grant lands under its own authority. The result was countless law suits, many entered by nonresident claimants, involving priority of right to specific plots of land.[115] The situation was further complicated in the 1790s by the enactment of state laws favoring

[112] An Act Concerning Certain Lands Lying in the Northern Neck, Dec. 10, 1796, in *Acts Passed At a General Assembly of the Commonwealth of Virginia* [1796] (Richmond, 1797), 14.

[113] The appeal from the circuit court decision pending before the Supreme Court (Hunter *v.* Fairfax's Devisee, 3 Dallas 305) was non pros'd in February 1797. Supreme Court Appellate Records, Dockets. The appeal from the decision of the lower court of Virginia, pending before the Virginia Court of Appeals, abated because of appellee's death. In 1803, the action was revived against the next Fairfax heir, and in 1810 the Court of Appeals reversed the 1794 decision of the lower court. Hunter *v.* Fairfax's Devisee, 1 Munford (Va.) 218. This judgment was overturned by the Supreme Court of the United States. Fairfax's Devisee *v.* Hunter's Lessee, 7 Cranch 603 (1813). The subsequent challenge of the Virginia Court to the Supreme Court's appellate jurisdiction over state tribunals in Hunter *v.* Martin, Devisee of Fairfax, 4 Munford (Va.) 1 (1814) led to the powerful enunciation of nationalism in Martin *v.* Hunter's Lessee, 1 Wheaton 304 (1816). See Beveridge, *Life of Marshall*, I, 191–196, II, 202–213, 551, IV, 145–161; Crosskey, *Politics and the Constitution*, II, 785–817; William E. Dodd, "Chief Justice Marshall and Virginia, 1813–1821," *American Historical Review*, XII (1906–7), 776–787; Warren, *Supreme Court*, I, 151–153, 444–453; H. C. Groome, *Fauquier During the Proprietorship: A Chronicle of the Colonization and Organization of a Northern Neck County* (Richmond, 1927), 218–240.

[114] The Ordinance of Separation declared that the rights and interests of lands derived from the laws of Virginia should be decided by the laws in force when the compact was made. An Act Concerning the Erection of the District of Kentucky into an Independent State, sec. 4 in *Laws of Kentucky*...(Lexington, 1799), xxxiii. This subsequently was incorporated into Art. VIII, sec. 6 of the Kentucky constitution. *Ibid.*, lvi.

[115] Triple adverse claims were not unusual. One example: "A, a non-resident has a claim on a certain tract of land, he enters a caveat in the Federal court, against the plat of B, a resident and recovers judgement – B, the resident, enters his caveat against A's, plat in the state court, and recovers judgement. C, is in possession of the land, whose claim is confessedly inferior to that of A, or B, or perhaps C, has no legal claim at all. Quere. Will not C, hold this land forever? or what measure can be taken to oust him!" *Kentucky Gazette* (Lexington), July 17, 1800.

the occupying settler[116] and by decisions of the state courts,[117] which, it was feared, might be overturned by federal judges on the grounds that Kentucky had violated the compact of separation from Virginia.[118] Were that to happen, many Kentucky land titles would be disturbed.

In 1800, then, private interests, frequently on a grand scale, stood opposed to the interest of the state government in Pennsylvania, Georgia, Virginia, and Kentucky. In the formulation of its public policy, each state had exercised the right to determine an issue that it clearly regarded as "local" and legitimately within its province. To a considerable degree, the Judiciary Act of 1789 had protected the states and the role of their judiciaries through its failure to provide the circuit courts with trial jurisdiction over private civil litigation arising under the Constitution and the laws of the United States and through its stringent restrictions on diversity suits to be tried in federal courts. Indeed, its basic principle had been that litigants must look primarily to the state courts in the first instance, subject to limited review by the Supreme Court.

The Judiciary Act of 1801, on the other hand, radically altered this principle. By giving the circuit courts original jurisdiction over such civil litigation, by greatly expanding the definition of diversity suits which could be heard in those courts, and by reducing the necessary jurisdictional amount, the new Act supplied the alternative of a national forum for many suits that heretofore could have been tried only in state courts. In so doing, it threatened state control over many areas of litigation involving basic questions of public policy. Furthermore, certain procedural changes made more effective this extension of federal power. Although the proposal for empowering federal judges to issue writs to state judges compelling removals was abandoned, nevertheless the new removal provisions struck more deeply at the autonomy of the state judiciaries. Under

---

[116] *Laws of Kentucky*, 202–206, 291–342.

[117] The Kentucky legislature had threatened the removal of judges of the Kentucky Supreme Court who failed to uphold the legislation. E. Polk Johnson, *A History of Kentucky and Kentuckians* ... (Chicago, 1912), I, 141–142.

[118] For this reason, some Kentuckians sought to end federal jurisdiction over suits in diversity. Warren, *Supreme Court*, II, 96. In 1823, in Green *v*. Biddle, 8 Wheaton 1, the Supreme Court declared the Kentucky "Occupying Claimants Law" of 1797 an unconstitutional violation of the contract clause. This set off efforts on the part of the state to curb the appellate jurisdiction of the Court. See William Ayres, "Land Titles in Kentucky," in Kentucky State Bar Association, *Proceedings* (Louisville, 1909), 160–191; Johnson, *History of Kentucky*, I, 141–144; Beveridge, *Life of Marshall*, IV, 371–382; Warren, *Supreme Court*, II, 97–101, 117–119.

the Act of 1801, an alien or out-of-state defendant who had not been
served with process or who had not appeared in state court, if the judgment of the state court was rendered for more than four hundred dollars,
could remove his case after judgment to the circuit court;[119] and any
defendant in a federal question case commenced in a state court could
remove his suit before trial without regard to citizenship or jurisdictional
amount. These provisions of the Judiciary Act of 1801 tied the state courts
far more closely to the federal system at the inferior level than had the
Act of 1789.

So major a revision may be interpreted as the result, in part, of the
desire of certain interests within the Federalist party to enlarge the amount
of private civil litigation that could be tried in the federal courts apart
from state courts then dominated by interests considered hostile to their
own. The new Act specifically invited to the federal courts all diversity litigation involving land titles, regardless of the monetary amount
involved. This was no insignificant technicality. Influential members of
the Sixth Congress were experienced lawyers; they were also land speculators. Robert Goodloe Harper and James Gunn, for example, were
heavily involved in the Yazoo lands purchase; James Bayard, William
Bingham, and James Ross were investors in the Holland Land Company,
and Ross was counsel for the Company; John Marshall, at one time counsel for Fairfax, had been one of the chief purchasers of the Fairfax claim
in Virginia.[120] Harper, Bayard, and Marshall had served on the House
committee that had drawn the initial judiciary revision bill in March
1800. These men were hardly unaware of the current of local hostility
to their speculative ventures. Having purchased lands on a vast scale,
their anticipated fortunes hung in the balance in 1800, jeopardized by
state action. Frightened by the pattern of action in some of the states,
such land merchants seemingly responded just as swiftly as the states had

---

[119] In 1796, Kentucky passed legislation regarding the method of proceeding in its courts
against absent debtors or other absent defendants. Passed at the same time as legislation
favorable to occupying claimants of land, this act made it possible in any suit upon
affidavit that the defendant could not be served with process, and the defendant did not
appear, for the complainant to proceed as if an appearance by the defendant had been
entered. *Laws of Kentucky*, 354–359. The removal provisions of the Act of 1801 made
it possible to circumvent the intention of the Kentucky legislature and the judgment of
its courts. It is possible, though not demonstrable, that this particular removal provision
was included as federal remedy to combat such state legislation.

[120] For the extent of land speculation during the Federalist decade, see Sakolski, *Great
American Land Bubble*, chaps. 2–7.

responded to the Supreme Court decision in the Chisholm case and in identical manner – by altering jurisdictions.

It would be a mistake, however, to view the Judiciary Act of 1801 solely in terms of its benefits to the speculative interests of Federalist members of Congress. It is not the only point. During the early national period, thousands of citizens, Federalist and Republican, invested in land that they purchased with cash or credit. Not until one contemplates the countless bona fide purchasers who obtained lands either from speculators or directly from the states, assuming that they had purchased clear titles, can the full dimension of this problem be realized. It was not only certain large land speculators who faced ruin in 1800 by virtue of state action; so did many others who had purchased land in small amounts from them. The Act of 1801 offered many of these smaller purchasers the choice of a federal court in which to litigate their titles.[121] Yazoo claimants, for example, to whom Georgia courts were closed and for whom the 1789 jurisdictional amount of five hundred dollars might have been too high, could now take their cases directly to federal court. So could nonresident claimants to every single acre of disputed lands throughout the nation. The new trial jurisdiction over cases arising under the Constitution, laws of the United States, and treaties could, at the choice of the plaintiff, put other land suits, irrespective of value, into the federal system for determination. Because of the intensity of land mania in the 1790s and the great number of people in one way or another involved, it is not unreasonable to suppose that the new judiciary act might have aroused public support as well as opposition, depending upon whether the individual stood to gain or lose by the lowering of the barriers to federal adjudication of land titles.

---

[121] It would be extremely difficult to determine the actual number of citizens who would have been affected. This would depend upon the authority under which each purchaser claimed title and the relationship between his claim and state law, which might give federal jurisdiction over the question or the existence of diversity of citizenship to give federal jurisdiction over the parties. Manuscript records indicate that in the federal court in Delaware, three ejectment suits, prompted apparently by the absence of jurisdictional limit on land cases, were brought against local citizens. Another case, Penn's Lessees *v.* Pennington, was similarly entered but was not tried until 1804. By then the Act had been repealed and Justice Chase granted a nonsuit for want of jurisdiction. Richard S. Rodney, "The End of the Penns' Claim to Delaware, 1789–1814: Some Forgotten Lawsuits," *Pennsylvania Magazine of History and Biography*, LXI (1937), 196. Existing court records for this period are so scanty that it is impossible to measure the effect of the Act during its brief existence.

Similarities can be noted when one considers commercial litigation. The efforts of the Federalists to abolish the "assignee clause" and to lower the requirement in diversity suits, other than land cases, to 100 dollars failed. Yet the Act as passed reflects some gains for those who wished to expand federal jurisdiction over litigation derivative from commercial enterprise. Through the increase in the number of federal courts, it promised greater uniformity of decisions, a major convenience to commercial litigants. Although subject to a jurisdictional amount of four hundred dollars, diversity suits were no longer restricted to suits between a citizen of the state where suit was brought and a citizen of another state. With federally-granted rights, irrespective of amount, no longer left only to state courts for trial, the federal judiciary might have become more attractive to, and useful for, men of business whether the business was small, medium, or large. State infringement on contractual obligations involving small sums, for example, could henceforth be freed from trial before state courts.[122] Together with the passage of a uniform national bankruptcy act,[123] administered through the federal courts, advantages can be seen for those who viewed the future of the nation, in Bayard's phrase, as "one great commercial republic."[124] Many, outside the inner councils of the Federalist party, might have welcomed such changes.

---

[122] After Ware *v.* Hylton in 1796, British creditors were safe in the federal courts, which took no cognizance of debts under $500. Many of these debts were for sums under that amount that the state courts had refused to take on the ground that no compensation had been given for slaves taken during the war. Samuel Flagg Bemis, *Jay's Treaty: A Study in Commerce and Diplomacy* (New York, 1923), 316–317. The Act of 1801 would have enabled such longstanding suits to be tried by the federal courts, but more important to the overall question is the nature of difficulties, if any, out-of-state litigants faced within the different states. Only when more extensive research is completed, will conclusions on this point be possible. The degree to which state court decisions would be accepted as guides to decisions in the circuit courts was an issue not settled at this early date. What law would be applied by the federal courts is a question of major importance. For a controversial interpretation, see Crosskey, *Politics and the Constitution*, I, chaps. 18–20, II, 763.

[123] Our knowledge of the national economy and the problems of federalism would profit from detailed investigation of both the first uniform national bankruptcy act, *U.S. Stat.*, II, 19–36 (Apr. 4, 1800), and the laws of the states governing the relationship between creditor and debtor. At a time when the reach of federal law within the states was in so undetermined a stage, the implications of federal bankruptcy legislation, at the same time as a more comprehensive judiciary policy was being presented, created extreme nervousness among those who feared the threat to state determination of such questions. For debate on the measure, see Jan. 14–15, 1799, in *Annals of Congress*, IX, 2649–2677. In 1803, the Bankruptcy Act was repealed by the Republicans. *U.S. Stat.*, II, 248 (Dec. 19, 1803).

[124] Feb. 18, 1803, in *Annals of Congress*, XII, 549.

All of this suggests that the innovations of the Judiciary Act of 1801 may reveal an underlying purpose of the Federalists to popularize the federal courts throughout the nation. Hitherto, neither its organization nor the scope of its jurisdiction had brought the federal judiciary very close to the average citizen. By expanding both, the Act of 1801 extended the benefits of a presumed uniformity of decision to litigants who formerly were deprived of the use of federal courts either because of their inconvenient location or because of jurisdictional restriction. The Act of 1801 made possible the diversion of an increased number of suits from the state courts to the federal system. In so doing, it potentially neutralized the power of state courts over a great mass of suits of the most ordinary variety, suits touching the legal interests of a great many citizens. Many simple commercial and property disputes could be more easily litigated in the federal courts, now made the "steady asserter of the federal rights" for which Attorney General Randolph had called a decade earlier.[125] By making the federal judiciary an effective shield against state action where it touched the tangible concerns of the individual citizen, and particularly by offering federal adjudication for many of the land suits that plagued the nation at this time, the Federalists may well have felt that they had rendered federal justice "acceptable to the people." In addition, such a judicial system could effectively serve the nationalist impulse of the Federalist party. By drawing the private citizen to the national government, it might strengthen the bonds of national union.

Not unconnected with this nationalist impulse were Federalist desires for more efficient execution of the criminal jurisdiction of the federal courts. This was equally well served by the new organization. The more circuits, the more judges, the greater the efficiency of national courts to the national government. Tax collection had been a continuing national problem; so was sedition. Federalist references to the desirability of a more comprehensive judiciary in lieu of an army are not without point at a time when some feared actual rebellion. There is no way of knowing how many would have favored the new policy on these grounds alone. However, it is no accident that effective pressure to revise the original judiciary system comes in 1799–1800 when peace with France was in the making, when the argument for an army was severely weakened, when the interests of powerful Federalist leaders were being threatened by the very states in which Republicans simultaneously challenged the

[125] Edmund Randolph to Washington, Aug. 5, 1792, in Sparks, ed., *Writings of Washington*, X, 513–514.

Federalist concept of union, and when there was a scramble to strengthen party support before the forthcoming election.

The Judiciary Act of 1801, then, was not conceived in the exigencies of defeat to compensate for that catastrophe. Rather, it was introduced long before the election. Political defeat then gave a driving urgency to the fight for its passage. The appointment of the midnight judges, considered so insulting by the incoming party, was a byproduct of wider aims and became the target for fundamental opposition to the new judicial structure.[126] Just as empiric response to their needs had stimulated the Federalist drive for a more comprehensive national judiciary, so opposition to the federal courts, already sharp because of their exercise of criminal jurisdiction, became heightened at the threat of federal adjudication of civil litigation involving issues regarded by state governments as concerns of their own. At the center of the political maelstrom in 1801, the role of the federal judiciary had become one of the most concrete manifestations of the division between the proponents and opponents of the extension of federal power. Passage of the Judiciary Act of 1801 was the last major policy achievement of the Federalists; its repeal was the first major action taken by the victorious Republicans.

[126] On the appointments, see my article "The Midnight Judges," *University of Pennsylvania Law Review*, CIX (1960–61), 494–523.

The Appointment of Chief Justice Marshall

Kathryn Turner

At the port of Le Havre in October 1800, wearied after the labors of negotiating the Convention with France,[1] and stricken with that "excruciating malady," the gravel, Oliver Ellsworth abruptly altered his plans for the future. He was too feeble, in the opinion of his physician, to attempt the long voyage home over stormy autumn seas. Consequently, Ellsworth sent by his returning son his resignation as Chief Justice of the Supreme Court to President John Adams and left France for England hoping to improve his health at the mineral waters of Bath.[2] Sympathetic though his personal feelings toward the ailing Ellsworth may have been, the President might well have regarded a resignation from the highest judicial office at this particular time a regrettably inopportune occurrence.

By mid-December 1800, when the resignation was received, it was apparent that the Federalist President was not to have a second term and that the Federalists were reduced to the minority party in the Congress

Kathryn Turner is a member of the History Department, Wellesley College, Massachusetts.

[1] The Convention had been signed in Paris on Sept. 30, 1800.

[2] Oct. 16, 1800, Letters Received and Other Loose Papers, Adams Papers, Massachusetts Historical Society, Boston; hereafter cited as Letters Received, Adams Papers (available on microfilm). Permission to quote from this and all subsequent references to the Adams Papers has been granted by the Adams Manuscript Trust at the Massachusetts Historical Society. The author wishes to express her gratitude to Mr. Lyman Butterfield, the editor of the Adams Papers, for his generous assistance while this study was in preparation. See also the Memoir of Ellsworth by his son-in-law Joseph Wood, Bancroft Transcripts, New York Public Library, N.Y.C. This memoir was drawn from the journal of Oliver Ellsworth, Jr., who served as private secretary to his father during the period Ellsworth was in France.

that would convene the following year.[3] A peaceable, but nonetheless feared, "revolution" had removed the Federalists from power in two of the three branches of government. Meanwhile, the proposed judiciary bill for strengthening the power of that branch immune from the popular will, the federal court system, was still before Congress. Convinced that now only in "a solid judiciary" was security to be found against "visionary schemes or fluctuating theories,"[4] Adams lost no time in attempting to fill the vacancy on the high court with a trusted and therefore suitable Federalist. The President at once nominated John Jay, then completing his term as governor of New York, to the very office Jay had resigned in 1795.

This decision was apparently reached by Adams without consultation with either his cabinet or party leaders in Congress. Indeed, he did not even learn Jay's sentiments before sending the nomination to the Senate.[5] It is not difficult to understand why Adams exercised his power of appointment without seeking advice or suggestions from others. By the end of 1800, the tensions within Federalist ranks had developed into an open and public split,[6] leaving the President alienated politically from many in his party and personally suspicious and hostile toward many others whom he now considered enemies. Neither is it difficult to understand why Adams, faced with the necessity of making a speedy decision to fill the chief justiceship, should have selected John Jay as his first choice.

[3] Ellsworth's letter of resignation to Adams is endorsed at the head of the text by John Adams, "Rcd. Dec. 15, 1800"; Letters Received, Adams Papers. The defeat of Adams and the tie between Burr and Jefferson for the presidency was known by Dec. 12, 1800; Thomas Jefferson to Henry Knox, Mar. 27, 1801, *The Writings of Thomas Jefferson*, ed. Paul Leicester Ford (New York and London, 1892–99), VIII, 36–37. The official counting of electoral votes did not take place until Feb. 11, 1801; U.S., Congress, *Annals of the Congress of the United States*, 6th Congress, 2d session (Washington, 1851), pp. 1022–30; hereafter cited as *Annals*. For details regarding the election, see Manning J. Dauer, *The Adams Federalists* (Baltimore, 1953), pp. 246–259; Morton Borden, *The Federalism of James A. Bayard* (New York, 1955), pp. 73–95.

[4] Adams to John Jay, Dec. 19, 1800, *The Works of John Adams . . .*, ed. Charles Francis Adams (Boston, 1850–56), IX, 91–92.

[5] *Ibid.* ". . . nobody but Mr. A would have made the nomination without consulting Mr. Jay," commented Timothy Pickering testily; Pickering to Rufus King, Jan. 5, 1801, *The Life and Correspondence of Rufus King . . .*, ed. Charles R. King, III (New York, 1896), 367.

[6] For the most recent analysis of Federalist politics, see Stephen G. Kurtz, *The Presidency of John Adams* (Philadelphia, 1957). The split within the Federalist party is covered in this work as well as in Dauer, *Federalists*; John Spencer Bassett, *The Federalist System, 1789–1801* (New York and London, 1906); and Claude Bowers, *Jefferson and Hamilton* (Boston and New York, 1925).

Jay, who had served as chief justice from 1789 to 1795, was qualified by experience. Since he was planning to retire as governor of New York in 1801,[7] he was also qualified by availability for an office providing tenure for life. Probably of equal importance in the mind of the President was the fact that Jay had not aligned himself with the Hamiltonian faction of the party, and hence Adams felt no sense of having been "betrayed" by him. In fact, the attacks of Hamilton upon Jay may well have served to bind more tightly Adams's affections for his old friend.[8] Judicially, politically, and personally, the reappointment of Jay was a move that seemed pleasing to Adams, and he strongly urged Jay to accept the opportunity to return to the Court: "Nothing will cheer the hopes of the best men so much as your acceptance of this appointment," Adams wrote. He added that "it appeared to me that Providence had thrown in my way an opportunity, not only of marking to the public where, in my opinion, the greatest mass of worth remained collected in one individual, but of furnishing my country with the best security its inhabitants afforded against the increasing dissolution of morals."[9]

Some surprise was indicated at the appointment. Oliver Wolcott, commenting that it was unlikely Jay would accept, wrote that "The nomination is here considered as having been made in one of those 'sportive' humors for which our Chief is distinguished."[10] Timothy Pickering felt sure that Jay would refuse the nomination and that Judge William Paterson of the Supreme Court would then be appointed.[11] Thomas Boylston Adams, unaware that his father had acted to fill the vacancy created by Ellsworth's resignation, wrote his mother that he presumed Paterson would be promoted to the chief justiceship.[12] Jefferson damned the nomination with faint praise. "We were afraid of something worse," he wrote to Madison.[13] The outspoken *Aurora* sneered: "John Jay, after having through decay of age, become incompetent to discharge the duties

---

[7] Frank Monaghan, *John Jay* (New York and Indianapolis, 1935), p. 424.
[8] Adams wrote Jay that among the few truths in Alexander Hamilton's pamphlet of 1800 were the remarks regarding the merits of Jay in the negotiations for peace, which Adams said he would "ever acknowledge with pleasure." Adams to Jay, Nov. 24, 1800, Adams, *Works of Adams*, IX, 90–91.
[9] Dec. 19, 1800, *ibid.*, pp. 91–92.
[10] Wolcott to Pickering, Dec. 28, 1800, George Gibbs, *Memoirs of the Administrations of Washington and John Adams, Edited from the Papers of Oliver Wolcott . . .* (New York, 1846), II, 461.
[11] Pickering to King, Jan. 5, 1801, King, *Life and Correspondence*, III, 367.
[12] To Abigail Adams, Dec. 20, 1800, Letters Received, Adams Papers.
[13] Dec. 19, 1800, Ford, *Writings of Jefferson*, VII, 471.

of Governor, has been appointed to the *sinecure* of *Chief Justice* of the United States."[14]

Although the nomination of Jay was approved by the Senate without delay, considerable doubt existed in the inner circles of the Adams administration that Jay would choose to forego his plans for retirement in favor of returning to the Court. On the day the nomination was presented to the Senate, Secretary of State John Marshall wrote that Jay would probably decline the office.[15] Only four days after writing Jay of his nomination, the President himself indicated to his son, Thomas, the possibility of a refusal.[16] In a Christmas Day letter to Thomas, Abigail Adams also expressed in confidence the fear that Jay would refuse the appointment.[17] Should the awaited reply from Jay bring a refusal early in the new year, Adams would again be faced with the problem of selecting a suitable Federalist for the position, a decision made more pressing and more complicated as each remaining week of his presidency slipped away.

Since the President had failed to ensure acceptance before making the nomination, time would have been lost, when there was no time to lose, if Jay decided to decline the post. During the interval in which President Adams awaited a reply from Jay[18] it is clear that consideration was given to the problems that would arise in such an eventuality. Either from cautious foresight or, despite his hopes, from a conviction that Jay would refuse his commission, Adams, without waiting for the reply from Albany to reach Washington, began to work out a possible alternative to be followed if it became necessary.

With the chief justiceship vacant, the Supreme Court at this time consisted of, in order of seniority, William Cushing of Massachusetts, William Paterson of New Jersey, Samuel Chase of Maryland, Bushrod Washington of Virginia, and Alfred Moore of North Carolina. Two

[14] *Aurora* (Philadelphia, Pa.), Jan. 8, 1801. The *Aurora* also circulated the Republican charge that Jay had been recommended in connection with a Federalist plan to prevent the election and place the Chief Justice in the presidency instead. Later, James Callender, writing in the *Examiner* (Richmond, Va.), Feb. 6, 1801, was to assert that Adams had nominated Jay with "the previous certainty" that Jay would refuse, thus facilitating the introduction of John Marshall to the office.

[15] To Charles Cotesworth Pinckney, Dec. 18, 1800, Pinckney Family Papers, Box 1, Library of Congress, Washington, D.C.

[16] Dec. 23, 1800, Letters Received, Adams Papers.

[17] Dec. 25, 1800, *ibid.*

[18] The letter from Adams to Jay is dated Dec. 19, 1800, Adams, *Works of Adams*, IX, 91–92. Jay's reply refusing the appointment was dated Jan. 2, 1801, *The Correspondence and Public Papers of John Jay*, ed. Henry P. Johnston (New York and London, 1890–93), IV, 285–286. There is no date of receipt marked on the original of this letter in the Adams Papers.

obvious courses lay open to the President: he could fill the vacancy by a promotion from among the associate justices or from outside the ranks of the Court. It may be that Adams felt that through the selection of Jay, who had the prestige of having been Washington's own choice as the first chief justice, he had avoided any party antagonism over the appointment. In addition, he had avoided wounding the sensibilities of any of the associate justices who might have looked less favorably upon the elevation of some other outsider to the highest rank.[19] In the event that Jay did not choose to return to the judiciary, the same choices for action would await the presidential decision, but as easy a solution was by no means evident. It seems quite clear that Adams fully intended at this time to select one of the associate justices to be chief justice should Jay refuse the nomination. As early as December 23, in fact, he was actively attempting to fill the subsequent vacancy in the Court that such a move would create.

While the outcome of the election had hung in the balance, officeholders under Federalist appointments had considered their future; some concluded that under a change of administration, they would not wish to continue service even if the Republicans permitted them to retain their offices. Among these was Jared Ingersoll, the noted leader of the Philadelphia bar and the United States district attorney for Pennsylvania.[20] Ingersoll had earlier requested Thomas Adams, then a young lawyer in Philadelphia, to tell the President of his intention to resign as district attorney as soon as it was clear that the Federalists would lose the election.[21] This news had brought an immediate response from the President that his son request Ingersoll not to resign at least until March 3, 1801. He added a hint that he might have a message to send to Ingersoll before that time.[22] Apparently, even before nominating Jay, Adams had considered that Ingersoll might be persuaded to take a seat on the Court should a vacancy occur.[23] On December 23, the President, then awaiting word from Jay, wrote again

---

[19] I am not convinced that the question of prestige of being chief justice weighed this heavily with the judges. I have taken the possibility into account because John Adams was subsequently to use it as a reason for action.

[20] The district attorneys held their appointments at the pleasure of the president. As Federal district attorney, Ingersoll had been responsible for initiating proceedings against William Duane, editor of the *Aurora*, in Oct. 1800, under the Sedition Act. See James M. Smith, *Freedom's Fetters* (Ithaca, 1956), pp. 301–302.

[21] Thomas Adams to John Adams, Dec. 14, 1800, Letters Received, Adams Papers.

[22] Adams to Thomas Adams, Dec. 17, 1800, *ibid.*

[23] Before he learned of the appointment of Jay, Thomas B. Adams had suggested Ingersoll or Edward Tilghman, two noted Philadelphia lawyers, or Samuel Dexter, then Secretary of War, to fill the place left at Ellsworth's resignation, though he believed Ingersoll would not accept the position; Thomas Adams to Abigail Adams, Dec. 20, 1800, *ibid.*

to his son. "I have appointed Mr. Jay chief Justice. He may refuse, if he should I shall follow the line of judges most probably & then there will be a vacancy I wish to know if Mr. Ingersoll would accept an appointment as one of the assistant Judges of the superior court.... I hope Mr. Ingersoll will not resign till the 3rd March at any rate unless he should do it a little sooner in order to fill the place with a thoroughly good man."[24] Replying to his father that he had "ventured in confidence" to show the letter to Ingersoll, young Adams reported that the Philadelphia lawyer requested more time to consider the subject, adding his own opinion that Ingersoll would not refuse to be considered. "Should this gentleman ... consent to accept the contingent proposal, which has been made to him, *at this time*, I shall view it as no common sacrifice of private feeling, domestic & retired habits and pecuniary benefit, to an imperious conviction, that an upright judiciary is the only bulwark that can oppose & restrain the impetuous torrent of division & disorganization with which this Continent is threatened. He has a stake in the common weal, and cannot be indifferent as to its protection from wild theories, and no less extravagant practise. I hope he may come in."[25]

Writing to his mother two days later, Thomas again mentioned the negotiations to secure a favorable reply from Ingersoll and the latter's desire to delay giving the President a decisive answer. "It is confidential business, but I presume you are in the secret.... He has not fully formed a resolution, what answer to give, and his greatest difficulty arises from the uncertainty whether any change will take place in the Judiciary system, during this session. If that were certain he would not scruple to give an affirmative answer, but said he, 'with my habits of life to be six months in the year absent from my family, I know of nothing scarcely that could induce the sacrifice.'"[26] It was also the understanding of Abigail Adams,

---

[24] Dec. 23, 1800, *ibid.*

[25] Dec. 28, 1800, *ibid.*

[26] Dec. 30, 1800, *ibid.* For Adams to have used his youngest son as his emissary in sounding out Jared Ingersoll does not seem unusual in view of the personal and political situation at the time. By this time, Adams trusted very few persons outside the family circle. Abigail had always been his political confidante as well as his "dear friend." Now, with John Quincy abroad, and with the promising Charles so recently dead, the ties of affection between John Adams and Thomas B. Adams seem to have grown even closer. "Indeed every letter I receive from you increases my esteem for your character, for an understanding discretion & benevolence.... The melancholy decease of your brother is an affliction of a more serious nature to this family than any other. Oh! that I had died for him if that would have relieved him of his faults as well as his disease." John Adams to Thomas Adams, Dec. 17, 1800, *ibid.*

her husband's political confidante, that if Jay declined, William Cushing would be named chief justice; if he should refuse, William Paterson, next in seniority, would be offered the highest office, with Ingersoll brought to the Court as associate justice.[27] Although Thomas Adams stated that his father would disregard the rule of geographical locality, "the narrow principle which has heretofore prevailed with regard to such appointments & which I know was never approved by him,"[28] the choice of a reputable legal figure who was outside the bitter intraparty war and was from the important state of Pennsylvania seemed wise. However, an affirmative reply from Ingersoll apparently would have to await not only the refusal from Jay that would make a place available to him but also the enactment of the judiciary bill, which would end the peregrinations to the circuits endured for a decade by the judges of the Supreme Court. Until Jay's answer was received, the President could officially do nothing further; until the judiciary bill was passed, he could not feel sure that his persuasions would be great enough to bring Ingersoll to the Court.[29]

Quite apart from its provision to free the Supreme Court justices from circuit duties, the judiciary bill had an important bearing on the appointment to be made at this time. The legislation included a provision to reduce the Supreme Court after the next vacancy from six members to five.[30] This bill, postponed by the House at the first session of the Sixth Congress, was due to be brought to the floors of Congress for debate and vote in January 1801. It became imperative that the membership of the Court be assured, with nominations made, approved, and accepted, before debate in Congress began. Although the reduction in the number of judges has been defended in terms of a means to prevent a tie vote on the Court,[31] only the most avid Federalist partisan could fail to attribute a political motivation to the proposed change. Certainly the provision was not intended to limit the Federalist power of placement. Should Jay refuse the commission tendered to him, and should the President follow his plan to elevate the new chief justice from among the membership of the Court, this would leave an associate justice to be appointed. Were the President to delay this decision until the judiciary bill came up for debate, it was

---

[27] Abigail Adams to Thomas Adams, Dec. 25, 1800, *ibid.*
[28] To Abigail Adams, Dec. 20, 1800, *ibid.*
[29] I have found nothing to indicate that John Adams thought of any other figure for the vacancy.
[30] 2 Statute 89, sec. 3 (Feb. 13, 1801), *Annals*, 6th Cong., 2d sess., Appendix, p. 1534.
[31] For example, William W. Crosskey, *Politics and the Constitution in the History of the United States* (Chicago, 1953), II, 759.

likely that the Republicans would willingly accede to the reduction of membership, thereby preventing Adams from adding another Federalist member to the Court. With a crowded calendar for action in the weeks remaining to the Federalist majority,[32] it was imperative that the judiciary bill be not delayed. It thus became urgent that the question of the appointment, whether to the office of chief justice or associate justice, be clarified as quickly as possible so that the Federalist leaders in Congress could carry the bill for reorganizing the federal courts without suffering from their own provision to cut the membership of the Supreme Court.

Of additional concern in this matter was the position of the elderly senior judge, William Cushing, now sixty-eight, whose infirmities had frequently prevented his attendance upon judicial duties, and whose voluntary retirement was not without the realm of possibility. Indeed, the wish was expressed that a successor might be appointed for Cushing as well as Ellsworth before the administration changed hands.[33] John Marshall "feared" that the President would nominate the senior judge as chief justice if Jay declined,[34] and clearly this is what the President had in mind. There were, indeed, to the Federalists, grounds for concern. Should Cushing be appointed to the high post with the membership of the Court reduced, upon his death or retirement (either of which could reasonably be considered imminent) the path would then be open for the incoming president to appoint to the highest judicial post in the nation.[35] Nevertheless, President Adams seems to have regarded it as awkward to plan to bypass Cushing by offering the chief justiceship directly to William Paterson of New Jersey, next in order of seniority, fifty-six years old, and in good health.[36] No other objection to Paterson for the office appeared

---

[32] Duties on licenses, the resolution to continue the Sedition Act, the election of Burr or Jefferson as president, the engrossment and recommittal of the Bankruptcy Act, and ratification of the Convention with France were measures in addition to the Judiciary Act that were acted upon by the lame duck session of the Sixth Congress.

[33] Samuel Sewall to Theodore Sedgwick, Dec. 29, 1800, Sedgwick Papers, Box D, p. 144, Mass. Hist. Soc., Boston.

[34] Marshall to C. C. Pinckney, Dec. 18, 1800, Pinckney Family Papers, Box 1.

[35] Whether the next president would be Jefferson or Burr was not known at this point, but it was generally assumed that Jefferson, if elected, hoped to name Spencer Roane, chief justice of the Virginia Court of Appeals, to the Supreme Court; David Mays, "Judge Spencer Roane," Virginia State Bar Association, *Reports*, XL (1928), 446–464.

[36] John Marshall recalled that he had suggested Paterson at the time of Ellsworth's resignation in 1800, but the President objected then that Judge Cushing's feelings would be wounded at being bypassed. For this reason, Jay had been selected instead; *An Autobiographical Sketch by John Marshall, Written at the Request of Joseph Story*, ed. John Stokes Adams (Ann Arbor, 1937), pp. 29–30.

at this time. Although Samuel Otis, secretary of the Senate and father of
Harrison Gray Otis, relayed to the President the request for a place on
the Supreme Court for Jacob Read, the recently defeated senator from
South Carolina, "sacrificed for his support of Government,"[37] there is no
evidence that John Adams heeded the suggestion. Making his decisions
alone, he had acted to reappoint Jay as chief justice. If this proved unsuccessful, Cushing would be offered the post and the vacancy on the Court
would be filled by Ingersoll, if he could be persuaded to accept. But these
were plans of the President, not achievements. By the end of December
1800, the chief justiceship was still vacant, the judiciary bill was still
unassured of passage, and Ingersoll as yet withheld an affirmative answer
because of the arduous duties assigned the Supreme Court judges by the
Judiciary Act of 1789. Only Jay's reply could determine the next course
of action.

By January 3, 1801, no answer had yet come from Jay.[38] On January
9, Thomas Adams wrote again that he still had no definite answer from
Ingersoll. The young emissary reminded his father that Ingersoll would
be in Washington early in February for the Supreme Court session; presumably the President could speak with his friend directly at that time.[39]

However, to prolong such an uncertainty until February was simply
to complicate the situation further. If Ingersoll decided to accept the
nomination, well and good. If he did not, then it would be necessary
to select another figure, assure his willingness to accept, and have the
nomination approved by Congress. If the judiciary bill should have passed
by that time, as the President hoped it would, then ironically he might be
spared by law the problem of appointing another associate justice. This
would in turn create the probability that the next appointment would
be that of a Republican justice. Amid such tangled eventualities, John
Adams continued to wait for the answer from Jay to arrive.

Jay's reply, written from Albany on January 2, was finally received
by the President.[40] As is well known, it brought a refusal to return as

[37] Jan. 13, 1801, Letters Received, Adams Papers.
[38] Abigail Adams to Thomas Adams, Jan. 3, 1801, *ibid.*
[39] Thomas Adams to John Adams, Jan. 9, 1801, and Thomas Adams to Abigail Adams,
Dec. 30, 1800, *ibid.*
[40] The date when Adams actually received Jay's reply is difficult to determine. Contrary to
his usual custom, Adams marked no date of receipt on the original. Newspapers reported
the fact on various dates, but it is impossible to separate the publication here of rumor
and/or wishful thinking from known or announced fact. The *Palladium* (Boston, Mass.),
Jan. 29, 1801, printed a report dated Phila., Jan. 9, stating that "We hear that Mr. Jay
has declined the acceptance of the office of Chief Justice." The *Philadelphia Gazette*

chief justice. The reasons Jay presented to the President are illuminating. Commenting upon the original federal court system, which had seemed so defective to him when he had resigned the office in 1795, he wrote:

Such was the temper of the times, that the Act to establish the Judicial Courts of the United States was in some respects more accomodated to certain prejudices and sensibilities, than to the great and obvious principles of sound policy. Expectations were nevertheless entertained that it would be amended as the public mind became more composed and better informed; but those expectations have not been realized, nor have we hitherto seen convincing indications of a disposition in Congress to realize them. On the contrary, the efforts repeatedly made to place the judicial department on a proper footing have proved fruitless.... I am induced to doubt both the propriety and the expediency of my returning to the bench under the present system; especially as it would give some countenance to the neglect and indifference with which the opinions and remonstrances of the judges on this important subject have been treated.[41]

Evidently, Jay took with little seriousness the effort to pass the judiciary bill for reforming the court system that had been introduced in 1800 – took with more seriousness, indeed, the fact that the bill was still not acted upon as the Sixth Congress drew to a swift conclusion.[42]

Adams now was faced with the necessity of choosing a chief justice who would accept the office. He could hardly afford the delay in time that a new nomination and possibly another rejection would entail. To carry out his initial plan of following the line of current members of the Court

---

and *Daily Adveriser* (Pa.), Jan. 16, 1801, printed the information from Washington over the date of Jan. 12. The *Gazette of the United States* (Philadelphia, Pa.), Jan. 13, 1801, reported that Jay had declined, but on Jan. 17, 1801, stated "The President *has received* (italics mine) Jay's declension." The *Aurora*, Jan. 13, 1801, included a notice that Jay had refused. The *National Intelligencer* (Washington), Jan. 14, 1801, stated that "The President *has received* (italics mine) Jay's declension." The *Washington Museum*, Jan. 16, 1801, reported the fact also under the date Jan. 14. On Jan. 19, 1801, Poulson's *American Daily Advertiser* (Philadelphia, Pa.), announced the news, and in other papers more distant the report naturally appeared at later dates. Although the *National Intelligencer* was an opposition paper, the wording of its report, together with its location at the seat of the government, together with the identical information in the *Washington Museum* also on the identical date, is reason enough to presume, I think, that this date (Jan. 14) is approximately correct. Marshall's reminiscences 27 years later of the sequence of events give the impression that Jay's refusal was received on Jan. 19, the day before his own appointment was made, but memory of detail of this sort may well not be precise; Adams, *Autobiographical Sketch by Marshall*, p. 30.

41 Jay to Adams, Jan. 2, 1801, Johnston, *Correspondence of Jay*, IV, 285–286.

42 When Jay wrote his reply on Jan. 2, 1801, the judiciary bill, postponed at the first session of the Sixth Congress, had not even been brought again from committee. Debate in the second session began in the House on Jan. 5; *Annals*, 6th Cong., 2d sess., p. 878.

and bringing Ingersoll in as an associate judge had a double disadvantage. Cushing's age and ill health made it likely that his years were numbered. He might again refuse to take the chief justiceship although wishing to remain on the Court as he had done in 1796.[43] In that case, Paterson would be selected. In either event, Ingersoll had not given assurance that he would accept a nomination as associate if it were made, and apparently, Adams had no other choice in mind.

Meanwhile, since the Federalist leaders in Congress were not in the confidence of the President on the court appointment, there was no way for the party to know Adams's plans. Their sentiments, nonetheless, for securing a firm composition for the supreme bench were equal to those of the President, and they were acutely aware that an immediate decision on this point was essential. If the President was thinking in terms of adding a new member to the Court, thus preserving the membership at six, any delay was a risk to be avoided. Benjamin Stoddert, the Secretary of the Navy, was at this point enlisted by some members of Congress to call upon the President and mention to him that the judiciary bill would be brought to a vote in the House on January 20, 1801. Prevented by bad weather from paying a personal visit with the news, Stoddert dispatched a note to this effect on January 19 and somewhat gingerly added a reminder of the importance of an immediate presidential decision regarding the Supreme Court before the House should act the next day: "As the bill proposes a reduction of the Judges to five – and as there are already five Judges in comission, it is suggested that there might be more difficulty in appointing a chief Justice without taking him from the present Judges, after the passage of this bill *even by one Branch of the Legislature*, than before."[44]

The sequence of this combination of circumstances makes clear that the action of the House of Representatives on the judiciary bill had direct bearing on the appointment the President did make to the vacant seat on the bench. It also clarifies the reason why John Adams failed to follow his plan of selecting the chief justice from the membership of the Court. Indeed, it seems likely that it was the timing of the House action alone

---

[43] Cushing had rejected the chief justiceship at that time, after the Senate had refused to confirm the appointment of John Rutledge, assigning ill-health as his reason for refusal. Henry Flanders, *The Lives and Times of the Chief Justices of the Supreme Court of the United States* (Philadelphia, 1855–58), II, 46.

[44] To Adams, Jan. 19, 1801, Letters Received, Adams Papers (italics added).

that forced him at this point to select a figure from *outside* the Court as
the new chief justice. When Jay's refusal was received, the judiciary bill
was still before the House in debate. Under the circumstances, even if
Jared Ingersoll could be reached in Philadelphia, he could not be pressed
for his final answer, since he had made clear that this was contingent upon
the passage of the bill. This made it unwise to risk sending his nomination
as associate justice to the Senate (together with that of Cushing as chief
justice) only to have Ingersoll later decline.[45] On January 19, the President
received Stoddert's reminder from the members of Congress, who urged
an immediate decision before the vote on the judiciary bill should be
taken the next day. A change of plans had to be made and made at
once.

Late in his life, in an autobiographical letter to Justice Joseph Story,
John Marshall recalled the details of his appointment to the highest judicial office as follows: "When I waited on the President with Mr. Jay's
letter declining the appointment he said thoughtfully 'Who shall I nominate now?' I replied that I could not tell, as I supposed that his objection
to Judge Patteson [*sic*] remained. He said in a decided tone 'I shall not
nominate him.' After a moments hesitation he said 'I believe I must nominate you.' I had never before heard myself named for the office and had
not even thought of it. I was pleased as well as surprized, and bowed
in silence. Next day I was nominated, . . ."[46] Marshall's reference to his
nomination "next day," if his memory is to be trusted, would point to
the conclusion that following Jay's refusal, the pressure from Congress
relayed by Stoddert, the impossibility of getting an immediate commitment from Ingersoll, and the physical presence of his Secretary of State all
confronted John Adams on January 19, 1801. "Next day," the 20th, in
the House of Representatives, the judiciary bill was brought to a vote and
passed fifty-one to forty-three;[47] in the Senate, the astonished gentlemen
received the nomination of John Marshall as Chief Justice of the Supreme
Court.[48]

---

[45] I have found no evidence that Adams discussed his plans with Cushing or other members
of the Court, and there would have been no vital necessity for his doing so. However,
an assurance from Ingersoll that he would accept a nomination was necessary to ensure
that six members could be kept on the Court.

[46] Adams, *Autobiographical Sketch by Marshall*, pp. 29–30.

[47] *Annals*, 6th Cong., 2d sess., p. 915.

[48] U.S. Congress, Senate, *Journal of the Executive Proceedings of the Senate . . .*, I
(Washington, 1828), 371.

There is no evidence to indicate that President Adams had, in the interval between Ellsworth's resignation and the moment he appointed Marshall, given any careful thought to filling the judicial vacancy with the Virginian who served him as Secretary of State. On the contrary, it is clear that in December 1800, at the time the nomination of Jay was made, Adams had thought of Cushing, and then Paterson, if Jay should decline. By January 1801, however, desiring to preserve the court membership at six before the passage of the judiciary bill should reduce this to five, Adams took no chance that a new appointee might refuse a nomination, thereby possibly forcing him into the position of selecting the chief justice from the five commissioned judges already on the Court. Under these circumstances, he appointed Marshall, since he could be sure, when Marshall "bowed in silence," that the office would be accepted. In this way, the aim of preventing a Republican nomination to the Court was achieved. Thus Marshall, who had in 1798 refused an opportunity to become an associate judge to fill the vacancy left at James Wilson's death,[49] was started on the path in which he was to achieve enduring fame. His selection can hardly be attributed to much deliberation or forethought on the part of the President; it seems clearly more the accidental result of a decision forced upon Adams by the cumulating necessities of the moment.

The Federalists, however, were somewhat less than pleased with the appointment. In 1799, during his campaign for a Congressional seat, John Marshall had publicly opposed the Alien and Sedition Acts.[50] Throughout the turbulent period prior to the election of 1800, he had walked as cool and independent a line between the two factions within the Federalist party as he had between the Federalists and Republicans. During his

---

[49] Marshall to Pickering, Sept. 28, 1798, Adams, *Works of Adams*, VIII, 598n. Marshall said that he was offered the office left vacant at the death of James Iredell; Adams, *Autobiographical Sketch by Marshall*, p. 26. However, here memory was at fault. Iredell did not die until 1799, and this vacancy was filled by Alfred Moore of North Carolina. Adams wanted either Marshall or Bushrod Washington to succeed James Wilson in 1798 and stated that "As Virginia has no judge at present, she is as much entitled as Pennsylvania to attention." Adams to Pickering, Sept. 14, 1798, Adams, *Works of Adams*, VIII, 596. This tends to discount the claims made by Thomas Adams that rules of locality were not approved by his father; Thomas Adams to Abigail Adams, Dec. 20, 1800. Letters Received, Adams Papers.

[50] Albert J. Beveridge, *The Life of John Marshall* (Boston and New York, 1916–19), II, 387–397. See *ibid.*, pp. 574–577 for Freeholder's Questions to Marshall and Marshall's answers.

six months in Congress from December 1799 to May 1800, Marshall
had supported the Federalists against Republican attempts to reduce the
army, had served on the committee to revise the judiciary system, and was
influential in drafting the National Bankruptcy Act, but had voted against
his party for repeal of the Sedition Law and also joined the opposition in
killing the disputed elections bill. Furthermore, against much of his party,
he had supported the decision of John Adams to send a second mission to
France and had vigorously defended the President's conduct in the return
of Thomas Nash-Jonathan Robins to British jurisdiction in that heated
cause célèbre,[51] action that did not go unnoticed by the President.

Federalist leaders of the Hamiltonian wing of the party held distinctly
ambivalent views toward the man now nominated as chief justice. "In
Congress, you see Gen. M. is a leader," wrote George Cabot to Rufus
King. "He is I think a virtuous & certainly an able man; but you see in him
the faults of a Virginian. He thinks too much of that State & he expects
the world will be governed according to the Rules of Logic. I have seen
such men often become excellent legislators after experience has cured
their errors."[52] Theodore Sedgwick, the Speaker of the House, although
he acknowledged the importance of Marshall in that body, blamed him
for the restrictions written into the Bankruptcy Act and related that some
members "thought him temporizing, while others deemed him foolish."
"He is attached to pleasures, with convivial habits strongly fixed. He is
indolent, therefore, and indisposed to take part in the common business
of the house. He has a strong attachment to popularity but indisposed
to sacrifice to it his integrity; hence it is that he is disposed on all popular subjects to feel the public pulse and hence results indecision and
an expression of doubt. Doubts suggested by him create in more feeble
minds those which are irremoveable."[53] At the time Marshall was chosen to replace the ousted Timothy Pickering as Secretary of State in May
1800, Charles Cotesworth Pinckney had felt it necessary to assure James
McHenry, recently dismissed as Secretary of War, of Marshall's political
soundness: "You may rely on his federalism," he wrote, "& be certain
that he will not unite with Jefferson & the Jacobins."[54] In that office

[51] See *ibid.*, chap. 11, for a full account of Marshall's activity in Congress.
[52] Cabot to King, Jan. 20, 1800, King, *Life and Correspondence*, III, 184.
[53] Sedgwick to Rufus King, May 11, 1800, *ibid.*, p. 237. See also Cabot to King, Apr. 26,
1799, *ibid.*, p. 9; Sedgwick to King, Dec. 29, 1799, and Feb. 6, 1800, *ibid.*, pp. 163,
189–190.
[54] C. C. Pinckney to McHenry, June 10, 1800, *The Life and Correspondence of James
McHenry*, ed. Bernard C. Steiner (Cleveland, 1907), p. 460.

from May 1800 to March 1801,[55] Marshall served the harried President well. Adams, outraged over the disloyalty of his cabinet, and distraught because of the illness of his beloved Abigail, had hurried to his Quincy home, where he remained until November 1800. In the absence of his chief, Marshall took no part in the machinations of the Hamiltonian Federalists to substitute Pinckney for Adams as the Federalist candidate in the election of 1800, nor was he a party to the diatribe against Adams that Hamilton wrote before the election.[56] At no time was Marshall's personal loyalty to the President questioned. The objections from within Federalist ranks in the Senate to his appointment to the Supreme Court, however, arose not on this score, nor even from suspicions regarding his political orthodoxy, but primarily from the fact that John Adams had failed to appoint Justice Paterson to the highest office.

There had been wide expectation among the Federalists that William Paterson would be named chief justice if Jay refused the office. "As Mr. Jay will certainly refuse the Chief Justiceship, I presume Judge Paterson will be appointed," wrote Pickering to Rufus King.[57] James Gunn wrote Hamilton that either Paterson or Pinckney should have received the appointment; "but both those worthies were your friends."[58] Samuel Sewall wrote to Theodore Sedgwick his pleasure at the prospect of Paterson's succession as chief justice, adding, "The Judiciary is now almost the only security left us – and it is at all times the most important branch of the federal government."[59] McHenry commented, "Here it was expected by everybody, that he [Adams] would have named Mr. Patterson to the vacant seat on the bench," facetiously adding, "except by Mr. —, who

---

[55] After his approval as chief justice, Marshall continued, at Adams's request, to hold the office of secretary of state until "another appointment can be made." Adams to Marshall, Feb. 4, 1801, Adams, *Works of Adams*, IX, 96. No other appointment was made, and Marshall served in this capacity until the end of the administration.

[56] Details for this part of Marshall's career will be found in Beveridge, *Life of Marshall*, II, 485–547. In Oct. 1800, Hamilton wrote an extravagant attack on Adams that was to be privately circulated among Federalist leaders in the states in order to persuade them against supporting Adams for re-election. After Aaron Burr secured a copy and published portions of it, Hamilton made public the entire pamphlet. This, of course, lent more virulence to the campaign and weakened even further the possibility of a Federalist victory over the Republicans in the election of 1800. See "The Public Conduct and Character of John Adams," *The Works of Alexander Hamilton*, ed. Henry Cabot Lodge, Federal ed. (New York and London, 1904), VII, 309–365.

[57] Jan. 5, 1801, King, *Life and Correspondence*, III, 367.

[58] Dec. 18, 1800, *The Works of Alexander Hamilton*, ed. John C. Hamilton (New York, 1851), VI, 492.

[59] Dec. 29, 1800, Sedgwick Papers, Box D, p. 144.

thought he should have been appointed, and by me, who thought the President should have appointed himself...."[60] In outraged tones, Senator Jonathan Dayton of New Jersey relayed the news of Marshall's appointment to Paterson "with grief, astonishment & almost indignation...contrary to the hopes and expectation of us all." Continuing, Dayton assured Paterson that he was consulting with other Federalists as to the propriety of making a stand against the President's nomination of Marshall, fearful though they were that a Senate rejection at this juncture would only induce Adams to nominate "some other character more improper & more disgusting." The bitterness of feeling toward Adams had reached, in this move, the breaking point. The appointment of Marshall, in what must have seemed a deliberate defiance of the known sentiments of the party favoring Paterson, led Dayton to castigate the retiring President. "The nominations and whole conduct of Mr. Adams during the present session have manifested such debility or derangement of intellect, that I am convinced, in common with the most of our Federal members that another four years of administration in his hands would have exposed us to destruction."[61]

For a full week, the Senate delayed in approving Marshall's nomination while Federalist leaders tried unsuccessfully to persuade Adams to choose Paterson instead. The reason for the President's adamant attitude is difficult to understand for earlier he had indicated that, if necessary, Paterson would have been offered the post.[62] According to Marshall, some suspected that Adams's objections rested on his belief that Paterson was connected with the Hamiltonians, who opposed the second attempt at negotiation with France. However, Marshall himself never heard the President express any objection to Paterson other than that his

[60] McHenry to Wolcott, Jan. 22, 1801, Steiner, *Life and Correspondence of McHenry*, p. 491.
[61] Jan. 20, 1801, William Paterson Papers, 1784–1803, Bancroft Transcripts, pp. 619, 621.
[62] Adams to Thomas Adams, Dec. 23, 1800, Letters Received, Adams Papers; Abigail Adams to Thomas Adams, Dec. 25, 1800, *ibid.* Charles Warren recounts this opposition of the Federalists who delayed the confirmation of Marshall, if by such action they could have brought about the elevation of Paterson, but he does not explain the inflexibility of Adams. Both Warren and Beveridge recount the story of the appointment as one totally unexpected by Marshall, but probably neither was aware of the earlier negotiations with Ingersoll, the evidence for which lies in the Adams Papers, only recently available. Nor does either draw a connection between Marshall's appointment and the passage of the judiciary bill. See Beveridge, *Life of Marshall*, II, 553; Charles Warren, *The Supreme Court in United States History* (Boston, 1924), I, 171–178.

elevation would have wounded the feelings of Judge Cushing.[63] The *Aurora* explained that Paterson failed to secure the nomination because certain Federalists resented his decision in 1795 in holding unconstitutional a Pennsylvania statute enacted in favor of Connecticut settlers.[64] Had either of these reasons been significant in the President's mind, it would have been so earlier, at the time when Adams expressed no serious objection to Paterson as a possible chief justice. It seems more probable that the President, confronted now by a request that he alter the nomination, and resenting this as an unwarranted intrusion upon his authority, flew into one of the tempers for which he was noted at the implied criticism of his judgment, and refused any suggested compromise.

When the hopelessness of their persuasion could not be ignored, the Senators had reason to take second thought at their delay in approving Marshall's nomination. The judiciary bill had been received in the Senate, after its passage by the House on January 21, the day after Marshall's nomination, and had been sent to committee. Federalist leaders may very likely have seen the advantages of approving the nomination before bringing the bill to the floor for debate for the same reasons that leaders in the House had desired that the appointment be made before that body voted on the bill. If the mind of the President could not be altered in favor of Paterson, was it not better to approve the nomination at hand rather than continue such a stalemate with the inflexible Adams? With little more than a month left to the administration, there seemed no point to be gained by continuing to oppose the appointment. The conclusion agreed upon, the Senate, on January 27, 1801, gave unanimous approval to the nomination of Marshall to be chief justice. On January 29, the judiciary bill was reported out of committee to the floor of the Senate for the consideration of the upper house. The Supreme Court was composed of six Federalist members; contingent upon the passage of the bill, the

---

[63] Adams, Autobiographical Sketch by Marshall, pp. 29–30.

[64] *Aurora*, Jan. 24, 1801, Jan. 22, Sept. 20, 28, 1803, quoted in Warren, *Supreme Court*, I, 176n. The case was John Dorrance *v.* Cornelius Van Horne's Lessees, 2 Dallas (Pa.), 304, which was tried in the circuit court for Pennsylvania district before Paterson and Richard Peters, the district judge. The case reached the Supreme Court on a writ of error at the August term, 1796, from which it was continued several terms until Feb. 1799. The Court then ordered the claimants to present their case within two days if they did not wish the case dismissed. As they still failed to do so, the Court dismissed the case for a failure to prosecute. In May 1800, five years having passed, the decision of the Federal court before Judge Paterson in 1795 became final and conclusive; *Gazette of the United States*, Mar. 5, 1801; Warren, *Supreme Court*, I, 69n.

proposed reduction to five members after the next vacancy would definitely apply to the incoming Republican president, and no Republican
could be appointed to that bench until the death or retirement of two
members.[65]

The previous day Dayton had written again to Paterson to explain the
reasons for the Senate action in approving Marshall:

The delay which has taken place was upon my motion for postponement, and
was intended to afford an opportunity for ascertaining whether the President
could be induced under any circumstances whatever to nominate you. If we could
have been satisfied of this, we should have taken measures to prevail upon Mr.
Marshall to have himself declined *the highest*, for a *lower seat*, upon the bench,
or in case of his refusal, have negatived him. This would have been a course of
proceeding, painful indeed to the Federalists on account of their esteem for that
gentleman & their respect for his talents, & to which nothing could have brought
them but their very strong attachment to you, & their very high sense of your
superior title & pretensions. It must be gratifying to you to learn that all voices,
with the exception of one only, were united in favor of the conferring of this
appointment upon you. The President alone was inflexible, & declared that he
would never nominate you. Under these circumstances we thought it adviseable
to confirm Mr. Marshall lest another not so well qualified, & more disgusting to
the Bench, should be substituted, & because it appeared *that this gentleman was
not privy to his own nomination, but had previously* exerted his influence with
the President in your behalf.[66]

Despite the activity of his friends on his behalf, Paterson himself seemed
to have been neither hurt nor angered by the appointment of Marshall.
Nor did he resign from the bench as some feared he might.[67] Quite the
contrary. He reproved Dayton for the strong terms in which he had
referred to both Marshall and the President[68] and warmly congratulated
Marshall on receiving the honor.[69]

There was some speculation that although his nomination had been
approved, Marshall would not take his seat on the bench until after

---

[65] The bill was passed by the House on Jan. 20 and by the Senate on Feb. 7, 1801; *Annals*,
6th Cong., 2d sess., pp. 915, 742. After receiving the signature of President Adams, An
Act for the More Convenient Organization of the Courts of the U.S. became law on
Feb. 13, 1801; *United States Statutes at Large*, II (Boston, 1845), 89.

[66] Jan. 28, 1801, William Paterson Papers, 1784–1803, Bancroft Transcripts, pp. 619,
621. See also James Bayard to Andrew Bayard, Jan. 26, 1801, American Historical
Association, *Annual Report . . . 1913*, II (Washington, 1915), 122.

[67] Dayton to Paterson, Feb. 1, 1801, William Paterson Papers, 1784–1803, Bancroft
Transcripts, pp. 627, 629.

[68] *Ibid.*

[69] Marshall to Paterson, Feb. 2, 1801, *ibid.*, pp. 635, 637; Adams, *Autobiographical Sketch
by Marshall*, pp. 30–31.

the administration changed on March 4, 1801.[70] But on February 4, the new appointee wrote his official acceptance to President Adams and immediately entered upon the office,[71] authorized by the President to continue to discharge the duties of the Secretary of State.[72]

Despite a few subsequent mutterings of disappointment over the failure to secure Paterson's appointment to the high bench,[73] there was little sentiment expressed regarding the new Chief Justice. Most newspapers simply stated the fact of his appointment. The *Aurora* merely noted that the Senate had confirmed the nomination, adding petulantly: "It is not said who is to be the Secretary of State in the room of Mr. Marshall for 34 days! Nor who is to receive the salary of Chief Justice from the time of Mr. Ellsworth's mission to France, until the appointment of his successor."[74] James Callender, that archfoe of the Federalists, then cooling his heels in the Richmond jail, snarled, "we are to have that precious acquisition, John Marshall as Chief Justice.... The very sound of this man's name is an insult upon truth and justice."[75]

With seeming pleasure, John Adams wrote that he had nominated "a gentleman in the full vigor of middle age, and whose reading in the science is fresh in his head."[76] There were others who were pleased. Richard Stockton, a leading Federalist from New Jersey, assured the President that the appointment of Marshall as chief justice "merits the certain approbation of all impartial men *here* who know what high qualifications are required in him who shall execute this office with dignity and advantage to the nation."[77] From Savannah, Charles Cotesworth Pinckney wrote Theodore Sedgwick, "I hope nothing will prevent his acceptance of that office at a time when attempts are making to construe away the energy of our constitution, to unnerve our Government, & to overthrow that system by which we have risen to our present prosperity, it is all important

---

[70] Hazen Kimball to Pickering, Jan. 29, 1801, Pickering Papers, XXVI, 248, Mass. Hist. Soc., Boston.

[71] Marshall to Adams, Feb. 4, 1801, Adams, *Works of Adams*, IX, 96. On this date, John Marshall took the oath of office and the first term of the Supreme Court to be held in Washington began. See Warren, *Supreme Court*, I, 184–185.

[72] Adams to Marshall, Feb. 4, 1801, Adams, *Works of Adams*, IX, 96.

[73] H. van Schaak to Sedgwick, Feb. 17, 1801, Sedgwick Papers, Box D, p. 171.

[74] *Aurora*, Feb. 3, 1801. Marshall drew only his salary as chief justice during this time; Beveridge, *Life of Marshall*, II, 559.

[75] Scots correspondent in the *Examiner* (Richmond), Feb. 6, 1801.

[76] To Elias Boudinot, Jan. 26, 1801, Adams, *Works of Adams*, IX, 94. This comment was made in Adams's reply denying a prevailing report that he himself would become chief justice after leaving office on Mar. 4. Boudinot to Adams, Jan. 20, 1801, *ibid.*, p. 93n.

[77] Feb. 2, 1801, Letters Received, Adams Papers.

that our supreme Judiciary should be filled by men of elevated talents, sound federal principles & unshaken firmness."[78] In after years, Marshall was to be described as "A man born to be the Chief Justice of any country into which Providence should have cast him."[79] Toward the end of his life, John Adams would reflect that it was the pride of his life to have given the nation a chief justice "equal to Coke or Hale, Holt or Mansfield."[80] But the sentiments of Marshall himself as the Federalist administration drew to a close were of a different kind. Shortly before Christmas 1800, he had written to a good friend about his plans to return to Richmond and the practice of law. "If my present wish can succeed so far as respects myself I shall never again fill any political station whatever."[81] A few weeks later, having accepted an office the power of which was necessarily political as well as legal, John Marshall began his work as Chief Justice of the Supreme Court of the United States.

[78] Feb. 12, 1801, Sedgwick Papers, Box D, p. 169.
[79] William Pinkney of Maryland, quoted in Charles Warren, *A History of the American Bar* (Boston, 1911), p. 252.
[80] Adams to Marshall, Aug. 17, 1825, Gray-Glines Collection of Autographs, Vol. A, No. 2, Connecticut State Library, Hartford.
[81] To Charles Cotesworth Pinckney, Dec. 18, 1800, Pinckney Family Papers, Box 1. Permission to quote here and on page 150 has been kindly granted by Dr. Morton Morris Pinckney of Richmond, Va.

3

The Midnight Judges

Kathryn Turner

"The Federalists have retired into the judiciary as a strong-hold . . . and from that battery all the works of republicanism are to be beaten down and erased."[1] This bitter lament of Thomas Jefferson after he had succeeded to the Presidency referred to the final legacy bequeathed him by the Federalist party. Passed during the closing weeks of the Adams administration, the Judiciary Act of 1801[2] provided the Chief Executive with an opportunity to fill new judicial offices carrying tenure for life before his authority ended on March 4, 1801. Because of the last-minute rush in accomplishing this purpose, those men then appointed have since been known by the familiar generic designation, "the midnight judges." This flight of Federalists into the sanctuary of an expanded federal judiciary was, of course, viewed by the Republicans as the last of many partisan outrages, and was to furnish the focus for Republican retaliation once the Jeffersonian Congress convened in the fall of 1801. That the Judiciary Act of 1801 was repealed and the new judges deprived of their new offices in the first of the party battles of the Jeffersonian period is well known. However, the circumstances surrounding the appointment of "the midnight judges" have never been recounted, and even the names of those appointed have vanished from studies of the period. It is the purpose of this essay to provide some further information about the final event of the Federalist decade.

Kathryn Turner is Assistant Professor of History, Wellesley College. A.B. 1946, Goucher College; M.A. 1951, Ph.D. 1959, University of Wisconsin.
[1] Letter From Thomas Jefferson to John Dickinson, Dec. 19, 1801, in 10 LIPSCOMB, WRITINGS OF THOMAS JEFFERSON 302 (1903).
[2] Judiciary Act of 1801, ch. 4, 2 Stat. 89.

A cardinal feature of the Judiciary Act of 1801 was a reform long advocated – the reorganization of the circuit courts.[3] Under the Judiciary Act of 1789, the judicial districts of the United States had been grouped into three circuits – Eastern, Middle, and Southern – in which circuit court was held by two justices of the Supreme Court (after 1793, by one justice)[4] and the district judge of the district in which the court was sitting.[5] The Act of 1801 grouped the districts into six circuits;[6] it freed the Supreme Court Justices from circuit duty and created new circuit court judgeships for this purpose.[7] Three circuit judges were assigned to each of the first five circuits; in the sixth, which was comprised of Kentucky, Tennessee, and the Territory of Ohio, there was provision for only one circuit judge, who would hold court with the district judges of the two states.[8] Sixteen circuit appointments, therefore, were available to the Federalists. Passed by the House on January 20 and by the Senate on February 7, the Judiciary Act became law on February 13, 1801, with scarcely more than two weeks remaining to the Adams administration. To the outgoing party it was of utmost importance that all the new offices be filled by Federalists. On February 17, the final frantic balloting in the tied Presidential contest was completed; Jefferson was now elected.[9] Writing this news to his wife, President John Adams, the lonely occupant of the splendid new White House, plaintively protested the burden that nominations to judicial and diplomatic offices represented.[10] Such a burden doubtless was increased

[3] See, e.g., the 1790 report of Attorney General Randolph, in 1 AMERICAN STATE PAPERS – MISCELLANEOUS 23–24 (1832); memorials of the Chief Justice and Associate Justices of the Supreme Court to Congress on November 7, 1792, and February 19, 1794, in *id.* at 52, 77–78.

[4] Act of March 2, 1793, ch. 22, §1, 1 Stat. 333.

[5] Act of Sept. 24, 1789, ch. 20, §4, 1 Stat. 74.

[6] Judiciary Act of 1801, ch. 4, §6, 2 Stat. 90.

[7] Judiciary Act of 1801, ch. 4, §7, 2 Stat. 90.

[8] Judiciary Act of 1801, ch. 4, §7, 2 Stat. 90. This section also provided that when the office of district judge should become vacant, circuit judges should be appointed to fill the places. Although five additional districts were created by this bill, no provision was made for the appointment of new district judges. Judiciary Act of 1801, ch. 4, §4, 2 Stat. 90.

[9] For a detailed account of the contest between Aaron Burr and Thomas Jefferson, see BORDEN, THE FEDERALISM OF JAMES A. BAYARD 73–95 (1955).

[10] Letter From John Adams to Abigail Adams, Feb. 16, 1801, in Adams Papers, Letters Received and Other Loose Papers, on microfilm at the Massachusetts Historical Society, Boston, Mass. [hereinafter cited as Adams Papers, Letters Received]. Permission to quote from this and other papers herein cited has been granted by the Adams Manuscript Trust. The author wishes to express her gratitude to Mr. Lyman Butterfield, editor of the Adams Papers, for his generous assistance while this study was in preparation.

for the President since petitioners for the available offices were by no means lacking. Inquiries or outright requests for office filled the mails even before the judiciary bill was passed, and it is clear from some of these that Adams had let be known his desire to receive suggestions of suitable persons for the judicial appointments.[11] However, the exact means by which the decisions on the midnight appointments were reached are impossible to determine precisely.

John Marshall's biographer states that the new Chief Justice appeared to be influential in determining the appointments,[12] and there is evidence that Marshall played some part. During the period of the nominations, he was in the unusual and fortuitous position of holding the two offices potentially most significant for assisting the Executive in the selection of those to hold the new offices. Marshall was not only Chief Justice but also Secretary of State,[13] an administrative role that made possible close cooperation with the President as the decisions were made.[14] As Marshall had helped formulate the Judiciary Act of 1801 while in Congress[15] and now held the office of Chief Justice, it would be foolish to suppose him to have been without interest in the selection of the circuit judges. The

[11] See, e.g., Letter From John Dennis to John Adams, Feb. 17, 1801; Letter From William Barry Grove to John Marshall, Feb. 16, 1801; Letter From Jonathan Mason, William Shepherd, and others to John Adams, Feb. 9, 1801 – all in Adams Papers, Letters Received. Adams wrote that the selection of the judges would cost him "much anxiety and diligence" and that he could make no promises nor give any encouragement until the merits of all candidates were weighed. Letter From John Adams to Rev. John Rodgers, Feb. 6, 1801, in Adams Papers, John Adams Letterbook.

[12] 2 BEVERIDGE, THE LIFE OF JOHN MARSHALL 559 (1916).

[13] When Marshall was appointed Chief Justice, John Adams requested that he continue as Secretary of State until another appointment could be made. Letter From John Adams to John Marshall, Feb. 4, 1801, in 9 THE WORKS OF JOHN ADAMS 96 (Adams ed. 1854). No other appointment was made, and Marshall continued in office until the end of the administration.

[14] At this time, many duties relating to domestic affairs were vested in the Department of State. The Secretary of State had charge of the preparation and authentication of all commissions issued by the President. In addition, federal marshals and attorneys received their instructions from the Department of State, and federal judges corresponded with this office – not that of the Attorney General – on matters of judicial business. HUNT, THE DEPARTMENT OF STATE OF THE UNITED STATES 128–29 (1914); WHITE, THE FEDERALISTS 128–44 (1948). Incoming correspondence regarding the judicial appointments came to Marshall when it was not addressed to the President himself.

[15] Marshall was a member of the committee in the House of Representatives that was appointed in December 1799 to consider revisions of the judiciary system. 6 ANNALS OF CONG. 197 (1799) [1799–1801]. Beveridge, although he devotes a chapter to Marshall's career in Congress, does not there mention the fact that Marshall served on this committee. See 2 BEVERIDGE, *op. cit. supra* note 12, at 432–84.

degree of his influence, however, cannot be established. It may have been more substantial than evidence indicates or it may have been relatively small. In the close association the two men shared during these weeks, discussion of those under consideration for the circuit court positions *may* have taken place; together they *may* have arrived at some of the decisions. Adams, in a state of mind wherein hurt, anger, and humiliation appear to have been mixed in equal portions at the trying end of his administration, and bereft of the comforting presence and counsel of his wife, may well have relied on the advice of the highly esteemed and trusted Marshall. There is, however, no way of knowing.[16]

The new First Circuit was composed of Massachusetts, New Hampshire, Rhode Island, and the district of Maine.[17] From each of these states came letters from local and national political figures interested in securing offices for themselves or for Federalist worthies. New Hampshire men were anxious that the appointment of a judge from their state be made with particular care, for it was no secret that John Pickering, the district judge, had suffered for some time from a regrettable combination of drunkenness and insanity that rendered him incapable of performing his judicial duties.[18] Samuel Livermore, Senator from New Hampshire, joined four congressmen from his state in recommending his own son[19] as one of the judges for the new circuit court and Jeremiah Smith, the United States District Attorney for New Hampshire,[20] as another.[21] Senator John Langdon also urged Samuel Dexter, Secretary of the Treasury, to recommend Smith to the President.[22]

[16] As both Marshall and Adams were in Washington at this time, there is no written correspondence between the two on the question of the selection of the judges.

[17] Judiciary Act of 1801, ch. 4, §6, 2 Stat. 90.

[18] See MORISON, LIFE OF JEREMIAH SMITH 147 (1845); PLUMER, THE LIFE OF WILLIAM PLUMER 273 (Peabody ed. 1857). Pickering was not officially removed until his impeachment in January 1804 by the Jeffersonian Congress. 14 DICTIONARY OF AMERICAN BIOGRAPHY 564 (1934).

[19] Edward St. Loe Livermore served as United States District Attorney from 1794 to 1797, then as judge of the New Hampshire Superior Court until 1798, when he resigned because of the low salary. In September 1798, John Adams appointed him naval officer of Portsmouth. 11 DICTIONARY OF AMERICAN BIOGRAPHY 305 (1933).

[20] Smith, a Federalist, had served in Congress from 1790 until 1797, when he was appointed United States Attorney and resigned the seat. In 1800, he became a judge of probate. 17 DICTIONARY OF AMERICAN BIOGRAPHY 292–93 (1935).

[21] Letter From Samuel Livermore, Abiel Foster, Samuel Tenney, Jonathan Freeman, and James Sheafe to John Adams, Feb. 10, 1801, in Adams Papers, Letters Received.

[22] Letter From John Langdon to Samuel Dexter, Feb. 10, 1801, in Adams Papers, Letters Received. Langdon also suggested the names of Benjamin West and William Gordon as others agreeable to the state.

Happy as he was to know of the activity of friends in his behalf, Jeremiah Smith was anything but reluctant to engage in vigorous office-seeking for himself. In January, he had written to Dexter stressing the disabilities of Judge Pickering in order to warn that the execution of federal laws, particularly the revenue acts, was being seriously jeopardized in New Hampshire.[23] Simultaneously the eager applicant directed these views to John Marshall and offered himself as circuit judge.[24] Pleas went to Federalist Senators Uriah Tracy of Connecticut and Dwight Foster of Massachusetts, and Smith renewed acquaintance with his former congressional colleague Jonathan Dayton, now Senator from New Jersey,[25] albeit sheepishly confessing, "There is something awkward in applying ... for an office before it is created...."[26] Fisher Ames, another who had received a bald plea for support, reported that he had written Dexter requesting him to contact Marshall and "to do all that he possibly can for you," playfully concluding, "I wish you a Judge, though you have not gravity."[27] Doubtless aided by such combined good offices, Jeremiah Smith was selected as one of the judges of the First Circuit, and to John Marshall he declared himself "particularly grateful" – believing that it had been Marshall who had selected the right man for the job.[28] Edward St. Loe Livermore was named federal district attorney in place of the pleased and promoted Smith.

Selection of the two other judges for the circuit also followed local desires as well as national recommendation. The day the Judiciary Act became law, the Federalist senators and congressmen from Rhode Island wrote directly to the President reminding him of the "natural pretensions" of each state to a share in the judicial appointments. Their candidate was Benjamin Bourne, district judge of Rhode Island and former member of

[23] Letter From Jeremiah Smith to Samuel Dexter, Jan. 27, 1801, in Adams Papers, Letters Received. At this date of writing, Smith would not have been aware that the new Judiciary Act provided that in such cases, one of the circuit judges could perform the duties of the district judge during the continuance of his disability. See Judiciary Act of 1801, ch. 4, §25, 2 Stat. 97.

[24] Letter From Jeremiah Smith to John Marshall, Jan. 27, 1801, in Adams Papers, Letters Received.

[25] Dayton served as a Federalist in the House of Representatives from 1791 to 1799, when he went to the Senate. 5 DICTIONARY OF AMERICAN BIOGRAPHY 166 (1930).

[26] Letter From Jeremiah Smith to Jonathan Dayton, Jan. 30, 1801, in the Gratz Collection, Box 5, Historical Society of Pennsylvania, Philadelphia, Pa.

[27] Letter From Fisher Ames to Jeremiah Smith, Feb. 16, 1801, in 1 AMES, WORKS OF FISHER AMES 291–92 (Ames ed. 1854).

[28] 1 S. EXECUTIVE JOUR. 381 [1800–1801]; Letter From Jeremiah Smith to John Marshall, Feb. 20, 1801, in MORISON, *op. cit. supra* note 18, at 144.

Congress, a man of "extensive information, strong attachment to the Government and amiable manners."[29] President Adams was also requested to appoint Senator Ray Greene to the district judgeship that would become vacant if Bourne were nominated to the new circuit court. In addition to his political qualifications as a pronounced Federalist, Greene had earlier served as the federal district attorney while concurrently holding the elective office of attorney general of Rhode Island. His friends assured the President that this appointment would be welcome within the state.[30] Evidently acting immediately upon these suggestions, the President sent the nominations to the Senate on February 18. Bourne thus became the second judge of the First Circuit and Senator Greene moved to the vacated office of district judge.[31]

Available sources reveal that it was Harrison Gray Otis, Federalist member of the House of Representatives from Massachusetts, who was most influential in guiding the future judicial composition in that state. Either at the request of the Executive or upon his own initiative, Otis acted as agent to ascertain a recipient for the judicial largess to be bestowed after the judiciary bill should pass. The two most noted leaders of the Massachusetts bar at this time were District Judge John Lowell and Theophilus Parsons, who was engaged in the practice of law in Newburyport and Boston.[32] Both were professionally well equipped to become circuit judge. Both were Federalists with distinguished political careers

---

[29] Letter From Theodore Foster, Ray Greene, John Brown, and Christopher Champlin to John Adams, Feb. 13, 1801, in Adams Papers, Letters Received.

[30] Letter From Theodore Foster, John Brown, and Christopher Champlin to John Adams, Feb. 16, 1801, in Adams Papers, Letters Received. Greene was attorney general of Rhode Island from 1794 to 1797, then was elected to the Senate to complete the term of William Bradford who had resigned. In 1799, he was elected to a full term. 2 APPLETON, CYCLOPEDIA OF AMERICAN BIOGRAPHY 755 (Wilson & Fiske ed. 1889).

[31] 1 S. EXECUTIVE JOUR. 381 [1800–1801]. Greene resigned his seat in the Senate on March 5, 1801. However, an error had been made in the commission itself and Greene received one to the newly created circuit court rather than to the district court. By the time he returned his commission to have the error rectified, the administration had changed hands. Letter From Levi Lincoln to Thomas Jefferson, April 8, 1801, in 111 JEFFERSON PAPERS, Library of Congress, Washington, D.C. Jefferson refused to remedy the mistake and nominated Republican David Barnes to this position. 1 S. EXECUTIVE JOUR. 401 [1801–1802]. As he had already resigned from the Senate, Greene was without any job at all.

[32] Otis had first known Lowell nearly twenty years earlier when he read law in Lowell's office and later, at the invitation of the older lawyer, took over some of Lowell's practice before the lower courts. He had also known Parsons and was aware that although the two men were rivals at the bar, they were warm personal friends. Letter From Harrison Gray Otis to Charles Lowell, Nov. 10, 1846, in 11 MONTHLY LAW REPORTER 425 (1849).

behind them,[33] and to each "Harry" Otis dispatched inquiries about the possible court position sometime before the judiciary bill passed the House.[34] Explaining that poor health together with the low salary offered by the new bill forced him to refuse consideration, Parsons mentioned other factors: "If J. Lowell is not appointed, he will certainly believe himself neglected & will resign which would be disagreeable to us all. And may I not ask how long the present system is to last, if it be established this session?"[35] Actually, Lowell's intention to resign was prompted by the proposed creation of the circuit courts, which markedly reduced the duties and prestige of the district judges. Writing Otis that he would accept appointment to the circuit court but intended to resign his present office, Lowell stressed the importance of accomplishing the appointments under the Federalist administration. He left to Otis the use to be made of his sentiments and plans.[36]

---

[33] John Lowell had served as a delegate to the Continental Congress and had been one of the three members chosen to make up the Court of Appeals in the Cases of Captures established by the old Congress. In 1789, he was appointed district judge of Massachusetts. 11 DICTIONARY OF AMERICAN BIOGRAPHY 464–65 (1933). The noted "Lawyer Parsons" was called by John Adams "one of America's greatest lawyers." Letter From John Adams to Adrian Van der Kemp, April 20, 1806, in ADAMS-VAN DER KEMP CORRESPONDENCE, Historical Society of Pennsylvania, Philadelphia, Pa. Parsons had served in the Massachusetts constitutional convention and the convention for the ratification of the federal constitution. PARSONS, MEMOIRS OF THEOPHILUS PARSONS 46–106 (1859). In 1806, Parsons became chief justice of the Supreme Judicial Court of Massachusetts.

[34] Parsons' reply to Otis is dated Boston, January 23, 1801. 1 MORISON, THE LIFE AND LETTERS OF HARRISON GRAY OTIS 213 (1913). This indicates that Otis's letter would have been written at least a week earlier while the bill was being debated in the House. Lowell's reply is in response, he says, to Otis's letter of January 14, 1801. Letter From John Lowell to Harrison Gray Otis, Jan. 26, 1801, enclosed in Letter From Harrison Gray Otis to John Adams, Feb. 16, 1801, in Adams Papers, Letters Received.

[35] Letter From Theophilus Parsons to Harrison Gray Otis, Jan. 23, 1801, in 1 MORISON, *op. cit. supra* note 34, at 213.

[36] Letter From John Lowell to Harrison Gray Otis, Jan. 26, 1801, enclosed in Letter From Harrison Gray Otis to John Adams, Feb. 16, 1801, in Adams Papers, Letters Received. John Lowell, Jr., had written to Otis to assure him of the desirability of his father for the office and the office for his father. He stated that continuation as district judge under the new system would be so derogatory to his father's character that nothing would induce him to retain it. Furthermore, the exercise (travelling the circuit, one presumes) would be "promotive of his health and would probably prolong his life." Letter From John Lowell, Jr., to Harrison Gray Otis, Jan. 26, 1801, in Otis Papers, Box 3, Massachusetts Historical Society, Boston, Mass. The reference to the life-giving properties of jouncing the circuit is a unique interpretation. Certainly no judge who had been on circuit duty ever regarded these travels as beneficial to his health. Indeed, the complaints of the Supreme Court Justices about this element of their circuit duties had been constant since the Judiciary Act of 1789.

Sometime after receiving this letter, Otis discussed the entire matter with President Adams.[37] It was imperative that a decision be reached quickly in order to fill the judicial positions at both circuit and district levels; in all likelihood the decision was then made to nominate Lowell as circuit judge because his acceptance was assured.[38] Otis, meanwhile, had already written to John Davis, the United States District Attorney for Massachusetts, apparently to inquire whether he might be interested in the district judgeship should the opportunity occur. Davis indicated interest provided that the salary of the office were made equivalent to that of circuit judge. He too left his future to the "friendship and good judgment" of Otis.[39] In the course of a single week, however, Davis, having discovered the diminished duties and lower salary of the district judges, wrote Otis emphatically that he now refused to be considered.[40] In Washington, Otis was hurried into action when he learned that John Lowell had sent his official resignation as district judge in order that there be no delay in filling that vacancy as soon as the Judiciary Act passed the Senate.[41] Despite the fact that in all probability Otis had also received Davis's letter excluding himself from consideration for that office, on February 18 the nominations of Lowell as circuit judge and Davis as district judge went to the Senate. In reply to Otis's announcement of his appointment, the outraged John Davis minced no words.

[T]he information was as unwelcome as it was unexpected. I could not imagine that I should be displaced from my present office and advanced to the office to which you inform me I am now nominated upon the mere *conjecture* that a bill before the house for augmenting the salary might pass in this sess[ion]; or if not that it would probably pass in the *next*: and I must consider it as extremely unfortunate for me that you should infer from the *tenor* of my letter that I would be "pleased with the appointment on its present establishment taking all chances." It certainly was not my intention to submit myself to an anxious dependency on any of the chances which you have supposed would have an influence on my decision. . . .[42]

---

[37] Otis refers to this meeting in a letter to Adams. Letter From Harrison Gray Otis to John Adams, Feb. 16, 1801, in Adams Papers, Letters Received.

[38] John Lowell had also been recommended by the Massachusetts members of Congress. Letter From Theodore Sedgwick and others to John Adams, Feb. 9, 1801, in Adams Papers, Letters Received.

[39] Letter From John Davis to Harrison Gray Otis, Feb. 2, 1801, in Otis Papers, *supra* note 36.

[40] Letter From John Davis to Harrison Gray Otis, Feb. 9, 1801, in Otis Papers, *supra* note 36.

[41] Letter From John Lowell to Harrison Gray Otis, Feb. 11, 1801, in Otis Papers, *supra* note 36.

[42] Letter From John Davis to Harrison Gray Otis, March 1, 1801, in Otis Papers, *supra* note 36. (Emphasis that of Davis.)

Davis expressed a hope that his nomination would be revoked before it was "too late."

But too late it was indeed – not only because time had run out for the Federalists, but also because on the same day that Harrison Gray Otis informed Davis of the unwelcome honor bestowed upon him, Otis had written his wife that the President had nominated *him* to be the district attorney for Massachusetts.[43] It was he who was to step into Davis's place! Otis, who had refused to run for re-election in 1800, was now provided with an office congenial to his desire to return to Boston, and Davis was confronted with the alternative of accepting the judgeship foisted upon him, or going without any appointment at all.

John Marshall's urging that Otis accept the office without delay was unnecessary.[44] Otis accepted his commission and returned to Boston prepared to enjoy the rewards of his new position with only the dark cloud of possibility at his back. The one disadvantage, he ruefully commented, was that his place was held at the pleasure of the President, "and though his friends say he [Jefferson] will not change any officers but the *heads of departments*, yet I presume in the course of a twelve-month he will *oust them all.*"[45] John Davis, preferring to take a small salary rather than none at all, also accepted his commission and began a forty-year career as district judge in which he was subsequently to distinguish himself.[46]

The Second Circuit was composed of Vermont, Connecticut, and two districts comprising the state of New York.[47] Obviously, geographical patronage became important; it was a fair and fitting division that each state be represented by one judge. The appointment from Vermont occasioned no difficulty; Samuel Hitchcock, the federal district judge, was

---

[43] Letter From Harrison Gray Otis to Sally Foster Otis, Feb. 18, 1801, in 1 MORISON, *op. cit. supra* note 34, at 203. Whether Otis had not received Davis's letter of February 9 in which Davis refused to be considered, and had honestly advised the President to risk Davis's acceptance of the nomination, or had simply seized an opportunity to insinuate himself into a profitable situation by trickery must remain in the realm of speculation.

[44] Letter From John Marshall to Harrison Gray Otis, Feb. 21, 1801, in Otis Papers, *supra* note 36. It was the state office of solicitor general that Otis originally desired, but this went to another. 1 MORISON, *op. cit. supra* note 34, at 202. Perhaps his failure to obtain the state office prompted Otis's search for some other appointive post in the Boston area.

[45] Letter From Harrison Gray Otis to Sally Foster Otis, Feb. 18, 1801, in 1 MORISON, *op. cit. supra* note 34, at 203. This prediction proved correct. Before the year was out, Jefferson removed Otis despite a letter from Samuel Otis, the secretary of the Senate, requesting that his son be continued in the office.

[46] See 5 DICTIONARY OF AMERICAN BIOGRAPHY 133 (1930).

[47] Judiciary Act of 1801, ch. 4, §6, 2 Stat 90.

the sole choice of the Vermont congressmen for the post.[48] Assuming that this suggestion would be followed, Senator Nathaniel Chipman of Vermont applied to both Marshall[49] and President Adams[50] in the hope that he might be chosen to replace Hitchcock. His entreaties, however, were to no avail; that appointment was given to Senator Elijah Paine, a former member of the Superior Court of Vermont.[51]

The selection of the judges from New York and Connecticut proved less simple. As soon as the new Judiciary Act had passed the House, the Speaker, Theodore Sedgwick, wrote to Egbert Benson, Revolutionary patriot and former congressman, who had served as justice of the New York Supreme Court since 1794, to ask if he would accept the office of circuit judge should this be tendered to him. Judge Benson replied that he would think it "prudent" to accept.[52] Simultaneously, pressure in behalf of Samuel Bayard, judge of the court of common pleas for Westchester County, was reaching the President. By marriage, Bayard was related to Elias Boudinot, the director of the mint, a long-time friend of John Adams. He was also a cousin of James A. Bayard's, an important Federalist member of the House and a man who, in his own opinion at least, was highly esteemed by the President.[53] Nor were character references for this well-connected aspirant lacking. Colonel John Bayard wrote the President in his son's behalf;[54] so did Senator Theodore Foster of Rhode

---

[48] Letter From Chauncey Goodrich to Oliver Wolcott, Feb. 18, 1801, in 2 GIBBS, MEMOIRS OF THE ADMINISTRATIONS OF WASHINGTON AND JOHN ADAMS 491 (1846).

[49] Letter From Nathaniel Chipman to John Marshall, Feb. 17, 1801, in Adams Papers, Letters Received.

[50] Letter From Nathaniel Chipman to John Adams, Feb. 16, 1801, in Adams Papers, Letters Received.

[51] 1 S. EXECUTIVE JOUR. 384 [1800–1801].

[52] Letter From Egbert Benson to Theodore Sedgwick, Jan. 31, 1801, in Sedgwick Papers, Box D, No. 162, Massachusetts Historical Society, Boston, Mass. This reply indicates that Sedgwick's letter was written on January 22, two days after the passage of the bill by the House. Two weeks later, Benson wrote again repeating that he would accept such an appointment. Letter From Egbert Benson to Theodore Sedgwick, Feb. 16, 1801, in Sedgwick Papers, Box D, No. 293, Massachusetts Historical Society, Boston, Mass.

[53] Letter From James A. Bayard to Andrew Bayard, Feb. 8, 1801, in *Papers of James A. Bayard, 1796–1815*, in 1913-2 ANNUAL REPORT OF THE AMERICAN HISTORICAL ASSOCIATION 123–24 (Donnan ed. 1915) [hereinafter cited as *Bayard Papers*]. When James A. Bayard was three years old, his father died. From that time on, James was raised in Philadelphia by his uncle, Colonel John Bayard, who treated him as a foster son, raising him with his cousins Samuel, Andrew, and Margaret Bayard. BORDEN, *op. cit. supra* note 9, at 9, 21.

[54] Letter From John Bayard to John Adams, Jan. 25, 1801, in Adams Papers, Letters Received.

Island.[55] The president of Princeton assured Adams of Bayard's attachment to the federal government,[56] and a noted clergyman reported Bayard's life to be "one such as the gospel of our Lord requires," a person well suited to judicial offices to be awarded to "men of legal abilities, Friends to Government & good order & of unstained moral Characters & enemies to the fatal philosophy of the Day."[57] Although Adams responded that he could neither make promises nor give encouragement until the merits of all candidates had been weighed, he acknowledged that "the character of 'an enemy to the fatal philosophy of the day' has great weight with me, although it appears to have none with our nation."[58] Urged by Andrew Bayard, Samuel's brother, their cousin in Congress James A. Bayard talked with President Adams, confidently reporting that "the President assured me that unless the N York delegation should press upon him some man whom with propriety he could not resist, Samuel should be appointed. I have little doubt of his success."[59]

After the Judiciary Act had been sent for presidential signature, however, twelve members of Congress from New York, Connecticut, and Vermont requested that the President appoint Egbert Benson as chief judge of the Second Circuit.[60] Doubtless Speaker of the House Sedgwick had informed this group that Benson would accept the nomination, for this fact was understood by the Federalist members from New York.[61] From the point of view of the President, the fact that Benson faced retirement from the New York bench[62] and the expressed desire

---

55 Letter From Theodore Foster to John Adams, Feb. 16, 1801, in Adams Papers, Letters Received. Foster enclosed a letter in which Bayard, although suggesting some improvements, expressed his approval of the judiciary bill. Letter From John Bayard to Theodore Foster, Jan. 22, 1801, in Adams Papers, Letters Received.

56 Letter From Samuel Smith to John Adams, Feb. 3, 1801, in Adams Papers, Letters Received.

57 Letter From John Rodgers to John Adams, Jan. 31, 1801, in Adams Papers, Letters Received.

58 Letter From John Adams to John Rodgers, Feb. 6, 1801, in Adams Papers, John Adams Letterbook.

59 Letter From James A. Bayard to Andrew Bayard, Feb. 8, 1801, in *Bayard Papers* 124.

60 Letter From Chauncey Goodrich, Samuel Dana, and others to John Adams, Feb. 11, 1801, in Adams Papers, Letters Received.

61 Letter From Chauncey Goodrich to Oliver Wolcott, Feb. 18, 1801, in 2 GIBBS, *op. cit. supra* note 48, at 491.

62 Later, William Cushing, Associate Justice of the Supreme Court, wrote: "I understand by Mrs. Adams...that the president had him [Bayard] in mind & wished there was a place for him; – but that he would not pass by that old faithful servant of the public, Mr. Benson, whose [age] of *Sixty* must soon put him out of office under the Constitution

of the New York congressmen furnished persuasive reasons for this nomination, and the appointment of Bayard, regretfully perhaps, went by the board. Although James A. Bayard, in a disgruntled mood, attributed the presidential change of mind to pressure from the New York delegation,[63] Adams may well have felt that the Congressman should rest content with the appointment of his father-in-law as judge in the Third Circuit[64] and with his own appointment at the same time as Minister to France.[65]

The third judgeship in the Second Circuit presumably would be filled by a Connecticut figure equally experienced at the bench as Hitchcock and Benson. Charles Chauncey, who had served on the Supreme Court of Connecticut until 1793, offered himself to the President for this honor,[66] but there is no evidence that he was seriously considered. The senators and representatives from Connecticut conferred and, in a move supported by the congressmen from Vermont and New York,[67] agreed to recommended Jonathan Sturges, formerly a congressman and now judge of the state superior court.[68] However, in the week's interval between this decision and the date on which the nominations were sent to the Senate, a different choice had occurred to President Adams.

In December 1800, Oliver Wolcott had resigned as Secretary of the Treasury under heavy fire from the political opposition. Earlier in that year, when James McHenry and Timothy Pickering had been flung from the cabinet by the President, Wolcott escaped and apparently continued

of New York." Letter From William Cushing to William Paterson, March 18, 1801, draft copy in the Robert Treat Paine Papers, Box 4, No. 19, Massachusetts Historical Society, Boston, Mass. (Emphasis that of Cushing.)

[63] Letter From James A. Bayard to Andrew Bayard, Feb. 22, 1801, in *Bayard Papers* 131.
[64] See notes 109–11 *infra* and accompanying text.
[65] Bayard immediately declined this appointment. Letter From James A. Bayard to Andrew Bayard, Feb. 22, 1801, in *Bayard Papers* 131. Bayard, who had played an important role in the election of Jefferson rather than Burr, wanted no implication that he had been persuaded by the promise of an appointment. BORDEN, THE FEDERALISM OF JAMES A. BAYARD 88–89, 97–98 (1955).
[66] Letter From Charles Chauncey to John Adams, Jan. 27, 1801, in Adams Papers, Letters Received.
[67] Letter From Chauncey Goodrich to Oliver Wolcott, Feb. 18, 1801, in 2 GIBBS, *op. cit. supra* note 48, at 491.
[68] Letter From Chauncey Goodrich, Samuel Dana, and others to John Adams, Feb. 11, 1801, in Adams Papers, Letters Received. Such joint action had been undertaken in the hope that "a recommendation thus circumstanced, could not be wholly disregarded." Letter From James Hillhouse to Oliver Wolcott, Feb. 19, 1801, in 2 GIBBS, *op. cit. supra* note 48, at 492.

to enjoy the confidence of Adams at the same time that he was continuing his deeper loyalty to Alexander Hamilton.[69]

It is not clear that Adams, even as late as the last month of his administration, was aware of the depths to which Wolcott had been involved in the labyrinth of intrigue against him. However, the resignation of the cabinet officer amid suspicions of defalcations in the public accounts[70] and accusations about the fires in the war office and treasury buildings had clearly done the Federalist party no good in the eyes of the public.[71] Resignation had left Oliver Wolcott unemployed and in serious financial straits,[72] a circumstance his friends were apparently not reluctant to remedy. Senator James Hillhouse of Connecticut explained that only the Connecticut group's fear lest efforts in Wolcott's behalf be in vain and "produce an irritation that would be attended with unpleasant consequences" had led to its initial support of Judge Sturges.[73] Possibly – but not necessarily – because he surmised such sentiments or because he chose to make a belated gesture to party solidarity, the President himself suggested that Oliver Wolcott be tendered the nomination as circuit judge from Connecticut.

The final substitution of Wolcott for Sturges was not actually made until the evening before the nominations were sent to the Senate; Secretary of the Treasury Dexter and Senator Hillhouse maneuvered the change in

---

[69] Wolcott had participated in the effort to select Pinckney over Adams as the Federalist presidential candidate in 1800, and prior to the election had collaborated in the preparation of Hamilton's circular letter in October. When this scheme failed, Wolcott offered his resignation to become effective December 31, 1800. This traditional interpretation of the role played by Wolcott in the Adams cabinet is followed by DAUER, THE ADAMS FEDERALISTS 123 (1953). A subsequent examination of the period, however, points out that Wolcott opposed Hamilton on the issue of a standing army and the plan for an attack on the Spanish empire. KURTZ, THE PRESIDENCY OF JOHN ADAMS 320, 323, 370–71, 388 n.45 (1957). Despite the information in the latter work that Wolcott may have been more loyal to Adams than scholars have hitherto assumed, there is no evidence that the objections of Wolcott to certain Hamiltonian plans resulted in a break between the two. Nor is there any evidence that indicates that Adams was fully aware of Wolcott's relationship with Hamilton, whatever it may have been.

[70] Upon Wolcott's invitation, the House of Representatives appointed a committee to investigate the Treasury. This committee reported on January 28, 1801, that all was in good order. 6 ANNALS OF CONG. 979–86 (1801) [1799–1801]. Later, a committee of the Jeffersonian Congress criticized the administration of the Treasury. 7 ANNALS OF CONG. 1255–85 (1802) [1801–1802].

[71] 2 GIBBS, *op. cit. supra* note 48, at 478–84.

[72] *Id.* at 476–77.

[73] Letter From James Hillhouse to Oliver Wolcott, Feb. 19, 1801, in 2 GIBBS, *op. cit. supra* note 48, at 492.

obedience to the wishes of the President. After Adams had received the recommendation favoring Sturges, Hillhouse was approached in confidence by Dexter to sound the sentiments of the Connecticut men if the President were to nominate Wolcott. The Federalist senator assured Dexter of their friendly feelings for Wolcott but candidly admitted he was less sure of that gentleman's qualifications for the bench.[74] Although Wolcott had studied law under Tapping Reeve and had been admitted to the bar in 1781, the fact that he had never practiced law – and much less enjoyed any experience at the bench – might have constituted good grounds for concern over his qualifications for the office. If any such concern existed, it was swiftly overborne in this eleventh-hour opportunity to make charitable provision for Wolcott. Three days later, after meeting with his Connecticut colleagues, Hillhouse informed Dexter of their approval of the nomination, only to have Dexter report that Adams was concerned over the order of the judges, feeling that Wolcott, in view of his former high public station, should not be an associate judge. Here, Hillhouse did take the candidate's absence of legal experience into account. Later, Hillhouse explained to Wolcott that the appointment as an associate judge was upon the former's suggestion, not simply because New York expected Benson to be chief judge, but also because "it would in some measure place you in a situation to be protected from the mistakes and errours to which you might be exposed, until you should have had an opportunity to make yourself acquainted with the technical rules of proceeding...."[75] On the morning of February 17, authorized by Adams, Dexter again asked Hillhouse to assure the approval of Wolcott with the Connecticut group before the following day, on which Adams intended to make the nomination.[76] The unanimous decision was that Wolcott's appointment would be "perfectly agreeable to them; he being in their estimation a person well qualified for such appointment."[77] In this, New York and Vermont Federalists concurred.[78]

---

[74] *Id.* at 492–93. Letter From Chauncey Goodrich to Oliver Wolcott, Feb. 18, 1801, in 2 GIBBS, *op. cit. supra* note 48, at 491.
[75] Letter From James Hillhouse to Oliver Wolcott, Feb. 19, 1801, in 2 GIBBS, *op. cit. supra* note 48, at 493. The sequence of events discussed in text is drawn from this lengthy explanatory letter.
[76] Letter From Samuel Dexter to James Hillhouse, Tuesday Morning [Feb. 17, 1801], in 2 GIBBS, *op. cit. supra* note 48, at 494.
[77] Letter From James Hillhouse to Samuel Dexter, Tuesday Evening [Feb. 17, 1801], in 2 GIBBS, *op. cit. supra* note 48, at 494. Hillhouse enclosed a copy of this note in his letter to Wolcott of February 19, 1801. The original is in Adams Papers, Letters Received.
[78] Letter From James Hillhouse to Oliver Wolcott, Feb. 19, 1801, in 2 GIBBS, *op. cit. supra* note 48, at 494.

In the decision to appoint Oliver Wolcott, personal or political motivations were obviously primary; both the President and the Connecticut Federalists preferred to take Wolcott and drop Jonathan Sturges, whose qualifications at bench and bar were far superior. Unabashed by the possible complications resulting from so unlearned a judge, the Senate approved the nomination and Wolcott received immediate congratulations from his brother-in-law, Chauncey Goodrich, and from Senator Uriah Tracy.[79] The former, swept aloft by a balloon of enthusiasm, wrote Wolcott that even though certain "embarrassments" might be experienced for want of knowledge of practice, all Wolcott's friends expected to see in him "the *American Mansfield*."[80]

Transmitting the commission "with peculiar pleasure," John Marshall hoped that "this high, and public evidence given by the President, of his respect for your services and character, will efface every unpleasant sensation respecting the past, and smooth the way to a perfect reconciliation."[81] Conscious of his deficiencies but promising to try to overcome them, Wolcott accepted the commission[82] and, secure in the future, wrote grateful thanks to his benefactors.[83]

Adams's appointment of Wolcott has been described as one of "astounding magnanimity or blindness,"[84] and either interpretation is certainly possible. However, if we can accept the sincerity of Adams's own statement on the matter, it is possible to explain the appointment simply on the basis of strong personal conviction:

When the public discards or neglects talents and integrity, united with meritorious past services, it commits iniquity against itself by depriving itself of the benefit

---

[79] Letter From Uriah Tracy to Oliver Wolcott, Feb. 20, 1801, in 2 GIBBS, *op. cit. supra* note 48, at 495.

[80] Letter From Chauncey Goodrich to Oliver Wolcott, Feb. 20, 1801, in 2 GIBBS, *op. cit. supra* note 48, at 495. (Emphasis that of Goodrich.)

[81] Letter From John Marshall to Oliver Wolcott, Feb. 24, 1801, in 2 GIBBS, *op. cit. supra* note 48, at 495. On the basis of the tone of this letter, Beveridge concludes that Marshall induced the President to nominate Wolcott: "Thus did Marshall end one of the feuds which had so embarrassed the Administration of John Adams." 2 BEVERIDGE, THE LIFE OF JOHN MARSHALL 559–60 (1916). There is no direct evidence that it was Marshall rather than Adams who decided upon the appointment, and it was clearly Samuel Dexter, not Marshall, to whom Adams had entrusted the mission of gaining the approval of the Connecticut delegation for his action.

[82] Letter From Oliver Wolcott to John Marshall, March 2, 1801, in 2 GIBBS, *op. cit. supra* note 48, at 496.

[83] Letter From Oliver Wolcott to James Hillhouse, March 18, 1801, in 2 GIBBS, *op. cit. supra* note 48, at 497; Letter From Oliver Wolcott to John Adams, March 28, 1801, in 2 GIBBS, *op. cit. supra* note 48, at 497.

[84] 2 BEVERIDGE, *op. cit. supra* note 81, at 559.

of future services, and it does wrong to the individual by depriving him of the reward which long and faithful services have merited. Twenty years of able and faithful service on the part of Mr. Wolcott, remunerated only by a simple subsistence, it appeared to me, constituted a claim upon the public which ought to be attended to.[85]

John Adams, forcibly retired from further service to the country whose cause he had so long advanced, had himself tasted the ingratitude of the public – the statesman's cup of woe. Perhaps from his own personal bitterness had come a reflective compassion in which he concluded that to Oliver Wolcott was owing some token of gratitude from the Executive in behalf of a thankless nation.

The selection of judges for the Third Circuit, consisting of Pennsylvania, Delaware, and New Jersey,[86] drew the careful personal consideration of President Adams. As early as December 1800, the Chief Executive had turned his attention to federal court problems in Pennsylvania when he received word from his son, Thomas Boylston Adams, that Jared Ingersoll, the noted district attorney, planned to resign his office as soon as it was certain that Adams had been defeated.[87] Tentatively offered a seat on the United States Supreme Court, Ingersoll, at the behest of Adams, delayed action on his resignation while deliberating this possibility.[88] Meanwhile, the President took immediate steps to shore up the underpinnings of the federal judiciary in Pennsylvania consequent upon Ingersoll's imminent resignation.

It was Adams's hope to fill this important position with "a thoroughly good man" – perhaps Joseph Hopkinson[89] – but he was warned by his son that so outspoken a Federalist, were he appointed, would instantly

---

[85] Letter From John Adams to Oliver Wolcott, April 6, 1801 in 2 GIBBS, *op. cit. supra* note 48, at 497.

[86] Judiciary Act of 1801, ch. 4, §6, 2 Stat. 90.

[87] Letter From Thomas B. Adams to John Adams, Dec. 14, 1800, in Adams Papers, Letters Received. Ingersoll had been responsible for initiating proceedings under the Sedition Act against William Duane, editor of the *Aurora*, in October 1800. Duane's trial, however, was postponed until the next session of the court. SMITH, FREEDOM'S FETTERS 301–02 (1956).

[88] See Turner, *The Appointment of Chief Justice Marshall*, 17 WM. & MARY Q. 143, 147–54 (1960).

[89] Letter From John Adams to Thomas B. Adams, Dec. 23, 1800, in Adams Papers, Letters Received. Joseph Hopkinson was famed as the author of the popular patriotic song, "Hail Columbia." A leading figure at the Philadelphia bar, in 1804, he – together with Luther Martin, the noted Maryland advocate – was to defend Justice Samuel Chase at his impeachment trial. 9 DICTIONARY OF AMERICAN BIOGRAPHY 223 (1932).

"become a mark for all the venom & spite of the Democrats."[90] The young man suggested William Tilghman as "a very fair character of temperate politics, good professional repute, and far less obnoxious to strong partisans than Hopkinson," whom Ingersoll himself strongly favored.[91] With the appointment of John Marshall as Chief Justice of the Supreme Court on January 20, the tentative plan to bring Ingersoll to the high bench collapsed, and early in February, Ingersoll met with his old friend, John Adams, and reiterated his determination to resign.[92] "If the result of the late presidential election had been conformable to my wishes & my ideas of what was best for the publick, I would have continued to execute the duties of that office," Ingersoll commented in his resignation. "I do not feel the same obligations nor the same inclination towards your successor...."[93] On the very day Ingersoll resigned, the Judiciary Act with its new organization of the circuits became law.

While the judiciary bill had been before the Senate, Senator William Bingham had written to that fervent Federalist, District Judge Richard Peters, that "the federal party wish the appointments to be made under the present administration, expecting the President will give due weight to the Recommendations of the Members of the Senate ... of the Importance of filling these Seats with federal characters must be obvious."[94] Nonetheless, there is no evidence that Adams was in communication with the Pennsylvania Federalists in Congress at this time. Nor is there evidence that Adams suggested a circuit court appointment to Ingersoll

---

[90] Letter From Thomas B. Adams to John Adams, Dec. 28, 1800, in Adams Papers, Letters Received.

[91] *Ibid.*; Letter From Thomas B. Adams to Abigail Adams, Dec. 30, 1800, in Adams Papers, Letters Received. William Tilghman was a master of equity jurisprudence who became chief justice of the state in 1806. WARREN, HISTORY OF THE AMERICAN BAR 246 n.1 (1911).

[92] Ingersoll mentions this meeting in a letter written after his return to Philadelphia. Letter From Jared Ingersoll to John Adams, Feb. 13, 1801, in Adams Papers, Letters Received.

[93] *Ibid.*

[94] Letter From William Bingham to Richard Peters, Feb. 1, 1801, in 10 PETERS PAPERS No. 65, Historical Society of Pennsylvania, Philadelphia, Pa. Peters was appointed federal district judge of Pennsylvania in 1792. His opinion in United States v. Worrall, 2 U.S. (2 Dall.) 384 (C.C. Pa. 1798), that there was a common-law jurisdiction over crimes in addition to that bestowed by federal statute, was the basis for the prosecutions for libel against the federal government prior to the passage of the Sedition Law in 1798, ch. 74, 1 Stat. 596. 14 DICTIONARY OF AMERICAN BIOGRAPHY 509–10 (1934). As district judge, Peters had issued the warrant for the arrest of Benjamin Franklin Bache, the editor of the *Aurora* in June of 1798, and subsequently presided at the trial of Thomas Cooper and the arraignment of William Duane. SMITH, *op. cit. supra* note 87, at 200–02, 285–86, 317–19.

when the two talked in Washington. Granting the possible inducement of an appointment with life tenure, there is no record that Ingersoll desired, solicited, or was even asked his opinion regarding such an appointment. Because he had returned to Philadelphia, it was impossible now for Adams to contact him instantly; his resignation as district attorney having been received, there were now two openings in Pennsylvania that had to be filled. There was no time to be lost. Unwilling to lose the services of so distinguished a Federalist, Adams apparently gambled that Ingersoll, confronted with a *fait accompli*, would accept appointment as chief judge of the Third Circuit. Acting solely on his own initiative, it seems, the President sent Ingersoll's name to the Senate.[95] To fill the vacant district attorney's office, he recommended not William Tilghman, Ingersoll's own choice as the best successor, but John Wilkes Kittera, a Federalist congressman who had been defeated for re-election.[96] The presidential gamble, if such it was, was anything but successful. Learning of his nomination, Ingersoll wrote immediately to Adams requesting that his name be withdrawn "without giving the appearance of a negative from the Senate."[97] Simultaneously Senator Bingham was worrying: "Why is not Some Person designated to Supply the Place of Mr. Ingersoll....is it intended to place the feature nomination within the power of the new administration?"[98] The predicament caused by the President's action and Ingersoll's refusal made it likely that the Federalists might depart from power with no nomination whatever from Pennsylvania.

To one and all in this confused melee, to allow such an important appointment to fall into the hands of the Jeffersonians would have been unthinkable. Fortunately, there was still time for remedy. On February 26, the Chief Executive sent to the Senate the name of Edward Tilghman in place of Jared Ingersoll.[99] Whether the President wrote the name of

---

95 1 S. EXECUTIVE JOUR. 381 [1800–1801].

96 *Ibid.* Kittera had been recommended by a congressional colleague for some appointment following his congressional service, "being advanced to that time of Life that opposes descending into the Minutia of the business of the Law – and also of an Age that Matures the Judgment and Understanding." Letter From Richard Thomas to John Adams, Jan. 17, 1801, in Adams Papers, Letters Received.

97 Letter From Jared Ingersoll to John Adams, Feb. 23, 1801, in Adams Papers, Letters Received.

98 Letter From William Bingham to Richard Peters, Feb. 23, 1801, in 10 PETERS PAPERS No. 69, Historical Society of Pennsylvania, Philadelphia, Pa.

99 Message of John Adams to the Senate, Feb. 26, 1801, Senate Files 6B-A1-A2-A3, Nominations and Papers, Dec. 5, 1799-March 3, 1801, National Archives.

Edward Tilghman rather than that of William Tilghman by mistake in the disordered scramble of those last pressing days or by express intention, we cannot know;[100] but that confusion was now confounded, there need be no doubt. At this point, Senator Bingham, having learned that Edward Tilghman would also decline, hurried to the President while the nomination awaited Senate approval. Because of the consequences of another refusal at so late a date, Bingham persuaded Adams to withdraw Edward Tilghman's name instantly and substitute that of William Tilghman.[101] The following day, February 27, the Chief Executive rushed a note to the Senate requesting that the name "William" be inserted in the nomination in place of "Edward."[102] Writing to the beneficiary of these latest developments, Bingham testily made it plain that *he* was expected to *accept* the honor: "I assured the President (& I was authorized in So doing, from the Tenor of Letters I had received) that you would accept the appointment – Another Consideration of primary Importance, is that it will be too late, to make any other Change, under the present administration."[103] Indeed, only four days remained to the Federalists after this appointment was approved, but its purpose had been fulfilled – a Federalist had been tucked into the new court, and upon the Philadelphia bar had been bestowed the honor and prestige of chief judge.

Members of the New Jersey bar were also interested, of course, in the judgeship that could be expected to come from their state. The probable passage of the Judiciary Act induced Richard Stockton, former congressman and Federalist leader from New Jersey, to recommend William Griffith, a Federalist lawyer of Burlington, to the Chief Executive. "It will give pleasure to the most substantial friends of your administration if he should be appointed. To those who under one name or another have perpetually opposed the Government, and calumniated its administration from its adoption to the present time it will be the cause of sorrow.... Your public conduct Sir has fully evinced that you never dreaded the

[100] William and Edward Tilghman were cousins and both were members of the Philadelphia bar. Edward Tilghman was "the consummate Pennsylvania authority on all points connected with estates, tenures, uses and remainders." WARREN, *op. cit. supra* note 91, at 245 & n.2, 246.

[101] Letter From William Bingham to William Tilghman, Feb. 27, 1801, in Gratz Collection, Box 32, Historical Society of Pennsylvania, Philadelphia, Pa.

[102] Message of John Adams to the Senate, *supra* note 99. This correction was duly recorded in 1 S. EXECUTIVE JOUR. 386 [1800–1801].

[103] Letter From William Bingham to William Tilghman, Feb. 27, 1801, Box 32, Gratz Collection, Historical Society of Pennsylvania, Philadelphia, Pa.

frowns, nor courted the smiles of such men."[104] Elias Boudinot, director
of the mint, recommended both Griffith and also his own brother, Elisha
Boudinot, one of the judges of the Supreme Court of New Jersey. Either
man, he assured the President, would "give general satisfaction to that
state – I mean to the friends of the present government."[105]

Adams, however, replied by asking Richard Stockton himself to consider the office.[106] In the absence of evidence that New Jersey leaders
in Congress or elsewhere importuned Adams to appoint Stockton, it is
likely that this offer was initiated by the President. Pleased though he was
to receive this confidential testimonial of high regard, Stockton was not
inclined toward an office that promised to be temporary. "It is true that
a Judge cannot be removed from office by a new President but the law
under which he is appointed may be repealed by a predominant party –
and his life may be embittered by unmerited censure and slander...." He
renewed his appeal in favor of Griffith, "whose character, talents and
virtuous exertion in stemming the tide of folly which overflows this land
are not inferior to those of any man in this state."[107] President Adams
learned just before the judiciary bill passed the Senate on February 7 that
his first choice for a judge from New Jersey was not anxious to accept.
This, coupled with the attendant risk that if nominated, Stockton would
refuse, probably determined the official decision. Doubtless assuming an
acceptance from the tone of Stockton's solicitation, the President sent the
nomination of William Griffith to the Senate.[108]

104 Letter From Richard Stockton to John Adams, Jan. 17, 1801, in Adams Papers, Letters
Received. To this Adams responded: "I may have been too indifferent to the smiles of
some men, and to the frowns of others, but neither will influence my judgment, I hope,
in determining nominations of judges, characters at all times sacred in my estimation."
Letter From John Adams to Richard Stockton, Jan. 27, 1801, in 9 THE WORKS OF
JOHN ADAMS 94–95 (Adams ed. 1854).
105 Letter From Elias Boudinot to John Adams, Jan. 20, 1801, in Adams Papers, Letters
Received. A portion of this letter is reprinted in 9 THE WORKS OF JOHN ADAMS 93 n.1
(Adams ed. 1854), but the quoted passage is not included.
106 Letter From John Adams to Richard Stockton, Jan. 27, 1801, in 9 THE WORKS OF
JOHN ADAMS 94 (Adams ed. 1854). Stockton's legal reputation was such that a legal
education in New Jersey was considered incomplete unless it included a course of study
in his office. Students from other states as well frequently applied for training under his
direction. WARREN, *op. cit. supra* note 91, at 114.
107 Letter From Richard Stockton to John Adams, Feb. 2, 1801, in Adams Papers, Letters
Received. In addition, Stockton was planning to run as Federalist candidate for governor
of New Jersey later in the year. He did this and was defeated. 18 DICTIONARY OF
AMERICAN BIOGRAPHY 47 (1933).
108 1 S. EXECUTIVE JOUR. 381 [1800–1801]. Unknown to the President, Associate Justice
William Paterson of the Supreme Court of the United States had suggested the name

"Delaware will be exceeding offended, if she has not a Judgeship allotted to her . . . ," wrote Senator William Bingham of Pennsylvania.[109] There was little likelihood, however, that the small state was to be forgotten. Nor did the selection of a member of the court from that state appear to have occasioned any inquiry, doubt, or choice. While the judiciary bill was before the Senate, Congressman James A. Bayard already had firmly in mind its possibilities for his father-in-law, Richard Bassett, the Governor of Delaware.[110] On February 6, he confidently wrote: "If it is good news I can assure you of a seat upon the Bench of the Circuit Court. 2,000 dollars are better than anything Delaware can give you, and not an unpleasant provision for life."[111] Two days later, in the midst of the frenzied balloting to determine whether Burr or Jefferson would be president, Bayard took a moment to dash off another note to tell his father-in-law that the appointment was "secure."[112] On February 15, the Delaware Congressman visited President Adams, who at that time, according to Bayard, expressed his intention to nominate Bassett as chief judge of the circuit.[113] On February 18, the nomination of Richard Bassett was sent to the Senate.[114] His nomination confirmed, Governor Bassett received congratulations from William Hill Wells, the Senator from Delaware,[115] and explanations from his son-in-law that the President had changed his mind about the title of chief judge.[116]

Delighted at his appointment, Bassett, anticipating the comfortable years ahead, resigned instantaneously as Governor and wrote a friendly letter to his future colleague, Tilghman. Despite some experience on the court of common pleas in Delaware, he acknowledged himself "very

of Judge Andrew Kirkpatrick of the New Jersey Supreme Court to William Cushing. Letter From William Paterson to William Cushing, Feb. 11, 1801, in Robert Treat Paine Papers, Box 4, No. 18, Massachusetts Historical Society, Boston, Mass. Having left Washington, Cushing did not receive the letter until March, two weeks too late to exert any possible influence upon the selection of a judge from New Jersey. Letter From William Cushing to William Paterson, March 18, 1801, draft copy in the Robert Treat Paine Papers, Box 4, No. 19, Massachusetts Historical Society, Boston, Mass.

[109] Letter From William Bingham to Richard Peters, Feb. 1, 1801, in 10 PETERS PAPERS No. 65, Historical Society of Pennsylvania, Philadelphia, Pa.

[110] Letter From James A. Bayard to Richard Bassett, Feb. 6, 1801, in *Bayard Papers* 123.

[111] Letter From James A. Bayard to Richard Bassett, Feb. 10, 1801, in *Bayard Papers* 124.

[112] Letter From James A. Bayard to Richard Bassett, Feb. 12, 1801, in *Bayard Papers* 125.

[113] Letter From James A. Bayard to Richard Bassett, Feb. 16, 1801, in *Bayard Papers* 127.

[114] 1 S. EXECUTIVE JOUR. 381 [1800–1801].

[115] Letter From William Hill Wells to Richard Bassett, Feb. 20, 1801, in the Dreer Collection, American Statesmen, Historical Society of Pennsylvania, Philadelphia, Pa.

[116] Letter From James Bayard to Richard Bassett, Feb. 22, 1801, in *Bayard Papers* 130.

unequal to the Task of filling a Seat in the Circuit Court of the United States. . . ." Relying on the chief judge to correct his errors and bear with them, Richard Bassett jocularly concluded: "I am a great Enemy to the Adjournement of Causes when once begun, well knowing it leads to corruption and injustice, and I also am opposed to adjournments for Dinner, but More of these things when we Meet. . . ."[117]

Less information exists regarding the appointments to the remaining three circuits. For the Fourth Circuit, consisting of Maryland and Virginia,[118] the President's first choice was Charles Lee, Attorney General of the United States since 1795.[119] Maryland congressmen and Supreme Court Justice Samuel Chase strongly supported Philip Barton Key, a Federalist who had narrowly lost his seat in the Maryland legislature in the election of 1800.[120] Federalist congressmen from Virginia requested John Marshall to urge the appointment of George Keith Taylor and Charles Magill.[121] Marshall, a brother-in-law of Taylor's,[122] may have added his personal recommendation to the Chief Executive. The initial nominations sent to the Senate were Lee as chief judge, Key and Taylor as associate judges.[123] The nomination of Key, who had captained the Loyalist regiment of Maryland during the Revolution, was the only one of the circuit appointments that occasioned active opposition on the floor of the Senate; nine Republicans voted against his confirmation.[124] With the refusal

[117] Letter From Richard Bassett to William Tilghman, April 20, 1801, in Gratz Collection, Box 28, Historical Society of Pennsylvania, Philadelphia, Pa.

[118] Judiciary Act of 1801, ch. 4, §6, 2 Stat. 90.

[119] 1 S. EXECUTIVE JOUR. 381 [1800–1801]. Charles Lee, not to be confused with General Charles Lee of Revolutionary War fame, was the brother of Henry ("Light Horse Harry") Lee and Richard Bland Lee.

[120] Letter From John Dennis to John Adams, Feb. 17, 1801, in Adams Papers, Letters Received; Letter From John Chew Thomas to John Adams, Feb. 17, 1801, in Adams Papers, Letters Received; Letter From Samuel Chase to John Adams, Feb. 17, 1801, in Adams Papers, Letters Received.

[121] Letter From Thomas Evans, Leven Powell, Henry Lee, Robert Page, Josiah Parker, and Samuel Goode to John Marshall, Feb. 10, 1801, in Adams Papers, Letters Received.

[122] In 1799, Taylor married Jane Marshall, the younger sister of John Marshall. 2 BEVERIDGE, *op. cit. supra* note 81, at 175 n.1.

[123] 1 S. EXECUTIVE JOUR. 381 [1800–1801].

[124] *Id.* at 381. Both the National Intelligencer and Washington Advertiser, Feb. 25, 1801, a Republican paper, and the Philadelphia Gazette and Daily Advertiser, Feb. 28, 1801, a Federalist organ, reported that the Senate "divided" on most of the appointments. The *Senate Executive Journal* does not indicate division except in the appointment of Key. Key, the uncle of Francis Scott Key, had not only served against the patriot cause until he was taken prisoner, but upon his release on parole had gone to England and retired on half pay. He returned to Maryland in 1785. 10 DICTIONARY OF AMERICAN BIOGRAPHY 363 (1933).

of Charles Lee to accept his appointment, the places were reshuffled in order to leave no judgeship to be filled by the incoming President. Key was advanced to chief judge and Charles Magill of Virginia was nominated to the third place of the circuit.[125]

For appointment to the Fifth Circuit, which drew together North Carolina, South Carolina, and Georgia,[126] the most frequently mentioned name was that of Samuel Johnston, judge of the superior court of North Carolina, who through service in the state legislature, the Senate, and as governor had well proved his worth. Johnston was the choice of both Republican senators from North Carolina and the outstanding Republican leader in the House, Nathaniel Macon, as well as that of other congressmen of both parties from the state.[127] Two other members of the House supported John Sitgreaves, the district judge for North Carolina, and there was apparently some understanding that the President had in mind the promotion of Sitgreaves.[128] Selection of a judge representing South Carolina seems to have been made by the President alone.[129] The district judge of South Carolina, Thomas Bee, was named chief judge of the circuit, perhaps an acknowledgment of judicial and political services rendered in the extradition of Jonathan Robins, which had brought both Bee and John Adams so much vituperative abuse from the Republicans in 1800.[130] District Judge Sitgreaves of North Carolina and District Judge

---

[125] 1 S. EXECUTIVE JOUR. 385 [1800–1801].

[126] Judiciary Act of 1801, ch. 4, §6, 2 Stat. 90.

[127] Letter From Nathaniel Macon to John Adams, Feb. 18, 1801, in Adams Papers, Letters Received; Letter From Timothy Bloodsworth to John Adams, Feb. 13, 1801, in Adams Papers, Letters Received; Letter From Willis Alston to John Adams, Feb. 14, 1801, in Adams Papers, Letters Received; Letter From R. Stanford to John Adams, Feb. 18, 1801, in Adams Papers, Letters Received; Letter From Jesse Franklin to [John Marshall?], Feb. 17, 1801, in Adams Papers, Letters Received.

[128] Letter From William Barry Grove to John Adams, Feb. 20, 1801, in Adams Papers, Letters Received; Letter From Richard Dobbs Spaight to John Adams, Feb. 18, 1801, in Adams Papers, Letters Received.

[129] Despite the fact that Senator Jacob Read of South Carolina was a Federalist and that five of the six members of the House from that state were of the President's party, no letters from South Carolinians have been discovered.

[130] In 1797, the crew of a British ship mutinied, murdered the officers and sold the ship. Among the crew members was Thomas Nash, a British subject. Two years later, when Nash appeared in Charleston, South Carolina, as a member of the crew of an American vessel, he was jailed at the request of the British consul under the twenty-seventh article of the Jay Treaty. Nash swore that he was an American citizen, Jonathan Robins, born in Danbury, Connecticut. However, on evidence that the seaman was a British subject and a murderer, President Adams requested Judge Bee to deliver Nash to the British consul pursuant to the terms of the treaty. Nash-Robins was hanged without delay, and

Joseph Clay of Georgia were also advanced to the new circuit court.[131]
Assuming Bee's acceptance of his commission, the defeated Federalist senator from South Carolina, Jacob Read, was appointed district judge of
the state, and Thomas Gibbons, who had been recommended by Senator
James Gunn,[132] was nominated to that position in Georgia, now vacated
by the promotion of Joseph Clay to the circuit court.[133]

   The Sixth Circuit established by the Judiciary Act of 1801 included
the districts of East Tennessee, West Tennessee, Kentucky, and Ohio.[134]
Its organization differed from the others in that the circuit function
was to be performed by one circuit judge and the judges of the district
courts of Kentucky and Tennessee, any two of whom could constitute
a quorum.[135] In the spring of 1800, when the new judiciary bill was
first presented to Congress, it was known that a new circuit judge was
planned for the region still far removed into the wilderness. At that time,
the federal district judge of Kentucky, Harry Innes, a fervent Republican,
had recommended Buckner Thruston, one of the state judges, to the

    both Adams and Bee were denounced by the Republicans for truckling to the British.
    See 2 BEVERIDGE, *op. cit. supra* note 81, at 458–75.

[131] 1 S. EXECUTIVE JOUR. 383–84 [1800–1801]. In the records of the Department of State,
    Applications and Recommendations, Miscellaneous: Adams and Jefferson Administra-
    tions, Box 1 at the National Archives, there is a fragment in an unidentified hand dated
    February 23 that lists the appointments to the fifth and sixth circuits. Beside the name
    of Clay there is a "plus" mark; beside those of Bee and Sitgreaves, there is a "qu." It
    would be hard to say whether this might indicate that there was question about their
    approval by the Senate or of their acceptance of the office.

[132] Letter From James Gunn to John Adams, Feb. 21, 1801, in Adams Papers, Letters
    Received. The *Aurora*, March 2, 1801, described Gibbons as "a man whose most
    flatterings recommendations were, that he had adhered to the cause of George III in our
    Revolution, was attainted and his estate confiscated; but that through supplications, a
    steadfast Whig confiscation was annulled, tho' Thomas still remains a Tory in thought,
    word and deed."

[133] 1 S. EXECUTIVE JOUR. 383, 385 [1800–1801]. Earlier, Read had been suggested to fill
    a vacancy on the Supreme Court of the United States. Letter From Samuel Otis to John
    Adams, Jan. 19, 1801, in Adams Papers, Letters Received. Thomas Bee, who did not
    receive his commission until after Jefferson had taken office, returned it preferring to
    continue as district judge. Letter From Thomas Bee to James Madison, March 19, 1801,
    in 22 MADISON PAPERS, Library of Congress, Washington, D.C. Jacob Read then had
    received a commission to an office not actually vacant and was out of luck.

[134] Judiciary Act of 1801, ch. 4, §6, 2 Stat. 90.

[135] The United States district courts in Tennessee and Kentucky were abolished and all
    powers of those courts were vested in the circuit court that was to sit in East Tennessee,
    West Tennessee, and Kentucky. The salaries in the Sixth Circuit were less than in the
    others, both the circuit judge and the district judges receiving $1,500 instead of $2,000.
    See Judiciary Act of 1801, ch. 4, §41, 2 Stat. 100.

President.[136] A year later, Innes again argued in Thruston's behalf,[137] as did Republican members of Congress from Kentucky.[138] Senator John Brown wrote the President that hopefully Thruston was distinguished for his political moderation, belonged to no party, and was not involved in land disputes within the state – "which will probably constitute the chief business of the Court for that District."[139] Kentucky's other senator, an obdurate Federalist defeated in the election of 1800 and a bitter enemy of Brown's,[140] had other views. Senator Humphrey Marshall wrote his cousin and brother-in-law, Secretary of State (and Chief Justice) John Marshall, to ensure that the President would not neglect William McClung, "whom I wish to be appointed." After elaborating on the geographical advantage of a resident of Kentucky as circuit judge, the senator closed on a more significant note: "If you can conceive that political opinions often have an influence in decisions ... upon private rights, you will readily perceive the importance of placing in the circuit courts a man well apperted [*sic*] to the federal government by way of Counterpoise. Mr. McClung is a man of good temper great firmness and a friend to the Government."[141] So thinly veiled a reference doubtless contributed

[136] Letter From Harry Innes to John Adams, April 30, 1800, in Adams Papers, Letters Received.

[137] Letter From Harry Innes to John Adams, Feb. 10, 1801, in Adams Papers, Letters Received. On the same day, Innes wrote more frankly to Jefferson. He solicited the aid of the latter in preventing, if possible, the appointment of William McClung as his superior. Innes described McClung, the brother-in-law of both John and Humphrey Marshall, as "a mere creature to party & faction" and a failure at the bar as well. "H. Marshall and myself are not on speaking terms – that family have imbibed all his dislikes & are my avowed enemies. ... I fear if he [McClung] meets with the appointment he will be governed by family influence. ..." Innes urged the appointment of Thruston. Letter From Harry Innes to Thomas Jefferson, Feb. 10, 1801 (marked "recd. Mar. 6"), in 109 JEFFERSON PAPERS, Library of Congress, Washington, D.C.

[138] Letter From Thomas Davis and John Fowler to John Marshall, Feb. 18, 1801, in Adams Papers, Letters Received.

[139] Letter From John Brown to John Adams, Feb. 19, 1801, in Adams Papers, Letters Received.

[140] Perverse by temperament, sharp of tongue, and a total stranger to tact, Humphrey Marshall could number more enemies than friends. Of all his enemies, according to his biographer, "Marshall hated John Brown the best – or worst." QUISENBERRY, THE LIFE AND TIMES OF HUMPHREY MARSHALL 51 (1892).

[141] Letter From Humphrey Marshall to John Marshall [January or February] 1801, in Adams Papers, Letters Received. Tennessee men in the Congress approved McClung as an alternative to their first choice, Archibald Roane, judge of the superior court of errors and appeals of their state. Letter From William Cocke, Joseph Anderson, and William Claiborne to John Marshall, Feb. 17, 1801, in Adams Papers, Letters Received.

to the geographical and personal advantages of the candidate. There was no need for the senator to mention specifically that William McClung, his own brother-in-law, was also a brother-in-law of John Marshall's.[142] Although Republican congressmen protested that they had not even been consulted[143] and Senator Brown reported that "Mr. Adams was deaf to every argument in opposition to the recommendation made by Messrs. J. & H. Marshall,"[144] a desire to please the political opposition was no part of these appointments. Care had been taken that this position would be filled with a reliable Federalist, and McClung was duly nominated to the Senate.[145]

In addition to addressing the Judiciary Act, the Sixth Congress devoted some of its last weeks to legislation regarding the administration of the territory that, upon the removal of the government from Philadelphia to Washington in 1800, had become the nation's capital. On February 27, with only four days of the Federalist administration remaining, the act concerning the District of Columbia became law.[146] It provided for the establishment of a court composed of three judges, resident in the district, having all the powers of the circuit courts and circuit judges of the nation.[147] "I trust your excellency will not pass me by ...," one applicant wrote the President,[148] but this plea as well as the recommendations from

---

[142] Raised in the Virginia home of his uncle, Thomas Marshall, Humphrey Marshall had grown up with his cousins John, James, Anna Maria, and the other Marshall children. After service in the Revolution, he settled in Kentucky, married his cousin Anna Maria (Mary) in 1784, and became deputy surveyor in the office of his uncle. He received from Virginia a warrant for 4,000 acres of land for his military services, and later became one of the greatest landholders and wealthiest citizens of the state. According to tradition, he measured his money by the peck. A Federalist in a Republican state, Marshall had accused his opposition of intrigues with the French and Spanish and as a result had been elected to the Senate in 1795 over John Breckinridge. Nearly lynched at home for his support of the Jay Treaty, and the victim of further political complications in the state, Marshall was defeated by Breckinridge in the election of 1800. QUISENBERRY, *op. cit. supra* note 139, at 10–17, 57–69. William McClung was married to a sister of Mrs. Humphrey (Mary Marshall) Marshall and John Marshall.
[143] Letter From Thomas Davis to John Adams, Feb. 20, 1801, in Adams Papers, Letters Received.
[144] Lexington, Kentucky Gazette, March 30, 1801.
[145] 1 S. EXECUTIVE JOUR. 383 [1800–1801].
[146] This bill was passed by the Senate on February 5, 1801, and by the House on February 24. After receiving the signature of the President, it became law on February 27. 6 ANNALS OF CONG. 739, 1052, 1552 (1801) [1799–1801].
[147] For other provisions of this act regarding the judicial structure of the District, see Act of Feb. 27, 1801, ch. 15, 2 Stat. 103.
[148] Letter From Richard Bland Lee to John Adams, Feb. 14, 1801, in Adams Papers, Letters Received.

Maryland senators and Virginia congressmen clearly went unheeded.[149] Early in January, Adams had nominated his nephew, William Cranch, to the position of commissioner of the city of Washington,[150] thereby risking charges of nepotism by his enemies.[151] Impervious now to any criticism, the President did not hesitate to make the young man a judge.[152] A warm endorsement by Secretary of the Navy Stoddert[153] was added to whatever solicitation may have been made by John Marshall in behalf of the latter's brother James, who also received an appointment to this court.[154] As chief judge, Adams named the elderly Thomas Johnson of Maryland, who had resigned from the Supreme Court in 1793 and because of ill health had refused in 1795 to become Secretary of State. Failure to assure Johnson's acceptance before making the nomination resulted in his rejection of the office and a vacancy that would be filled by Thomas Jefferson.[155]

---

[149] Both Senators from Maryland had recommended John Rousby Plater, a noted Maryland attorney. Letter From William Hindman and John Eager Howard to John Adams, Feb. 25, 1801, in Adams Papers, Letters Received. Virginia Congressmen had sought the nomination of Colonel Charles Simms of Alexandria. Letter From Leven Powell and Robert Page to John Marshall, Feb. 26, 1801, in Adams Papers, Letters Received.

[150] Letter From John Marshall to William Cranch, Jan. 8, 1801, in Cranch Papers, Massachusetts Historical Society, Boston, Mass. William Cranch was the son of Richard and Mary Cranch; Mrs. Cranch and Abigail Adams were sisters.

[151] Letter From Abigail Adams to Mary Cranch, Jan. 15, 1801, in NEW LETTERS OF ABIGALL ADAMS: 1788–1801 at 263, 264 (Mitchell ed. 1947); Boston Independent Chronicle, Jan. 19–22, 1801.

[152] The commission, dated March 3, 1801, is in the Cranch Papers, Massachusetts Historical Society, Boston, Mass. With this appointment, Cranch began a fifty-four year tenure in this court. In 1805, Jefferson appointed him as chief judge, and from 1802 until 1817, Cranch was also reporter for the Supreme Court of the United States.

[153] Letter From Benjamin Stoddert to John Adams, Feb. 28, 1801, in Adams Papers, Letters Received. Stoddert himself received appointment as justice of the peace of Washington County on March 3, 1801.

[154] 1 S. EXECUTIVE JOUR. 387 [1800–1801].

[155] That Johnson's refusal was not received until after Jefferson had taken office vexed Chief Justice Marshall considerably. "I am excessively mortified at the circumstances relative to the appointment of the chief Judge of the district. There was a negligence in that business arising from a confidence that Mr. Johnson would accept which I lament excessively. When Mr. Swan parted with us at your house I thought he went to send an express the next morning...." Letter From John Marshall to James Marshall, March 18, 1801, in Marshall Transcripts and Photostats, Library of Congress, Washington, D.C. Republican William Kilty was appointed barely in time for the meeting of the first session of the new court in 1801. Letter From William Cranch to William Shaw, May 15, 1801, in 18 MISCELLANEOUS BOUND COLLECTION, Massachusetts Historical Society, Boston, Mass. This recess appointment was not officially presented to the Senate until January 6, 1802. 1 S. EXECUTIVE JOUR. 401 [1801–1802].

The passage of this act also created the opportunity for countless appointments of marshals, clerks, attorneys, registers of wills, and justices of the peace. Such an abundance of new offices drew applications from many, some of whom were out of office, out of money, or both. In accordance with the recommendations and wishes of local Federalists,[156] these lesser but lucrative offices were filled with deserving recipients by various definitions of the word. On March 2 and March 3 until their final adjournment, the senators approved the remaining nominations of marshals, registers of wills, and forty-two midnight justices of the peace.[157] As the day dwindled, the last crumbs from the Federalist feast table were distributed to eager waiting hands, and hurriedly, in the office of Secretary of State John Marshall, commissions were signed and sealed before the term of President Adams expired on March 3, 1801. Of these, at least four had not been delivered when Thomas Jefferson became the third president of the nation.[158]

As the nominations of "the midnight judges" were swiftly being approved by the Senate, Republican leaders manifested their dismay and disgust. "Instead of smoothing the path for his successor, he [Adams] plays into the hands of those who are endeavoring to strew it with as many difficulties as possible; and with this view does not manifest a very squeamish regard to the Constn," Madison wrote to James Monroe.[159] Reporting to his constituents, John Fowler asserted that the insidiousness of the design was equalled only by "the shameless manner of its being carried into execution."[160] Senator Stevens Thomson Mason of Virginia grumbled vigorously because careful provision had been made

---

[156] See, e.g., Letter From Leven Powell to John Marshall, Feb. 27, 1801, in Adams Papers, Letters Received; Letter From Henry Lee and Leven Powell to John Marshall, Feb. 27, 1801, in Adams Papers, Letters Received; Letter From G. Dent to John Marshall, Feb. 27, 1801, in Adams Papers, Letters Received; Letter From Thomas Dyson to John Marshall, Feb. 28, 1801, in Adams Papers, Letters Received; Letter From Benjamin Stoddert to John Adams, Feb. 27, 1801, in Adams Papers, Letters Received.

[157] 1 S. EXECUTIVE JOUR. 388 [1800–1801].

[158] This circumstance led to the celebrated case of Marbury v. Madison, 5 U.S. (1 Cranch) 137 (1803), which, in declaring the Supreme Court's power to void unconstitutional legislation, held that Congress could not by statute create original jurisdiction in the Supreme Court to issue a writ of mandamus directing the Secretary of State to deliver an undelivered commission.

[159] Letter From James Madison to James Monroe, Feb. 28, 1801, in 22 MADISON PAPERS, Library of Congress, Washington, D.C. Three years later, Jefferson wrote that only one act of Adams's life had ever given him displeasure, the last appointments to office. Letter From Thomas Jefferson to Abigail Adams, June 13, 1804, in 1 THE ADAMS-JEFFERSON LETTERS 270, 271 (Cappon ed. 1959).

[160] Philadelphia Aurora and General Advertiser, April 9, 1801.

for John Marshall's relatives.[161] Republican newspapers screeched casti-
gations at the President. "In all these instances he named men opposed
in political opinion to the national will, as unequivocally declared by his
removal and the appointment of a successor of different sentiments."[162]
"Mr. Adams is determined to do all the mischief in his power to the
last of his administration."[163] "Judge of them [the appointments] from
a declaration which he [Adams] has made that 'no man that would be
admitted into decent company, was likely to be nominated under the
new administration, and that he would continue his appointments to the
last.'"[164]

To the Republicans, not only the fact of the appointments but also
the character of them seemed a matter for public outrage. In addition
to the attacks on the former Loyalists Philip Barton Key and Thomas
Gibbons, Thomas Bee was singled out for special attention – Matthew
Lyon charged that Adams would be tortured forever by the ghost of
Jonathan Robins.[165] The appointments of Jacob Read, Elijah Paine, Ray
Greene, and John Wilkes Kittera were bitterly attacked as sinecures
given in deliberate violation of the Constitution.[166] The *Aurora* pro-
claimed that nominations such as these were null and void and that, even
were the law not repealed, these men were removable by the courts.[167]
Monroe warned President-elect Jefferson of the implications of the retreat
of the Federalist party into the judiciary: "While in possession of that
ground it can check the popular current which runs against them & seize
the favorable occasion to promote reaction, which it does not despair

[161] Letter From Stevens Thomson Mason to John Breckinridge, Feb. 19, 1801, in 20 BRECKINRIDGE PAPERS, Library of Congress, Washington, D.C.
[162] National Intelligencer, Feb. 25, 1801.
[163] Lexington, Kentucky Gazette, March 30, 1801.
[164] Aurora, Feb. 28, 1801.
[165] Baltimore American and Daily Advertiser, March 7, 1801. For an account of Matthew Lyon's trial and imprisonment earlier under the Sedition Act, see SMITH, FREEDOM'S FETTERS 221-46 (1956).
[166] U.S. CONST. art. I, §6, provides that "no senator or representative shall, during the time for which he was elected, be appointed to any [federal] civil office...created during such time." See the Federalist denial of this charge in Gazette of the United States and Philadelphia Daily Advertiser, March 4, 1801, which pointed out that those in Congress had received appointment as district judges, an office created in 1789. No members of Congress were appointed as circuit judges.
[167] Aurora, March 3, 1801. The National Intelligencer, Feb. 20, 1801, questioned whether appointments to offices not actually vacant at the time, even if afterward vacated, were not null. Madison also raised this point. Letter From James Madison to James Monroe, Feb. 28, 1801, in 22 MADISON PAPERS, Library of Congress, Washington, D.C.

of...."[168] That expectation of a repeal of the Judiciary Act and an abolition of the offices created by it was current in the Republican press is
not surprising.[169] Instantaneous removal of those officers of the federal
courts who held their positions "at pleasure" was, of course, taken for
granted.[170] Stated Jefferson: "The only shield for our Republican citizens
against the federalism of the courts is to have the Attornies and Marshals
republicans...."[171]

Federalist newspapers were not surprised at the "Jacobin" reaction:
"They well know that the judges are equally independent upon the *officers of the government* and the *people*, and can be influenced in their
actions, by no other motives than the love of justice and desire for the
strict execution of law."[172] In tones of lofty dignity appropriate to his
pseudonym, Aristides, one Federalist defended the appointments of those
who were "respectable from their age and...venerable for their talents
and services,...[whose] conduct has been marked by a mild, able, and
impartial administration of justice...."[173] Privately, Gouverneur Morris
wrote a friend that the Federalists were about to experience "a heavy gale
of adverse wind; can they be blamed for casting many anchors to hold
their ship through the storm?"[174]

All these "anchors" were indubitably of the Federalist elite, and the
haste with which the Federalist party filled the appointments – resem-
bling in many ways the last act of a comic opera – was without doubt a
crude exercise of their last moment of voting strength and understandably

168 Letter From James Monroe to Thomas Jefferson, March 3, 1801, in 110 JEFFERSON
    PAPERS, Library of Congress, Washington, D.C.
169 Lang's New York Gazette and General Advertiser, March 7, 1801; Aurora, March 3,
    1801; National Intelligencer, Feb. 20, 1801; Baltimore American, Feb. 17, 1801.
170 Lover of Truth and Justice, Georgetown, D.C. Museum, April 10, 1801; National
    Intelligencer, as reprinted in Aurora, March 28, 1801.
171 Letter From Thomas Jefferson to A. Stuart, April 8, 1801, in 111 JEFFERSON PAPERS,
    Library of Congress, Washington, D.C. To Benjamin Rush, Jefferson wrote that he
    would "expunge the effect of Mr. A's indecent conduct in crowding nominations after he
    knew that they were not for himself." Letter From Thomas Jefferson to Benjamin Rush,
    March 24, 1801, in 111 JEFFERSON PAPERS, Library of Congress, Washington, D.C.
    He expressed similar sentiments in letters to Gideon Granger (March 29, 1801); Henry
    Knox (March 27, 1801); William Findley (March 24, 1801); Thomas N. Randolph
    (March 12, 1801) – all in 111 JEFFERSON PAPERS, Library of Congress, Washington,
    D.C.
172 Gazette of the United States and Philadelphia Daily Advertiser, Feb. 6, 1801.
173 Georgetown, D.C. Museum, April 17, 1801.
174 Letter From Gouverneur Morris to Robert Livingston, Feb. 20, 1801, in 3 LIFE OF
    GOUVERNEUR MORRIS 153–54 (Sparks ed. 1832).

regarded by the Republicans as a gratuitous insult to their chieftain. The appointment of former Loyalists might well be regarded as a "prostitution of justice." Richard Bassett of Delaware, James Marshall of Virginia, William McClung of Kentucky, George Keith Taylor of Virginia, and William Cranch all owed their appointments to direct action on the part of their respective relatives. Oliver Wolcott, the personal choice of President Adams, had had neither legal nor judicial experience; he could scarcely have been expected to be a luminous ornament to the federal bench. However, Benjamin Bourne of Rhode Island, John Lowell of Massachusetts, Samuel Hitchcock of Vermont, John Sitgreaves of North Carolina, Thomas Bee of South Carolina, and Joseph Clay of Georgia already held permanent judicial appointments as federal district judges. Egbert Benson of New York held high judicial office in the state. Jeremiah Smith of New Hampshire and William Tilghman of Pennsylvania were held in high professional regard by local bench and bar, and each was destined later for a distinguished career as chief justice of his respective state. Certainly Republican tempers mounted at their helplessness to do more than raise outraged cries of "Jobbery" and "Foul!" This may well have inspired an impulse to immediate political revenge. Nonetheless, it should be stressed that these appointments did not include any of the particular *bêtes noires* of the Republican party and press. None of the detested Federalists zealots – Timothy Pickering, Gouverneur Morris, Theodore Sedgwick, or Robert Goodloe Harper – would confront Republicans from behind a federal bench. As a whole, the group of midnight judges reflected the relatively moderate political positions of the men who had selected them. They were not facsimiles of the fanaticism that had led the Federalists to prosecute the Whiskey Rebels and John Fries for treason and to enforce the Sedition Act with such vigor. One might have expected that some Republicans would even have sighed relief that Samuel Chase, Associate Justice of the Supreme Court, would ride the circuit no more!

To comment that the group who received these judicial appointments was not as partisan as might have been is not to applaud the action;[175]

---

[175] A vigorous defense of the partisan nature of the "midnight appointments" has been made in 2 CROSSKEY, POLITICS AND THE CONSTITUTION IN THE HISTORY OF THE UNITED STATES 761 (1953). Crosskey argues that because the power of judicial review had not yet been established, the view of "fairness" through a party division of national judgeships did not exist and hence censure of Adams for failing to include any

its timing was understandably a source of outrage to the incoming party. But whether the appointment of "the midnight judges" alone is sufficient to explain either the determination of the Federalists for the passage of the Judiciary Act of 1801 or the vehemence of the Republican determination for its repeal is questionable. Be that as it may, the last action of the one administration was to provide the first major issue of the next, and a wry reflection of attitudes can be seen in respective toasts offered during the last days of the Adams administration. The Federalists drank to "the judiciary of the United States – independent of power and independent of popularity."[176] At a Republican festival, at about the same time, the ardent Jeffersonian, William Branch Giles, lifted his glass: "The Judiciary of the United States – from the 4th of March next, may the judges lose their political sensibilities in the recollection that they are Judges, not political partisans."[177] Not until the future, amid circumstances even more highly charged politically, would such a sentiment become infused with its full meaning.

At the immediate present, however, according to ancient story, the Secretary of State continued to sign commissions until interrupted by Levi Lincoln, the incoming Attorney General, who carried Jefferson's watch, the hands of which showed midnight, March 3, 1801.[178]

Whether this part of the story be true or not, the clocks that tolled midnight on that date tolled the final end of more than a decade of Federalist predominance in the nation. Before daybreak, President John

Jeffersonians among the judges is unwarranted. Furthermore, "other differences between conditions then and now" would have made Adams's appointment of any Jeffersonians "reprehensible in a high degree." In Crosskey's estimation, the judges were an "extraordinarily able group of men" of whom "there can be no possible doubt, will bear comparison with any equal number of judges ever chosen by any President before or since." *Ibid.*

176 New York Daily Advertiser, Feb. 10, 1801.
177 Richmond, Virginia Argus, Feb. 6, 1801. In the House of Representatives in 1802, Giles would lead the victorious Republican fight to repeal the Judiciary Act.
178 PARTON, LIFE OF THOMAS JEFFERSON 585–86 (1874). Parton repeats the version told by Jefferson's great-granddaughter, Sarah M. Randolph. See RANDOLPH, THE DOMESTIC LIFE OF THOMAS JEFFERSON 307–08 (1871). These accounts come complete with dialogue presumed to have taken place between John Marshall and Levi Lincoln. This "household gossip" has been perpetuated by serious historians, says Beveridge, who calls the account "an absurd tale." 2 BEVERIDGE, THE LIFE OF JOHN MARSHALL 561 n.2 (1916). Beveridge's spirited biography does not perpetuate the last part of the account in the earlier works – that in after years, John Marshall, "laughing," used to say that he had been allowed to pick up nothing but his hat.

Adams set out alone for Quincy, his carriage wheezing through the spring mud along the road that led away from the capital. Behind him, he left in the dawn of a new day a quickened mood of public excitement as the members of Congress gathered to witness the ceremony at which Chief Justice John Marshall would administer the oath of office as President of the United States to Thomas Jefferson.

4

United States v. Callender: Judge and Jury in a Republican Society*

Kathryn Preyer

It is universally acknowledged that the English background of American law and institutions was foundational to important American constitutional developments. For pride of place, we would surely include trial by jury and the concept of trial by jury as a substantial right. Less understood, however, are important related questions: What was the proper role of the jury? The role of the judge? What was the appropriate relationship between the two? Both in the pre-Revolutionary period and in the years of the early republic, such questions are joined in the American context, and it is these questions that are at the core of this chapter.

My focus is a case tried in one of the federal circuit courts established by the Judiciary Act of 1789. *United States v. Callender*[1] was a prosecution under the Sedition Act of 1798, tried in Richmond in the spring term 1800, five months before the election that would bring Thomas Jefferson

* Originally published as "*U.S. v. Callender*. Judge and Jury in a Republican Society," in *Origins of the Federal Judiciary: Essays on the Judiciary Act of 1789*, ed. Maeva Marcus (New York: Oxford University Press, 1992), 173–195. Copyright © 1992 Oxford University Press. Reprinted by permission of Oxford University Press.

The author wishes to thank Thomas Andrew Green, Wythe Holt, and Henry Lee Conway for valuable comments and suggestions. The reader is directed to two relevant works published after this book [*Origins of the Federal Judiciary: Essays on the Judiciary Act of 1789*, ed. Maeva Marcus (New York: Oxford University Press, 1992)] went to press: S. C. Stimson, *The American Revolution in the Law: Anglo-American Jurisprudence Before John Marshall* (1990), and M. Durey, "*With the Hammer of Truth*": James Thomson Callender and America's Early National Heroes (1990).

[1] F. Wharton, *State Trials of the United States during the Administrations of Washington and Adams*... (1849; reprint, 1970), 688–718; United States v. Callender, 25 Fed. Cas. 239–58 (C.C.D. Va. 1800) (No. 14,709).

to the presidency. Callender's trial has been frequently described by others, but all too often it has served chiefly as a way station to a discussion of Justice Samuel Chase's later impeachment.[2] Yet some of the most important issues arising under the Judiciary Act of 1789 are to be discovered in the case: the relationship of federal and state authority, the relationship of judge to jury, the power of the judge at trial, the role of the jury, and the place of federal judicial authority.

It is important to note that the English tradition of trial by jury was anything but uniform or static over the 400 years of its history before the settlement of the first North American colony.[3] It is important to emphasize as well that even though jury trials took place in most of the American colonies almost from their inception, it is clear that an extremely wide variation in colonial practice existed. For example, Puritan New Haven abolished juries altogether, even for capital crimes, relying for its criminal procedure on an inquisitorial process carried out by its magistrates, who played all the roles – charged suspects, examined witnesses, rendered judgment, and imposed punishment. In Quaker West Jersey, on the contrary, magistrates had virtually no discretionary powers. The magistrates presided and could offer advice to the jury if requested, but it was the jury that determined both law and fact. In Virginia, after a period of martial law followed by one of summary justice, common law jury trial for capital offenses was in use by 1630; use of the civil jury developed far more slowly. The same was the case for the noncapital criminal jury.[4] John Murrin's careful study of trial by jury in New England suggests that colonies organized by settlers without strong leadership from a magisterial elite (Rhode Island, West Jersey, North Carolina) "warmly embraced" juries, whereas colonies dominated by powerful magistrates (New Haven, Massachusetts, Virginia, early Maryland) were suspicious

[2] C. Warren, *The Supreme Court in United States History* (1924), 1:282; J. Haw, F. Beirne, R. Beirne, and R. Jett, *Stormy Patriot: The Life of Samuel Chase* (1980), 202–6; R. Berger, *Impeachment: The Constitutional Problems* (1973), 224–51. For more extensive discussion, see J. M. Smith, *Freedom's Fetters: The Alien and Sedition Laws and American Civil Liberties* (1956), 334–58; S. B. Presser and B. B. Hurley, "Saving God's Republic: The Jurisprudence of Samuel Chase," *University of Illinois Law Review* 1984:808–14; J. Goebel, Jr., *Antecedents and Beginnings to 1801*, vol. 1 of *The Oliver Wendell Holmes Devise History of the Supreme Court of the United States* (1971), 640–45, 649–51.

[3] For discussion of the evolving English tradition, see T. A. Green, *Verdict According to Conscience: Perspectives on the English Criminal Trial Jury, 1200–1800* (1985).

[4] J. M. Murrin and A. G. Roeber, "Trial by Jury: The Virginia Paradox," in J. Kukla, ed., *The Bill of Rights: A Lively Heritage* (1987), 110–15.

of juries, and their widespread use developed more slowly.[5] Diversity within a multifaceted English tradition characterized most of the colonial period, and diversity would continue to persist.

New imperial policies after 1763 as well as patterns of local usage precipitated a heightened ideology around the idea of trial by jury as a right of Englishmen, and no right was made more central in the configuration of rights created by lawyers, legislators, and pamphleteers in the decade of the American rebellion.[6] In their view, the right to trial by jury constituted the most effective mode of popular check on arbitrary power, securing both liberty and property to the citizen. Countless examples demonstrate the passionate reaction to the loss of jury trial as the British attempted to enforce revenue measures in juryless vice-admiralty courts.[7] Most conspicuously, the Declaration of Independence included among the array of charges against King George III that he had assented to laws depriving the colonists of trial by jury.[8]

It is hardly surprising, therefore, that the new states secured this right immediately in their individual declarations of rights and constitutions.[9] Moreover, some states, as part of their Revolutionary efforts to restructure institutions of colonial days, expanded the jury's role by provisions to try admiralty and equity to juries.[10] Such innovations also bespeak ideas about the nature of law itself in a republican society, about the very nature of popular sovereignty. And they constitute a starting point for a congeries of problems that the new states would encounter in the 1780s. Convinced of an intrinsic equitableness of all law and committed to popular participation as a basis *for* law, the new states were committed to legislative supremacy. Because of their colonial experience, they

[5] J. M. Murrin, "Magistrates, Sinners, and a Precarious Liberty: Trial by Jury in Seventeenth Century New England," in D. D. Hall, J. M. Murrin, and T. W. Tate, eds., *Saints and Revolutionaries: Essays on Early American History* (1984), 152–206.

[6] J. P. Reid, *Constitutional History of the American Revolution*, vol. 1, *The Authority of Rights* (1986), 47–49. For other conflicts involving local juries, see G. S. Rowe, "Rex v. John Clowes, Jr., and the Shape of Politics in Pre-Revolutionary Sussex County," *Delaware History* 17: 215–35, 1977.

[7] C. Ubbelohde, *The Vice-Admiralty Courts and the American Revolution* (1960); D. S. Lovejoy, "Rights Imply Equality: The Case Against Admiralty Jurisdiction in America, 1764–1776," *William and Mary Quarterly*, 3rd ser., 16:459–84, 1959; Reid, *Authority of Rights*, 177–83.

[8] H. S. Commager, ed., *Documents of American History*, 3rd ed. (1947), 101.

[9] These documents can be conveniently located in F. N. Thorpe, ed., *The Federal and State Constitutions, Colonial Charters, and Other Organic Laws of the States, Territories, and Colonies Now or Heretofore Forming the United States of America*, 7 vols. (1909).

[10] Goebel, *Antecedents and Beginnings*, 154–55, 161–63, 484, 500.

were particularly apprehensive of the discretionary power of judges and the *uncertainties* of judicial discretion.[11] Yet the language of fundamental principles – or aspirations – in declarations of rights or constitutions left much to be clarified in the day-to-day life of the citizenry. The right to trial by jury "shall remain inviolate forever." What did this mean? Despite the greater tendency at the time to look to legislative bodies for remedy for grievances, a few cases tried in state courts in the 1780s touch the subject. *Trevett v. Weeden* (1786) and *Bayard v. Singleton* (1787)[12] would later become familiar for their precedential utility in discussions of the power of judicial review by the Supreme Court over acts of Congress. Here, I want to emphasize that the issue raised in both was the right to trial by jury. State courts proved instrumental in the process of enforcing the right *to* trial by jury,[13] but the cases did little to clarify the power or the right *of* the jury. The presentation, moreover, of a new Constitution, which so profoundly altered the relationship between the individual states and the proposed central authority, skewed attention in an entirely new direction.

Article III established a Supreme Court with minimal original jurisdiction but extensive appellate jurisdiction, as to both *law and fact*. It provided a jurisdiction that extended "to all cases, in Law and Equity, arising under the Constitution, the Laws of the United States, and Treaties made," in addition to all cases of admiralty and maritime jurisdiction. It guaranteed jury trial in *criminal* cases, with trials to be held in the *state* where the crime was committed. Powerful objections to each of these provisions flourished in state ratifying conventions, especially to the omission of provision for trial by jury in civil cases.[14]

When we turn to the Judiciary Act of 1789, it is important to keep in mind that the First Congress was simultaneously drawing up this statute, the Process Act, the first Crimes Act, and the constitutional amendments that would become the Bill of Rights. These closely interrelated measures responded to some of the criticism strongly voiced in the ratification

---

[11] G. S. Wood, *The Creation of the American Republic, 1776–1787* (1969), 291–305, 453–67.
[12] J. M. Varnum, *The Case, Trevett against Weeden... Tried before the Honorable Superior Court in the County of Newport, September Term, 1786* (1787); Bayard v. Singleton, 1 N.C. (Mart.) 42 (1787); see also A. Scott, "Holmes v. Walton: The New Jersey Precedent," *American Historical Review* 4: 456–69, 1899.
[13] R. Rutland, *The Birth of the Bill of Rights, 1776–1791* (1955), 93–97.
[14] For a few examples, see J. Elliot, ed., *The Debates in the Several State Conventions on the Adoption of the Federal Constitution*, 2nd ed. (1881), 3:446–47, 543–46, 568–70; H. J. Storing, ed., *The Complete Anti-Federalist* (1981), 2:7–9, 5:14.

debates in some states. The Fifth Amendment added procedural flesh to the bones of the provision for jury trial in criminal cases, the right to jury trial in civil cases became the Seventh Amendment, and no fact tried by a jury was to be reexamined in any court. The Judiciary Act excluded jury trial from admiralty and maritime cases (Section 9) and provided that in capital cases the trial had to be "in the *county*" where the offense was committed (Section 29). Marshals were authorized to summon jurors "designated by lot or otherwise" in each state according to state practice, as far as that was deemed "practicable" by the courts or marshals (Section 29).[15] None of the legislation, however, dealt specifically with a definition of Article III's jurisdictional language, and neither the amendments nor the statute clarified exactly what the role of the jury was in either civil or criminal cases. At the state level, the question of the powers of the jury in relation to those of the judge remained ambiguous. Procedural devices known in England for controlling the civil jury varied widely among the individual states. In some, motions before or after verdict obtained. In others, the jury was subject to little control.[16] In criminal cases, a jury's power to render a general verdict and acquit, even against the judge's instructions, was a strong safeguard against the power of the bench, but it did not eliminate the court's power to arrest judgment, to award new trial, or to reverse on writ of error when a jury convicted. These matters were not clarified by the Judiciary Act. Although Section 17 allowed new trials in the federal courts "for reasons for which new trials have usually been granted," there was no provision for writ of error in criminal cases. Despite the specification that state procedures be followed in process of arrest, bail, venue in capital crimes, and directions for selection of jurors, the statute may have assumed considerable discretion for the judge as a lawsuit moved from initial writ to final judgment.

For many years in America, as had long been so in England, there were reiterated arguments that jurors were the judges of law in criminal cases. In English history, the claim that it was the right of the jury to decide the law predates the Tudor period but was brought to the forefront of debate in seventeenth-century attacks on the judiciary in criminal cases as a response to the power and behavior of the bench. It was intensified there during the eighteenth century as part of the seditious libel crisis.[17] There

---

[15] Act of September 24, 1789, 1 Stat. 73 (1789); Act of April 30, 1790, 1 Stat. 112 (1790).
[16] E. Henderson, "The Background of the Seventh Amendment," *Harvard Law Review* 80:299–300, 1966.
[17] Green, *Verdict According to Conscience*, esp. chaps. 5, 8.

were counterpart conflicts between judge and counsel in American trials, notably that of John Peter Zenger in 1735.[18] In 1771, John Adams had argued that a juror had the right and the duty to find a verdict according to his best understanding, even though it might be in opposition to the direction of the court.[19] In 1794, in a civil case tried in original jurisdiction before the Supreme Court, Chief Justice John Jay instructed the jury on the roles of the jury and the court and stated that both the law and the facts were "lawfully within your [the jury's] power of decision."[20] The issue of the right of the jury surfaced heatedly in Congress during the debates on the Sedition Act of 1798. Those who feared that federal judges would follow Lord Mansfield's doctrine on libels rather than be guided by the principles of the recent Fox's Libel Act (1792)[21] were eager to amend the initial proposal to ensure that juries, in libel cases, should judge the law as well as the fact.

Federalist Nathaniel Smith argued that this would give the jury "a strange power indeed,... so that in case of any doubt as to legality of testimony, it would seem as if the jury were to be judges of the matter in dispute." James Bayard of Delaware warned that the effect of the amendment would be "to put it into the power of a jury to declare that this is an unconstitutional law, instead of leaving this to be determined, where it ought to be determined, by the Judiciary."[22] Two years later, such concerns would become reality when Associate Justice of the Supreme Court Samuel Chase presided in the circuit court at Richmond in the trial of James Callender for seditious libel. The subtext of controversy to this trial was what contemporaries often referred to as "Virginia theory,"[23] that of limited federal authority, particularly the limits of federal judicial authority. Perhaps it is the trial that is subtext to the political controversy.

The persistence of these political antagonisms is crucial. In the First Congress, this had resulted in the compromises of the Judiciary Act of

---

[18] S. N. Katz, ed., *A Brief Narrative of the Case and Trial of John Peter Zenger* (1970).

[19] L. K. Wroth and H. B. Zobel, eds., *The Legal Papers of John Adams* (1965), 2:230.

[20] Georgia v. Brailsford, 3 Dall. 3. For discussion of cases in several jurisdictions, see M. D. Howe, "Juries as Judges of Criminal Law," *Harv. L. Rev.* 52:582–616, 1939.

[21] It was the interpretation of Chief Justice Mansfield of the Court of King's Bench that the role of the jury was simply to find whether or not the defendant had printed, published, or written the matter charged in the indictment. Fox's Libel Act, 32 Geo. 3, c. 60, enabled the English jury in libel cases to render a general verdict on the whole matter in issue, as in all other ordinary criminal cases.

[22] 8 *Annals of Congress*, 5th Cong., 2nd sess., 2136 (1798).

[23] Theodore Sedgwick to Rufus King, May 11, 1800, in C. R. King, ed., *The Life and Correspondence of Rufus King* (1894–1900), 3:236.

1789, but even so, antagonism to the federal courts mounted steadily as their decisions countered doctrines central to the policies of a growing opposition party. By the spring of 1800, Federalists had embarked on their effort to reorganize radically the federal courts and to supply them with the more extensive federal question jurisdiction withheld by the Judiciary Act of 1789.[24] Simultaneously, the Uniform Bankruptcy Act gave jurisdiction over bankruptcy proceedings exclusively to the federal courts, although forced on the bill by southern Federalists, led by Congressman John Marshall, was provision for trial by jury of the question bankrupt or not.[25] The introduction of a bill to establish a uniform mode of drawing federal juries by lot,[26] no matter what the state practice, added to the nervousness of those who feared the loss of local control. Enthusiastic prosecution by the Federalists of their opponents first at common law, and then under the Sedition Act, determined Republicans, led by Jefferson and Madison, to organize to take the presidency and the Congress away from the party in power.

The piercing conflict generated by the passage of the Alien and Sedition Acts of 1798 furthermore evoked formal resolutions from Virginia and Kentucky that presented a compact theory of union in which the states were the legitimate source of popular authority.[27] The question of the proper authority to determine constitutionality had not yet been resolved; it was neither novel nor unreasonable for those who feared centralization to insist that the states were the proper agencies to decide this question. When we read chronologically all the extant grand jury charges delivered by Supreme Court justices on circuit, we can hear their markedly quickened tempo of concern *after* 1798. Exhortations become more specifically political rather than general, more emphatic in their warnings of danger to the new republic from abroad and from enemies within.[28]

---

[24] K. Turner, "Federalist Policy and the Judiciary Act of 1801," *William and Mary Quarterly* 22:3–32, 1965.

[25] Act of April 4, 1800, 2 Stat. 19–36 (1800), see sec. 52. S. T. Mason to James Madison, March 7, 1800, James Madison Papers, Library of Congress; James A. Bayard to Richard Bassett, February 1, 1800, in E. Donnan, ed., *The Papers of James A. Bayard* (1913), 95; Theodore Sedgwick to Rufus King, May 11, 1800, in King, *Life and Correspondence,* 3:236.

[26] 10 *Annals of Congress,* 6th Cong., 1st sess., 106–7 (1799–1800).

[27] For texts, see Elliot, *Debates in the Several State Conventions,* 4:528–29, 540–45.

[28] Compare, for example, those given by Ellsworth, J., April 25, 1796 (Savannah) with May 7, 1799 (Charleston); by Cushing, J., November 7, 1794 (Providence) with November 23, 1798 (Richmond); by Iredell, J., May 7, 1798 (Charleston) with April 11, 1799

This is the context for Callender's trial. Samuel Chase had been in Philadelphia in April and May 1800; he then went on to Maryland and Virginia. As his biographer puts it, "[H]e roamed the Middle Circuit stamping out sedition wherever he could."[29] His behavior and rulings in the trials of Thomas Cooper and of John Fries[30] were widely publicized among his friends and his foes. As Chase went south through Annapolis, his old friend Luther Martin gave him a copy of the campaign pamphlet *The Prospect Before Us*, a savage attack on President Adams written by a Scottish-born radical émigré, James Thompson Callender, and published in Richmond.[31] Chase arrived in the Old Dominion, the taproot for Republican doctrine, home of its leaders and spokesmen. Here, the Virginia Resolutions of 1798 against the Sedition Act were still a prominent part of public discussion.

The presence of Samuel Chase as circuit judge at this juncture struck a particular nerve in the commonwealth, for Virginia was a state in which judicial control over juries had been limited. Directed verdicts were ruled out in 1793; compulsory nonsuit was ruled out in 1794. There were no cases in which verdicts were set aside as against law or against evidence, although demurrers to evidence and special verdicts were in use.[32] Early practice in criminal cases is not clear, but some later cases in Virginia seem to indicate that the jury had the right to determine questions of criminal law.[33] Although no legislation governed charges, instructions, or fact evaluation, it apparently was not the custom in Virginia courts for judges to make observations to the jury concerning

---

(Philadelphia). G. J. McRee, ed., *Life and Correspondence of James Iredell* (1949), 2:523–27, 551–70. Many hitherto unpublished charges have been collected by the staff of *The Documentary History of the Supreme Court of the United States, 1789–1800* (1985); I am grateful to Maeva Marcus, the editor of the series, for enabling me to use the collection in advance of publication. Charges cited above are now published and can be found in volume 3, *The Justices on Circuit, 1795–1800* (1990).

[29] Haw et al., *Stormy Patriot*, 197.
[30] Wharton, *State Trials*, 659, 610.
[31] Haw et al., *Stormy Patriot*, 202–3.
[32] Henderson, "Background of the Seventh Amendment," 301, 319. See Wroe v. Washington, 1 Va. (1 Wash.) 357 (1794), judgment of nonsuit reversed. M. Horwitz discusses the increasing power of judge over jury by the turn of the century, but cites no Virginia cases, in *The Transformation of American Law* (1977), 140–43.
[33] Harrison Dance's Case, 5 Munf. (Va.) 363 (1817); Davenport v. The Commonwealth, 1 Leigh (Va.) 596 (1829). As late as 1831, this question remained unsettled in the Old Dominion. In Commonwealth v. Garth, 3 Leigh (Va.) 765 (1831), see the written argument as *amicus curiae* submitted by Benjamin Watkins Leigh, the distinguished lawyer and reporter for the Virginia Supreme Court.

evidence.³⁴ Jefferson had long held the view that trial by jury was one of the "fences" that experience proved "peculiarly efficacious against wrong, and rarely obstructive of right," one that governing powers were ever ready to weaken.³⁵ In his proposed Bill to Proportion Crimes and Punishments (1786), he had gone to great lengths to make the judge "a mere machine," and the bill's successful offspring in 1796 gave to the jury, not the judge, discretion over punishments within limits set by the legislature.³⁶

The stage was set for serious combat when court convened and a grand jury was sworn.³⁷ The next day, Chase charged the jury in a very long, very lucid, and very assertive manner. He emphasized that it was the duty of the court to advise the trial jury on all questions of law and that should juries in a criminal cause disregard the advice of the court or find against the weight of the evidence, the court would grant a new trial. Chase acknowledged that the trial jury in criminal cases, including prosecutions for libel, had the right to decide the law as well as the fact and to give a general verdict. He instructed the grand jurors and onlookers that should Congress pass a law in violation of the Constitution, such a law would be void. And he emphasized that

[b]ecause the Constitution is the fundamental Law of the United States superior to any act of the Federal Legislature whose authority is derived from the Constitution... certain restrictions on the legislative authority can only be preserved through the medium of the Courts of Justice.... The Judicial power, therefore, are the only proper and competent authority to decide whether the Constitutionality of any Law made by Congress, or any of the State Legislatures is contrary to or in Violation of the federal Constitution.³⁸

³⁴ K. A. Krasity, "The Role of the Judge in Jury Trials: The Elimination of Judicial Evaluation of Fact in American State Courts from 1795 to 1913," *University of Detroit Law Review* 62:606, 1985.
³⁵ Thomas Jefferson to Noah Webster, December 4, 1790, in J. P. Boyd et al., eds., *The Papers of Thomas Jefferson* (1950-), 18:132.
³⁶ K. Preyer, "Crime, the Criminal Law and Reform in Post-Revolutionary Virginia," *Law and History Review* 1:56, 77, 1983.
³⁷ United States Circuit Court for the District of Virginia [C.C.D. Va.], May 22, 1800, order books 1–3, 1790–1800, 341 (microfilm; originals in the Virginia State Library, Richmond). Chase held court alone until District Judge Cyrus Griffin arrived a week later. For a detailed account of the trial of Callender, see Smith, *Freedom's Fetters*, 334–58.
³⁸ No printed record of this charge has existed, but an undated charge in Chase's charge book at the Maryland Historical Society, Baltimore, has been identified by the editors of *The Documentary History of the Supreme Court of the United States* as one that Chase gave in Philadelphia, on April 12, 1800. Goebel has dated this charge to 1799, but internal evidence is more persuasive in favor of 1800. Goebel, *Antecedents and*

This seems basic civics to us today, but in Richmond in 1800 it directly repudiated with considerable force the doctrine of the Virginia Resolutions and the Republican party. Chase did not stop with this. He told the jurors that should they exercise such a role (judging the validity of a law), they would be usurping the authority entrusted by the Constitution to the legislature to judge the justice of its laws, and to the judiciary to determine their constitutionality. The next day the grand jury returned a true bill, Callender was immediately indicted, and a bench warrant was issued for his arrest.[39]

It was Governor James Monroe's idea that Callender's trial could be used to give exposure and conspicuous success to Virginia theory. He and Jefferson decided that Callender should be "substantially defended" by the state.[40] Callender was located, arrested, and brought to court on May 27, where Meriwether Jones, the publisher of the most widely circulated Republican newspaper in the state, and Republican congressman William Branch Giles gave recognizance bonds for him. A lengthy indictment for a seditious libel against the president was read. Callender entered a plea of not guilty, and his counsel requested a continuance in order to procure witnesses and other materials that were needed to prove the truth of the charges in the indictment.[41]

The dramatis personae deserve far more attention here than space permits. Callender was not a youthful first offender. He was forty-two years old, and ten years earlier, when he had been prosecuted and outlawed in Scotland for violating the royal proclamation against seditious writings, he fled Edinburgh for Dublin. He then went to Philadelphia, where he became part of the network of émigré radicals. Jefferson became his supporter, and it was under Jefferson's patronage that *The Prospect Before Us* was published.[42]

Beginnings, 647. It was a general custom of the justices to prepare a single grand jury charge each time they rode a cricuit and to repeat it at each court on that circuit. I believe this charge to be the one that Chase also delivered on May 23, 1800, in Richmond. Reference to his charge appeared in *The Virginia Federalist* (Richmond), May 28, 1800.

[39] C.C.D. Va., May 23 and 24, 1800, order books 1–3, 1790–1800, 341, 350.

[40] James Monroe to Thomas Jefferson [May 25, 1800], in S. M. Hamilton, ed., *The Writings of James Monroe* (1898–1903), 3:179. Thomas Jefferson to James Monroe, May 26, 1800, in P. L. Ford, ed., *The Writings of Thomas Jefferson* (1904–1907), 9:136–37.

[41] C.C.D. Va., May 27 and 28, 1800, order books 1–3, 1790–1800, 370, 381.

[42] D. Malone, ed., *Dictionary of American Biography* (1928–1936), 2:425–26 (hereafter cited as *DAB*). After his inauguration, Jefferson pardoned Callender and remitted his fine, but was subsequently attacked by him. Callender died, intoxicated, by drowning

Samuel Chase was sixty years old, with more than thirty-five years of public life behind him. He had signed the Declaration of Independence, had opposed the Constitution out of fear of a stronger central government, and was chief judge of the Maryland General Court when Washington appointed him in 1796 to the Supreme Court of the United States. Chase's conversion to Federalism was gradual, but by 1800 he had become a fervent adherent to that party. He was known to his contemporaries as a man of passionate views, strong ego, and quick temper.[43]

Thomas Nelson, Jr., the federal attorney for the district, the second son of a Virginia patriarch who had bankrupted himself during the war, had been appointed to this federal office by his father's friend George Washington in April 1796.[44] David Meade Randolph, another child of the mighty Virginia gentry, had held the marshal's post since 1791,[45] and the important office of clerk had been held since 1790 by the younger brother of John Marshall.[46]

The highest ranking member of Callender's defense was the twenty-five-year-old attorney general of the commonwealth of Virginia, Philip Norborne Nicholas, the youngest brother of the powerful Republican triumvirate of Nicholases from Williamsburg. He was the chairman of the Republican party organization in the state and had recently been appointed attorney general by Monroe.[47] At his side was another office holder indebted to Jeffersonian friends, twenty-eight-year-old William Wirt, the clerk of the Virginia House of Delegates. Wirt was admitted to federal practice only the day before the trial began.[48] The senior and most experienced of Callender's defense team was George Hay of Williamsburg. A confirmed Jeffersonian, Hay was radical enough to believe in

in the James River. For his obituary, see *Examiner* (Richmond), July 27, 1803. See also M. Durey, "Thomas Paine's Apostles: Radical Emigrés and the Triumph of Jeffersonian Republicanism," *William and Mary Quarterly* 44:683, 1987.

43 The most recent biography is Haw et al., *Stormy Patriot*. See also Presser and Hurley, "Saving God's Republic," 771–822.

44 E. G. Evans, *Thomas Nelson of Yorktown: Revolutionary Virginian* (1975); *Senate Executive Journal* 1:205, 206.

45 *Senate Executive Journal* 1:86, 88, 194, 195, 325–26.

46 C. F. Hobson, ed., *The Papers of John Marshall* (1987), 5:269, 270.

47 *DAB*, 7:484–85; James Monroe to Philip N. Nicholas, March 16, 1800, in Hamilton, *Writings of James Monroe*, 3:170; N. Cunningham, *The Jeffersonian Republicans: The Formation of Party Organization* (1957), 152–54. For biographies of George, John, and Wilson Cary Nicholas, see *DAB*, 7:482–87.

48 C.C.D. Va., June 2, 1800, order books 1–3, 1790–1800, 409; J. P. Kennedy, *Memoirs of the Life of William Wirt* (1849), 1:36–38, 72–85.

complete freedom of political expression, even if maliciously motivated and harmful; he had written attacks on the Sedition Act before he took on Callender's defense.[49] During the trial, he told Justice Chase that he had "long ago" determined to defend the first man indicted in Virginia under the Sedition Act.[50]

The prosecutor's case was an easy one. Evidence was ample that Callender had written the pamphlet and had had it published. "Malicious intent" (required by the statute) would not be hard to show. The task of the defense was the reverse. To prove the truth of the charges (as permitted by the statute) was contingent on testimony, which, in turn, was contingent on the admission of witnesses and the admissibility of evidence. Determination of each, Chase viewed as solely within the province of the judge. Of Callender's seven witnesses, only three resided in the state. When the Court denied a continuance, Hay renewed his argument on the grounds that it was customary in Virginia (after indictments for misdemeanors) for the individual not to be arrested and immediately tried, but to be given a summons returnable at the next term (241).[51] Hay also argued that the purpose of the Sedition Act was to punish not for erroneous *opinion*, but for false and malicious assertion of *fact*. It was his intention to distinguish between fact and opinion because an indictment that charged error in opinion as well as falsehood in fact was defective and should therefore be ignored by the jury in assessing the fine (242).

Here, Chase interrupted to tell Hay that whatever the jury's power was to assess fines in Virginia, "it is a wild notion as applied to the federal

[49] *DAB*, 4:429–30; "Hortensius" [G. Hay], *An Essay on the Liberty of the Press* (1799); L. Levy, *Emergence of a Free Press*, rev. ed. (1985), 313. Hay would be appointed the United States attorney for Virginia when Jefferson took office in 1801.

[50] Fed. Cas. 241. For the method by which Wharton pieced together his report of Callender's trial, see *State Trials*, 688–89. This report is reprinted in 25 Fed. Cas. 239 as No. 14,709. The citations that appear in the text are to the pagination of 25 Fed. Cas.

[51] The Virginia custom followed the traditional English practice as set forth by Blackstone. T. A. Green, ed., *William Blackstone, Commentaries on the Laws of England* (1979), 4:345. Judge St. George Tucker of the General Court of Virginia noted this fact and commented that in *United States v. Callender* in the federal circuit court, "a different course was pursued," although Section 34 of the Judiciary Act of 1789 "may be interpreted otherwise." St. G. Tucker, ed., *Blackstone's Commentaries: With Notes of Reference to the Constitution and Laws of the Federal Government of the United States and of the Commonwealth of Virginia* (1803), 4:350n. Section 34 provided that "the laws of the several states, except where the constitution treaties or statutes of the United States shall otherwise require or provide, shall be regarded as rules of decision in trials at common law in the courts of the United States in cases where they apply."

court. It is not the law." Hay, perplexed, then attempted to state to the
judge his ideas about the importance of the difference between fact and
opinion (242). If assertions made by the defendant were not facts subject
to proof, the privilege of giving the truth in evidence was a nullity. The
judge reiterated to Nicholas that the right of juries in Virginia to assess
fines did not apply in the federal courts. He dismissed with contempt
Hay's discrimination between fact and opinion in the indictment and
ordered the marshal to call the jury.

In Virginia, jurors were selected in the ancient common law fashion.
"Good and lawful" jurors of the neighborhood (free, white, male, age
twenty-one, not alien, with property of $300)[52] were selected by the
sheriff after the clerk had issued the venire. If the array was challenged,
the number could be made up of bystanders.[53] It was a simple system,
and it worked simply. In federal court, these functions were performed by
the marshal and clerk. Following state practice, the marshal selected men
thought to be friendly to the prosecution.[54] Nicholas's effort to challenge
the array (244) resulted in sharp dispute between bench and bar, and
another followed over the challenge to an individual juror whom Chase
ordered seated despite protest of counsel (245).

After Callender's single witness, John Taylor of Caroline, was sworn,
Chase demanded that questions that counsel intended to ask Taylor first
be put in writing so that he could determine whether they led to admissible
evidence. Counsel once more tried to impress on Chase that this was not
the practice in Virginia. Nicholas said that he wished his witness to state
all he knew that would be useful to his client. If the court insisted, he
agreed to furnish written questions, but he made it plain that he did not

---

[52] For inferior courts (the county courts and examining courts of the lowest local level),
property of at least $150 was required. An Act Concerning Grand Juries, Petit Juries,
and Venire-men, November 29, 1792, *Laws of Virginia 1792*, ch. 73, sec. 12, was a new
code for old practice. Tucker, *Blackstone*, 3:362n. The recent Act of Congress, May 13,
1800, 3 Stat. 82 (1800), directed that federal jurors "be designated by lot or otherwise"
according to the mode of forming juries to serve in the highest court of the state, as
far as the laws of the state "shall make the designation practicable by the courts, or
marshals of the United States." The new legislation allowed broad discretion for judges
and marshals to define "practicable."

[53] Tucker, *Blackstone*, 3:352n, 358–59; *Laws of Virginia 1792*, ch. 73, sec. 11.

[54] *Aurora* (Philadelphia), June 2, 1800; *Examiner* (Richmond), June 4, 1800. To thwart
such an outcome at the hands of a Federalist marshal, Jefferson had prepared a petition
to the Virginia legislature in 1798 urging that juries of the commonwealth be elected
rather than chosen by officers of the court. The petition was not acted on. See also
Thomas Jefferson to James Madison, October 26, 1798, in Ford, *Writing of Thomas
Jefferson*, 7:284–87.

wish to be confined to those questions when he examined Taylor (251). But the judge had no intention of providing a forum for Republican doctrine elicited by counsel's unconfined questions.[55] When Nicholas did give the judge written questions, Chase declared Taylor's evidence to be inadmissible because it did not attempt to prove the whole of one charge. Chase said that if his ruling was not correct, counsel could state the proceedings on the record in order to show error, and "I shall be the first man to grant you the benefit of a new trial by granting you a writ of error in the supreme court [sic]." Next, young William Wirt rose and began to attack the Sedition Act directly by reminding the jurors that a part of their inquiry would relate to the *powers* of a jury over cases before them, whether they had the *right* to determine the law as well as the fact. In Virginia, he told them, the legislature had adopted the common law, which therefore possessed the same force as a legislative act. By an act of Congress, the rules of proceeding for the federal courts were required to conform to the rules of the state. It followed that for the jury to ascertain its own powers *as a federal jury*, it was only necessary to refer to the common law as adopted by Virginia. Since by the common law of England and of Virginia juries had the power to decide the law as well as the fact "in every case which may come before them," so too did the present jurors in this federal case. Wirt did not even pause for breath as he took a giant leap to push the concept of jury right well beyond the power to render a general verdict:

The federal constitution is the supreme law of the land; and a right to consider the law, is a right to consider the constitution: If the law of congress under which we are indicted, be an infraction of the constitution, it has not the force of a law, and if you were to find the traverser guilty, under such an act, you would violate your oaths.... (253)

Chase told him to sit down; the jury had no such right. Such a power would be "extremely dangerous." The judge read a long prepared opinion to this effect, after which he invited argument that might show he was mistaken (253). Wirt popped up again: "Since, then, the jury have a right

---

[55] John Taylor of Caroline had been senator from Virginia from 1792 to 1794. Long identified as a proponent of radical changes such as a wider franchise and a more equal system of representation, he had opposed the federal Constitution and condemned Hamilton's financial policies. In the 1790s, he wrote pamphlets attacking Federalist measures, and in 1798 he introduced to the legislature the Virginia Resolutions in support of the doctrine of delegated powers and the rights of the states to interpose their interpretation of the Constitution against acts of the Congress. *DAB*, 9:331–33. R. Shalhope, *John Taylor of Caroline: Pastoral Republican* (1980), 218–19.

to consider the law and since the constitution is law, the conclusion is certainly syllogistic, that the jury have a right to consider the constitution." When Chase told him that was a non sequitur, Wirt sat down.

Philip Nicholas, the young attorney general of Virginia, took up where Wirt stopped and told Chase that in the exercise of the power to decide the constitutionality of an act of Congress, the jury could not be controlled by the court. The jury had the right to act "as they think right"; if the jurors found contrary to the directions of the court and to the law of the case, the court could set aside the verdict and grant a new trial: "Juries are to decide according to the dictates of conscience and the laws of the country, and to control them would endanger the right of this most invaluable mode of trial" (253). He continued: "I do not deny the right of the court to determine the law, but I deny the right of the court to control the jury.... I am perfectly convinced that the jury have the right I contend for; and consequently, that counsel have a right to address them on that subject" (254).

George Hay followed. He intended to try to convince the jury that Callender's case was not a libel because there was no law in force under the national government that defined this crime or set its punishment (254). Interrupted by Chase several more times, Hay left the courtroom followed by his youthful associates.[56] The judge then proceeded to address the jurors on his reasons for not allowing counsel to argue the point:

> ...I admit that the jury are to compare the statute with the facts proved, and then to decide whether the acts done are prohibited by the law; and whether they amount to the offence described in the indictment. This power the jury necessarily possesses in order to enable them to decide on the guilt or innocence of the person accused. It is one thing to decide what the law is on the facts proved, and another and a very different thing, to determine that the statute produced is no law....

If this power were admitted, petit jurors, he emphasized, would be superior to Congress; the power to nullify laws was equal to the authority to make them.

Chase then moved to a ringing enunciation of federal judicial power, and it is clear that his target was a good deal broader than James Callender's conviction. To surrender to a petit jury the judicial power of the United States entrusted by the Constitution to the federal courts alone was in his view unthinkable. Only these courts had the power to determine the constitutionality of any law of the United States or of any particular

---

[56] Kennedy, *Life of William Wirt*, 83.

state. His reference to the Judiciary Act rested only on Section 8, which stipulated the oaths for the federal justices (256).

Ignoring his own opinion in the carriage-tax case of 1796 that it was unnecessary "at this time" to declare whether or not the Supreme Court had a constitutional power to declare an act of Congress void for unconstitutionality,[57] Chase now used that decision as evidence for "the general and prevailing opinion in all the Union" that the power now being argued for as the right of the jury properly belonged to the federal courts alone (257). He emphatically charged the jury that if it decided on the constitutionality of the Sedition Act, it would be usurping the authority given by the Constitution to the federal courts. The jury returned a verdict of guilty, and Callender was sentenced to a fine of $200, an imprisonment of nine months, and a stiff good-behavior bond for two years.[58]

What of significance is to be said about this overtly political trial? *United States v. Callender* vividly presents the quandary, still unsettled in 1800, of the locus for the determination of constitutionality. Judicial review of acts of Congress was, as is well known, not provided for by the Constitution or by the Judiciary Act of 1789. Of the federal judges of this time, Samuel Chase was particularly conscious of this dilemma and uncertain about its solution. In *Calder v. Bull* in 1798,[59] he had refrained from giving an opinion "at this time" whether the Supreme Court had jurisdiction to decide that a law made by Congress contrary to the Constitution was void. Just four months before *Callender*, in *Cooper v. Telfair*,[60] Chase had regarded the question as still unsettled and apparently felt that a declaration by the Supreme Court itself of its power to void an act of Congress would first be necessary. This may shed light on some of Chase's rulings in *Callender*. Chase knew perfectly well that under the Judiciary Act, no writ of error lay to the Supreme Court in a criminal case. Did he urge counsel to state the proceedings on the record and offer him a writ of error[61] in order to get a case to the Supreme Court

---

[57] Hylton v. United States, 3 Dall. 175 (1796). Chase had stated there that if the Court had such power he would "never exercise it except in a very clear case."

[58] The account in Wharton, *State Trials*, makes no mention of the bond, which was $600 for himself and $300 for each of two sureties. C.C.D. Va., June 4, 1800, order books 1–3, 1790–1800, 413. For Chase's castigation of Callender at the sentencing, see *The Virginia Federalist* (Richmond), June 7, 1800.

[59] 3 Dall. 391 (1798).

[60] 4 Dall. 17 (1800).

[61] 25 Fed. Cas. 251. This comes at the point where Chase had ruled that in both civil and criminal cases, the truth of an entire charge had to be proved by a single witness or the defense was not justified.

in which such a declaration might be made? He and Richard Peters, the district judge of Pennsylvania, in *United States v. Worrall* (1798) had not been successful in their efforts to have counsel put that case in a form that would enable it to go to the Supreme Court.[62] Chase may have been trying the same strategy again. He was now clearly willing – indeed, given the criticism of the president, *eager* – to pick up the thorny question of constitutionality. He, who had denied passionately in 1798 the existence of a federal common law of crimes and had demanded a congressional statute to prosecute, was now confronted by resolutions adopted by the Virginia legislature that challenged the constitutionality of the very act of Congress that Chase's own opinion in *Worrall* had done so much to bring about. This, in his view, was outrageous enough, for it threatened the delicate fabric of union. How much more outrageous to have before him the argument that the local jury was to determine questions of such magnitude! Chase pulverized the argument to the jury's right, but the bulk of his opinion is its bold justification of judicial review by the federal courts. In this last case tried under the Sedition Act, Chase's opinion represents the strongest repudiation we have of republican doctrine and "Virginia theory." It is a document of nationalist persuasion that bears comparison with hallmarks more famous, notably John Marshall's opinion in *Marbury v. Madison* in 1803.[63]

Consider also Chase's rulings on admissibility of evidence. What kinds of evidence may go before a jury, and in what form, is a subject with a long history of its own. Suffice it to say that rules of evidence at the end of the eighteenth century were by no means as commonly concurred in as is the case today. Nor did they necessarily protect defendants in a fashion more familiar to us. Nonetheless, Chase's ruling that strikes us as preposterous – to keep Callender's only witness from testifying in order to hamper the defense in questioning its own witness – probably has an extralegal explanation. In two earlier trials under the Sedition Act, Justices Bushrod Washington and William Paterson had permitted arguments against the act's constitutionality to be made to the jury.[64] Chase was determined to

---

[62] Wharton, *State Trials*, 198–99 (C.C.D. Pa. 1798). For differing interpretations, see S. B. Presser, "A Tale of Two Judges: Richard Peters, Samuel Chase, and the Broken Promise of Federalist Jurisprudence," *Northwestern Law Review* 73:68–69, 1978, and K. Preyer, "Jurisdiction to Punish: Federal Authority, Federalism and the Common Law of Crimes in the Early Republic," *Law and History Review* 4:233–35, 1986.

[63] 1 Cranch 137 (1803).

[64] In the trial of Matthew Lyon for a seditious libel (C.C.D. Vt. 1798), Lyon had defended himself by saying that the Sedition Act was unconstitutional. Paterson charged the jury

have none of this in the hotbed of Republican Virginia. He would allow in this court no further platform for the views of John Taylor, the very man who had proposed the Virginia Resolutions!

Chase was a political animal, to be sure, but he and others were frightened animals, gravely concerned with internal threats to the union that the Virginia and Kentucky Resolutions represented. Virginia had begun to arm its militia. Fears were rampant that federal troops of Hamilton's "New Army" would be sent to the state.[65] Hostile nations ringed the country's borders. France loomed large in fears of the external – not simply the outward and visible source of republicanism turned to anarchy, popular sovereignty become the Terror, established traditions of Christianity (albeit Catholic) reduced to atheism, but also the collapse of Geneva, the only republic in Europe, before the armies of France. Bonaparte had become first consul. Only present-mindedness or lack of imagination leads us to dismiss casually such fears as paranoia. It is not without point that concern with the First Amendment appears so slight in judicial attention to the Sedition Act. When reference is made to it, this is generally countered with emphasis on the "sweeping clause" (general welfare clause) and the necessity for the nation to protect itself against destruction by its enemies.[66]

The opposite side of the coin was the situation of the Virginia Republicans. Callender's case is important not only because of Chase's enunciation of the powers of the federal courts, but also because of the centrality of Virginia and Virginians to the continuing debate over federalism and to the struggle for control of the national scene in 1800. The contest

that they had nothing to do with the constitutionality of the act: "until this law is declared null and void by a tribunal competent for the purpose, its validity cannot be disputed. Great would be the abuses were the constitutionality of every statute to be submitted to a jury, in each case where the statute is to be applied." Wharton, *State Trials*, 335–36; A. Austin, *Matthew Lyon: "New Man" of the Democratic Revolution, 1749–1822* (1981), 113, 115–17. In the prosecution of Charles Holt for a seditious libel in the Circuit Court for Connecticut in April 1800, counsel argued that the Constitution conferred no power on Congress to pass a sedition statute, nor could the "sweeping clause" be extended to the subject. In his charge, Bushrod Washington upheld the act. Smith, *Freedom's Fetters*, 379–81.

[65] R. R. Beeman, *The Old Dominion and the New Nation, 1788–1801* (1972), 201–4; Smith, *Freedom's Fetters*, 343n; S. G. Kurtz, *The Presidency of John Adams, The Collapse of Federalism, 1795–1800* (1957), 354–58; R. H. Kohn, *Eagle and Sword: The Federalists and the Creation of the Military Establishment in America, 1783–1802* (1975), 249–52, 262–63, 279–82.

[66] See the charges of Justice Cushing at Richmond, November 23, 1798; Justice Iredell at Philadelphia, April 11, 1799; and Chief Justice Ellsworth, May 15, 1799. Marcus, *Justices on Circuit*.

between bench and bar in the trial itself dramatically illustrates the force of localism and reminds us of the heterogeneity of legal practices among the various states. This has to be noted as much as Chase's roughneck courtroom manner and the political use made of the trial by leaders of the opposition party. It is hardly surprising that collision between federal and state authority would be especially acute in Virginia by the time Chase rode in to do battle. This state had provided the most strenuous opposition to the Constitution, its assent gained only by bargains requiring the amendments we know as the Bill of Rights. Both Virginia senators voted against the Judiciary Act because of the centralizing potential provided by the establishment of federal trial courts. Formidable Virginia opposition to the centralizing thrust of Hamilton's financial plan was grudgingly assented to only by Jefferson's deal that located the national capital in the South. But behind all this lay a strong tradition of localism, a cultural tradition far older and far better established than Chase's nationalism.

It is the persistence of such localism that helps us better understand this trial. The Virginia lawyers, that "aristocracy of talent" that was replacing the plutocracy of colonial Virginia, believed themselves to be the defenders of the republican experiment – a small-scale republic, self-governed by an elite corps of the locality. There was an irregular state of procedure in Virginia courts at that time; no rigid rules were enforced or technicalities observed.[67] Yet everyone knew and understood the custom of the country, the common law, in short, of Virginia. Chase seemed intent on deconstructing the conventional ways of doing legal business. Caught with having to prepare his case over the weekend instead of in six months, as Virginia custom would have allowed, George Hay was ill-prepared for argument. It was not that he was ill-prepared for the law of libel, as he claimed. (He had written about that the year before, anonymously, as "Hortensius.") He was ill-prepared for the Judiciary Act in the hands of Samuel Chase. He made insufficient use of Section 34 with respect to Virginia procedures regarding evidence, witnesses, jurors, fines, and continuances.[68] Chase's repeated stomping of Virginia customs and repeated references to their being of no account in the federal court include a lot of nonsense. It is more often simply the blast of an angry

---

[67] A. G. Roeber, *Faithful Magistrates and Republican Lawyers, Creators of Virginia Legal Culture* (1981), 220, 254.

[68] Modern lawyer and legal historian Julius Goebel believed that this would have strained the meaning of Section 34. Goebel, *Antecedents and Beginnings*, 651. This would not necessarily have been the case in 1800; Virginia judge St. George Tucker believed that procedures fell within the language of Section 34. Tucker, *Blackstone*, 4:350n.

judge, "Not in *my* court!" One of the great might-have-beens of our legal history is that Hay was prevented from making a sustained argument in favor of the jury's right to determine the constitutionality of an act of Congress. Such a logical but radical extension of doctrines of popular sovereignty and states' rights would have carried each principle into a new dimension well beyond the arguments of the Virginia and Kentucky Resolutions. One wonders how many Republicans would actually have favored such an expansion of the doctrine of "popular will." *United States v. Callender* has nothing to do with democrats versus aristocrats, or liberals versus republicans. Be that as it may, we can see in counsel's effort to apply the jury's right to render a general verdict to the larger goal of defeating Federalist policy the same technique of attack by jury that colonists had used to defeat British policy during the colonial period.

Scholars may point to a continuity of nationalist sentiment from 1776 through the framing of the Constitution to the works and ways of the Federalist party in power. But twenty-five years is a short time, far too short to create a *national* tradition, an inherited, customary pattern of thought and action that exemplifies cultural continuity in both institutions and attitudes. I would stress rather the weakness of nationalist sentiment during the first decade of the nation's history. It is from the perspective of the nationalizing *process* that both the Judiciary Act of 1789 and *United States v. Callender* are best studied. The creation of national law and legal institutions is in all new nations a central element of this process. In the United States, the far older and more powerful tradition of localism gave this process its own texture, distinguishable from that of nation building in nineteenth-century Europe, even though there are certain similarities. The politicization of the federal justice system by the Federalists and later by the Republicans is well documented,[69] but the nature of federal law and the problems of its enforcement simply reflected the formal political structure of federalism itself, a decentralized national polity, which, in turn, was an outgrowth of the specific political and local cultures of the time.

By 1800 there were few national institutions of any substance at all. The Judiciary Act of 1789 was a states' rights document, emblematic of no more than a potential for national judicial action. Its efforts to come to grips with the realities of the complex structure of federalism created by

---

[69] R. E. Ellis, *The Jeffersonian Crisis: Courts and Politics in the Young Republic* (1971); D. Henderson, *Courts for a New Nation* (1971); D. Henderson, *Congress, Courts and Criminals: The Development of Federal Criminal Law, 1801–1829* (1985).

the Constitution make it one of the significant documents of the origin of a nation. It would in time permit a body of interpretation, a rudimentary federal law, to begin to build within decisions of federal courts that the First Congress had created, and it would permit a national legal culture to begin to develop. The struggle to establish harmony between nationalism and localism, the whole and its parts, is the single greatest link between past and present in this country's traditions. *United States v. Callender* takes its place in that great game.

PART II

THE LAW OF CRIMES IN POST-REVOLUTIONARY AMERICA

Introduction

R. Kent Newmyer

The three essays in this part, like those throughout this book, are systematically organized and thematically related to one another. Taken together they also constitute an integral part of Kathryn Preyer's effort to understand the process that the founding generation employed to fashion a legal culture suitable for the new nation. Her three essays on criminal law in early America, if read in the order of their appearance, not only track Preyer's scholarly approach to the problem, but stand as a valuable guide to those who follow in her footsteps.

The first essay, "Penal Measures in the American Colonies," undertakes the daunting task of surveying the scholarship dealing with penal law in each of the British North American colonies, from their first settlement to the Revolution. It is a masterly synthesis that treats key scholarly work on each of the colonies and identifies subjects for further investigation, the availability of sources, and the pitfalls of doing work in this field.

Several working assumptions inform Preyer's synthesis – starting with the recognition that each colony put its own spin on the English legal heritage. English law is the base point of her analysis, but her emphasis is on the "nature and pace of change" in each colony – change influenced by the unique social, economic, and demographic factors in each colony, and by the "profound decentralization of power" in all of them (with the result that local communities played a large role in the process of transplantation). Finally, Preyer invites scholars to recognize the "significance of a sense of scale" in the colonies compared to pre-industrial England and the Continent. The absence of large metropolitan centers in the colonies – London is her comparative point of reference – is a major factor in the development of colonial penal law.

Historical context in all its variety, complexity, and change over time is therefore the central theme of the second essay – and Preyer's synthesis sets the conceptual stage for her detailed exploration of criminal law reform in post-Revolutionary Virginia. "This essay," in Preyer's words, "concerns the nature of crime within the free population of Virginia, the operation of the system of criminal justice, and the efforts in the new Commonwealth to replace the English criminal code with one based on the doctrine of proportionality. It seeks also to suggest linkages between the specific problems of crime and the criminal law and the broader social development of post-Revolutionary Virginia." By focusing on the effort of Thomas Jefferson, George Wythe, and Edmund Pendleton to revise the Virginia criminal code (an effort that failed in 1786 by only one vote), we see the liberating force of the Revolution at work – alongside the persistent operation of ingrained practice and the English legacy. Explaining why criminal reform succeeded in Virginia in 1796 when it had failed ten years earlier permits Preyer to explore the process of change during one of the most remarkable decades in Virginia's history.

This essay is full of substance, but it also illustrates by way of example, Preyer's determination to avoid both overgeneralizing and undergeneralizing. She is equally at home analyzing crime statistics at the district level and tracing the liberating influence of foreign theorists such as Beccaria on Virginia's legal reformers. Equally worthy of emulation is her discriminating use of sources and her willingness to acknowledge the limits of her own research. Her insightful statement about what she was unable to do – and what remains to be done – is vintage Preyer.

The final essay in this part, "Jurisdiction to Punish," addresses what is perhaps the central theme of Preyer's entire corpus of scholarship: the effort by the founding generation to modify English law to fit the needs of the new republic. As she saw it, the process of transplantation was played out in the struggle between the states and the new nation created by the Constitution.

In this ongoing struggle, law and politics were inseparable. Nowhere was this more apparent than in the question Preyer explores in this enduringly valuable essay – whether the courts of the new nation could, in the absence of federal criminal statutes, exercise a common law criminal jurisdiction. In answering this question, Preyer challenges received wisdom, which held that prior to the decision of the Supreme Court in *Hudson v. Goodwin* (1812), a federal criminal common law was generally accepted.

Her brilliant analysis of the key cases proves this assumption wrong. She does not, however, replace one un-nuanced assertion with another. What she demonstrates instead – and what she willingly lets stand as the truth of history – is that for twenty years the matter was unresolved and open for debate. Only time, experience, and a changed political environment settled the issue.

5

Penal Measures in the American Colonies: An Overview

Kathryn Preyer

Several considerations that frame the subject of penal measures in the American colonies differentiate it from the subjects of the papers concerned with England, France, and the Netherlands. It is useful to emphasize the obvious at the outset. First, we deal with a colonial context of a singular sort. These English colonies, the colonial inhabitants of which were predominantly, although by no means exclusively, English, were physically separated from England by the distance of the Atlantic. Formal institutional connections with England were minimal and the administrative bureaucracy of a colonial service that would characterize British colonialism elsewhere during the nineteenth century was virtually non-existent. Despite the fact that each of the colonies by the provisions of its charter was required to establish laws "not contrary" to those of England, there is not a uniformity between the legal systems of the colonies and that of the mother country, nor is there uniformity among the separate legal systems of the thirteen colonies themselves. Diversity of practice among the different colonies might therefore be anticipated.

A second significant point is historical time. The "colonial period" covers more than a century and a half. From the establishment of Virginia in 1607 until after that of Georgia in 1733 (Dutch New Netherland had become English New York in the mid-seventeenth century), all colonies experienced considerable individual development long before their successful rebellion, beginning in 1775, severed them from colonial status.

Kathryn Preyer is Professor of History, Wellesley College.

The character of each colony at its earlier and later stages needs to be considered in order to assess the process of change through time.

The nature and pace of change within each colony requires emphasis as well, for the American colonies are not static, traditional pre-industrial societies. Geographical expansion, economic growth, both agricultural and commercial, substantial internal physical mobility, and rapid population increase marked by widespread religious and ethnic diversity from the continuing immigration of newcomers from England, the Continent, and Africa: these are features that characterize colonial development and identify societies quite different from those of the European world. Nonetheless, as Richard Hofstadter has emphasized, the American colonies came into being in a period of European history that was post-Reformation, post-nationalist, post-capitalist;[1] each factor has a shaping effect on the future. So do the particular founding auspices of individual colonies. The Puritan origin of Massachusetts, for example, or the Quaker beginnings of Pennsylvania, or the greedy entrepreneurship of Virginia may have bearing on the question of penal measures and their implementation. The profound decentralization of power in the institutional structure within each colony and the widespread dispersal of authority to local communities, towns or counties, resulted from the application of familiar English models as response to colonial realities. This may account for certain similarities in colonial penal measures and in the operation of all bodies of formal authority. Be that as it may, such widespread local authority, the absence of a national or "centralizing" presence, and local conditions themselves, as well as the English legal inheritance, complicate the consideration of the actual operation of the disparate colonial systems of criminal justice.

Finally, I want to allude to the significance of a sense of scale as we attempt to consider problems of crime and punishment in the American colonies in comparison to the problems and solutions in pre-industrial England and the Continent. Increasingly complex commercialized capitalism, class stratification, and urbanization are dynamics of American colonial society as they are elsewhere, yet it does have bearing on our subject to note that each of these features is to be measured on a far smaller scale. Poverty is less widespread and the degree of it less abject. In comparison to other cities, American "cities" were small. As late as 1760, there were only seven "cities" of more than 3,000 people in the colonies. Rapid growth in the next fifteen years would add a few more urban

---

[1] Richard Hofstadter, *America at 1750: A Social Portrait* (New York, 1971), xii.

areas, yet at the outbreak of the revolution in 1775, Philadelphia, the largest, had a population only slightly over 23,000, New York, 22,000 and Boston, 16,000.[2] This is a far cry from London's 900,000 or the 600,000 of Paris or the 200,000 of Amsterdam in the late eighteenth century. Probably only a small proportion of colonists lived in concentrated population settlements greater than 1,000 people. If we are to consider the problems of crime and its punishment, or the relationship between urbanization and crime, or the patterns of urban crime and rural crime, it is important not to think in terms of modern cities or towns or eighteenth century London or Paris. The size, complexity, and quality of London and Paris have no American counterparts.

If it is assumed that the deterrence of crime in the interest of preserving social peace is the chief end of punishment, important questions are raised by the nature of penal measures imposed by the authority of the law and the judgment and sentence of a court, no matter which society, at whatever time or place, is being investigated. What penalties does the formal law inflict upon those who transgress the laws of the community for the breach of which the law provides that the offender shall make satisfaction to the community? What variety of pains and sufferings, corporal and noncorporal, are made available by a particular society? To what extent do judgments in practice mirror the prescriptions of the formal law? To what degree are different members – or groups – of society reached differently by the punitive power of the law in practice? Most importantly, to what degree does the penal law *per se* permeate the society?

There is considerable difficulty at present, however, in addressing such questions about the American colonies in detail. Although the recent renaissance of legal history in American scholarship has provided several valuable studies of the criminal law in this period, anyone attempting a synthesis of the application of penal measures in the thirteen colonies is confronted instantly with a dearth of scholarship on this particular subject. Simple descriptions of punishments inflicted during the colonial period, with illustrative examples drawn from one colony alone or from a

---

[2] Lester Cappon, et al., eds., *Atlas of Early American History* (Princeton, 1976), 97. City is here defined as a concentrated settlement of 3,000 people or more, constituting an economic unit. In 1760, the seven were, in order of size, Philadelphia, Boston, New York, Charleston, S.C., Newport, Rhode Island, Marblehead, Mass., and Salem, Mass. A colonial town or county might have a larger population but not be urban because the population was scattered over a large area, with only a tiny nucleated settled area.

variety of colonies often scattered widely over time, are no substitute for more systematic analyses that would help us toward greater understanding of penal measures in their relationship to colonial society. It is this kind of analysis of available legal materials that is only at its beginning.[3] The broad paradigm of colonial penal measures is, however, common knowledge. A wide range of punishments, capital, corporal, and non-corporal – death, whippings, brandings, pillory, stocks, public cages, the wearing of symbols, cutting of ears, fines, banishment – are indeed the staples of formal criminal codes. Imprisonment, although provided for as a punishment in some colonies, was not a central feature of criminal punishment until a later time.[4] David Rothman has argued that corporal and noncorporal punishments were limited ways of enforcing public safety and that, owing to the weakness of colonial law enforcement agencies, the most punitive measures of the law were resorted to, particularly through a broad definition of capital offenses. The result was "imbalance and inflexibility, a vacillation between lenient and harsh punishment.... In the absence of punishments in the middle range, they [the colonists] depended extensively upon the discipline of the hangman."[5] It may be helpful to see what further information can be added to this assessment by looking at the penal measures employed in several colonies.

If we look first at the seventeenth century, what can we discover? Mutinous conditions, starvation, Indian hostility, and extremely quarrelsome personal relationships characterize the initial years of the colony of Virginia and account for the extraordinarily harsh variations from the common law crimes and punishments that are to be found. The *Lawes Divine, Morall and Martiall* were appropriate to the needs of a military

---

[3] See, for example, Douglas Greenberg, *Crime and Law Enforcement in the Colony of New York, 1691–1776* (Ithaca, N.Y., 1974); William E. Nelson, *Americanization of the Common Law; The Impact of Legal Change on Massachusetts Society, 1760–1830* (Cambridge, Mass., 1975); David H. Flaherty, *Privacy in Colonial New England* (Charlottesville, Va., 1972) and "Law and the Enforcement of Morals in Early America," *Perspectives in American History*, V, 201–53 (1971); Michael Stephen Hindus, *Prison and Plantation, Crime, Justice and Authority in Massachusetts and South Carolina, 1767–1878* (Chapel Hill, N.C., 1980).

[4] See the interesting discussion of colonial practice in David Rothman, *The Discovery of the Asylum: Social Order and Disorder in the New Republic* (Boston, 1971), ch. 1–2. Rothman examines penal measures in the context of the development of institutional confinement for deviants and dependents in the nineteenth century that replaced self-policing community practices of the seventeenth and eighteenth centuries.

[5] Rothman, *The Discovery of the Asylum*, 50–51.

outpost in hostile territory, and need not detain us.[6] By 1619, under a new charter, this code had been abandoned, the Virginia Assembly took over the lawmaking process, courts were established, and in 1624, the Crown assumed control of the colony. Virginia from that time on became one of the American colonies that adhered most closely to the legal system of England. English common and statute law constituted the basis of the law of Virginia; criminal legislation passed by the Assembly had to do with the question of public morals (adultery, bastardy, drunkenness), with the regulation of special classes of persons (slaves, servants, Indians) and other matters applicable to the colony alone, and with the clarification of the applicability of English statutory law within the colony. Treason, murder, arson, rape, burglary, robbery, larceny, horsestealing, witchcraft, assault and battery, and other English offenses were crimes and were punishable, as they were in England, by capital punishment for the more serious or by a variety of corporal and noncorporal means known or unknown to traditional English law. Like the mother country, Virginia permitted minor criminal cases to be tried in the county courts (composed of the justices of the peace) but, in contrast to England, in Virginia all criminal cases involving punishments of "life or member" could only be tried at the General Court (initially called the Quarter Court), which sat only at the capital. There were no assizes in the colony of Virginia. The prisoner, guards, witnesses, all persons relevant to the case had to travel to the judges; the judges did not travel to them. Although the county courts had no felony jurisdiction, by mid-seventeenth century they had begun to play a crucial role in the process, serving as examining courts (or "called courts") to examine arrested suspects to determine whether or not they should be sent to be tried before the General Court. Until 1692, slaves as well as freemen were sent to Jamestown (the seventeenth-century capital) when charged with a felony, and like freemen were tried before a jury. The consequences of this procedure, its delay and expense, and the withdrawal of the slave's labor from his master then resulted in the creation of special Courts of Oyer and Terminer, and commission of the justices of county courts to the special purpose of a court to try slaves accused of capital offenses. Trials of slaves were henceforth held in the county where the

---

[6] David H. Flaherty, ed., *For the Colony in Virginea Britannia: Lawes Divine, Morall and Martiall, etc.,* by William Strachey, 1612 (Charlottesville, Va., 1969). Flaherty provides a good discussion of these laws in his introduction. See also Darrett Rutman, "The Virginia Company and its Military Regime," in Darrett Rutman, ed. *The Old Dominion: Essays in Honor or Thomas P. Abernethy* (Charlottesville, Va., 1964), 1–20.

offense had taken place, but were not held before a jury. Trials of freemen, whether white or black, accused of serious crimes continued to be heard only at the capital (first Jamestown and later Williamsburg) until after the American Revolution.[7] Given expanding population, implementation of penal measures is affected by a judicial structure of this sort.

Surviving records of seventeenth-century county courts are sparse, yet it is clear that the infliction of pain, payment of money, or labor and humiliation were the measures employed. Whippings of up to 40 lashes were most frequently administered for immorality, being the form of payment that could be made by servants, who accounted for most of these cases. More severe application of the lash appears to have been reserved for insubordinate behavior: the scattered instances of mutiny of slaves against an overseer, a wrongful accusation of bastardy, a servant woman's false accusation of her mistress of acts of unchastity were punished by 100 lashes on the bare back. Servants who could not pay fines could have additional time added to their term of service, and for a wide range of offenses the justices provided individualized utilitarian punishments of temporary work beneficial to the county – e.g., to build a ferry boat for fornication, to repair church for illegal carrying of arms, to build stocks and sit in them, to pull weeds in the churchyard. Where master and servant were charged with the same offense, the master was sentenced to pay a fine in tobacco, the servant was whipped. Only occasionally does a case of petty theft appear in the records; it was slander that was prevalent. For the latter, as well as for moral offenses, imaginative penalties of humiliation such as being drawn across a creek at the end of a boat or begging pardon in church while standing on a stool wrapped in a white sheet were imposed.[8]

The almost complete destruction in 1865 of all General Court records will leave forever unmeasurable the disposition of cases involving serious crime. Only fragmentary sources provide clues. In the earlier years, only a handful of felonies appears to have been tried – four in five years: two

---

[7] This bare sketch is drawn from Oliver P. Chitwood, *Justice in Colonial Virginia*, (Baltimore, 1905 reprinted New York, 1971); Arthur P. Scott, *Criminal Law in Colonial Virginia* (Chicago, 1930), ch. 3–4; Philip A. Bruce, *Institutional History of Virginia in the Seventeenth Century*, 2 vols. (New York, 1910), I, Part III; Susie M. Ames, *Studies of the Virginia Eastern Shore in the Seventeenth Century* (Richmond, 1940), ch. 6; Albert O. Porter, *County Government in Virginia*, (New York, 1947).

[8] Susie M. Ames, ed. *County Court Records of Accomack-Northampton, Virginia 1632– 1640*, (Washington, D. C., 1954), li-liv. Chitwood, *Justice*, 88–91. The extensive power of the master to discipline servants and slaves must be kept in mind when considering effective modes of social control in Virginia society.

convicted of manslaughter received benefit of clergy,[9] one convicted of rape and another convicted of sodomy were hanged. The severe corporal penalties imposed on those who criticized the Governor and Council reflect the continuing insecurity of those in authority – e.g., lying in bolts, loss of rank as lieutenant together with a fine of 1,000 pounds of tobacco, pillory with ears nailed and cut off unless a fine of £1,000 sterling was paid. As the population increased during the century, it is not surprising that the number of felonies tried increase, although the total number between 1699 and 1701 is small (13). Homicide predominates; in addition to those executed for murder, another, who was found guilty of manslaughter but was deprived of benefit of clergy because he could not read, was reprieved and transported. Each of the handful tried for grand larceny was either acquitted or pardoned. During serious uprisings, those convicted of treason at the time of Birkenhead's Plot (1663), Bacon's Rebellion (1676), and plant cutter disturbances (1682) were hanged and their property confiscated. One of Bacon's rebels was hanged in chains; otherwise there was no utilization of the full measure of English law, disemboweling and quartering.[10]

[9] The English doctrine of benefit of clergy, originally a privilege of the clergy, had been extended to free men from certain crimes punishable by death if they could read or recite a verse from the Bible. During the reign of William and Mary, women were admitted by statute to clergy on an equal basis with men, and in 1707 (5 Anne, ch. 6) the reading test was abolished. In 1732, to clarify the operation of the English reform in the colony, Virginia statute abolished the reading test and extended the privilege to women, slaves, and Indians. After conviction of a "clergyable" felony, the prisoner would "plead his clergy," be sentenced instead to be burned in the thumb, and then released. The burning served as a punishment and as permanent evidence that the person had received his clergy, a privilege that could be claimed only once. The device is an extremely important means of mitigating in practice the use of the death penalty in both England and in the American colonies. Since the common law earlier had developed the doctrine that all felonies should be clergyable for the first offense, it was necessary to take away by statute the benefit of clergy in such serious crimes as treason, murder, rape, arson, burglary, robbery. The long history of benefit of clergy shows innumerable statutes enacted that declared certain crimes to be clergyable or non-clergyable and the status could change, depending on the degree to which legislative bodies perceived the need for a harsher or more lenient criminal code. In England during the seventeenth and eighteenth centuries, although the classes of persons who could claim the privilege was enlarged, the number of offenses for which it might be claimed was reduced. This would come to be the case in many of the colonies as well. The Virginia statute of 1732, for example, although it extended the privilege to women, slaves, and Indians, denied it to slaves and to Indians for manslaughter of a white person, breaking and entering a house in the night, and breaking and entering a house in daytime if more than 5s. was taken. For discussion of the subject in the colonies, see George Dalzell, *Benefit of Clergy in America* (Winston-Salem, N. C., 1955).
[10] Scott, *Criminal Law in Virginia*, 154–60, 314–18.

Massachusetts in the seventeenth-century presents a different picture. Legal reform had been a central, although ultimately unsuccessful, goal of both Puritans and Levellers in early seventeenth-century England and during the period of the Commonwealth.[11] Among other matters, the enormous variety of capital felonies, ranging from treason and murder to one shilling thefts, was protested by many. Others wished to introduce into English law capital punishment for such biblical offenses as adultery, sodomy, and blasphemy. English criminal penalties had borne heavily on dissenters, and there was no wish in colonies such as Massachusetts and Pennsylvania, which were the result of the dissenting tradition, to duplicate the English criminal law. Furthermore, these colonies were founded in order to put into practice revolutionary conceptions of society itself. Penal codes represent not simply the basic general task of the maintenance of proper order but also the effort to implement the overall goals of a new society in a new land. The departure from English norms reflects Puritan determination to eliminate the harsh capriciousness of English penal measures and to replace them with a system of sanctions in accord with Puritan conceptions of righteousness implicit in the law of God. Equating crime with sin and regarding the state as the instrument of God on earth, the Puritan criminal code represents in certain respects a formal break with traditional English law. The Body of Liberties of 1641 provided punishment of death for only twelve offenses, each accompanied in the document with appropriate Biblical authorization: idolatry, witchcraft, blasphemy, willful murder, slaying "in anger or Cureltie of passion," slaying through guile "either by poysoning or other such divelish practise," bestiality, sodomy, adultery, man-stealing, false witness in capital cases, conspiring or attempting insurrection against the commonwealth. No one could be put to death without the testimony of two or three witnesses. We know that Massachusetts followed the English practice of hanging; stoning to death or burning to death, mentioned in the Pentateuch, were not adopted, nor is there, in noncapital offenses, a replica of the precise proportionality of the Mosaic code. Torture, if not "barbarous and inhumane," was permitted only after conviction for a capital crime and only to force disclosure of names of accomplices and conspirators. Corporal

---

[11] Donald Veall, *The Popular Movement for Law Reform, 1640–1660* (London, 1970), ch. 3–5, 7, 11; Barbara Shapiro, "Law Reform in Seventeenth Century England," *American Journal of Legal History* XIX, 280–312 (1975). G. B. Warden has argued that the Puritan Revolution had a profound immediate effect on "English law" if the term includes legal reforms adopted by the English settlers in New England before 1660. "Law Reform in England and New England, 1620 to 1660," *William and Mary Quarterly*, 3d ser., XXXV, 668–90 (1978).

punishments that were "inhumane, Barbarous or cruell" were not permitted and whippings were limited to the Biblical maximum of 40 stripes. No gentleman was to be punished with whipping "unless his crime be very shamefull, and his course of life vitious and profligate." There was no provision for benefit of clergy.[12]

Most striking about the list of capital offenses is the absence of crimes against property. Robbery, larceny, burglary, and countless others for which Englishmen went to the gallows were punishable in the Bay colony by fines of up to £5 or a whipping of 20 stripes and payment of treble damages to the victim in money or in services; on the other hand, penalty of death was mandated for manslaughter, blasphemy, and adultery, which were not punished capitally in England. The population of Massachusetts, however, did not consist only of Puritan zealots, and the initial code of its deeply religious power elite soon proved insufficient to the maintenance of order and ideology. During the course of the century, statutes added capital punishment for other Biblical offenses (cursing or smiting parents, being a stubborn or rebellious son) and for those dictated by the realities of wrongdoing in the Commonwealth (arson, rape, burglary, robbery, piracy and mutiny, heresy, defiance of order of banishment, defiance by Quakers, treason against the King). By 1684, the Bay Colony had enacted 25 capital laws, 21 of which provided no penalty but death. In the remainder, alternatives duplicated the mitigating role of benefit of clergy: for rape, "other grievous punishment" could be imposed at the discretion of the court; banishment was the alternative to death on second offense for heretics, for burglary and robbery on the third. The laws of God regarding obstreperous children were mitigated by making them applicable only to children over sixteen.

How widely were these capital statutes utilized? Was there a discrepancy between the punishment prescribed by formal law and its implementation in practice? Edwin Powers's analysis of the seventeenth-century county courts of Essex, Suffolk, and Plymouth counties and the Court of Assistants, which held sessions for the entire Bay Colony, concludes that

---

[12] The Body of Liberties, sec. 43, 45, 46, 47, 94 in *The Book of the General Lawes and Libertyes Concerning the Inhabitants of the Massachusets*, printed according to the order of the General Court, Cambridge, 1660, reprinted ... with the Body of Liberties of 1641, with introduction by William H. Whitmore, ... (Boston, 1889). No instance of torture is known in Massachusetts, although one person accused of witchcraft in the Salem outbreak in 1691 was pressed to death in an effort to force him to enter a plea to the charge. In England, torture of prisoners during interrogation was authorized by the Privy Council in connection with offenses of state during the reign of the first two Stuarts. Orders indicate that torture was employed *before* a defendant's trial in order to obtain either confession or evidence to be used at the trial.

between 1630 and 1692, only 9 of the capital laws were actually used in sending a total of 56 persons in the sixty-year period to the gallows for the following crimes: "witchcraft (23), murder (11), piracy (6), rape (4), defiance of banishment by Quakers (4), bestiality (2), adultery (2), arson (2), treason (2)."[13] There is no way of ascertaining the degree of possible "hidden" statistics.[14] The two-witness rule as well as practical problems of law enforcement, may have saved suspects or known offenders from formal prosecution. It is equally possible that serious crime was infrequent. Powers wisely uses his data to establish relative rather than absolute incidence of the most frequent crimes and punishments, and it is abundantly clear that it is not serious crime that dominates the records but prosecutions for violations of the moral codes of Puritan society. Fornication, lewd behavior, drunkenness, Lord's Day violations, petty theft, assault and battery lead all else. Surprisingly, analysis of sentences shows *almost three times* the number of fines as the number of corporal punishments. Of the latter, whipping was the most frequent; nearly half – 46% – of those sentenced to whippings had been convicted of sex offenses. Some offenders were sentenced to both fine and whipping. Data drawn both from the early and later seventeenth century show the persistence of this pattern. Other corporal punishments – stocks or pillory, branding (B for burglar, for example), cleft stick on forked tongue (swearing), heavy lock on leg (runaway servant), cutting off of ears, whipping at cart's tail through the town were unusual sentences. So, too, were the shaming punishments for which Massachusetts is probably best known. Sentences such as the wearing of emblems on the clothing or placards on the head or sitting on the gallows with a rope around the neck appear only rarely in the records. Good behavior bonds with sureties were employed occasionally as punishment, as was imprisonment for short terms determined by the judges.[15] Other penal measures employed might be categorized as penitential punishments for admonition by the constituted

---

[13] Edwin Powers, *Crime and Punishment in Early Massachusetts, 1620–1692, A Documentary History* (Boston, 1966), 294. See also the tables on pp. 404–08.

[14] See the discussion of this problem in J. M. Beattie, "Towards a Study of Crime in Eighteenth Century England: A Note on Indictments," in David Williams and Paul Fritz, eds. *The Triumph of Culture: Eighteenth Century Perspectives* (Toronto, 1972), 299–314.

[15] Powers, *Crime and Punishment in Early Massachusetts*, ch. 12. One example was found of a man convicted of attempted rape, swearing, and house breaking who was sentenced to multiple punishment of severe whipping, a year's imprisonment at hard labor, and wearing an iron collar. The length of this sentence was extremely rare. Powers makes clear, however, that imprisonment was used as a criminal punishment not simply as a means for confining persons awaiting trial or as a penalty for debtors.

court, or the requirement of public confessions were sentences, not an absence of them.[16] Perhaps contrite attitudes induced judges to mitigate punishments. We know that, in the first decade of the colony's history, sentences actually carried out were frequently at variance with the sentences originally imposed, nearly 50% of them being remitted in part or in full.[17] Perhaps it was only the obstinate for whom corporal punishment or emblems of shame were reserved. George Haskins has emphasized the degree to which magistrates utilized the criminal law less in the direction of concepts of retribution, which permeated English criminal law, than toward practices that emphasized moral persuasion in order to reform the offender.[18] The fact that white, non-servant offenders from all levels of society were prosecuted may bespeak the equality of all sinners before God, but economic circumstance would ensure that the impetus to reform was expedited by fines for those with property who could pay, and corporal punishments for those who, lacking property, could not.[19]

In New Haven, another Puritan colony, the distribution of crime was similar to that in Massachusetts; capital cases were few in number, sex offenses appear more frequently than drunkenness. As in Massachusetts, punishments of humiliation were few, but corporal punishments were employed more frequently (41%) than fines (35%). Higher status citizens were more likely to be fined, and those of lower status whipped. When given corporal punishment, higher status citizens were however the more likely to be sentenced to more severe whippings, and their fines were also heavier. Imprisonment, posting of peace bonds, and multiple restitution in cases of theft were sanctions for higher status defendants;

[16] George Lee Haskins, *Law and Authority in Early Massachusetts, A Study in Tradition and Design* (New York, 1960), 209–10.
[17] Jules Zanger, "Crime and Punishment in Early Massachusetts," *William and Mary Quarterly*, 3d ser., XXII, 470, 473 (1965). The records examined were those of the General Court, 1630–1641. How long this pattern persisted has not been investigated.
[18] Haskins, *Law and Authority*, 204.
[19] See Eli Faber, "Puritan Criminals: The Economic, Social and Intellectual Background to Crime in Seventeenth Century Massachusetts," *Perspectives in American History* XI, 103, 135 (1977–78). Faber's study of the convicted population of Middlesex county concludes that apart from the servant category, a greater number of offenders belonged to the county's middle and upper social ranks than to the bottom and that the likelihood of a fine increased with the offender's social status. Between 1650 and 1686, the proportions in social rankings of those who received public punishments: servants – 59.3%; lower – 14.2%; middling – 10.2%; prominent – 5.2%. Faber also discusses the degree to which the Puritans viewed convicted offenders leniently after they had been punished by the courts, reintegrating them into the community in one fashion or another rather than condemning them to ostracism for long years afterwards.

admonition was administered to lower status persons but not to those of higher status.[20]

Like the Puritans in Massachusetts, the Quakers arrived in America with new conceptions of society and penal sanctions. William Penn's initial criminal code for Pennsylvania was grounded in Quaker religious belief, which minimized the traditional Christian doctrine of original sin, saw causes of crime in poverty, and believed that under proper treatment, the worst criminals could be reformed. At its origin in 1682, Pennsylvania had the mildest criminal code of any of the colonies. Murder alone was punishable by death. Crimes against property, arson, forgery, and counterfeiting were penalized by multiple restitution. Rape and sodomy were punished by combinations of whipping and imprisonment, and for a second offense, by imprisonment for life. Breaches of the peace were punishable by fines and whippings, moral offenses by fines. Adulterers were to be whipped and wear the letter A on their garments. Prisons were to be workhouses devoted to rehabilitation.[21] Both religious conviction and English experience led to Quaker distrust of courts; it was believed that persons could reconcile their differences by reasoning together, with the aid of arbitrators if necessary, and abide by those agreements. Within the Quaker meeting, such communal procedures were exercised in minor criminal matters as well as in civil disputes,[22] and echoes of such attitudes are reflected in the legal system through efforts to extend Quaker theory to the larger colonial society, to those who were not within the communal discipline of the meeting. "Peacemakers" were appointed yearly in every

[20] M. P. Baumgartner, "Law and Social Status in Colonial New Haven, 1639–1665," *Research in Law and Sociology*, I, 168–70 (1978). In Newtown, Long Island, a town settled by dissidents from Massachusetts, crime of any sort was infrequent over a thirty-year period. The few punishments recorded show that when the poor committed crimes against those much better off they were publicly punished, while those who were wealthier or those who committed offenses against "middling" citizens were fined. Public apology, restitution, and some form of corporal punishment were meted out. Out of 517 cases heard by the town court, the offenses punished were defamation (10), slander (9), theft (4), assault (4), improper fencing (4), abuse (4). Jessica Kross Ehrlich, "To Hear and Try All Causes Betwixt Man and Man; the Town Court of Newtown, 1659–1690," *New York History*, LIX, 282, 302 (1978).

[21] H. W. K. Fitzroy, "The Punishment of Crime in Provincial Pennsylvania," *Pennsylvania Magazine of History and Biography*, LX, 247–48 (1936). Pennsylvania settlers were less committed than reformist English Quakers to the theory that prisons should be workhouses. Although Penn's law of 1682 provided for this possibility as well as for the plan that there should be no fees for food and lodging, by 1700 Penn had to appeal to the Council to put the law into effect. Sydney James, *A People among Peoples: Quaker Benevolence in Eighteenth Century America* (Cambridge, 1963), 151.

[22] Frederick Tolles, *Meeting House and County House* (Chapel Hill, 1948), 64–65, 79–80.

precinct by judges of county courts to settle disputes; their decisions were to be as valid as judgments of the county justices.[23] Quaker usage of the peace bond, *before* a person had been criminally accused, was an effort to render criminal court action unnecessary. The frequent use of this bond (unlike those imposed as punishment following conviction or for those acquitted as a guarantee of good behavior in the future) was intended to make the peace bond an alternative to prosecution in the interest of harmonious community goals. Minor offenders would thus not be prosecuted at all.[24]

Social realities in the colony and political struggle over Penn's control of it resulted in changes toward greater severity as early as 1700. A first offense of theft was to be punished by branding, the second by life imprisonment. A third conviction of adultery was punishable by branding with an A on the forehead. Those unable to pay restitution for arson were to be sold as servants to the benefit of the injured party. Sodomy was punishable by life imprisonment with a whipping every three months if the offender were single, with castration if he were married. Rape was punishable by 39 lashes, seven years imprisonment and forfeiture of the entire estate of a single man, half of the estate if the convicted were married; second offenders were to be castrated and branded with an R on the forehead.[25] Amelioration came, ironically, not from Quakers but from the Privy Council, which in 1705 disallowed the sanctions of castration and sale into servitude because these punishments were no part of English law. Otherwise this code remained in force until 1718.

New York alone of the colonies of British North America had not been originally settled by the English. At the time of its conquest in 1664, its population was more heterogeneous than any other colony, and pluralistic complexities characterized the unstable colony from its inception. Several changes in government marked its initial turbulent years and culminated in the briefly successful rebellion of Jacob Leisler in 1689–91. With this brief exception, however, the adoption and application of English law had proceeded apace, and in 1691 the adoption of a new Judiciary Act restructured the court system toward a greater similarity

[23] Lawrence H. Gipson, "Crime and Punishment in Provincial Pennsylvania," *Lehigh University Publications*, IX, 2 (1935).

[24] Paul Lermack, "Peace Bonds and Criminal Justice in Colonial Philadelphia," *Pennsylvania Magazine of History and Biography*. C, 173–77 (1976).

[25] J. T. Mitchell and Henry Flanders, eds. *Statutes at Large of Pennsylvania from 1682 to 1801*, (Harrisburg 1896–1908), III, 199–214.

with that of England.[26] The sparse court records before 1691 that have survived provide a general if imprecise picture. Practice in the Sessions appears to have been modeled on English summary procedure. Defendants were generally fined; whippings were more frequently imposed than stocks, branding, standing at whipping post, or banishment for assorted misdeeds. Occasionally, punishments were remitted. Numerous entries show that part of the penalty was a public acknowledgment of fault, sometimes an alternative to fine, and it is possible that this as well as banishment from the county served the role of judicial mercy. Julius Goebel has drawn attention to varying patterns of severity in different local jurisdictions, but with the exception of a slave executed for arson, has found no example of capital punishment in remaining court records before 1691. At the Oyer and Terminer, the most severe penalty was whipping.[27] Leisler and one of his lieutenants were hanged for treason by Special Commission of Oyer and Terminer; six other convicted rebels were reprieved and eventually pardoned by the crown.[28]

Two important facts about the evolution of English penal measures need to be noted as we look at the American practices in the eighteenth century. In 1706 (5 Anne, ch. 6), the requirement of reading or reciting the Biblical "neck verse" in order to receive benefit of clergy was abolished. This brought all British subjects in England who were convicted of clergyable crimes within the privilege for first offenses.[29] A decade later in 1717 (4 George I, ch. 11), Parliament made transportation for seven years an alternative punishment to being burned in the hand. This statute also allowed courts to order that those convicted of non-clergyable offenses but conditionally pardoned be transported for fourteen years or for any

---

[26] For a good general discussion of seventeenth century New York, see Michael Kammen, *Colonial New York* (New York, 1975), ch. 1–6. On the court system, see Julius Goebel and T. Raymond Naughton, *Law Enforcement in Colonial New York, A Study in Criminal Procedure, 1664–1776* (New York, 1944), ch. II; Julius Goebel, "The Courts and the Law in Colonial New York," in David H. Flahery, ed. *Essays in the History of Early American Law* (Chapel Hill, NC., 1969), 245–77; Robert Summers, "Law in Colonial New York: The Legal System of 1691," *Harvard Law Review*, LXXX, 1757–1772 (1967).

[27] Goebel and Naughton. *Law Enforcement*, 689–91. In 1680, the Esopus court ordered a jail built for drunken Christians and Indians; those imprisoned for debt were to be kept in the church loft. 690n.

[28] Goebel and Naughton. *Law Enforcement*, 83–84, 582, 692–693. In the formal sentence pronounced, Leisler and Milborne were to be hanged, their bodies cut down while still alive, their bowels burned before their faces, their heads cut off and their bodies quartered. The parts of the sentence in excess of hanging were respited by the Governor.

[29] Dalzell, *Benefit of Clergy*, 25–26.

other term specified in the pardon.[30] Taken together, these provisions broadened the utility of the American colonies as a dumping ground for illiterate convicts and provided a handy solution to the penal problems faced by the mother country at this time. Simultaneously, British importation of African slaves into her labor hungry colonies, although begun well before the end of the seventeenth century, increased dramatically through each decade of the eighteenth century.[31] More slaves, more convicts, the continuing increase of indentured servants, and laboring and dependent classes[32] offer partial explanation of both the speed and character of population growth in eighteenth-century colonies. These factors are related to the perception of the cause of criminal activity and the most effective measures of its punishment as well.

An increase in categories of serious crime as well as an increase in severity of punishments provided by formal law describe the general trend in most of the colonies in the eighteenth century. It is hard to evaluate the degree to which various changes in the structure or procedures of the judicial systems were related to effective implementation of sanctions in actual practice, if they were at all. Techniques of law enforcement remained primitive by present standards in many areas, particularly at the necessary first step in the criminal process, catching the suspect. We are here concerned, however, with the last step of that process.

Virginia penal measures continue to resemble the English in their harshness and in their stylized leniency through the use of benefit of clergy for first offenders in certain crimes. But clergyable offenses, as in England, became more limited. Arson of a dwelling had always been unclergyable, but the significance of tobacco in Virginia and the instances of suspected arson led the legislature to make arson of a tobacco warehouse a felony, although clergyable, in 1714; by 1730, clergy had been ousted and the crime was extended to the burning of any building containing grain.[33] Breaking and entering and theft of less than five shillings had originally been petit larceny, not capital, on first offense.

[30] Originally, transportation of convicts under sentence of death was not a substantive punishment but a form of conditional pardon. It was first provided with statutory authority in 1679. Leon Radzinowicz, *A History of the English Criminal Law*, 4 vols. (London, 1948–68), I, 108–110. Some felons were transported in the seventeenth century, but the years of greatest growth of the practice are in the eighteenth.
[31] Philip Curtin, *The Atlantic Slave Trade* (Madison, Wis., 1969), ch. 5, esp. 151–54. The increase is steady, except for years of warfare when control of sea lanes was at issue.
[32] Abbot E. Smith, *Colonists in Bondage* (Chapel Hill, 1947), 116–17, 335–37.
[33] Scott, *Criminal Law in Virginia*, 211–12.

Eighteenth-century statutes made the offense capital if the theft was more than 20 shillings. When benefit of clergy was extended to slaves in 1732, stealing of over five shillings was ousted of clergy, although in 1748 this too was raised to the 20 shilling limit. Horsestealing had always been a felony; in 1748, clergy was ousted for accessories as well. Negro-stealing was made a non-clergyable felony. The distinction between grand larceny (a clergyable felony) and petit larceny (thefts under 13 pence) remained, but the severity of corporal punishment was increased for the frequent offense of hogstealing. The number of prosecutions for grand larceny increased, and often, in practice, though technically triable only by the General Court, those charged with this crime received summary judgment at the county court level, where the prisoner was sentenced to be whipped. In England, counterfeiting was treason, but in Virginia, where little of the King's coin circulated, the counterfeiting of tobacco notes or issues of paper money was made a felony in 1730 and ousted from clergy by 1765. In the courts, according to the investigation of Arthur Scott, crimes of violence remained high, but prosecutions for crimes against property increased absolutely as well as in proportion to the population. Of those convicted, perhaps as many as half were granted clergy as first offenders. Virginians of high status were inclined to blame convict servants for much of the crime, and the legislative intent to control it by increasing the punishment is clear. If convicted of non-clergyable felonies, slaves probably enjoyed greater access to pardon, not simply because of the intercession of the master or the justice but because the colony was required to compensate the master for the value of a slave who was executed. Slaves who were convicted of attempted rebellion, arson, or crimes against a white person such as murder or rape were dealt with in extraordinarily harsh fashion in the eighteenth century; their heads were sometimes cut off and placed on poles as *in terrorem* examples to others.[34] As might be

---

[34] For further details see Scott, *Criminal Law in Colonial Virginia*, ch. 9, 13 and Hugh Rankin, *Criminal Trials Proceedings in the General Court of Colonial Virginia* (Charlottesville, 1965), ch. 3, 4. In the absence of records of the General Court before which these felonies were tried, both authors have used newspaper accounts that do not lend themselves as satisfactorily to quantitative analysis. Furthermore, this source of information has no bearing on the numbers who were either not sent on for trial by the examining courts in the counties or who were punished there by the justices, who frequently exceeded their statutory authority over felonies. My own research convinces me that the proportion of felony prosecutions hidden at the lower court may prove substantial. Kathryn Preyer, "Crime, the Criminal Law and Reform in Post-Revolutionary Virginia," *The Law and History Review* (forthcoming). See also A. G. Roeber, "Authority, Law and Custom: The Rituals of Court Day Tidewater, Virginia, 1720 to 1750,"

expected, the patterns of economic growth and of stratification by class and caste are mirrored in the attempts to enforce social control through penal sanctions imposed by judicial authority.

By the latter half of the eighteenth century, there were fewer prosecutions for adultery, fornication, Sabbath breaking, gambling, and swearing, even though none of the laws was a dead letter. From time to time there would be spasmodic efforts by governors, justices, or clergy to carry out "crusades" against immorality, but none of these were prosecuted with much consistency. The penalty against servant women who had an illegitimate child was reduced in the eighteenth century from a two-year to a one-year extension of service or fine of 1,000 pounds of tobacco. Free women were fined as well, but the penalties were reduced, and by 1769 it was provided that no whipping should be inflicted for failure to pay. The social cost of the child, not the moral code, seems to have been the greater offense. The high incidence of assaults to be found in the county court records is generally in the form of private civil suits for damages, although in the eighteenth century the Commonwealth began to attempt criminal prosecutions. In 1752, the Virginia Assembly reenacted the Coventry Act, which made malicious wounding and maiming a felony without benefit of clergy, and in 1772 the legislature attempted again to deal with this offense, but the statute was disallowed.[35]

Following the reorganization of the government of Massachusetts in 1692 and the disintegration of the Puritan synthesis, many of the earlier

---

William and Mary Quarterly XXXVII: 35n. In any event, the question of "crime rate" *per se* may be less significant than the nature of crimes committed. I should add that arson, horsestealing, and counterfeiting are complained of with frequency in newspapers but seldom are found in court records. The difficulties of catching these wrongdoers were substantial. With the larger number of slaves, the problems of runaways and potential rebellion became the greater. A 1705 statute made it possible for a runaway to be killed if he resisted recapture, with compensation to the owner and no penalty for the person who killed the runaway. If recaptured alive, he might be "dismembered" in any way not taking his life by order of the court. In 1769, the latter provision was repealed except for castration, which could be the sentence in conviction of attempted rape of a white woman. No case of this punishment has been found. Scott, 301. In 1748 in an effort to stem another problem "by which many persons have been murdered," for a slave to administer any medicine without the direct order of the master was made a felony without benefit of clergy. If it could be proved that it was given without ill intent or if the outcome was not seriously harmful, the offense was clergyable. There are a number of prosecutions under this act. Scott, 310–11. See Ulrich B. Phillips, "Slave Crime in Virginia," *American Historical Review* XX, 336–40 (1915). When the current research of Philip Schwarz is completed, we will have a far more fruitful analysis of slave crime in Virginia than we have at present.

35 Scott, *Criminal Law in Virginia*, 279–81, 284–92.

capital laws were either abandoned or disallowed by the Privy Council. Idolatry, witchcraft, blasphemy, manslaughter, man-stealing, cursing parents, false witness in capital cases, and adultery were no longer capital crimes. Increasing Anglicization of the law can be noted; benefit of clergy first appears in 1686 in a few cases of larceny.[36] Though no longer capital, adultery was regarded seriously, to be punished with a whipping of 40 stripes, an hour on the gallows with a rope around the neck, and the wearing of a large letter A on the upper garment. New capital laws not only bring the formal Massachusetts law closer to the English but perhaps reflect the degree to which different offenses were perceived as more threatening to a more complex colonial society. Arson became capital in 1705. Burglary and robbery, capital only on third conviction, had been made capital on the first by the mid-eighteenth century; the fines, triple restitution, and whippings earlier provided for stealing were reinforced in 1736 by the death penalty on third offense if the object stolen was at least £3 in value. Counterfeiting of paper money of the province was made punishable in 1704 by branding on the cheek with the letter F for forgery; in 1736, this too was made an unclergyable felony.[37]

David Flaherty's ongoing work concerning crime in provincial Massachusetts concludes that the amount of serious crime in Massachusetts was very low in the eighteenth century, occurring at roughly similar levels throughout the province, with Suffolk County (Boston) the main exception. A relatively homogeneous population living in small organized townships, the outmigration of potentially disruptive young persons, low population density, and the absence of substantial poverty, Flaherty argues, account for the low levels of serious deviant behavior. Within an overall declining rate of serious crime in the first half of the eighteenth century, Flaherty's data do show a general rise in both the rate of prosecutions and convictions for property crimes at the Court of Assize from 1693 to 1769. Although total numbers are small, the increase may explain the new legislation. The use of fines continued to be the punishment most commonly imposed on persons convicted of non-capital offenses; the most substantial financial punishments occurred in property offenses, the rule being restitution to triple the amount of stolen goods. Those who could not pay fines, court costs, or restitution were sold into servitude for a term of years or had their terms extended if they were already servants. The incidence of those sold into servitude for property

---

[36] Dalzell, *Benefit of Clergy*, 181.
[37] Powers, *Crime and Punishment in Early Massachusetts*, 189–90, 304–08.

crimes was on the increase in the 1730s and 1740s, and the terms were longer. Instances in the 1730s ranged from four to seven years, in the 1740s from four years to life. Whippings were frequent, but the incidence of humiliating punishments remained low; few persons were hanged for a limited range of crimes. The total is 56 persons from 1693 to 1769: murder–26, infanticide–15, rape–3, arson–3, burglary–8, sodomy–1, a total somewhat less than in the seventeenth century. Benefit of clergy was used with increasing frequency. Prison terms formerly imposed for counterfeiting ceased when the crime was made capital.[38]

Another investigation of Massachusetts has shown the remarkable continuity between the seventeenth and eighteenth centuries in the prosecution of moral offenses. In one populous county between 1760 and 1774, almost two-thirds of all prosecutions in the Superior Court and General Sessions were for fornication, and prosecutions were brought against married as well as single women even when no economic interest of the town was at stake.[39] Fines and/or whippings continued to be the punishments, with no apparent increase in severity.

In Pennsylvania, the Act of 1718 was in effect a codification of much of the English criminal law, importing both its rigorous formal punishments for serious crimes and the standardized mitigation of benefit of clergy for first offenders in clergyable crimes. One important exception is to be noted: grand larceny was to be punished with flogging, branding or imprisonment, restitution or sale into servitude, but not with death. Petit larceny was defined as theft of goods less than 5 shillings in value, with a maximum of 15 lashes, 20 shilling fine and, "if able," restitution. The earlier counterfeiting statutes had punished with 39 lashes, ears cut off on the pillory, £100 fine, and double damages to the party injured or sale for service until satisfaction was made; in 1757, counterfeiting became punishable by death without benefit of clergy. What is known of the actual pattern of prosecutions, convictions, and punishments in Pennsylvania in the eighteenth century? One investigation finds that capital punishment

---

[38] David H. Flaherty, "Crime and Social Control in Provincial Massachusetts," *The Historical Journal*, XXIV, 339–360 (1981); "The Punishment of Crime at the Massachusetts Assizes: An Overview, 1692–1750," unpublished paper, 1978–79.

[39] Only 14% of the total were prosecutions for property crimes. Not until after the Revolution, Nelson argues, did prosecutions for immorality taper off and the preservation of property rather than the preservation of morality become perceived as the basic function of the law. William E. Nelson, "Emerging Notions of Modern Criminal Law in the Revolutionary Era: An Historical Perspective," *New York University Law Review*, XLII, 452–53 458–59, (1967).

was imposed for murder, rape, arson, burglary, robbery, horsestealing, and counterfeiting of the 141 recorded convictions before the Revolution. Of these, 41 were pardoned, frequently on condition of leaving the colony, and 26 were reprieved. No information exists on the numbers receiving benefit of clergy during the period. It was not until 1736 that a convicted burglar was actually executed, and the execution rate seems to have been greater after the 1730s. Juries often voided the forfeiture penalties, finding, either accurately or piously, that the convicted had no goods or chattels.[40] Another study counting 112 convictions of capital felonies between 1745 and 1775 for the entire colony finds 61 executed, with burglary and murder the crimes of greatest frequency. The remaining 51 presumably were pardoned or had broken jail while awaiting execution.[41] The relative frequency of theft is highlighted in a study of Chester County, 1726–55. Here, theft accounted for 144 of the 694 cases heard by the Quarter Sessions. There were 59 sex crimes, with fornication, adultery, rape, and bastardy being grouped together by Alan Tully. The number of murders was so insignificant that Tully classified it with "miscellaneous," but the largest total of all was cases for assault and battery (192). The greatest number of cases fell within the 1745–55 period.[42] Fines ranged widely in amount and increased markedly by the middle of the century; so apparently did the number of lashes imposed by the justices, according to their perception of the gravity of the offense.[43]

The absence of adequate prisons, given the fact that this was a punishment provided by statute for theft, may have contributed to the increased severity of punishments noted by the 1740s; more likely is the fact that incarceration would have withdrawn servant labor and thereby directly penalized the master, as well as costing the community by keeping imprisoned those who could not pay fees. Much more investigation of Pennsylvania penal measures is needed, but the colony's phenomenal five-fold population increase in the first five decades of the century is relevant. The majority of this increase is due to immigrating servants of diverse

[40] Fitzroy, "The Punishment of Crime in Provincial Pennsylvania," *Pennsylvania Magazine of History and Biography*, LX, 250–57, 264.
[41] Gipson, "Crime and Punishment in Colonial Pennsylvania," *Lehigh Univ. Pub.*, IX, 2.
[42] Alan Tully, *William Penn's Legacy; Provincial Politics and Social Structure, 1726–1755* (Baltimore, 1977), 190–91. Tully's discussion of the control of Quaker deviance by the consensualism of the meeting is extremely interesting. With the exception of marrying outside the meeting, the offenses that drew most attention were the same as those tried in the Quarter Session: fornication, indebtedness, assault and cursing. 147, 197–206.
[43] Fitzroy, "Punishment of Crime," 262–63. Fines for assault and battery, for example, ranged from 6p to £100.

ethnic and racial backgrounds, although not convicts. In Philadelphia, the busy commercial port, poverty became an ever-increasing problem.[44] Philadelphians themselves believed that crime was on the increase – particularly that of theft – and attributed this to the poor. Newspapers continually reported robberies and burglaries.[45] The early Quaker use of peace bonds as a means of avoiding trial before a criminal court had become virtually anachronistic by the middle of the eighteenth century. Peace bonds had become by then routinely used as punishment following conviction – generally in addition to fine or whipping – and also routinely imposed upon persons who had been *acquitted* after trial.[46] Little appears to remain of early Quaker theory and practice except for the concept of confinement as punishment for crime. The stone prison for criminals in Philadelphia was opened in 1722, the larger Walnut Street prison in 1775.[47]

In New York, a comparable increase in the prosecution of all categories of serious crime and the increasing severity of punishments after 1750 has been noted by Douglas Greenberg. Particularly was this the case in punishments imposed for theft. Executions rose from 5% before that date to 22% afterward; whippings dropped from 70% to 25%, and the branding that accompanied benefit of clergy rose from 5% to 28.4%. The volume of cases handled by the courts between 1750 and 1754 was more than five times that between 1691 and 1695.[48] Among those sentenced to death, the most brutal vindictive punishments of English treason rituals were applied to some of the slaves convicted in the alleged conspiracies of 1712 and 1741: sixteen were burned alive, one hanged in chains until he was dead, another broken on the wheel. Slaves, furthermore, were

[44] Gary Nash, "Poverty and Poor Relief in Pre-Revolutionary Philadelphia," *William and Mary Quarterly*, 3d ser., XXXIII, 3–20 (1976).

[45] Carl Bridenbaugh, *Cities in the Wilderness* (New York, 1938), 220–24, 379–84.

[46] Lermack, "Peace Bonds and Criminal Justice in Colonial Philadelphia," *Pennsylvania Magazine of History and Biography*, C, 186–88.

[47] Carl Bridenbaugh, *Rebels and Gentlemen; Philadelphia in the Age of Franklin* (New York, 1942), 250–52. Each was regarded as a model penal institution for its separation of debtors and criminals.

[48] Greenberg, *Crime and Law Enforcement in the Colony of New York, 1691–1776*, 206–07, 223. The features of the court system remained the same, and Greenberg concludes that the system was an institutional anachronism that could not deal effectively with crime in a society undergoing the rapid transformations of provincial New York in the eighteenth century. Assaults were the most common crime in the countryside, and thefts and assaults in the city. 198–199. Many assault indictments were for assault on public officers. 52–53. See also Goebel and Naughton, *Law Enforcement in Colonial New York*. 99–101.

more often found guilty of other crimes than any other group within the colony.[49]

The vast increase in benefit of clergy that comes only after 1750[50] requires attention. Since illiterate defendants could claim the privilege after 1707, the increase of its use by mid-century may correlate to an increase in this class of defendants in the colony by that time. The economic sanctions of English law that accompanied felony convictions, escheat and forfeiture, were virtually non-existent in New York. Even when it was clear that property existed, juries invariably reported that no lands or chattels were owned by those convicted.[51] In convictions of non-capital offenses, it is the moderate use of corporal punishment that is striking. As in the seventeenth century, modest fines were imposed far more frequently – nearly twice as often – as whippings for the same offenses. Good-behavior bonds and imprisonment were slight by comparison, and punishments of pillory, carting, the wearing of labels or halters were minimal.[52] The disappearance of presentments and indictments for bastardy in the eighteenth-century New York records may reflect an increasing use of recognizance bonds by single magistrates for this offense. With the exception of cases against disorderly houses in New York City, prosecutions of other forms of immorality seem to dwindle after the Hanoverians had replaced "virtuous Anne."[53] New York

---

[49] Goebel and Naughton, *Law Enforcement in Colonial New York*, 703–04. In 1708, a black woman was sentenced to be burned to death for murder. Such a sentence appears to be exceptional. The case involved the murder of an entire family; an Indian male slave also convicted was sentenced to hang. Greenberg, *Crime and Law Enforcement in New York*, 119, 216.

[50] Goebel and Naughton, *Law Enforcement in Colonial New York*, 702n. Of convicted defendants at the Supreme Court, 87 were sentenced to hang and 78 were granted benefit of clergy. Of the latter, the majority were grand larceny cases. There were only 5 instances of clergy from 1691 to 1750.

[51] Goebel and Naughton, *Law Enforcement in Colonial New York*, 710–18. To have done otherwise would of course have thrown the support of the family on the public.

[52] Goebel and Naughton, *Law Enforcement in Colonial New York*, 702n–03n. Greenberg also finds stocks and pillory little used, *Crime and Law Enforcement in New York*, 39. Goebel and Naughton suggest that whippings may have been the sanction more often employed in summary proceedings before single magistrates, records of which are lacking. They also note that the widespead use of fines by the courts may be in part the result of confessions or *nolo* pleas on the part of defendants eager to avoid trial, to avoid costs, to avoid whippings if convicted. It is conceivable though not demonstrable that an early form of plea bargaining, with its savings of time and expense to the colony, resulted, and explains the substantial proportion of fines to whippings, 709–10.

[53] Goebel and Naughton, *Law Enforcement in Colonial New York*, 104–06. In 1708, the legislature enabled individual justices to deal with immorality. Other legislation in 1732 widened summary jurisdiction over criminal offenses under the degree of grand larceny.

in the eighteenth century witnessed decades of fairly continual tumult, rapid increase in its already heterogenous population, alleged slave conspiracies, the French and Indian war, land riots in Dutchess county, and fast-paced urbanization of New York City. Is it possible that the colony presents an interesting paradox of an increasing number of executions at the same time as severity of other penal measures was actually decreasing?

What is to be made of this compilation of penal measures in four colonies during the seventeenth and eighteenth centuries? Efforts to compare or generalize on the basis of the information reported above is doomed to frustration or disaster – and probably both. The data that different scholars have used are not sufficiently comparable. Some draw only on Superior/Supreme Court records, others include those of lower criminal courts. Some examine a single county jurisdiction, others attempt several. Some approach the subject as social historians, others from the more confined perspective of doctrines and procedures of the legal system. Methodological techniques vary widely. All confront problems of incompleteness of records, a caution that cannot be emphasized too often. We know all too little in detail about the actual imposition of penal measures over time in any given colony. Yet problems of comparability among the colonies will always continue even after we have more sophisticated quantitative studies of the incidence and types of punishments imposed in the American colonies. Cautiously I proceed.

It is safe, I think, to dispense with the idea that in the American colonies as a whole an extensive proportion of those convicted of serious crime was actually executed. In the earliest years, when the settlements were small and their existence precarious, penal measures were characterized by the desire to preserve labor necessary for the development of the community, not to take lives except for behavior that was perceived as constituting the most undeniable threat to the security of the group. This characteristic is common to many small economically precarious cultures, Western and non-Western alike. This stage of development would of course be far in the past by the latter eighteenth century, but even by then we know that of those convicted and sentenced to the gallows, an appreciable number were clergied and released; others were pardoned.[54] That this is so turns our attention to what seems to me to be central to this entire general

If the accused could not furnish bail within forty-eight hours, he could be tried without a jury and sentenced to corporal punishment. 119.

[54] The important subject of pardons or commutation has not been investigated. Governors did not have the power to pardon for treason or murder as they did for other crimes. They could recommend to the Crown pardons for the two most serious offenses.

problem: crimes against property in these preindustrial societies, larceny in all its specific legal categories – burglary, robbery, theft of goods or animals.

The core of the capital code in the colonies did not lie in offenses against property. Initially, Massachusetts and Pennsylvania in their formal codes provided restitution, fine, or corporal punishment; only later would capital punishment come to be the ultimate sanction. In New York and Virginia, executions for larceny do not overwhelm the data. The mitigation of benefit of clergy became the routinized first-offender rule, and it is possible, although not known at present, that pardons were granted to second offenders. Although we cannot demonstrate that harshness of possible capital punishment influenced juries to acquit against the weight of the evidence, they did on occasion convict of petit larceny rather than grand larceny, thereby removing the offense out of the capital category altogether. In short, it is possible to speculate that in the colonies over a considerable period of time, crimes against property were not in actuality regarded as *mala in se* like murder or rape. The harsh and oppressive criminal code of England had developed out of the efforts to control or intimidate a large landless and unemployed population with a sizable concentration in London. There the thrust of the capital code was centered with virtually unremitting increase in severity on crimes against property.[55] It was very different in the colonies. In an agricultural economy in which marginality was not tantamount to starvation for vast numbers of "the poor," the crime itself may have been committed with far less frequency in proportion to the population of any colony than was the case in England.[56] Theft might well have seemed less heinous, less deserving of the death penalty even to those members of the elite class who served as legislators, jurors, or judges. It is this perception that begins to alter in the course of the eighteenth century, if the passage of more stringent legislation provides any reflection of such change.[57]

Of possible corporal punishments in non-capital offenses, whipping was everywhere the method most frequently employed. This is not hard

---

[55] The focus of reformers was invariably on this aspect of the law as well. Most reformers did not advocate abolishing capital punishment entirely but abolishing it for crimes against property.

[56] Further exploration of so complex a comparison is, mercifully, beyond the scope of this article.

[57] I set aside here the question of an increase in the statistics of indictments and convictions since changes in the judicial and administrative systems take place in all colonies over time and complicate the subject substantially.

to understand. It was after all the most conventional mode of discipline in all authority relationships, master/servant or slave, parent/child, the military and naval services. Within the legal system it was the simplest, least costly, and most immediate form of punishment. This had not simply the virtue of considerable certainty in the Beccarian sense. The immediacy of punishment following instantly upon conviction could be expected to impress upon wrongdoers the direct connection between offense and punishment, a crucial ingredient in helping them to remember not to repeat the offense. Carried out in public, the deterrent effect of whippings was extended, in theory at least, to onlookers as well. But what about these sentences? Would different whipping patterns be discovered in different courts of different communities if we focused our attention on the question? How does the recorded sentence "to be severely whipped" differ from "to be whipped" where the number of stripes is unspecified in the record? Was 39 lashes "severe" and 20 not? Which offenders or which offenses were pegged to which number of lashes? Was a flogging of more than 40 always exceptional, dependent upon aggravated circumstances of the offense or the aggravating behavior of the person convicted? Does severity increase over time in any general way? Did formal law everywhere always specify the maximum? Whipping, intensely painful as well as humiliating, was at the discretion of the judge. It seems reasonable to infer that the number of lashes would vary according to judicial (or community) perception of the prevalence of the offense in general or the circumstances of the particular offense in particular, with a rough proportionality of scale resulting. The meaningful distinctions in the pain of the number of lashes given particular offenses may elude us, but they were well understood by those who imposed and those who received this particular punishment,[58] and the punishment lent itself to the vagaries of individual choice by judges.

So too of course did those corporal punishments commonly described as punishments of humiliation or shaming punishments – the stocks, pillory, wearing of labels or symbols, and so forth. The singularly significant point of note about these is their infrequent usage in Virginia, Massachusetts, Pennsylvania, and New York in either the seventeenth or eighteenth century. Though hardly in disuse, those punishments so dear to the lore about colonial America are, from the data we have at present,

---

[58] Goebel and Naughton, give 39 as the conventional limit, but note a range in New York from 5 to 150. *Law Enforcement in Colonial New York*, 705. Some slaves in Virginia died "under correction." Scott, *Criminal Law in Virginia*, 202–03.

clearly not a very characteristic mode of punishment. Perhaps reserved for more serious offenses or for those who were regarded as unusually disturbing or who exhibited no sign of respect, regret, or repentance, such punishments may possibly have served the purposes of retribution and deterrence. Sensitivity to the opinion of others might well be strong in the context of small communities. It is also possible to think about these punishments not simply in terms of the putative shame of the offender but in terms of the release of communal aggression, revenge, or tension. In each of these public punishments, the convicted person was after all placed at the mercy of others in the most literal physical fashion. The pelting with stones or other objects of those unfortunates confined by instruments of punishment may suggest milder parallels with ritual sacrifice or even torture in other societies. The "entertainment" aspect, furthermore, of such sport or of seeing the unfortunate sentenced to lie neck and heels or to sit in the stocks with stolen breeches wrapped around his neck was perhaps "beneficial" to community needs in deeply psychological ways well beyond shame and deterrence of the individual. At a less fanciful level, perhaps it is simply that carting and pillory had serious permanent consequences of future civil disabilities and were therefore little used by the judges except for crimes such as larceny, counterfeiting, receiving stolen goods, jailbreak, attempted murder, violent wounding.[59] Be that as it may, these penal measures seem to have been used only sparingly, and perhaps too much attention has been paid to them for the wrong reasons.

Too little attention on the other hand has been given to another phenomenon, which, given the current state of investigations, seems quite clear. This is the fine, overwhelmingly the most common of the noncapital punishments and far more significant to consideration of penal measures than hanging, whipping, or pillory. Also within the discretion of the judge, as with whipping, the precise amount of the fine was established by him and tailored individually to the particular case. The range was apparently without limit except insofar as it was within the expectation on the part of the court that it would be paid. This is extremely interesting, and a good deal more needs to be learned about the details of the actual workings of financial sanctions. We would reasonably

[59] These punishments rendered the person infamous in English law and unable to serve as witnesses or to own property. Whether such doctrines were followed in the colonies is not entirely clear. See Goebel and Naughton, *Law Enforcement in Colonial New York*, 706–07, 720–21.

conclude that any society in which economic sanctions are widely applied is one in which criminal defendants are known to be sufficiently prosperous to pay the sentence. The fine, after all, is a means of raising revenue to be used for community purposes as well as for punishing wrongdoers. As a punishment, it is obviously a discriminatory one, for not only can some pay and others not, but a heavier fine to the wealthier person will be less painful to his pocketbook than a smaller one to the poorer. The principal question, however, is what proportion of those fined from various social classes paid fines? Does the remission of fines when this occurs speak to the mercy of the judge who had the power to temper his justice or does it give evidence of the numbers who simply could not pay the fine at all?

There are other penal measures that are economic sanctions. Restitution to triple restitution was the punishment in Massachusetts for property crimes, for example. Sale into servitude or extension of servitude for the benefit of the victim was the alternative. By the 1730s, such sales to servitude were on the increase in the Commonwealth, and terms of service were longer.[60] Was inability to pay fines on the increase as well? Unlike corporal punishment, which was easily and inexpensively executed, financial sanctions for those without resources were impossible unless the defendant had friends or relatives in the community who were able and willing to pay. Peace bonds with the requirement of two sureties illustrate the problem even more. Only for those of sufficient economic status would this prove a functional device. It is not surprising that the usage seems relatively small. What is surprising is that the use of fines is as widespread as appears to have been the case, even in the context of the social and economic changes of the eighteenth century.[61]

---

[60] David H. Flaherty, "The Punishment of Crime at the Massachusetts Assizes: An Overview, 1692–1750," unpublished paper, 1978–1979. By 1772, according to William Nelson, judgments contain provisions that if an owner could not sell a defendant within 30 days of his conviction, the defendant was to be released unless the owner compensated the government for the costs of keeping him in jail. The dilemma of the government was whether to pay the costs of imprisonment or to free the defendant from punishment. The dilemma of the victim was the problem of selling a convicted thief as a servant or paying the costs of imprisonment for the person who had stolen from him. Nelson argues convincingly that it is this predicament that lies behind legislative action in 1785 that provided for the imprisonment of thieves at hard labor, the expectation being that the proceeds of such labor would pay the state the costs of imprisonment. In this resolution of the problem, the victim received nothing except the knowledge that the thief was laboring in prison. "Emerging Notions of Modern Criminal Law," *New York Univ. Law Review*, XLII, 460–61.

[61] It is conceivable that this was not so in proceedings before individual magistrates at the most local level, that it was here that statistics on whippings would be remarkably

However unequally financial sanctions or corporal punishments may have fallen on the lower classes in colonial society, no matter what the degree of class control penal measures represent within the white population, the greatest discriminatory power of the penal law is to be seen in the case of slaves. The master's virtually total power over the slave meant that much punishment was applied under authority of the law but was administered within the private domain of the master. Only severe offenses of public order came to court at all. Concern for the property of the master and consciousness of the cost of financial compensation to be awarded to the master when slaves were hanged contributed to the mercy of pardon for some who were convicted of unclergyable felonies.

By the last quarter of the eighteenth century, the colonies confronted serious problems of effective punishment of crime. Assumption of a rising rate of crime, whether accurate or not, particularly a rise in crimes against property, took on a far greater role than had been the case in the seventeenth century. Prosecution of crimes against morality had steadily dwindled throughout the entire century well before the Revolution.[62] In colonies other than Massachusetts, crime meant theft and burglary as well

---

higher. Given the wide jurisdiction individual magistrates exercised over vagrants and over petty crimes, the resort to expeditious whipping may have been standard practice and may have been more harshly administered. John Beattie points out that there is reason to think that the actual extent of the rise in rural property crime in the last third of the eighteenth century in England is not fully reflected by bills of grand juries at assizes and quarter sessions because of the number of offenses increasingly dealt with by magistrates acting summarily out of sessions. "The Pattern of Crime in England 1660–1800," *Past and Present* No. 62, 78 (1974). This is an important point and the role of the individual magistrate may be as significant in the colonies. See the comments in Goebel and Naughton, *Law Enforcement in Colonial New York*, 121, 705. David Flaherty, using assize records, finds no correlation between significant economic distress and the commission in Massachusetts. "Crime and Social Control in Provincial Massachusetts. *The Historical Journal* XXIV, 339–360 (1981). See, however, the suggestive evidence of Douglas Jones for an increase in transiency in the province. "The Strolling Poor: Transiency in Eighteenth Century Massachusetts," *Journal of Social History* VIII, 28–54 (1975). It may well be that those least able to pay fines were the ones who appeared most frequently before the single magistrate out of sessions and were the ones most frequently whipped rather than fined. It is also possible that the large proportion of fines is swollen by *nolo* pleas or confessions in order to avoid costs of trial, fees, the possibility of a whipping. Some early form of plea bargaining might have existed at all the jurisdictional levels where the penalty was fine and/or whipping.

[62] David H. Flaherty, "Law and the Enforcement of Morals in Early America," in *Perspectives in American History*, V, 203–53. Nelson dates this change from the Revolution in *Americanization of the Common Law*. It is a matter of regret that analysis of Massachusetts has so frequently been taken as a paradigm for "the colonies." Massachusetts was quite atypical in many respects.

as crimes of violence. Most of this was conventionally attributed by those in power to those of lower status, often immigrant newcomers, some of them convicts transported from England, some of them slaves. Perhaps it is only natural that many of these perceptions were most current in urban areas with a larger concentration of population, a greater number of poor, more varied economic activities that provided for crimes against property. It was in the urban areas that legislators met and attempted to remedy many of the problems with more severe penal legislation. The ousting of benefit of clergy for several capital crimes in the various colonies is evidence for this. But where clergy did remain, the mitigation of this particular form of corporal punishment carried the defect of its own virtue. So did whipping. Those convicted and so punished were instantly released, returned to their private pursuits so, it was often assumed, to prey again. The varying punishments imposed by judicial discretion, whether corporal or otherwise, came to be regarded as "ineffective," "irrational," and "inhumane" in American practice, charges that corresponded to the charges levelled against the English criminal law by its seventeenth-century critics. If the number of persons convicted of crimes who were able to pay fines, or make restitution in colonies where that had been the practice, actually was decreasing, this too would have proved an ineffective method of deterring crime. Neither certainty nor proportionality characterized penal measures in the late eighteenth century to those who made the laws and administered them. At the same time as in the European world, but particularly fuelled with the ideology of the beneficent potentialities of a newly independent American republic, some, although not all, former colonies joined other nations in the conviction that a more rational criminal code that made punishment certain but genuinely humane would not only increase enforcement of the law but could also reform the offender, and in so doing actually reduce the number of criminal offenses. It was easy in America to identify reason and humanity, the watchwords of the Enlightenment, with the successful republicanism of the new nation and to find in imprisonment the ideal embodiment of these new goals.

6

Crime, the Criminal Law, and Reform in Post-Revolutionary Virginia

Kathryn Preyer

Exhortations to maintain a reasonable balance between crimes and punishments, condemnations of excessive penal severity, and pleas for a reduction in the number of crimes for which death was the penalty do not originate in the eighteenth century.[1] Reform of the criminal law had been an unattained goal of both Puritans and Levellers during the Commonwealth period.[2] Reform efforts ironically paralleled the immense increase of new statutory felonies in eighteenth-century England,[3] and throughout the Western world a simultaneity of attention was paid to reformulating the nature and purpose of punishment.[4] A vigorous reformist sentiment can be observed among enlightened men in Europe and America regarding

Kathryn Preyer is Professor of History at Wellesley College. The author wishes to thank George M. Curtis for discussing the material of this essay, and David Flaherty, David Konig, and Paul Clemens for their comments on papers presented at the meetings of the American Society for Legal History in 1976 and the Organization of American Historians in 1981.

[1] A fine eighteenth-century example is William Bradford. *An Enquiry How Far the Punishment of Death is Necessary in Pennsylvania* (Philadelphia, 1793) 3, reprinted in *Reform of Criminal Law in Pennsylvania* (New York, 1972).

[2] Mary Cotterell, 'Interregnum Law Reform: The Hale Commission of 1652,' *English Historical Review* lxxxiii (1968) 689–704; Donald Veall, *The Popular Movement for Law Reform 1640–1660* (London, 1970) 65–141, 152–66 and 225–40; Barbara Shapiro, 'Law Reform in Seventeenth Century England,' *American Journal of Legal History* xix (1975) 280–312; Barbara Shapiro, 'Sir Francis Bacon and the Mid-Seventeenth Century Movement for Law Reform,' *American Journal of Legal History* xxiv (1980) 331–62.

[3] See Leon Radzinowicz, *A History of English Criminal Law and its Administration, Vol. I. The Movement for Reform* 4 vols. (London, 1948).

[4] Peter Gay. *The Enlightenment* 2 vols. (New York, 1969) ii, 423–47; Franco Venturi, *Utopia and Reform in the Enlightenment* (London, 1971) 95–116; Michael Kraus. *The Atlantic Civilization* (Ithaca, New York, 1979) 127–38.

the necessity of an amelioration in the criminal codes of their nations, and central to much of this was the principle of proportionality, that every penalty be proportioned to the offense. In the American colonies, the initiation of rebellion presented an unparalleled opportunity for change.

This essay concerns the nature of crime within the free population of Virginia, the operation of the system of criminal justice, and the efforts in the new Commonwealth to replace the English criminal code with one based on the doctrine of proportionality. It seeks also to suggest linkages between the specific problems of crime and the criminal law and the broader social development of post-Revolutionary Virginia.

During the colonial period, the substantive criminal law of Virginia resembled that of the mother country. Virginians were bound by the common and statute law of England insofar as that was applicable to their situation. English law was supplemented or amended by those laws of the General Assembly that were approved by the King in Council, but the basic law, including all the more serious criminal offenses, was the law of England. The bulk of criminal legislation passed by the Assembly was concerned with public morals or with the regulation of servants and slaves. The acts of the Assembly, furthermore, did not *define* offenses and make them penal. It was by virtue of the fact that English common law and statute law constituted a part of the law of Virginia that the numerous offenses known to the English criminal law were punishable in the colony. Virginia statutes having to do with crimes followed this pattern even when they modified it to fit colonial conditions or clarified the applicability of English statutes to Virginia.[5] In the colony, as in England, death was the penalty for a large number of crimes. The same standardized mitigation by way of benefit of clergy applied to first offenders in clergyable crimes,[6] and the possibility of pardon by the Governor likewise existed for those

[5] For example, that the statute of 21 James I, c. 27, women who attempted to conceal the fact that they had borne a bastard child that had died were tried for murder unless they could prove that the child had been stillborn. This statute was reenacted by the Virginia Assembly in 1710 after doubts were raised regarding its applicability to the colony. William Waller Hening, *The Statutes at Large; being a Collection of all the Laws of Virginia, from the First Session of the Legislature in the Year 1619*, 13 vols. (Philadelphia, 1809–1823) iii, Ch. XII, (October, 1710) 516–17.

[6] The English doctrine of benefit of clergy, originally a privilege of the clergy, had been extended to free men from certain crimes punishable by death if they could read or recite a verse from the Bible. During the reign of William and Mary, women were admitted by statute to clergy on equal basis with men, and in 1707 the reading test was abolished. In 1732, to clarify the operation of the English reform in the colony, Virginia by statute abolished the reading test and extended the privilege to women, slaves, and Indians. After conviction of a 'clergyable' felony, the prisoner would 'plead his clergy,' be sentenced

convicted of offenses short of treason or murder. In the latter cases, the Governor might grant reprieve while a pardon from the Crown was being sought. The same range of punishments used in England was employed in Virginia: fines, stocks or pillory, whippings, branding, banishment, death mitigated by benefit of clergy, death without benefit of clergy, and execution by hanging.

The General Court and the county courts were the important elements in the judicial machinery of the Colony. The county courts, consisting of the justices of the peace of each county meeting monthly, had no jurisdiction over freemen in cases in which punishment went to 'life or member.' It was, however, a regular part of the duties of the justices to meet as a special examining court (or 'called court') to consider the evidence against those charged with felonies. If it appeared that the evidence warranted trial before the General Court, it was the responsibility of the sheriff to take the accused to the capital (first Williamsburg, then after 1780, Richmond), where the Court sat; at the time of the examination, all necessary witnesses were required to give bond to appear at the trial.[7] Unlike in England, there were no assizes in Virginia, and the preliminary sifting

---

instead to be burned in the thumb, and then be released. The burning served as a punishment and as permanent evidence that the person had received his clergy, a privilege that could be claimed only once. The device was an extremely important means of mitigating in practice the use of the death penalty in both England and in the American colonies. Since the common law earlier had developed the doctrine that all felonies should be clergyable for the first offense, it was necessary to take away by statute the benefit of clergy in such serious crimes as treason, murder, rape, arson, burglary, and robbery. The long history of benefit of clergy shows innumerable statutes enacted that made certain crimes clergyable or non-clergyable, and the status could change, depending on the degree to which legislative bodies perceived the need for a harsher or more lenient criminal code. In England during the seventeenth and eighteenth centuries, although the classes of persons who could claim the privilege was enlarged, the number of offenses for which it might be claimed was reduced. This came to be the case in many of the colonies as well. The Virginia statute of 1732, for example, although it extended the privilege to women, slaves, and Indians, denied it to slaves and to Indians for manslaughter of a white person, for breaking and entering a house in the night, and for breaking and entering a house in daytime if more than 5s. was taken. For discussion of the subject, see George Dalzell, *Benefit of Clergy in America* (Winston-Salem, 1955).

[7] For the place of English law in Virginia and the functioning of the judicial system, see Arthur P. Scott, *Criminal Law in Colonial Virginia* (Chicago, 1930) 13–49; Oliver P. Chitwood, *Justice in Colonial Virginia* (Baltimore, 1905); Albert O. Porter, *County Government in Virginia: A Legislative History 1607–1904* (New York, 1947); Robert Wheeler, 'The County Court in Colonial Virginia,' in Bruce C. Daniels, ed., *Town & Country: Essays on the Structure of Local Government in the American Colonies* (Middletown, 1978) 111–13; Hugh Rankin, *Criminal Trial Proceedings in the General Court of Colonial Virginia* (Williamsburg, 1965); A. G. Roeber, *Faithful Magistrates and Republican Lawyers, Creators of Virginia Legal Culture, 1680–1810* (Chapel Hill, 1981).

before the called court was an attempt to guarantee that only when there was a reasonable prospect of conviction were prisoners taken before a grand jury and subsequently tried.

In his celebrated work, *On Crimes and Punishments*, published in 1764, Cesare Beccaria had emphasized that certainty of the law and infallibility of enforcement, not harshness of punishment, promised the most successful deterrence of crime. Others asserted that the proportioning of crimes and punishments would result in punishment of fewer crimes with death and therefore a penal system less fraught with judicial and executive discretion. In Virginia, as in England and elsewhere, equally compelling and more difficult than the restriction of capital punishment was an effort to deal with the problem of what to use in its place.[8]

With the Declaration of Independence behind him, and waiting in Philadelphia during the summer of 1776 for his replacement to arrive, Thomas Jefferson corresponded with Edmund Pendleton concerning desirable changes in the legal institutions of Virginia. Jefferson anticipated having a voice in the fashioning of the new government at home, and the correspondence is instructive, coming before Jefferson took his seat in the Virginia legislature and participated in drafting the bills revising the laws of Virginia. In one of these letters, Jefferson denied that he adhered to the 'fantastical' idea of virtue and the public good being a sufficient security to the state against the commission of crime. It was the 'sanguinary hue' of the penal law to which he objected.

… Punishments I know are necessary and I would provide them, strict and inflexible but proportioned to the crime. Death might be inflicted for murder and perhaps for treason if you would take out of the description of treason all crimes which are not in their nature: rape, buggery &c. punish by castration. All other crimes by working on high roads, rivers, gallies &c. a certain time proportioned

---

[8] Reform of the criminal law in the new United States is commonly listed as one of the humanitarian reforms generated by the American Revolution, but there are remarkably few efforts to analyze the subject in any detail. William E. Nelson, 'Emerging Notions of Modern Criminal Law in the Revolutionary Era: An Historical Perspective,' 42 *New York University Law Review* 450–82 (1967) is an exception, dealing in detail with Massachusetts; for New Jersey, see John E. O'Connor, 'Legal Reform in the Early Republic: The New Jersey Experience,' *American Journal of Legal History* 22 (1978) 95–105; for Connecticut see Richard Gaskins. 'Changes in the Criminal Law in Eighteenth Century Connecticut,' *American Journal of Legal History* 25 (1981) 330–42; generally, see Lawrence M. Friedman, *A History of American Law* (New York, 1973) 248–64; Allan Nevins, *The American States during and after the Revolution* (New York, 1924) 451–65. See also David B. Davis, 'The Movement to Abolish Capital Punishment in America, 1787–1861,' *American Historical Review* 28 (1957) 23, on this particular subject. On the necessity of certainty of punishment, see Caesare Beccaria, *On Crimes and Punishments*, trans. by Henry Paolucci (New York, 1963) 58–9.

to the offence. But as this would be no punishment or change of condition to slaves (me miserum!) let them be sent to other countries. By these means we should be freed from the wickedness of the latter, and the former would be living monuments of public vengeance. Laws thus proportionate and mild should never be dispensed with. Let mercy be the character of the lawgiver, but let the judge be a mere machine. The mercies of the law will be dispensed equally and impartially to every description of man; those of the judge, or the executive power, will be the eccentric impulses of whimsical capricious designing men. . . .[9]

The principles embodied in this letter would soon be incorporated in the Bill for Proportioning Crimes and Punishments in Cases Heretofore Capital, Bill No. 64 of the 126 bills of the revised laws of Virginia prepared by Jefferson, George Wythe, and Edmund Pendleton, Jefferson being responsible for the criminal law.[10] The committee having decided the broad principles of a crimes bill,[11] Jefferson's work on its details, he later recalled, took him longer than all the rest of his assignment,[12] and in 1778 he reported to Wythe that he had strictly observed the scale of punishments determined by the Committee even though he believed that the inclusion of the *lex talionis* would be 'revolting to the humanised feelings of modern times' and needed reconsideration.[13] In February 1779, the three revisors met at Williamsburg and reviewed their work, making amendments until agreement was reached. Copies were then made and

---

[9] Jefferson to Pendleton, Aug. 26, 1776, in reply to Pendleton's letter of August 10, 1776. Julian Boyd, ed., *The Papers of Thomas Jefferson* 20 vols. (Princeton, 1950) i, 489–90, 505. (Hereinafter referred to as Jefferson, *Papers* Boyd.)

[10] On October 15, 1776, the Assembly named Jefferson, George Wythe, Edmund Pendleton, George Mason, and Thomas Lightfoot Lee as the Committee of Revisors, but Mason soon resigned and Lee died shortly thereafter. Although the proposed revision was presented in 1779, its consideration by the legislature was delayed until 1785. For this intricate story, see Julian Boyd's comprehensive note, Jefferson, *Papers* (Boyd) ii, 308–24. For the subsequent history of the revisal, see Charles Cullen, 'Completing the Revisal of the Laws in Post-Revolutionary Virginia,' *Virginia Magazine of History and Biography* lxxxii (1974) 84–99.

[11] The deliberations of the committee are obscure. At a meeting in January, 1777, the revisors determined basic principles and divided their work. A memorandum kept by Mason is our only source of the plans agreed upon. This is printed in Jefferson, *Papers* (Boyd) ii, 325–28. Jefferson wrote in his autobiography that he had wished the committee to settle leading principles as a guide for his revisions of the law of descents and the criminal law. Paul L. Ford, ed., *The Writings of Thomas Jefferson* 12 vols. (New York and London, 1904–05) i, 59 (Hereinafter referred to as Jefferson, *Writings* (Ford).)

[12] Jefferson to Skelton Jones, July 28, 1809. Andrew A. Lipscomb and Albert Ellery Bergh, eds., *The Writings of Thomas Jefferson* 20 vols. (1903) xii, 298.

[13] Jefferson to Wythe, November 1, 1778. Jefferson, *Papers* (Boyd) ii, 230. His concern about severity of penalties may be seen in Jefferson's original outline for his proposal, which included 'death by burying alive' as the penalty for high treason, a penalty stricken out in favor of hanging, in conformity with the plan agreed to by the revisors. Ibid. ii, opposite 305.

presented to the legislature on June 18, 1779, together with the other bills of the entire work of revision.[14] Shortly before, on June 1, Jefferson had been elected governor.[15]

The proposed bill[16] substantially followed the plan initially established by the three revisors and is striking in its similarity to the ideas that Jefferson communicated to Pendleton in August of 1776. Treason and murder were specified as the only capital crimes. Treason was more narrowly defined than in the law of England and required evidence of two witnesses;[17] lands and goods of the condemned were forfeited to

---

[14] Jefferson, Autobiography, in *Writings* (Ford) i, 61. It is unnecessary here to detail the variant texts of the bill as included in the revision. These are indicated in Boyd's notes. Jefferson, *Papers* (Boyd) ii, 492–507. The text of the crimes bill as printed in the Report of the Revisors does not include the abundant notes and comments made by Jefferson. Jefferson's outline for his bill is reproduced by Boyd, ii, opposite 305, and the document is presented as literally as possible in Appendix 4, ii, 663–64. It was this list that Jefferson employed in preparing Query XIV of *Notes on the State of Virginia* in 1781.

[15] Dumas Malone, *Jefferson the Virginian* (Boston, 1948) 301.

[16] The entire bill is printed in Jefferson, *Papers* (Boyd) ii, 492–507. Jefferson scholars have customarily given brief attention to this bill in comparison to that accorded other Jeffersonian legislative reforms perhaps owing to the paucity of materials regarding it, perhaps because it failed to pass, or perhaps because it does not completely accord with modern, humanitarian standards. Notes that Jefferson apparently had in his personal archives have long since vanished, although he preserved two elegant manuscripts complete with detailed notes from his researches. Jefferson, *Papers* (Boyd) ii, 321, 492–504. Malone, Jefferson, supra note 15, 269–72 sees the main significance of the proposals in Jefferson's attempt to relax the severity of punishments making them more humane and rational, with the greatest weakness being the resort to the *lex talionis* in certain cases. Marie Kimball, *Jefferson War and Peace* (New York, 1947) 14, says that the bill 'eradicating the incredibly brutal survivals of an archaic conception of criminal law, is a monument to his [Jefferson's] humanity.' See also Marie Kimball, *Jefferson, Road to Glory* (New York, 1943) 224–25; Merrill Peterson, *Thomas Jefferson and the New Nation* (New York, 1970) 124–33 calls the bill 'definitely humanitarian in principle and design' and attributes its 'shocking lapses from humane and liberal standards' to the force of traditionalism in Jefferson's thinking and his passion for order and system. Gilbert Chinard, *Thomas Jefferson: The Apostle of Americanism* (Boston, 1929) 93–5, feels the bill, despite the reflection of the ideas of Montesquieu and Beccaria in the preamble, can hardly be called humanitarian 'in the modern sense of the word.' Kean, 'Jefferson as Legislator,' 11 *Virginia Law Journal* 714 (1887), praises the bill for its removal of the death penalty in the case of 27 felonies at a date more than a generation prior to similar changes in England but does not discuss the severity of some of the secondary punishments. Edward Dumbauld, *Thomas Jefferson and the Law* (Norman, Ok., 1978) 138–39, pays only slight attention to the bill.

[17] Treason was defined as: 'If a man do levy war against the Commonwealth or be adherent to the enemies of the commonwealth giving to them aid and comfort in the commonwealth, or elsewhere.' An overt act was required, and the language 'the said cases, and no other shall be adjudged treason' was intended to prevent what Jefferson in his notes called 'an inundation of Common Law Treasons.' Jefferson, *Papers* (Boyd) ii, 494.

the Commonwealth. Particular categories of murder were separated for different punishments. Petit treason (murder of master by servant or husband by wife) and the murder of wife by husband, parent by child, and child by parent were punishable by hanging, the body then to be anatomized. Those who committed murder by poison were to be punished with death by poison. Those who committed murder by duel were to be hanged; a convicted challenger's body was to be gibbeted as well. In all other cases of murder, hanging was the penalty. The forfeited lands and goods of convicted murderers did not go to the Commonwealth, as they went to the Crown under English law, but one-half of the land and goods of the offender went to the kindred of the victim, the remaining half to the offender's heirs. The only exception was for one who killed his challenger in a duel; in that case, the kindred of the slain challenger took nothing, but that half went to the Commonwealth. The punishment for manslaughter for a first offender was altered to provide a punishment of seven years hard labor in the public works; half of lands and goods forfeited to next of kin of the slain person, the other half sequestered during the period of labor for the use of the Commonwealth, save a reasonable allowance for the support of the convicted person's family.[18] A second offense was deemed to be murder. Involuntary homicide committed in the course of an unlawful act, so frequently made murder or manslaughter by British statutory law, was specifically restricted to the lesser crime unless an intention to commit these more serious crimes was proven. No punishment lay for justifiable homicide or for suicide, thus terminating the English punishment of forfeiture of chattels.[19]

Nowhere was the symmetry of proportionality so well displayed as in the punishments for other crimes against the person. For these, punishments went not to life, but very directly to limb. Rape was punished by castration; the penalty for sodomy, if a man, was castration; if a woman, by cutting through the cartilage of her nose a hole of at least one-half inch diameter. Bigamy and bestiality were eliminated from the list of felonious offenses, but maiming and disfiguring ('by cutting out or disabling the tongue, slitting or cutting off a nose, lip or ear, branding, or otherwise') was to be punished by retaliation in kind – 'or if that cannot be for want of the same part, then as nearly as may be in some other part of at least

[18] Jefferson made no note of the possible anomaly here. The family of one convicted of murder retained half the land and goods outright, whereas for seven years the family of one convicted of manslaughter would receive only a portion of profits on that portion. Manslaughter had been punishable by burning in the hand and forfeiture of chattels.
[19] Jefferson, *Papers* (Boyd) ii, 469*n*.

equal value and estimation in the opinion of a jury.'[20] Offenders were, moreover, to forfeit one-half their land and goods to the victim.

Counterfeitors were to be condemned to six years hard labor and to forfeit all land and goods to the Commonwealth. For those crimes against property that had hitherto been capital offenses, a precise scale of mandatory penalties, all combining labor in the public works with multiple restitution to the victim, was envisioned.[21] The bill distinguished burglary from housebreaking and applied different degrees of punishment for each offense. The definition of grand larceny raised the requisite value of goods stolen from the common law's 12 pence to $5.00. Slaves convicted of offenses punishable in the case of freepersons by labor were to be transported to the West Indies, South America, or Africa, there to be sold. Attainder was retained, although corruption of blood was prohibited. In all cases of forfeiture, the widow's dower was preserved.[22] Those who broke out of prison were not to be punished. ('The law of nature impels everyone to escape from confinement; it should not therefore be

[20] Jefferson notes that bigamy (being twice married, the former partner living) had not been penal until the statute of James I. Bestiality, he said, could never make any progress. 'It cannot therefore be injurious to society in any great degree, which is the true measure of criminality in *foro civili*, and will ever be properly and severely punished by universal derision.' Jefferson, *Papers* (Boyd) ii, 497–98.

[21] Jefferson, *Papers* (Boyd) ii, 499, 501. The scale of penalties is as follows:

> Arson – hard labor 5 years; triple restitution to victim
> Asportation of vessels or goods thereon or plundering wrecks – hard labor 5 years; treble restitution to victim
> Robbery – 4 years hard labor; double reparation to victim
> Burglary – 4 years; double restitution
> Housebreaking – 3 years hard labor; reparation to victim
> Horsestealing – hard labor 3 years and reparation to victim. Jefferson distinguished this offense from other larcenies in Virginia: 'Where these animals generally run at large, the temptation is so great and frequent, and the facility of commission so remarkable'
> Grand larceny – pillory for 1/2 hour, hard labor 2 years, and reparation to victim
> Petty larceny – pillory for 1/4 hour, hard labor 1 year, and reparation to victim
> Robbery or larceny of bonds, bills obligatory, bills of exchange, promissory notes, lottery tickets, paper bills issued as money, loan certificates issued by Virginia or any of the United States, or Inspector's tobacco notes to be punished in the same manner as robbery or larceny of the money or tobacco represented by such paper.

The bill made no provision for instances in which the convicted were unable to pay restitution.

[22] Jefferson, *Papers* (Boyd) ii, 500–1, 503–4, 506–7n. See Boyd's suggested linkage between Jefferson's work on this bill and the bill of attainder he prepared against Josiah Phillips, which was approved by the legislature on May 30, 1778.

subjected to punishment.') Those who broke into prison in order to aid the escape of felons, however, were to be punished as accessories after the fact to the felons whom they had assisted. Witchcraft was penalized by ducking and, at the discretion of the jury, by a whipping not exceeding 15 stripes.[23]

Unlike the plan agreed to initially by the revisors in which refusal to plead was to constitute a plea of not guilty, the proposed bill continued the English practice of entering a guilty plea.[24] Aid of counsel and examination of their witnesses on oath was to be allowed to defendants. Benefit of clergy was eliminated, and in a clarification of an important point undecided at the initial meeting of the revisors, pardons were completely abolished. The trial court was given the power to grant a new trial if there was suspicion that a verdict against a defendant was 'untrue for defect of testimony or other cause.'[25]

The proposed bill represented a substantial departure from colonial practice. It is important to remember that the bill was conceived by its three sponsors as a practical program of change, appropriate to the requirements of a republican state and representing only one part of the larger goal of establishing Virginia institutions 'indicative of the general pulse of reformation.'[26] Not the whimsy of theorists but the work of men who were lawyers experienced in the public life of the colony, the bill addressed what they perceived as current problems of the criminal law. The tone of the bill reflected the notion of retributive justice, with deterrence achieved through certainty of severe punishment. At the same time, it revealed greater humaneness in the abolition of the death penalty for many capital offenses.

---

[23] Jefferson, *Papers* (Boyd) ii, 502–04.

[24] Jefferson, *Papers* (Boyd) ii, 503. The author has no explanation as to why this change was made in the finished bill. The section applied also to those who peremptorily challenged more jurors than the allowed number. In his notes, Jefferson questioned whether it would not be better simply to consider additional challenges as void and proceed to trial, a question he also raised about refusals to plead. The entering of a guilty plea, of course, eliminated trial and the court proceeded to impose punishment.

[25] Jefferson, *Papers* (Boyd) ii, 503–04. It is not certain that this language carries precisely the same meaning as the modern 'against the weight of the evidence.' Laws of evidence at this time were by no means clear. In view of the restrictions on judicial discretion elsewhere in the bill, I doubt that the principal intent was to increase markedly the discretion of the judge. It seems more likely that this provision was included to ensure the defendant (now deprived of benefit of clergy and pardon) an opportunity for another trial in any case where irregularities in the testimony colored the outcome to his prejudice.

[26] Jefferson, 'Autobiography,' *Writings* (Ford) i, 57.

The bill proposed to abolish the death penalty for nearly all offenses because it was believed that the current prevalence of that severe penalty increased the likelihood of a failure to prosecute or a failure by juries to convict and, thus, ultimately failed to deter. The purpose of the proposed proportional scale of punishment was to achieve greater effectiveness and uniformity. If punishment were proportioned to injury, 'men would feel it their inclination as well as their duty to see the laws observed.' Capital punishment should be employed only as 'the last melancholy resource against those whose existence is become inconsistent with the safety of their fellow citizens.' Clearly recognizable in these quotations from the preamble to the bill is the classic doctrine of several eighteenth-century reformers, Montesquieu, Beccaria, Eden, and others with whose writings the elite of the American revolutionary generation was thoroughly familiar.[27] Closer to home, however, were the realities of the operation of the criminal system in colonial Virginia.

According to statistics compiled by Arthur P. Scott, during the nine years preceding the outbreak of the Revolution, of 240 persons bound over for grand jury action in capital cases in Virginia, 13 were not indicted. Of the 227 tried, almost one-third (79) were acquitted; of those found guilty, 42 were clergied, 9 pardoned, and 17 hanged, with no information remaining about the outcome of 45 trials. In the case of the crimes of greatest frequency, larceny, horse stealing, and murder, which constitute well over half (150) of the total number, there were 58 acquittals (slightly over one-third) and of the 82 convictions, 29 were clergied – 3 as a result of a finding of manslaughter rather than murder – 8 pardoned

---

[27] Jefferson, *Papers* (Boyd) ii, 492–93. Jefferson, prior to 1776, had copied into his Commonplace Book long extracts of Eden's and Beccaria's work. Gilbert Chinard, ed., *The Commonplace Book of Thomas Jefferson* (Baltimore, 1926). Blackstone's references to Beccaria's theories undoubtedly communicated knowledge of them to a wider American audience than may have read the original. Jefferson's bill differs from Beccarian doctrine, although the crucial principle of proportionality is present in both. Unlike Beccaria, Eden did not advocate abolition of the death penalty but advocated its restriction to seven felonies. For relevant dicussions of Beccaria, see Paul Spurlin, 'Beccaria's *Essay on Crimes and Punishments* in Eighteenth Century America,' *Voltaire Studies* xviii (1963) 1489–1504; Michael Kraus, *The Atlantic Civilization* (Ithaca, 1949) 127–38; Coleman Phillipson, *Three Criminal Law Reformers* (Montclair, 1923); Marcello Maestro, *Voltaire and Beccaria as Reformers of the Criminal Law* (New York, 1942); Marcello Maestro, *Cesare Beccaria and the Origins of Penal Reform* (Philadelphia, 1973). For efforts to reform the criminal law of England, see Radzinowicz, *History of the Criminal Law*, supra note 3, 1; Michael Ignatieff, *A Just Measure of Pain* (New York, 1978).

and 9 hanged, with the ultimate fate of 23 convicted horse thieves unknown.[28] Whatever the inadequacy of these statistics, neither certainty nor proportionality characterized the operation of the law as it bore on those apprehended and tried. Though a relatively small proportion of those convicted of capital felonies during these years were actually executed, the penalty was hardly in disuse; benefit of clergy and pardon considerably mitigated the implementation of full penalty for those whom jurors convicted.

Julian Boyd, the distinguished editor of *The Papers of Thomas Jefferson*, regarded the provisions of the proposed Bill to Proportion Crimes and Punishments as doing little more than restating generally accepted practice concerning capital offenses.[29] But this was not the case. Generally accepted practice of the time, in Virginia as in England, relied heavily on both benefit of clergy and the use of executive pardon, which increased the likelihood that punishments would be inflicted haphazardly and unevenly.[30] These two traditional modes of mitigating the severity of the English penal code were now to be swept away in order that, in the language of the bill, 'none may be induced to injure through hope of impunity.' An inflexible scale of proportional punishments established by the legislature would have need of neither judicial nor executive intervention in the criminal process. 'Let mercy be the character of the law-giver, but let the judge be a mere machine,' Jefferson had written earlier.[31] Mandatory sentences confined the judge to such a role. Limitations of the death penalty bespoke the mercy of the law-giver. Equally striking, however, is the use made of the doctrine of forfeiture and the resurrection of the long-vanished Saxon custom of restitution to the victim or his heirs as punishment for crime.

Only upon conviction of treason, counterfeiting, and murder by duel was the penalty of forfeiture of land and goods to the sovereign – now the Commonwealth – retained. Though the principle of forfeiture remained

[28] Scott, *Criminal Law in Colonial Virginia*, supra note 7, 319–21. In the absence of the records of the General Court before which these cases were tried, Scott has used the *Virginia Gazette*. Information given there would, of course, have no bearing on the numbers who were not sent on to the grand jury by the examining courts in the counties.

[29] Jefferson, *Papers* (Boyd) ii, 505.

[30] In England, transportation of convicts under sentence of death was not a substantive punishment, but a form of conditional pardon by the Crown. For the evolution of the statutory basis for this practice, see Radzinowicz, *History of the Criminal Law*, supra note 3, 108–10.

[31] Jefferson to Pendleton, August 26, 1776, Jefferson, *Papers* (Boyd) ii, 505.

in the case of convicted murderers, half of such estates were to be forfeited to the heirs of the victim, the remainder being retained by the family of the felon. Supplying to the heirs of the victim both more direct revenge and remedy, not available at common law, and at the same time protecting the family of the felon against destitution creating a public charge, this utilitarian scheme melded the *wergelt* of Jefferson's beloved Saxon past[32] with the intent of a short-lived Virginia statute under the Commonwealth in 1656 that had provided that the estate of an executed criminal was to remain in the possession and for the use of his family.[33] In another striking departure from the common law, double or triple restitution to the victim as part of the punishment for crimes against property similarly combined the ancient law with an extension of seventeenth-century Virginia statutory penalties for hog stealing and for taking boats, both of which had provided for payment to the owner as penalty.[34]

Multiple restitution to the victim as punishment for theft was prescribed by the Bible. In addition, Elizabethan and Jacobean statutes had imposed treble damages for certain property offenses; in a single prosecution, restitution of property was awarded and there was no necessity for a civil action. Unlike Massachusetts, however, where multiple restitution as punishment for theft had been the practice since the beginning of the colony, in eighteenth-century Virginia, as in England, the crime was

[32] Trevor Colburn discusses the force of Jefferson's convictions regarding the Saxon model and relates this to Jefferson's views on land tenure, representative government, annual elections, a standing army, and the disestablishment of the Anglican church. *The Lamp of Experience, Whig History and the Intellectual Origins of the American Revolution* (Chapel Hill, 1965) 158–84. Solutions to problems of crime and punishment can be seen as another dimension of the degree to which the Saxon past was significant to Jefferson's thinking. See also Peterson, Thomas Jefferson, supra note 16, 57–61. For the general English background of such views, see particularly J. G. A. Pocock, *The Ancient Constitution and the Feudal Law* (Cambridge, 1951) and Christopher Hill, 'The Norman Yoke,' *Puritanism and Revolution* (London, 1958).

[33] Hening, *Statutes at Large*, supra note 5, i, 397–98 (March, 1655–56). This statute was not reenacted in 1660, and thereafter, convicted felons forfeited their property according to English practice. Elsewhere the practice varied. See Richard B. Morris, *Studies in the History of Early American Law* (Reprint, New York, 1974) 247–50. At common law there was no recovery where death resulted from murder both on the ground that the right of action founded upon torts of any description terminated with the life of either participant and that any right of action had merged in the felony. The latter principle, however, was not carried out consistently because civil remedies were available after criminal prosecutions in such felonies as robbery and larceny.

[34] Warren Billings, 'Some Acts not in Hening,' *Virginia Magazine of History and Biography* lxxxiii (1975) 62; Scott, supra note 7, 225–29. In 1705, the penalty for hog stealing was increased to include whipping and fine as well as payment to the owner and informer. Hening, *Statutes at Large*, supra note 5, iii (October, 1705) ch. XIV, 276–77.

punished capitally and the owner of the chattels had to bring his action for restitution after the conviction of the felon.[35]

In the Jefferson bill, restitution was awarded the owner, but the larger public interest was served by an additional punishment of hard labor, ranging from one to five years according to the gravity of the offense. Penalties other than death extended mercy to the offender; compensation extended it to his victim. By incorporating such penalties, the need of a subsequent and separate civil action on the part of the victim was removed. The design supplied certainty of punishment of the wrongdoer and certainty of compensation for the victim, who was also spared the practical difficulties of litigation at the capital. In addition, restitution may have also provided an added inducement in apprehending suspects. Because of the raising of the common law's definition of grand larceny from 12 pence to $5.00, a larger number of offenses would be determined in accordance with the new rules governing petit larceny.

The punishments proposed for crimes against the person present a curiously interesting mosaic of ancient forms applied in the new state of Virginia. The punishments do not fit modern ideas of humanitarian reforms. What we doubtless regard as excess of punishment, anatomization of the body after hanging for petit treason, parricide, and 'saticide,' was deliberately chosen by men would could have omitted this. Indeed, there was never any special punishment for parricide in English law and, unlike French law, the murder of a parent by a child was not a special crime.[36] The distinction, though, that English law made between petit

[35] George Haskins, *Law and Authority in Early Massachusetts* (New York, 1960) 153–54; Morris, supra note 33, 53–54; William E. Nelson, *Americanization of the Common Law: The Impact of Legal Change on Massachusetts Society, 1760–1830* (Cambridge, Mass., 1975). The practice of selling free persons into servitude for a limited term if they could not pay appropriate restitution was also a part of Massachusetts law. Edwin Powers, *Crime and Punishment in Early Massachusetts, 1620–1692* (Boston, 1966) 404–08, 410; David Flaherty, 'Crime and Social Control in Provincial Massachusetts,' *Historical Journal* xxiv (1981) 349–51. In colonies spawned by the Bay Colony, restitution was also one of the penalties for theft. M. P. Baumgartner, 'Law and Social Status in Colonial New Haven,' *Research in Law and Sociology* (1978) 168–70; Jessica Kross Ehrlich, 'To Hear and Try All Causes Betwixt Man and Man: The Town Court of Newtown, 1659–1690,' *New York History* lix (1978) 282, 302. In the early criminal codes of Pennsylvania, crimes against property were also punished by multiple restitution. H. W. K. Fitzroy, 'The Punishment of Crime in Provincial Pennsylvania,' *Pennsylvania Magazine of History and Biography* lx (1936) 242–69; Lawrence H. Gipson, 'Crime and Punishment in Provincial Pennsylvania,' *Lehigh University Publications* ix (1935) 2.

[36] James Fitzjames Stephen, *A History of the Criminal Law of England* 3 vols. (New York, 1973) iii, 94–5. In 1752, however, 24 Geo. II, c. 37 made the punishment for murder more severe than the punishment for other capital crimes by providing that the body

treason – the murder of a master by a servant or a husband by a wife – and ordinary murder was retained in that the punishment for petit treason was analogous to that for high treason. Drawing and quartering and hanging in chains were not unknown for this offense in colonial Virginia; all of the recorded eighteenth-century cases involved slaves.[37] Though instances are few, black heads were cut off and put on poles in public places within the lifetime of the revisors.[38] These refinements were not specified in Jefferson's bill, nor was any distinction made between servant and slave, yet the deliberate retention of this crime and the particularly severe punishment for it suggest the seriousness with which the offense appears to have been regarded by slave-owning authors of the bill. Deterrence by terror in the interest of controlling a slave population may be the explanation.

Although murder by poison had been traditionally regarded as particularly heinous since it involved obvious planning, English law had not punished it in kind.[39] It is conceivable that in the proposed bill, the singling out of murder by poison, and only that, for death in kind was also aimed principally at slaves. We know that murder by poison was a technique employed by slaves who committed this crime.[40] Whether the special deterrent for this particular form of murder was attributable to a special dread of slaves with easy access to their owners is speculative, yet a purpose beyond the symmetry of proportionality seems evident. Death in kind was not meted out, for example, in the case of murder by shooting.

---

of a convicted murderer after death be dissected or hung in chains. An English judge had the power to remit these special severities; this was not so in the proposed Virginia legislation. The earlier colonial rule requiring the prosecuting for murder of any woman who concealed the death of a bastard child unless she could prove that the child had been stillborn was omitted. Jefferson, *Papers* (Boyd) ii, 494*n*.

[37] Scott, *Criminal Law in Colonial Virginia*, supra note 7, 195–96. See Elkanah Watson's account of seeing a slave hanging in chains, executed for the murder of his master in 1777. *Men and Times of the Revolution: or the Memoirs of Elkanah Watson, including Journals of Travels in Europe and America* (New York, 1856) 43.

[38] In his study of slaves and crime in Virginia, Professor Philip Schwarz has found 12 instances of this punishment between 1745 and 1784. Only five instances appear after that date. The author is very grateful to Professor Schwarz for sharing this information with her.

[39] Willam Blackstone, *Commentaries on the Laws of England, A Facsimile of the First Edition of 1765–1769*, 4 vols. (Chicago, 1979) iv, 196.

[40] Eugene Genovese, *Roll, Jordan, Roll, The World the Slaves Made* (New York, 1974) 224–25, 616; Ulrich B. Phillips, 'Slave Crime in Virginia,' *American Historical Review* xx (1915) 336–40. Phillips found that murders of masters and mistresses almost equalled the number of murders of other slaves. More detailed analysis of the subject of slaves and crime in Virginia is the subject of the ongoing work of Philip Schwarz.

Special and severe punishment was, however, provided for dueling. In English law, death by dueling was murder, and was punished, in theory at least, with death, although this penalty was seldom imposed. Unlike petit treason, English law did not distinguish between dueling and ordinary murder and it was difficult to obtain a conviction in dueling cases, apparently because the two offenses were not considered comparable by Englishmen.[41] Jefferson's bill provided the additional ignominy of gibbeting as well as denying forfeiture to the heirs of the challenger if slain in the contest. Perhaps this was done to provide more effective deterrence for which Blackstone had called in his denunciation of the custom.[42] Even if this is so, one cannot be sure why dueling was singled out for a special punishment, unless it was a notable problem in revolutionary Virginia.

It would be easy to neglect the particular significance of dueling in Virginia. We know something about dueling in general but not enough about its social evolution during the eighteenth century.[43] The revisors knew more. Although dueling may not have been a common offense during the colonial period, it occurred often enough to abandon the idea that the custom was brought here by European officers during the war for independence.[44] Dueling was not unknown in Virginia, and the casualness of a reference to a duel in a Virginia diary of 1774 supports the view

---

[41] Lorenzo Sabine, *Notes on Duels and Duelling* (Boston, 1859) 43; John R. Reed, *Victorian Conventions* (Ohio, 1975) 142–55.

[42] Blackstone, *Commentaries*, supra note 39, iv, 199.

[43] Discussion of dueling commonly focuses upon the Western frontier or the code of honor of the antebellum Southern elite. See, for example, Joe B. Franz, 'The Frontier Tradition: An Invitation to Violence,' in *Violence In America; Historical and Comparative Perspectives*, Hugh Davis Graham and Ted Robert Gurr, eds., (New York, 1969) 127–53; John Hope Franklin, *The Militant South* (Cambridge, Mass., 1958) 44–62; Rollin G. Osterweis, *Romanticism and Nationalism in the Old South* (New Haven, 1949) 96–98, 128–29, 168–69, 200–03; Jack K. Williams, *Dueling in the Old South* (College Station, 1980); Dickson D. Bruce, Jr., *Violence and Culture in the Antebellum South* (Austin, 1979); Steven M. Stowe, 'The "Touchiness" of the Gentleman Planter: the Sense of Esteem and Continuity in the Antebellum South,' *The Psychohistory Review* viii (1979) 6–15. Richard Buel has argued that dueling, with its close ties to social status in the South, provided a way in the early national period for members of the gentry to distinguish themselves from the common man. *Securing the Revolution* (Ithaca, 1972) 80–81. The most recent discussion of antibellum dueling is Bertram Wyatt-Brown, *Southern Honor, Ethics and Behavior in the Old South* (New York, 1982) 166–67, 328, 350–61.

[44] This is contrary to the views of Daniel Boorstin, *The Americans, The National Experience* (New York, 1965) 207. But see M. N. Stanard, 'A Virginia Challenge in the Seventeenth Century,' *Virginia Magazine of History and Biography* ii (1894–95) 96–97. Evarts B. Greene, 'The Code of Honor,' *Colonial Society of Massachusetts Transactions* xxvi (1927) 368–85; William O. Stevens, *Pistols at Ten Paces, the Story of the Code of Honor in America* (Boston, 1940) 9–14.

that it was a familiar custom.[45] The practice, however, was very likely on the increase during the eighteenth century and appeared to spread rapidly during the war period when the revisors were doing their work.[46] Franklin, Paine, and Washington all condemned dueling, and in 1776 a committee of the Continental Congress unsuccessfully urged the adoption of punitive legislation applicable to army personnel.[47] Alexander Graydon later recalled that during the war years 'among all the southerners, the point of honor was maintained,... with considerable punctilio.'[48] Disorderly social conditions of the revolutionary period may well have produced genuine concern over problems of private justice and public lawlessness.

The Jeffersonian bill, in sum, seems to have been aimed at curtailing dueling. The common law had long recognized that an individual should have a right to defend his person or his property, but unrestrained,

[45] Jack Greene, ed., *The Diary of Colonel Landon Carter of Sabine Hall*, 1752–1776, 2 vols. (Charlottesville, 1965) ii, 1143. In 1765, John Scott of Prince William County challenged a neighbor who had insulted his father, the Rev. James Scott. His brother-in-law, serving as a second, was so insulted by Scott's antagonist that he demanded satisfaction, took Scott's place, and killed the man. The episode took place in a churchyard and the malefactor was acquitted on a plea of self-defense. Mary Stanard, *Colonial Virginia, Its People and Customs* (Philadelphia, 1917) 159.

[46] In 1766, a naval officer challenged Maurice Moore, a North Carolina legislator. In 1768, Henry Laurens challenged Judge Leigh of the vice-admiralty court to a duel following the seizure of his vessels and the proceedings in that court. In 1771, John Hay had killed his friend, Peter DeLancy, deputy postmaster for the southern district of North America, in a duel. The young John Jay in 1773 was ready to defend his honor by duel. In 1777, Christopher Gadsden dueled with Major General Robert Howe and Button Gwinnett was killed in a duel with Lachlan McIntosh. Gen. Thomas Cadwalader seriously wounded Gen. Thomas Conway in a duel in 1778. Horatio Gates and James Wilkinson dueled in that year, as did Andrew Porter of Pennsylvania, who killed a fellow officer who had 'insulted' him by calling him a schoolteacher. In 1778, Gen. Francis Marion, 'the Swamp Fox,' accepted a challenge from a British officer, who then declined to meet him. John Laurens wounded Major General Charles Lee in a duel in 1778; the following year, Lee challenged Justice William Henry Drayton of Charleston, who declined, declaring that although custom sanctioned the duel for the army, it did not for the judiciary. The above list was compiled from Allen Johnson and Dumas Malone, eds., *Dictionary of American Biography* 22 vols. (New York, 1928–44) xi, 33; xi, 36; iii, 398; ix, 295; vii, 186; x, 82; viii, 68; Stevens, Pistols, supra note 44, 19; Richard Morris, *Seven Who Shaped Our Destiny* (New York, 1973) 150–51; Merrill Jensen, *The Founding of a Nation* (New York, 1968) 301–02. Lt. Thomas Anburey of the British army reported that among the British troops billeted in Charlottesville in 1779 there were six or seven duels fought in three or four days. *Travels through the Interior Parts of America*, 2 vols. (Boston, 1923) ii, 185–86.

[47] Stevens, Pistols, supra note 44, 15–25. For dueling in the army, see Charles Royster, *A Revolutionary People at War* (Chapel Hill, 1979) 208–10.

[48] John S. Littell, ed., *Memoirs of His Own Times, with Reminiscences of the Men and Events of the Revolution* (Philadelphia, 1846) 180.

unregulated individual combat might rend the bonds of social unity within the governing class and threaten social stability. Judging by the penalties proposed, dueling was perceived as a more significant threat to the state than counterfeiting or 'ordinary' murder.

While gentlemen dueled, men of other classes fought. It is interesting in this light to observe that the traditional punishment for manslaughter, burning in the hand and forfeiture of chattels to the state, was also increased in the Jefferson bill. Hard labor for seven years, the longest period of all labor sentences – surpassing that for counterfeiting and arson – together with forfeiture of half of lands and goods to the heirs of the victim was proposed. A second violation was deemed a murder, a deterrent formula unknown to the English law for this offense. Perhaps this was aimed at the instances when men fought in heat of passion and one was killed. Such episodes were not rare in Virginia, and a harsher penalty for this offense must have been designed to deter it.

The proposed provisions for maiming and disfiguring are worth highlighting as well. Atrocious acts of personal violence, not resulting in homicide, were not treated as very serious crimes until the English Coventry Act of 1670 made malicious maiming or disfiguring ('by disabling the tongue, putting out eyes, biting or cutting off nose and lip or disable any limb or member') a non-clergyable felony.[49] This statute was enacted in Virginia in 1752, and in 1772 the Assembly again attempted to deal with the offense of serious wounding. Along with broadening the definition of the crime to include the maiming customs of Virginia, 'gouging,[50] plucking or putting out an eye, biting, kicking or stamping,' the punishment was changed to provide that the injured party might sue for damages, and if the damage award was not paid, the guilty person could receive up to 39 lashes. The law was disallowed by the Privy Council because it applied a criminal penalty in a civil action.[51]

Jefferson's bill deleted mayhem from the list of capital crimes. On the other hand, it substituted the ancient and cruel *membrum pro membro* as a punishment. This may also have reflected a concern about the level of violence in Virginia. Retaliatory maiming or disfiguring in kind was

---

[49] 22 & 23 Chas. II, c.1 (December 21, 1670). This act was construed very narrowly. In 1722, the Waltham Black Act extended heavy penalties for violent offenses committed or likely to be committed. James Fitzjames Stephen, supra note 36, iii, 112–13; Radzinowicz, History of the Criminal Law, supra note 3, I, 69–73; E. P. Thompson, *Whigs and Hunters, The Origin of the Black Act* (New York, 1975) 245–58.

[50] William Fouchee, the surgeon of Richmond, for example, was one among many who had had an eye gouged out, this by a 'low fellow' who insisted on fighting him. Anburey, Travels, supra note 46, ii, 201–02.

[51] Hening, *Statutes at Large*, supra note 5, viii (February, 1772) 520.

combined with forfeiture of half of the land and goods to the victim as a punishment for mayhem.[52] No higher authority could now complain that criminal prosecution and civil remedy were combined in a single procedure or that the *lex talionis* was to be inaugurated in the independent state.

It is significant that in Jefferson's bill, all penalties for offenses against the person were extremely severe – castration for rape, for example. Apparently the revisors believed that these crimes constituted a greater threat to the social fabric of the new Commonwealth than crimes against property. The punishment for only the latter appears mild and humanitarian by comparison.[53] But the shame of public labor was intended only for free persons. Convicted slaves would be transported abroad, thereby, in Jefferson's phrase, freeing the Commonwealth from the 'wickedness' of slave offenders.[54]

Little is gained by further speculation about a bill, which, like Jefferson's Bill for the Diffusion of Knowledge, was destined not to pass, yet it is useful to disinter the Bill to Proportion Crimes and Punishments for thoughtful consideration for it was as serious a proposal as the successful new Act for the Establishment of Religious Freedom and the Statute of Descents. Like them, it was intended to supercede the immediate past by embracing ancient realities.

This bill was not considered by the Assembly until October of 1785, but Jefferson did not await legislative action. During his wartime term as governor (June 1779–June 1781), he assumed an executive prerogative and pardoned felons convicted of capital crimes on condition that they work for a term of years on a variety of public works – generally the

---

[52] Blackstone had written that the law of retaliation was an inadequate rule of punishment partly because on repetition of the offense the punishment could not be repeated. Blackstone, *Commentaries*, supra note 39, iv, 12–14. The revisors solved the problem by giving to the jury the power to decide which part of the body was of nearest value to be taken or disfigured in cases where the same part was already missing. Jefferson, *Papers* (Boyd) ii. 498.

[53] The doctrine of proportionality and discussion of the efficacy of capital punishment, particularly for theft, were staples of eighteenth-century reform literature. Closer in principle to the proposed bill than the more famous works of Beccaria and Eden are Lord Kames's 'History of the Criminal Law' in his *Historical Law Tracts* (Edinburgh, 1758, 1761) and Henry Dagge's *Considerations on the Criminal Law*, 2 vols. (London, 1772). There were advocates in eighteenth-century England of aggravated forms of the death penalty to maximize deterrence, but the author knows of no proposal that duplicated Jefferson's scale of precise retaliation for offenses against the person. See Radzinowicz, *History of the Criminal Law*, supra note 3, i, 231–59.

[54] Jefferson to Pendleton, August 26, 1776, Jefferson, *Papers* (Boyd) i, 505.

lead mines.[55] Given the need for bullets and the high cost of labor, the utility as well as the humaneness of conditional pardons was followed by successive governors[56] until 1785, when the Court of Appeals determined that conditions attached to pardons were unconstitutional.[57] By the time the Assembly began its consideration of the revised code in 1785, Jefferson was in France as Minister to the French court. James Madison, who was piloting the bill through the House, wrote optimistically of the speed with which the legislature was acting[58] before sharp dispute over the proportioning of crimes and punishments (Bill No. 64) brought action on the entire revision to a stop. 'Here the adversaries of the code exerted their whole force,' he reported, singling out the opposition of the speaker, Benjamin Harrison, James Mercer, and Charles Thruston.[59] By way of a special bill, to last only one year, the legislature empowered the governor to grant conditional pardons of those sentenced to death for felonies.[60] In the next session (1786), the bill was rejected by a single vote.[61] 'Our old bloody code is by this event fully restored,' Madison wrote to Jefferson,

---

[55] The first reference is June 26, 1780. H. R. McIllwaine, ed., *Journal of the Council of the State of Virginia* (Richmond, 1932) ii, 260.

[56] Ibid., iii, 74, 89, 201, 443, 456. After the war, conditional pardons were granted on terms of 'servile but useful labour' to be determined by the corporation of Richmond, prisoners being turned over to custody of the city. Gov. Patrick Henry to Mayor of the City of Richmond, January 13, March 28, May 12, 1785. Executive Letterbook 3. Microfilm, Virginia State Library. Some were apparently used on the construction of the James River Canal. Herbert A. Johnson, ed., *The Papers of John Marshall* (Chapel Hill, 1974) i, 205n.

[57] Commonwealth v. Fowler 4 Call (Va.) 36. A supporter of the reform of conditional pardons, Joseph Jones, a member of the council, wished to see the experiment continued only if sanctioned by the legislature. McIllwaine, ed., *Journal of the Council*, supra note 55, iii, 422–23.

[58] Madison to Washington, November 11, 1785, William T. Hutchinson et al., eds., *The Papers of James Madison* (Chicago, 1962-) viii, 403. (Hereinafter cited as Madison, *Papers*.)

[59] Madison to Jefferson, January 22, 1786, Jefferson, *Papers* (Boyd), ix, 195; to Monroe, December 9, 17, 1785, Madison, *Papers* viii, 436–37, 445–46. Madison mentions that amendments were made, but he does not explain what they were. Neither do legislative materials, published or unpublished, or newspapers. For the completion of the entire revisal in 1792, see Charles Cullen, 'Completing the Revisal of the Laws in Post-Revolutionary Virginia,' *Virginia Magazine of History and Biography* lxxxii (1974) 84–99.

[60] Hening, *Statutes at Large*, supra note 5, xii, 45–56.

[61] Madison to Washington, December 24, 1786, Madison, *Papers* supra note 58, ix, 225. Defeat of the bill came 'after being purged of its objectionable peculiarities' but Madison does not explain which ones he means. He had anticipated 'the most vigorous attack' in both houses of the legislature. To Jefferson, December 4, 1786, Jefferson, *Papers* (Boyd) x, 575.

adding that the rage against horse stealers had influenced the outcome and that the Assembly had not reenacted the law granting the executive the prerogative of conditional pardon.[62] Shortly before, Jefferson had written from Paris of the praise in Europe for Virginia's new Act for Establishing Religious Freedom and of the criticism that the principle of retaliation in the Bill for Proportioning Crimes and Punishments had received.[63]

More than 30 years later in his *Autobiography*, Jefferson attributed the legislative defeat to rejection of the Beccarian principle of the inefficacy of the death penalty. He did not recall, he wrote, how the 'revolting principle' of the *lex talionis* had been approved by the revisors, 'the modern mind having left it far in the rear of its advances.'[64] Despite Madison's reference to the rage against horse stealers, the failure of the bill by only a single vote is a clue as to the sharp division of opinion on alteration of the criminal code. The bill and its defeat remain something of a mystery. Its proposals may have been within the realm of a realistic criminal bill or may have been rejected as a harshly reactionary measure. It is also hard to relate the bill to the history of crime in Virginia and the eventual passage of a reform bill in 1796 without knowing the amendments attached by the legislature. The limitation of the death penalty, the principle of retaliation, forfeiture and multiple restitution, mandatory sentences, transportation of slaves, and absence of pardoning power may all have drawn objection.[65]

The main reason we have a hard time evaluating the Jefferson bill is the lack of knowledge about crime and the operation of the criminal system in Virginia at this time. The records of the trial court, the General Court, were burned during the Civil War.[66] Nevertheless, analysis of extant trial court records after 1788, when 18 new district courts were

[62] Madison to Jefferson, February 15, 1787, Jefferson, *Papers* (Boyd), xi, 152.
[63] Jefferson to Madison, December 16, 1787, Jefferson, *Papers* (Boyd), x, 603–04.
[64] Jefferson, *Writing* (Ford), i, 69.
[65] Legislative records for the period do not report debates. Newspapers that have been examined make no mention of the subject. Searches in unpublished letters of members of the assembly have produced nothing. Legislative and executive materials, both printed and unpublished, have shed no light on this bill.
[66] There are no published reports of the decisions of the General Court from 1777 to 1788. A selection of cases, chiefly criminal cases decided from 1789–1814, was published in 1815 by William Brockenbrough and Hugh Holmes, two of the judges; in 1826 Brockenbrough published a second volume including decisions from 1815 to 1826. By the revision of 1788, the General Court was given appellate jurisdiction over the district courts in criminal cases. *Virginia Cases* therefore does not supply the type of information necessary to evaluate the nature and extent of crime in the post-Revolutionary period. Manuscript notes on cases heard at the district court level were kept by St. George Tucker and other judges very likely did the same, but no comparable notes, to the author's knowledge, have ever come to light.

created (records of six of these have been located), together with the records of some of the examining courts of the counties sheds some light on that system. In 1788, the legislature revised the court structure creating district courts as the principal trial courts of the Commonwealth to replace the General Court.[67] The 18 districts created, each composed of several counties, afforded greater facility for trials throughout the Commonwealth and markedly altered the practice during the earlier period in which all felony trials had to take place at the state capital. It must be emphasized that the use of the records of these courts is fraught with difficulties familiar to legal historians. The data applies only to the period after 1788, and not all extant records are complete; imposed randomness complicates efforts to evaluate the significance of such material. Additionally, the increase of trial courts in itself alters many factors. There is no way of telling whether the number of prosecutions, for example, reflects any change in pattern or simply an increased ease of prosecution once the accused and witnesses no longer had to travel to the capital for trial.

The six districts for which records exist comprise 25 counties.[68] Of a total of 105 terms of court investigated from 1789 to 1800, in 28 terms

[67] Hening, *Statutes at Large*, supra note 5, xii, (December 22, 1788) 730–63. The purpose of the creation of the district courts was to alleviate congestion in the General Court. Courts were held in each district twice annually and cases were heard from the several counties in that district. The courts always met at the same place in the district and each district court was presided over by two General Court judges, each pair having responsibility for three or four districts. The act also increased the number of General Court judges from 9 to 12. The district courts were replaced in 1808 by the Superior Courts of Law. For discussion of these courts, see A. G. Roeber, *Faithful Magistrates and Republican Lawyers; Creators of Virginia Legal Culture, 1680–1810* (Chapel Hill, 1981) 203–30.

[68] In the Virginia State Library, Richmond, the records are located within the county records of the county in which the court was held and consist of Order Books; no case papers have been located. The six district courts are:

> Frederick: sat at Winchester; includes Frederick, Berkeley, Hampshire, Hardy, and Shenandoah counties
> Prince William: sat at Dumfries; includes Fairfax, Fauquier, Loudoun, and Prince William counties
> Northumberland: sat at Northumberland County Courthouse; includes Westmoreland, Lancaster, Northumberland, and Richmond counties
> Accomac: sat at Accomac County Courthouse; includes Accomac and Northampton counties
> Augusta: sat at Staunton; includes Augusta, Rockbridge, Rockingham, and Pendleton counties
> Fredericksburg City: sat at Fredericksburg; includes Spotsylvania, Caroline, King George, Stafford, Orange, and Culpeper counties.

(almost 25%) no action was taken by the grand jury:[69] in 16 cases, grand juries failed to return a true bill.[70] Of the total number of felonies prosecuted (147), about one-third (50) resulted in jury acquittals, with the outcomes of most of the rest distributed as follows: 16 nol pros'd (frequently witnesses failed to appear), 21 escapes before or after trial, 24 convicted and clergied, and 17 sentenced to be hanged. Thus, less than one-third received punishment. There is a rough parallel here with Scott's information about the pre-Revolutionary period.[71] Those sentenced to the gallows were murderers, horse thieves, and one rapist, who was a free black. The number of prosecutions for murder (35) nearly equalled those for grand larceny (39). Seventeen were prosecuted for horse stealing, and within the category specified only as felony (32), occasionally a brief reference in the record seems to indicate that the crime was larceny or horse stealing, a fact that could increase these totals. Other crimes are far fewer in number: burglary (10), rape (5), negro stealing (2), counterfeiting (2), and one instance each of prosecutions for mayhem, arson, and carnal knowledge of a child under ten. Close to half (63) of all felonies from these six districts were prosecuted in the Frederick District Court, sitting in Winchester.[72]

---

[69] Accomac District accounts for a sizable proportion of this number. Of the 25 terms in which that court sat between 1789 and 1801, in 16 of them no indictments were returned. In three terms, no grand jury was even impanelled. This may be because the required 24 members had not turned up in obedience to process; repeatedly, individuals were summoned to answer and pay fines for this offense. Accomac County Order Book 1789–1797; District Court Order Book 1797–1805, Reel #110. Virginia State Library, Richmond.

[70] Five were to charges of larceny, five murder (one a woman), two horse stealing, three unspecified felony, and one rape.

[71] See note 28 supra.

[72] In descending order for other districts: Fredericksburg City District there were 34, in Augusta 23, in Northumberland 15, in Prince William 8, and in Accomac 4. With the exception of rape, for each of the different felonies the numbers are greater also in the Frederick Court. The information presented here and elsewhere in the paper is compiled from the following manuscript records available on microfilm in the Virginia State Library, Richmond.

> Accomac County Order Book 1789–1797; District Court Order Book, 1797–1805, Reel #110
> Augusta County District Court Order Book 1789–1793, Reel #91; District Court Order Book, 1789–1803, Reel #92
> Frederick County Superior Court Order Book (District Court) 1789–1793, 1794–1797, Reel #95; 1797–1800, Reel #96
> Fredericksburg City District, Law Orders A, 1789–1793, one volume photostat Northumberland County District Court Order Book, 1789–1793, 1793–1802, Reel #67
> Prince William District Court Order Book, 1793, 1797–1798, 1799, Reel #30.

The criminal work of the district court was clearly one for the poor and lowly. Generally identified by race, sex, and occupation, there are only six black males among the offenders: two were convicted and hanged (one for 'felony,' the other for rape), two convicted of grand larceny and clergied, and two acquitted of larceny but convicted of the lesser offense of burglary. Only seven women, all white, were tried: one, identified as a laborer, was clergied after conviction of grand larceny; of the others, identified as spinsters, one was sentenced to the gallows for murder, two were acquitted of murder, another acquitted of the murder of her bastard child, and two acquitted of grand larceny. Of 100 white males, 56 are identified as laborers,[73] 16 as yeomen, and the balance a sprinkling – in the single numbers – of artisans: shoemakers, carpenters, saddlers, blacksmith, sailors, and so forth. Only one person is designated 'planter'; by special verdict he was acquitted of negro stealing.

The conclusions to be reached from such figures are modest. First, the district courts heard a small total number of cases. (I have used numbers rather than percentages in order not to mislead.) Making due allowance for those districts whose records for the decade are incomplete, this is especially striking when viewed in light of the total, free population within the districts; 63 felonies over a ten-year period for the district with the greatest number seems remarkably low. These records, of course, tell only of those charged with felony who had been apprehended, bound over by the examining court, successfully confined, and taken before the district court for trial. The degree of 'slippage' at each stage could be considerable.[74] Madison's reference to 'the rage against horse-stealers' may reflect anger derived from the difficulties of catching them as much as opposition to ending the death penalty for those convicted. Though the grand total of prosecuted horse thieves is small (17), the legislature repeatedly attempted to devise successful means of apprehending and punishing such wrongdoers. The crime was made unclergyable in 1789, and the death penalty was extended to accessories in

[73] The meaning of this word is not precise. The author is uncertain whether it should be understood simply as an unskilled laborer employed or not, or taken to mean vagrant, a word that never appears in these records. Comparable difficulties have plagued studies of eighteenth-century labor. See Billy G. Smith, 'Material Lives of Laboring Philadelphians, 1750 to 1800,' *William and Mary Quarterly*, 3d ser. xxxviii (1981) 166. In urban Philadelphia, Smith classified 'laborers' as an unskilled group.

[74] See the discussion of the problems related to the amount of unknown crime in J. M. Beattie, 'Towards a Study of Crime in Eighteenth Century England: a Note on Indictments,' in David Williams and Paul Fritz, eds., *The Triumph of Culture: Eighteenth-Century Perspectives* (Toronto, 1972) 302–04.

1792 since 'felons are much encouraged to steal horses, because a great number of persons make a trade to receive and buy of such felons.'[75] Edmund Randolph claimed that pardons for horse stealing multiplied in Virginia and hardly any horse thieves were executed.[76] Prosecuting counterfeiting seems to have been comparably difficult. Despite legislative efforts, only two people in six districts examined were tried for this crime. In 1792, burglary, arson at common law, burning of a court house, robbery, theft, and forgery were made unclergyable; malicious shooting, stabbing, maiming, and disfiguring were made felonies, although apparently clergyable.[77] These acts reflect legislative intent, but prosecutions on account of these crimes, except for theft, were negligible before and after 1792. The records may tell us what happened in a court but very little about crime in Virginia. Perhaps the severity of punishment contributed to the difficulties confronting the courts, perhaps not. It is possible that prosecutions for murder alone may approximate commissions of the offense. In comparison to other crimes, the relatively high number of murders prosecuted (particularly in comparison to larceny) conforms to the stereotype of Southern violence.[78] Reinforcing the stereotype all the more is the high proportion of those prosecuted criminally for assault, a major quotient of all misdemeanors.[79] In light of recent

75 Hening, *Statutes at Large* xiii, 30 (Nov. 27, 1789); *A Collection of All Such Acts of the General Assembly of a Public and Permanent Nature, as are Now in Force: Comprising the First Volume of the Revised Code* (Richmond, 1814) i, 251 (Dec. 10, 1792). The latter statute also provided for $20 rewards to those who aided in the apprehension of horse thieves and payment of $170 to the heirs of anyone killed in the effort to capture such offenders, a clue to the possible hazards of such an enterprise.

76 William Bradford, *An Enquiry How Far the Punishment of Death is Necessary in Pennsylvania* (Philadelphia, 1793). Randolph also told Bradford that in Virginia, the proportion of those acquitted for rape in comparison to those charged was 'very great.' These records show a low incidence of those formally charged with this crime (5), of whom only one, a black, was sentenced to death.

77 Hening, *Statutes at Large*, supra note 5, xiii, 30–32 (Nov. 27, 1789); *A Collection of All Such Acts of the General Assembly... of the Revised Code* (Richmond, 1814) i, 249–50 (Dec. 17, 1792); i, 350–53 (Dec. 19, 1792).

78 See note 72 supra. There were 35 prosecutions for murder and a total of 71 prosecutions for grand larceny (39) and unspecified 'felony' (32). To have prosecutions for murder as high as 50% of those for larceny is extraordinary. For rough comparison with Massachusetts and South Carolina, see Michael Hindus, *Prison and Plantation: Crime, Justice and Authority in Massachusetts and South Carolina, 1767–1878* (Chapel Hill, 1980) 64–65.

79 The number of indictments for assault is but a small patch on the countless number of civil suits brought in Trespass AB. The number of one-penny damages awarded by juries in these cases reflects the commonplace quality of this type of behavior and may also reflect jury condemnation of the one who brought such action in court. Of criminal

research about crime in Massachusetts, we were clearly in a very different world.[80]

The primitive techniques of law enforcement in Virginia may account for the fact that not all felonies reached the trial court. This raises the question of whether felonies might have been handled in some fashion at the local level. In grand larceny cases, for example, the examining or county court might have regarded the crime as being insufficiently serious to warrant the expense and inconvenience of trial and/or the penalty of death. County courts may have exercised jurisdiction without statutory authorization over felonies committed by lower-class whites analogous to that which they had been authorized to exercise over slaves. Perhaps they were not simply 'examining' but, in effect, trying felonies without juries and imposing penalties short of death.[81]

The records of the examining courts bear out such hypothesis only partially. It should be recalled that because county court records of the ten counties examined vary widely in completeness over time and span

prosecutions, only a few actually came to trial, often because of the failure of process to bring either the accused or the witnesses in for trial. Fines for those convicted were set by the jury and were generally small.

[80] David Flaherty, 'Crime and Social Control,' supra note 35, 339–60; William E. Nelson, *Americanization*, supra note 35, 37. For information about the incidence of crimes of violence elsewhere, see Rachel Klein, 'Ordering the Backcountry: The South Carolina Regulation,' *William and Mary Quarterly*, 3rd ser. xxxviii (1981) 661–80; Douglas Greenberg, *Crime and Law Enforcement in the Colony of New York, 1691–1776* (Ithaca, 1974); Hindus, *Prison and Plantation* supra note 78; Donna J. Spindel, 'The Administration of Criminal Justice in North Carolina, 1720–1740,' *American Journal of Legal History* 25 (1981) 141–62.

Flaherty argues that eighteenth-century Massachusetts was remarkably free of serious crime, and probably of all crime. He attributes this to a small and relatively homogenous population living within physical confines of townships, the out-migration of potentially disruptive young men who sought economic opportunities elsewhere, and an effective system of prosecuting serious breaches of the law. The commitment of elite groups in the towns and churches to law and order and the role of the family in inculcating standards of behavior are other components of the system of social control over criminal activity. Virginia by the latter eighteenth century presents limited parallels in the Tidewater and the polar opposite in western counties. David Flaherty, 'Crime and Social Control,' supra note 35, 339, 355–56.

[81] Prior to 1692, slaves, like free men, were tried for capital crimes only in Jamestown, and before a jury. To improve the speed of determination and punishment where necessary, the governor was empowered in 1692 to issue specific commissions of oyer and terminer to persons in the county (normally the justice of the peace) to try slaves there without juries and to order the execution of convicted slaves. In 1765, another statute provided that each county court be given a standing commission of oyer and terminer to try without a jury and acquit or execute any slave accused of a capital offense. Hening, *Statutes at Large*, supra note 5, ii, 102–03 (1692); viii, 137–39 (1765).

the period of two different organizations of trial courts, the data base is not fully satisfactory. Keeping this caveat in mind, it can be said that of 248 persons examined on suspicion of various felonies, somewhat less than one-third were discharged, and one-half of those examined were bound over for prosecution before the trial court. It is difficult to know whether the number bound over is high or low. There are a few instances each of confessions followed by immediate whippings, of individuals who being bound over for trial begged to be whipped instead, and of cases in which justices reduced the charge to bring it within the definition of a misdemeanor, thereby saving a person from being tried for his or her life. Such practices constituted less than 1/10 of the total number of individuals examined.[82] Even with a generous allowance for disparity in records, some regional patterns emerge. There are more examinations for felony in the more recently established counties: 60 over 11 years in Augusta, for example, 42 in a 9-year period in Frederick compared with 12 in 9 years in Caroline, 20 in 18 years in Northumberland. In Henrico County (Richmond city) in 13 years, 45 free persons were examined. Theft, murder, and horse stealing were the crimes of greatest frequency,

---

[82] Of 248 persons examined, 121 were bound over for trial, 88 discharged, 27 punished by the examining court, 12 held for the county grand jury. Figures drawn from the following county court records available on microfilm from the Virginia State Library: Caroline Co. Order Books (1778–1787), Reel #20, 21, 22; Frederick Co. Order Books (1781–1784; 1789–1795), Reel #74, 75, 76, 77; Albemarle Co. Order Books (1783–1785; 1793–1795), Reel #46, 47; King George Co. Order Books (1786–1792). Reel #26; Henrico Order Books (city of Richmond) (1781–1787; 1791–1799), Reel #69, 71, 72; Westmoreland Co. Order Books (1776–1795), Reel #61–62; Fairfax Co. Order Books (1783–1788), Reel #39; Northumberland Co. Order Books (1773–1797), Reel #56, 57, 58, 59; Augusta Co. Order Books (1774–1785), Reel #67; Fauquier Co. Minute Books (1773–1795), Reel #47, 48, 49. Compare with information given for an earlier period of the eighteenth century for Caroline, King George, and York counties in the Tidewater. A. G. Roeber, 'Authority, Law and Custom: The Rituals of Court Day in Tidewater Virginia, 1720 to 1750,' *William and Mary Quarterly*, 3d ser. xxxvii (1980) 35n. In Orange County between 1735 and 1775, an average of two persons a year were examined for felony, of whom less than half were held for trial at the capital. Arthur P. Scott, *Criminal Law*, supra note 7, 47n. Order Books and Minute Books do not include case papers. Extant case papers, few and far between and located in a handful of courthouses, are relevant to civil litigation rather than criminal prosecution. We therefore lack information about the exact nature of the proceedings, the facts of the case, examination of witnesses, the questioning of the accused, and the nature of evidence presented. For one early example of the process of examination before the called court of Westmoreland Co. June 3, 1715, see 'The Pulpit Cloth of Appomattox Church,' *William and Mary Quarterly*, 1st ser. xxvii (1918) 28–33.

other serious offenses appearing much less often.[83] An analysis of the records of the Hustings Court, with jurisdiction over the new city of Richmond, reveals a rise in the prosecution of major crimes in the late 1780s, followed by decreases for more than a decade after 1790.[84]

A combination of factors, therefore, may explain the passage of the act to amend the penal laws that was adopted in 1796. If colony-wide statistics bear out those presented here, if it is the case that roughly 1/3 of those examined for felony were being discharged at the county level, if 1/3 the number actually being tried were acquitted by the juries, if the harsh penalties of the Act of 1792 failed to improve the effectiveness of law enforcement, then perhaps people became convinced that these harsh punishments were part of the problem.

Sponsored by George Keith Taylor of Prince George County, the 1796 legislation[85] abolished the death penalty for all crimes committed by free

---

[83]

Augusta – 1774–1785	11 years	60 examined
Frederick – 1781–84; 89–91; 91–95	9 years	42 examined
Henrico – 1781–84; 84–87; 91–94; 95–99	13 years	45 examined
Fauquier – 1773–1793	20 years	30 examined
Northumberland – 1777–1795	18 years	20 examined
Westmoreland – 1777–1795	18 years	19 examined
Caroline – 1778–1787	9 years	12 examined
Albemarle – 1783–1785	2 years	4 examined
Fairfax – 1784–1788	5 years	3 examined

It is also interesting to observe the surprisingly low incidence of misdemeanors in these county records: slander, fornication, or other crimes of morality are few and far between. Most of those presented by grand juries of the county were charged with not keeping the roads or for selling liquor without a license and keeping a tippling house. Since drunkenness virtually never appears, one is left to think that the absence of revenue from licensing or an effort to contain the sale of liquor was the offense at issue.

[84] Robert M. Saunders, 'Crime and Punishment in Early National America, Richmond, Virginia 1784–1820,' *Virginia Magazine of History and Biography*, lxxxvi (1978) 33–38. The information presented is interesting, but the value of the article is diminished by its misunderstanding of the function of the Hustings Court, which served as an examining court for free people and as a trial court for slaves. For the increase in crime in Richmond during the Revolutionary war years, see Harry M. Ward and Harold E. Greer, Jr., *Richmond During the Revolution, 1775–1783* (Charlottesville, 1977) 109–25.

[85] Samuel Shepherd, *Statutes at Large of Virginia, 1792–1806: Being a Continuation of Hening Statutes at Large* 3 vols. (Richmond, 1835–1836), ii, 5–16 (Dec. 15, 1796). *Virginia Argus* (Richmond) Friday, Dec. 9, 1796. Details about the evolution and passage of this legislation are as elusive as for Jefferson's proposal almost 20 years before. No debate is reported in the Journal of the House of Delegates and none has been located

persons except murder in the first degree, defined as murder by poison and other premeditated killings. No special distinctions for the felonies of petit treason, parricide, and dueling were included. Directing the governor to purchase land for a penitentiary, the legislature inaugurated imprisonment as the punishment for all other crimes formerly capital, including treason. In place of the mandatory sentences proposed by the earlier revisors, minimum and maximum periods of confinement, according to the gravity of the offense, were established.[86] The power to set the sentence within this range was given to the jury, not the judge, continuing the idea in the Jefferson bill of restricting judicial discretion.[87] Restitution of value to the owner was coupled with imprisonment as punishment for crimes against property. Similarly, in the additional punishment for malicious

elsewhere. The bill passed the House on Dec. 7 by a vote of 95–66 and the Senate on Dec. 15, no vote being recorded. Blocs of opposition votes in the House centered in Grayson and Pittsylvania counties to the west along the North Carolina border, but as a whole the vote may illustrate the localized force of particular domestic issues in Virginia referred to by Richard Beeman, *The Old Dominion and the New Nation, 1788–1801* (Lexington, 1972) 92–93. See also Edward Wyatt, 'George Keith Taylor, 1769–1815, Virginia Federalist and Humanitarian,' *William and Mary Quarterly*, 2nd ser. xvi (1936) 1–18.

[86] The terms of imprisonment set forth:

> High treason – 6 to 12 years at hard labor or in solitude
> Arson: principals and accessories – 5 to 12 years
> Rape – principals and accessories before the fact: 10 to 21 years
> Second degree murder – 5 to 18 years
> Robbery or burglary – principals and accessories: restoration of full value and 3 to 10 years
> Horsestealing – principals and accessories before the *fact*: restoration of the animal or full value, 2 to 7 years
> Larceny above the value of $4 – restoration of full value, 1 to 3 years
> Petty larceny under $4 – restoration of full value and 6 months to 1 year
> Counterfeiting of gold or silver coin or notes of the banks of Alexandria or the United States – fine not exceeding $1,000, the amount of the fine to be set by the court; 4 to 15 years
> Malicious maiming or disfiguring – 2 to 10 years and $1,000 fine, 3/4 of which to party grieved
> Voluntary manslaughter – imprisonment at hard labor and solitary confinement for 2 to 10 years and security for good behavior during life, or for less time according to the nature and enormity of the offense, second offense: imprisonment at hard labor and solitary confinement for 6 to 14 years
> Involuntary manslaughter happening in consequence of unlawful act – attorney general may waive the felony and charge with misdemeanor; attorney general may charge both offenses in same indictment, in which case the jury may acquit on one and convict on the other.

[87] Virginia State Library House of Delegates, Loose Papers, 1796.

maiming or disfiguring – a $1,000 fine, 3/4 of which was to be paid to the party harmed – one sees vestiges of the Jeffersonian proposals. Benefit of clergy was abolished, but executive pardon was retained. Although Taylor's original bill kept transportation of convicted slaves and provided for jury trials for slaves arraigned for criminal offenses, the House of Delegates eliminated both from the bill.[88] The legislature appropriated $30,000 to construct a penitentiary large enough to hold 200 convicts. Shortly after passage. Governor Wood wrote to Dr. Caspar Wistar of Philadelphia requesting information about Pennsylvania's experience, as well as a copy of the plan of the Pennsylvania penitentiary.[89]

Taylor's description of the existing criminal code as 'unjust, impolitic, and barbarous' was accompanied by a new emphasis on the moral reform of the delinquent, totally missing in Jefferson's proposal.[90] The substitution of prison sentences for death sentences would lead, he argued, to more effective enforcement of the law. Pointing to Pennsylvania ('whose criminal system the bill before us contemplates to imitate and adopt'), Taylor identified reason and humanity with the successful republicanism of the new nation. 'How distressing it is to a Virginian,' he said, 'to reflect that his native state is likely to be distanced in this race for mercy.' He charged his colleagues with passively submitting to a system 'calculated to awe and crush the humble vassals of monarchy,' and urged them to revise the criminal law 'to comport with the principles of our government.' Using statistics from Philadelphia to show the sharp reduction in crime there since the inauguration of the penitentiary system in 1791, Taylor also praised the system of convict labor as both morally and financially desirable: 'while it corrects and reforms, it SAVES the citizen [a vast annual expense].'[91] With the passage of the bill, Virginia

---

[88] Virginia State Library House of Delegates, Loose Papers, 1796. This section provided also that convicted slaves, so transported, would be sold for the best price obtainable, the amount of the sale, after deduction for the price of transportation, to be applied to discharge the value of the slave, an amount to be fixed by the court on the condemnation of such slaves. The provision for jury trial also specified that slaves be allowed the same number of challenges allowed to others.

[89] 'I have been induced to take the liberty from an anxious desire that no time should be lost in bringing this humane law into operation, and which is not to be in force until the necessary Buildings are completed.' Wood to Wistar, Jan. 6, 1797. Virginia State Library Executive Letterbooks, Reel #5.

[90] George Keith Taylor, *Substance of a Speech... on the Bill to Amend the Penal Laws of this Commonwealth* (Richmond, 1796) 7, 10–11. Taylor listed as the objects of punishment: 1. Amendment to delinquent 2. Example to others 3. Retribution to the injured party 4. Retribution to the public.

[91] Ibid. 7, 25, 29, 30–31, 35–36.

joined Pennsylvania and New York in the faith that a more rational criminal code that made punishment proportional would not only make law enforcement more effective but also reduce the number of criminal offenses.[92]

Such a faith certainly reflects conviction about the beneficent potentialities of the new republic, an attitude characteristic of post-Revolutionary societies. With independence won, the turmoil of the war and the eighties behind,[93] the transition of leadership at the national level successfully achieved, an assured confidence in the powers of republicanism contributed potently to a mood of humanitarianism. It is also conceivable, although not demonstrable, that the perceived increase in the amount of crime over the course of the eighteenth century, so frequently linked to the British export of convicts, appeared to be diminishing with the end to this practice.[94] By 1796, successful experiments with leniency – in Tuscany, in France, in Holland, Ghent, England, and most of all the penitentiary system in Pennsylvania – were available as models for Virginia legislators. While in Europe, Jefferson had learned of the success of private English experiments with solitary confinement, and obtained from an architect in Lyons the plan of a prison adapted to this design, which he sent home to Virginia at the request of the legislature.[95]

The foregoing observations do not address the major questions about crime, the criminal law and its reform in Virginia. The role of legal institutions in the history of any society can only be fully understood in relation to the configuration of the total social system of which they are a part. Answers to historical inquiries do not lie in isolated bits of data but in the social reality that generated them. Only very recently has a reconstruction

[92] Pennsylvania had limited the death penalty to murder in 1794, the first state to do so. David B. Davis, 'The Movement to Abolish Capital Punishment in America, 1787–1861,' *American Historical Review* (1957) 23–46. New York in 1796 approved funds for a state prison and soon opened Newgate; New Jersey completed a penitentiary in 1797. The Virginia penitentiary provided for in the bill under discussion opened in 1800. See the brief discussion of this period in David Rothman, *The Discovery of the Asylum* (Boston, 1971) 57–62. For analysis of the creation of the penitentiary in England, see Michael Ignatieff, *A Just Measure of Pain; the Penitentiary in the Industrial Revolution 1750–1850* (New York, 1978).

[93] This subject deserves further attention. See Elizabeth Cometti, 'Depradations in Virginia during the Revolution,' in Darrett Rutman, ed., *The Old Dominion: Essays in Honor of Thomas P. Abernethy* (Charlottesville, 1964) 147–49.

[94] Fairfax Harrison, 'When the Convicts Came,' *Virginia Magazine of History and Biography* xxx (1922), 250–60; Abbott E. Smith, *Colonists in Bondage, White Servitude and Convict Labor in America 1607–1776* (Chapel Hill, 1947) 124, 128–33; Hugh Rankin, *Criminal Trial Proceedings in the General Court of Colonial Virginia* (Charlottesville, 1965) 124.

[95] Jefferson, 'Autobiography,' *Writings* (Ford) i, 71–74.

of the society and culture of eighteenth century Virginia begun to emerge that may enable us to describe the role of crime and the criminal law within the larger social framework.[96] In Virginia at this time, counties, not towns, were the geopolitical units that defined the daily realities of living, customary mores, and rituals knitting together inhabitants.[97] Characterized by diffusion of settlement and dominated by gentry, traditional and personal types of authority, within or without the formal legal process, were understood within this social space. In such a world, rural and preindustrial, networks of blood and marriage, kinship, and friendship at all levels of society were the most important and through which much else is best comprehended.[98] The personal and the institutional, the formal and the informal, and the individual and the communal overlapped at the

[96] See Rhys Isaac, 'Religion and Authority: Problems of the Anglican Establishment in Virginia in the Era of the Great Awakening and the Parsons' Cause,' *William and Mary Quarterly* 3d ser. xxx (1973) 3–36; Rhys Isaac, 'Evangelical Revolt: The Nature of the Baptists' Challenge to the Traditional Order in Virginia, 1765–1775,' *William and Mary Quarterly* 3d ser. xxxi (1974) 345–68; Jack P. Greene, 'Society, Ideology, and Politics: An Analysis of the Political Culture of Mid-Eighteenth Century Virginia,' in Richard M. Jellison, ed., *Society, Freedom, and Conscience: The American Revolution in Virginia, Massachusetts, and New York* (New York, 1976) 14–76; T. H. Breen, 'Horses and Gentlemen: The Cultural Significance of Gambling among the Gentry of Virginia,' *William and Mary Quarterly* 3d ser. xxxiv (1977) 239–57; Richard Beeman, 'Social Change and Cultural Conflict in Virginia: Lunenburg County, 1746–1774,' *William and Mary Quarterly* 3d ser. xxxv (1978) 455–76; A. G. Roeber, 'Authority, Law and Custom: Rituals of Court Day in Tidewater Virginia, 1720–50,' *William and Mary Quarterly* 3d ser. xxxvii (1980) 29–52; Richard R. Beeman and Rhys Isaac, 'Cultural Conflict and Social Change in the Revolutionary South: Lunenburg County, Virginia,' *Journal of Southern History* xlvi (1980) 524–50; A. G. Roeber, *Faithful Magistrates and Republican Lawyers: Creators of Virginia Legal Culture, 1680–1810* (Chapel Hill, 1981); Daniel Blake Smith, *Inside the Great House; Planter Family Life in Eighteenth Century Chesapeake Society* (Ithaca, 1980). Valuable overall accounts remain Charles Sydnor, *Gentlemen Freeholders: Political Practices in Washington's Virginia* (Chapel Hill, 1952) and Robert E. and B. Katherine Brown, *Virginia 1705–1786: Democracy or Aristocracy?* (East Lansing, 1964). The most recent analysis of Virginia society is Rhys Isaac, *The Transformation of Virginia 1740–1790* (1982).

[97] See the suggestive essay by Darrett B. Rutman, 'The Social Web: A Prospectus for the Study of the Early American Community,' in William L. O'Neill, ed., *Insights and Parallels: Problems and Issues of American Social History* (Minneapolis, 1973) 57–89. For the increase of incorporated towns after the revolution, see E. Lee Shepard, 'Courts in Conflict: Town-Country Relations in Post-Revolutionary Virginia,' *Virginia Magazine of History and Biography* lxxxv (1977) 184–99.

[98] See Daniel Blake Smith, *Inside the Great House: Planter Family Life in Eighteenth Century Cheasepeake Society* (Ithaca, 1980), for an examination of family life in planter households. See also the suggestive article by Bertram Wyatt-Brown, 'The Ideal Typology and Ante-bellum Southern History: A Testing of a New Approach,' *Societas*, v (1975) 1–29, and the author's discussion in his book, supra note 43, (1982) 117–324. Analysis of kin networks of those in more modest circumstances in Virginia society remains to be done.

bottom level of the legal system.[99] This Virginia world had its own peculiarities of crime and law enforcement not necessarily analogous to those of other colonies or of eighteenth century England, where an oppressive criminal code had developed out of the efforts to control or intimidate a large, landless, and unemployed population with a sizable concentration in London. Indeed, it would be reasonable to anticipate considerable variation among Virginia counties themselves, for there is a temporal as well as spatial framework to be considered. Virginia counties were not static but were undergoing considerable social change before, during, and after the Revolution. The nature of such change must be located in a continually changing space-time matrix, the pace of different developmental phases affected by many factors local to the various counties of Virginia.

Although we know that Virginia, by contrast to other colonies, was relatively untroubled by large scale discord in the years preceding the war, there are other special aspects of Virginia society as well. Population was expanding swiftly. The economy and indebtedness flucuated sharply. Ethnic and regional differences, including racial divisions, were intensified by increasing numbers of slaves. Class divisions were exacerbated by the arrival of convicted felons from England, as well as by the competition between Anglicans and Baptists.[100]

It is not necessary here to determine definitively whether the Virginia gentry was made anxious by some social and moral threat or whether there existed a confident and stable cohesion of a gentry-dominated white society attributable to the expansion of slavery and racism. Whether the Revolution was intended to bring profound moral regeneration of American society, or whether the degree of white solidarity in the eighteenth century has been overstated, it was assumed that the Revolution would ultimately lead to order and social stability.[101]

---

[99] See Sydnor, supra note 96, 74–85, for discussion of the multiple roles of the county oligarchies that dominated the local vestry, militia, and courts. See also Isaac, *The Transformation of Virginia,* supra note 96, 88–94 and 115–38.

[100] See Jackson T. Main, *The Social Structure of Revolutionary America* (Princeton, 1965) 45–7, 65–6, 183–85; Robert Sutton, 'Sectionalism and Social Structure,' *Virginia Magazine of History and Biography* lxxx (1972) 70–84; Robert D. Mitchell, *Commercialism and Frontier; Perspectives on the Early Shenandoah Valley* (Charlottesville, 1977) 93–132; Fairfax Harrison, 'When the Convicts Came; A Chapter from Landmarks of Old Prince William,' *Virginia Magazine of History and Biography* xxx (1922) 250–60; Robert McColley, *Slavery and Jeffersonian Virginia* (1964); Rhys Isaac, 'Evangelical Revolt,' *William and Mary Quarterly* 3d ser. xxxi (1974) 345–68; Beeman and Isaac. 'Cultural Conflict and Social Change...in Lunenburg County,' *Journal of Southern History* xlvi (1980) 524–50.

[101] See Gordon S. Wood, 'Rhetoric and Reality in the American Revolution,' *William and Mary Quarterly* 3d ser. xxiii (1966), 3–32 and more extensively. *The Creation of the*

In the context of the war, whose outcome was so uncertain and that produced further disruptions to the earlier social order, the original revisors attempted the first alteration in the criminal code in 1779. In their reconstitution of the criminal law, the heaviest penalties, as in many kinship systems, were retained for crimes against the person, or against natural relations, for, as in ancient laws, these were perceived as threats to the social stability of the community. It is this stability that the revisors endeavored to achieve by severe deterrents. A high degree of individual aggression constituted one of the chief aspects of Virginia culture and was shared among all classes of society in much the same fashion as gambling, racing, cockfighting, or other turbulent amusements.[102] Challenging questions remain concerning the reasons for widespread social acceptability of such mores in these Southern communities, where complex tribal customs of social and racial relationships were often considered more important than formal law.[103]

One is still impressed by the seemingly small number of serious crimes prosecuted, as well as by the high proportion of murders within the total. It may be that the vast distances to be traveled in taking a suspect and the prosecutor and witnesses from the called court to the trial court explains why only the most serious felonies or the most threatening suspects were

---

American Republic 1776–1787 (Chapel Hill, 1969) 46–90, 393–429; Jack P. Greene, 'Society, Ideology and Politics: An Analysis of the Political Culture of Mid-Eighteenth Century Virginia,' in Richard M. Jellison, ed., Society. *Freedom and Conscience: the American Revolution in Virginia, Massachusetts and New York* (New York, 1976) 65–75; Edmund S. Morgan, *American Slavery American Freedom; the Ordeal of Colonial Virginia* (New York, 1975) 363–86.

[102] Jane Carson, *Colonial Virginians at Play* (Williamsburg, 1965) 151–80; Breen, 'Horses and Gentlemen,' *William and Mary Quarterly* 3d ser. xxxiv (1977) 239–57. Historical scholarship on violence tends to fall on collective lawlessness related to major political concerns or on urban crime and riot in their relationship to the process of social and economic development. Richard Maxwell Brown, *Strain of Violence, Historical Studies of American Violence and Vigilantism* (New York, 1975); Hugh Graham and Ted Gurr, eds., *Violence in America* (New York, 1969). Of countless essays that discuss violence as a character trait attributed to Southerners, 'Southern Violence,' by Sheldon Hackney in the latter volume, 505–27, is particularly interesting on individual violence. See also Dickson D. Bruce, Jr., *Violence and Culture in the Antebellum South* (Austin, 1979); Wyatt-Brown, Southern Honor, supra note 43, 366–401.

[103] Charles S. Sydnor, 'The Southerner and the Laws,' *Journal of Southern History*, vi (1940) 3–23. Dealing with the antebellum period, Sydnor stresses the Southerner's steady assumption that a relatively large number of his deeds could be and had to be performed outside the written law. Sydnor explains much of this in terms of the slave-owner's individual power over his slaves. See also John Hope Franklin, *The Militant South* (Cambridge, 1956) 33–62. For comparison with South Carolina, see Hindus, Prison and Plantation supra note 78.

ever tried.[104] Given the inadequacies of law enforcement and the absence of close surveillance, one would also suspect a sizable quotient of unreported crime. Unlike Massachusetts, Virginia had a formal system of criminal justice that probably did not penetrate very far into the society and in which few institutional mechanisms were available for solving conflicts peacefully.[105] Here, private ties of kinship, friendship, or economic relationship may have been more significant in the preservation of social order and the control over serious crime than agencies of either church or state.[106] Virginia society, however, was evolving in such a way as to produce new groups of people who were beyond the reach of any of these relationships.

Consider the familial character of the county court in the social system of Virginia. This court represented more than a judicial institution in which criminal cases were evaluated to send only those in which there was a good chance of conviction to the trial court. The lay justices of the peace monthly meetings constituted one of the major social institutions of Virginia communities; it was a complex unity of undifferentiated governance organized in judicial form. Holding office for many years, often with members of the same families governing over several generations,[107] this influential gentry played a deeply personal and cohesive role in the

[104] In 1783, one man reported that to travel 140 miles with the witnesses in order to testify against a man he suspected of stealing his horse would have doubled the amount of the loss, and he preferred to let the matter go. J. D. Schoepf, *Travels in the Confederation* 2 vols. (Philadelphia, 1911) ii, 53. In 1788, Brissot wrote that he had heard more of crimes in Virginia than in the Northern states; he attributed criminal behavior to the large plantation, luxury, and slavery. J. P. Brissot De Warville, *New Travels in the United States of America* (Cambridge, Mass., 1964) 349.

[105] On Massachusetts, see the recent scholarship of David Flaherty, 'Crime and Social Control,' supra note 35, 339–60; William E. Nelson, *Dispute and Conflict Resolution in Plymouth County, Massachusetts, 1725–1825* (Chapel Hill, 1981); David Thomas Konig, *Law and Society in Puritan Massachusetts, Essex County, 1629–1692* (Chapel Hill, 1979); David Grayson Allen, *In English Ways, The Movement of Societies and the Transferal of English Local Law and Custom to Massachusetts Bay in the Seventeenth Century* (Chapel Hill, 1981).

[106] Daniel Blake Smith, supra note 98, 212–13, suggests this for the planter community. Evidence is lacking to demonstrate whether stronger or weaker kin connections existed among poorer families. Richard Beeman stresses the degree to which Baptists by the 1770s were turning to the meeting rather than to the court for settlement of secular disputes and disciplinary action. 'Social Change and Cultural Conflict in Virginia: Lunenburg County, 1746 to 1774,' *William and Mary Quarterly* 3d ser. xxxv (1978) 470. Whether such activity existed within the Anglican community at this time has not been investigated.

[107] Daniel Blake Smith, 'Changing Patterns of Local Political Leadership: Justices of the Peace in Albemarle County,' unpublished M.A. thesis, University of Virginia, 1973;

continuity of life in some Virginia counties.[108] It was the county court
that functioned as an informal, discretionary agency for solving the problems of community affairs. Its role in the criminal process, differentiating
more serious crimes as well as misdemeanors, must be seen in this light. It
was the unrestrained discretion of the justices that determined whether a
person charged with serious crime would be discharged, punished lightly
at the local level on a lesser charge, or sent to be tried for his or her
life.

Such a description of the county courts would not, however, apply to
every county. Research by Richard Beeman and Rhys Isaac in Lunenburg
County, established in 1746, finds a very different character of justices
there, undistinguished men who lacked the wealth, experience, and family background necessary to give a degree of authority like that present
in long settled eastern counties.[109] A careful examination of other counties on the moving Virginia frontier might reveal similar differences.[110]
In Frederick and Augusta counties, which show the highest number of
felonies prosecuted, settlers of English background were a minority in
the rapidly growing population of the Shenandoah Valley. In occupation, religion, and ethnicity, the composition of eastern Virginia was
more homogenous than that of the west.[111] This is not to say that ethnic
diversity guarantees a higher incidence of serious crime but to emphasize

Gwenda Morgan, 'The Hegemony of the Law; Richmond County 1692–1776,' unpublished dissertation, Johns Hopkins University, 1980, 79–100; Charles Sydnor, *American
Revolutionaries in the Making, Political Practice in Washington's Virginia* (New York,
1965) 74–85.

[108] For perceptive analyses of the Virginia courthouse culture, see Rhys Isaac, 'Evangelical
Revolt,' *William and Mary Quarterly* 3d ser. xxxi (1974) 354–68; Rhys Isaac, 'Dra-
matizing the Ideology of Revolution: Popular Mobilization in Virginia, 1774–1776,'
William and Mary Quarterly 3d ser., xxxiii (1976) 357–67; A. G. Roeber, 'Authority,
Law and Custom,' *William and Mary Quarterly 3d ser. xxxvii (1980) 29–52; Faithful
Magistrates and Republican Lawyers 73–111*; Robert Wheeler, 'The County Court in
Colonial Virginia,' in Daniels, ed., *Town and Country*, 111–34; although it deals with
Massachusetts, the important article by Hendrik Hartog, 'The Public Law of a County
Court; Judicial Government in Eighteenth Century Massachusetts,' *American Journal
of Legal History* 20 (1976) 282–329, is germane to the subject.

[109] 'Cultural Conflict and Social Change in the Revolutionary South: Lunenburg County,
Virginia,' *Journal of Southern History* xlvi (1980) 531–33; also Beeman, 'Social Change
and Cultural Conflict,' supra note 100, 458–61, 464–66.

[110] Freeman Hart, *The Valley of Virginia in the American Revolution 1763–1789* (Chapel
Hill, 1942) gives no attention to the subject.

[111] Robert Sutton, 'Sectionalism and Social Structure,' *Virginia Magazine of History and
Biography* lxxx (1972) 74; See the table of distribution of national groups in the Shenandoah Valley, 1775, in Robert D. Mitchell, *Commercialism and Frontier; Perspectives
on the Early Shenandoah Valley* (Charlottesville, 1977) 43.

that cultural homogeneity may make its control easier.[112] There would not necessarily be a replication elsewhere of whatever stability may have resulted from the integration of power and authority in the persons of 'tribal elders' in Tidewater communities.[113]

It is not surprising that the statistics identify more than half of those prosecuted as 'laborers' if we think only in terms of social class. Ranked at the bottom of the economic scale, owning little property, and rarely owning land, there were, in addition, others of unidentified occupation who were poorer yet.[114] In Richmond, propertyless white males, apparently an underclass of drifters, constituted the overwhelming proportion of those who were examined before the Hustings Court.[115] Even the meaning of the word laborers is unclear. The records do not indicate whether the designation implies one actually employed or not, a transported convict or second offender, a local resident or vagrant. Such distinctions are obviously important. For clergyable crimes, the rule was to burn the hand of a first offender and then discharge him or her. Sometimes the judge would add a whipping. Since the records used do not state whether the accused was a repeat offender previously convicted and clergied, there is no way to tell how many second offenders there may have been among the total number of convictions. Among those sentenced to hang there were undoubtedly some who had used up the privilege of benefit of clergy. We know virtually nothing in detail about the wandering poor in Virginia or about another important factor, the proportion of those appearing on criminal charges who were known to the community, as opposed to strangers.

The county court was one part of the formal legal structure, but it operated in an informal familial fashion as the justices questioned suspects and witnesses and reached their determination. Known to members of the community in long-established counties, the justices in turn knew them, often by personal associations of one sort or another. To what degree this influenced judgments rendered is unknown. Discrepancies in

---

[112] For conflicts occasioned by national prejudices, see Samuel Kercheval, *History of the Valley of Virginia* (2nd ed. 1850) 157–58.

[113] For discussion of differences in community organization between early Lunenburg County and the more settled older counties, see Beeman, 'Social Change and Cultural Conflict,' supra note 100, 455–61.

[114] The number owning property worth less than $50 has been estimated at 9% for pre-Revolutionary Virginia. Jackson Turner Main, *The Social Structure of Revolutionary Virginia* (Princeton, 1965) 72–73.

[115] Saunders, 'Crime and Punishment,' supra note 84, 42; Henry M. Ward and Harold E. Greer, Jr., *Richmond during the Revolution*, supra note 84.

the handling of identical offenses lead one to suspect that the reason for judicial differentiation lay in the identity of the accused more than in the nature of the offense. Wrongdoing members of the community may have been punished locally, while strangers were sent off to trial.[116] In less well-established counties, which by definition were communities of strangers,[117] where formal institutions and individual social relationships were only commencing to develop, the formal system of criminal justice was needed more and employed more. In each community, the social texture and evolving customs might well prove different, and given the limited state of our knowledge, speculation is unavoidable.

As the social organization of various counties moved through stages of growth toward greater resemblance to Virginia's older counties, a strengthened network of institutions and values helped to stabilize public order, replacing the disorderly traits of the frontier.[118] This process, imperfectly understood though it is, has a connection with the legislation of 1796, which virtually abandoned capital punishment as an instrument for control over serious crime. Agencies of social control, which have nothing to do with the criminal law *per se* but which aided in discouraging serious deviant behaviour, are important to this development: population growth and the pattern of settlement; the role of family, church, and school; the growth of towns; improved availability of legal redress and political representation; and particularly the role of the dominant groups that exercised power and authority. All play interrelated parts in this process. Comparative data is not extensive, yet the conclusion that the amount of serious crime in Virginia as elsewhere in eighteenth century America was low by comparison to that of England or the European countries is not startling. The United States of the eighteenth century had no cities even remotely the size of London or Paris or

---

[116] The work of Gwenda Morgan provides evidence of this in the mid-eighteenth century for Richmond County. Local men and women were most likely to be spared trial, non-residents or newcomers most frequently to be punished; in all known cases, convict servants and ex-convicts were sent on for trial. 'The Hegemony of the Law,' supra note 107, 209.

[117] The ritual process of stranger relations could be fruitfully examined in this connection. There is a substantial literature on strangers, the outgrowth from Georg Simmel's brief essay, 'The Stranger,' in Kurt H. Wolff, trans. and ed., *The Sociology of Georg Simmel*, (New York, 1950) 402–08. For a good overview, see Daniel Levine, 'Simmel at a Distance: On the History and Systematics of the Sociology of the Stranger,' in William A Shack and Elliott P. Skinner, eds., *Strangers in African Societies* (Berkeley, 1979) 21–36.

[118] See Beeman's discussion of this process in one county, 'Social Change and Cultural Conflict,' supra note 100, 463–68.

Amsterdam, with their large urban criminal problems. Even allowing for
probable increase in economic inequalities over the course of the eighteenth century, poverty was less widespread and the degree of it less severe
than elsewhere; economic incentives to serious crime and persistent, large-
scale transiency were thereby reduced.[119] Such social facts, coupled with
the continuation of the master's extensive power to punish his servants
and slaves within his private domain contribute also to the relative ease
with which change could come about in Virginia. Jefferson's proposed
bill had sharply limited capital punishment, took the principle of revenge
seriously, and provided that the state take this into account by making
retribution the basis of punishment. It is the Act of 1796 that signified the
modern approach to the problems of crime by providing imprisonment to
replace both hanging and benefit of clergy as punishment for all felonies
except murder in the Old Dominion.[120]

[119] See, E. P. Thompson, Whigs and Hunters, supra note 49; Douglas Hay et al., *Albion's Fatal Tree: Crime and Society in Eighteenth Century England* (New York, 1975); John Beattie, 'The Pattern of Crime in England, 1660–1800,' *Past and Present* lxii (1974) 47–95; Nicole Castan, 'Summary Justice,' and Andre Zysberg, 'Galley Rowers in the Mid-Eighteenth Century,' in Robert Foster and Orest Ranum, eds., *Deviants and the Abandoned in French Society*; Selections from the *Annales* Economies, Societies, Civilizations, iv (Baltimore and London, 1978) 83–110, 111–56; Olwen Hufton, *The Poor of Eighteenth Century France* (New York, 1874). See the critique of the latter by John Langbein, 'Albion's Fatal Flaws,' *Past and Present* xlvii (1983) 96–120.

[120] On this transformation in Western culture, see Michel Foucault, *Discipline and Punish; The Birth of the Prison* (New York, 1977).

7

Jurisdiction to Punish: Federal Authority, Federalism, and the Common Law of Crimes in the Early Republic

Kathryn Preyer

Discussion and debate over the nature of federalism is one of the staples of American public discourse. Among historians and lawyers, politicians and judges, this constant has remained. It is only the context of the discourse that has changed over time. Given the unusual framework of union provided by the Constitution, it is hardly surprising that debate over its nature should continue, for concepts of constitutionalism, federalism, and law in American culture have melded into an alloy from which it is often impossible to determine which is the baser metal. Continuing inquiry over the proper balance between state and national authority and over the proper reach of federal jurisdiction has prompted as many scholarly endeavors as ever the quest for the Holy Grail led brave knights to their adventures. The endless searches among scholars, lawyers, and jurists for 'the original understanding' of 'the Framers' has been an active industry for generations, seldom more so than in our own time. This is itself a striking cultural fact, and like the quest for the Grail, the center

Kathryn Preyer is Professor of History at Wellesley College. The author wishes to thank Kent Newmyer, Stephen Presser, Wythe Holt, and Sandra Van Burkleo for providing criticism and suggestions, and Maeva Marcus, Director of the Documentary History Project, Supreme Court of the United States, for making available the Project's files of grand jury charges, 1790–1800. These will be published in volume three of *The Documentary History of the Supreme Court*. This article was completed before the publication of Stewart Jay's recent study, 'Origins of Federal Common Law: Part One,' 133 *University of Pennsylvania Law Review* 1003–116; 'Part Two', 1231–333 (1985), to which the reader's attention is directed. The author expresses her gratitude to Professor Jay for conversations about a shared interest in the early federal common law and for providing her with material from Paterson manuscripts in the New York Public Library. A version of this article was presented at the conference 'The Law in America, 1607–1861' held at the New York Historical Society in May 1985.

around which a huge corpus of legend, romance, learned scholarship, and wishful thinking revolves.

That there were abundant differences of opinion and many 'original understandings' about the nature of federalism among the founders of the Republic is readily apparent from even the most cursory acquaintance with the debates in the Constitutional Convention, the ratifying conventions, and the early legislative and judicial materials of the states and the nation. Entangled in broad general problems of federalism in these early years was the more specific question, the reach of federal authority over crimes and punishments in the new nation. This was a question of significance in its own right, and it is the subject of this essay.

The applicability of the English common law in the new United States was a matter of much debate for many years for this was a subject less agreed upon among the individual states following independence than we are inclined to assume, and after 1789 the creation of two spheres of governance, state and federal, considerably magnified the uncertainties. Whether there was or was not a federal common law of crimes became a subject embedded in more general questions of the federal-state relationship as well as in those involving the relationship between the federal judiciary and the new federal representative body, the Congress. What *was* American law, how was it to be made, where was it to be made? Was there a difference perceived between the criminal law, including the common law of crimes, and other aspects of the general English common law?

It is important to bear in mind the full implications of the fact that the new forms of government at the time of the American Revolution required new conceptions of sovereignty; gone were doctrines and institutions that had derived historically from the theoretical structure of the Crown as sovereign. By either constitution or statute, various provisions, often ambiguous, were enacted in the individual states regarding the reception of English law.[1] Following the adoption of the federal Constitution in 1789, general problems of sovereignty and the particular problem of the reception of English law were further compounded by the structure of the new national government with its principle of separation of powers and with its novel relationship to the states of the union. The new formula

---

[1] For a convenient overview see Ford W. Hall, 'The Common Law: An Account of its Reception in the United States,' 4 *Vanderbilt Law Review* 791–825, (1951); for British statutory law, see Elizabeth Gaspar Brown, *British Statutes in American Law 1776–1836* (Ann Arbor, 1964).

required substantial future clarification of the relationship between the whole and its parts. It furthermore compelled efforts within both the individual states and the national government to define more precisely than had reception statutes or Constitutional provisions the operative force of English common law in the new republic.

The creation of the Supreme Court and the Congress of the United States was of course stipulated by the Constitution itself; the creation of its inferior courts was effected by legislation of the first Congress, the Judiciary Act of 1789.[2] Defining the *powers* of the federal courts, however, would constitute a profound part of the subsequent political-legal history of the nation from that day to this. One important aspect of this vast subject was the realm of the criminal law, where the source of much difficulty lay in the ambiguous understanding of the reception of the English common law at the federal level. Was there a federal common law jurisdiction over crimes? In the absence of statutes passed by Congress, what recourse to English tradition or to conceptions of the role of the judiciary were appropriate to the government of the United States? Was Article III of the Constitution in effect tantamount to a reception provision of the federal government, and if so, what did it receive? What exactly were 'the laws of the United States'?

The subject of a federal common law of crimes has been discussed over time by legal scholars, and the received wisdom on the subject has held that bench and bar during the early national period did recognize a federal common law of crimes in the absence of federal statutes, and that the jurisdiction of the federal courts embraced common law crimes until it was denied in 1812 by the Supreme Court in *U.S. v. Hudson and Goodwin*, 7 Cranch (U.S.) 32.[3]

---

[2] Art. III, §2. 'The judicial Power shall extend to all Cases, in Law and Equity, arising under this Constitution, the Laws of the United States, and Treaties made, or which shall be made, under their Authority; . . .'. 1 United States Statutes at Large 73 (Sept. 24, 1789). The relevant criminal jurisdiction appears in section 11 of the statute, which gave to the circuit courts exclusive cognizance over 'all crimes and offences cognizable under the authority of the United States' except as otherwise provided and where jurisdiction was concurrent with the district courts. It is the meaning of the quoted language that came into dispute as well as the language of Article III of the Constitution.

[3] Charles Warren, *The Supreme Court in United States History*, 3 vols. (Boston, 1924) i, 159n, 433–37; Charles Grove Haines, *The Role of the Supreme Court in American Government and Politics, 1789–1835* (Berkeley and Los Angeles, 1944) 125–28, 306–07; William Winslow Crosskey, *Politics and the Constitution*, 3 vols. (Chicago, 1953–80) ii, 782n; Julius Goebel Jr., *History of the Supreme Court of the United States, Antecedents and Beginnings* (New York and London, 1971) 623–33 [hereinafter: Goebel, *History*]; George Haskins and Herbert A. Johnson, *History of the Supreme Court of the United*

Let me first take a closer look at the shaping of this interpretation. In April 1790, Congress passed the first federal criminal statute, and the reach of it was carefully restricted to treason, counterfeiting or forgery of public securities, theft or forgery of judicial records, perjury in federal courts or in depositions taken pursuant to the law of the United States, bribery of federal judges, rescue of federal prisoners committed or convicted of capital crimes, and attempts to subject foreign ministers to arrest. In addition, on federal reservations and on navigable waters and the high seas, murder, manslaughter, robbery, mutiny, piracy, theft of federal implements of war, receiving stolen property, and harboring felons were defined as crimes against the United States. Treason, murder, robbery, piracy, mutiny, accessories before the fact to such felonies, and counterfeiting public securities were punished by death. Other offenses were punished by imprisonment and/or fine. Benefit of clergy was prohibited. So was corruption of blood.[4]

In view of the fact that the system of English criminal justice had so recently represented to Americans the might of centralized royal authority, it is not surprising that the legislation was narrowly restrictive. Any resuscitation of the doctrines of sovereignty that had made the royal power to punish so useful a tool of Crown politics was clearly to be

States, *Foundations of Power: John Marshall 1801–15* (New York and London, 1981) 158–59, 354, 633–40; Morton Horwitz, *The Transformation of American Law 1780–1860* (Cambridge, Mass., 1977) 9–12 [hereinafter: Horwitz, *The Transformation of American Law*]; Leonard Levy, *Freedom of Speech and Press in Early American History, Legacy of Suppression* (New York, Torchbook ed., 1963) 233–34, 238–46; Leonard Levy, *Emergence of a Free Press* (New York, 1985) 274–79. A detailed discussion of the issues involved is Stephen B. Presser 'A Tale of Two Judges: Richard Peters, Samuel Chase, and the Broken Promise of Federalist Jurisprudence,' 73 *Northwestern Law Review* 27–111 at 46–72 (1978) [hereinafter: Presser, 'Tale of Two Judges']; also Stephen B. Presser and Becky Bair Hurley, 'Saving God's Republic: The Jurisprudence of Samuel Chase,' 3 *University of Illinois Law Review* 771–822 at 796–99 (1984) [hereinafter: Presser, 'Saving God's Republic'].

4 1 *Stat.* 112 (April 30, 1970). Space precludes discussion of the procedural aspects of the legislation. See the brief mention in Goebel, *History*, supra note 3 at 609–11. The passage of the bill may be followed in Linda Grant DePauw, ed., *Documentary History of the First Federal Congress of the United States of America*, 3 vols. (Baltimore, 1972–77) i, *Senate Legislative Journal*, 44, 98, 120, 139, 227, 229–30, 285–87; iii, *House Legislative Journal*, 178, 180, 181, 207, 210, 359–63 [hereinafter. DePauw, ed., *Documentary History of the First Federal Congress*]. Debate in the House will be found in *Annals of Congress*, ii, 1572–74 (April 6–10, 1790) [hereinafter: *Annals*]. Brief references to the bill are to be found in William Maclay, *Sketches of Debate in the First Senate of the United States in 1789–90–91* (George W. Harris, ed. Harrisburg, 1880) 45, 128–29, 163–65 [hereinafter: Maclay, *Sketches of Debate in the First Senate*].

eschewed by the new Congress. Power to initiate prosecution by information, thereby avoiding action by a grand jury, appears to have been deliberately denied the federal government through an amendment to the bill as originally proposed. Felonies punishable if committed on the high seas were not punishable by federal authority if committed on land, except on federal reservations as specified by amendment.[5] Punishable offenses committed – presumably on land – were very carefully attached to a precise federal interest – public securities, perjury in *federal* courts, bribery of *federal* judges, rescue of *federal* prisoners convicted of capital crimes. It is instructive to note also that the only reported debate we have about the first Crimes Act is the disagreement expressed in the House regarding the wisdom of making counterfeiting a capital crime and opposition to a clause in the Senate bill that permitted, at the discretion of the court, bodies of convicted murderers to be dissected following their execution.[6] To date, I do not know of any discussion of the question of the *extent* of federal jurisdiction to punish. It seems to have been commonly assumed that federal authority over crimes and punishments was to be limited, and limited solely to that which was specified by statute.

In their efforts to determine contemporary views regarding federal common law jurisdiction over crimes, scholars have used pretty much the same evidence, a few charges to grand juries made by some of the federal judges and a handful of cases decided in the federal circuit courts. It is hazardous, however, to fashion this type of evidence too tightly into abstract doctrinal logic, for the evidence itself takes on appropriate meaning only from its historical context. Most important of all it is necessary to keep firmly in mind the degree of uncertainty about 'federal law' that afflicted the first federal judges as they took up their duties. Supreme Court Justice William Cushing, for example, wrote to the District Judge

---

[5] DePauw, ed., *Documentary History of the First Federal Congress*, supra note 4 at i, 286, note 42. Note that the twelve amendments to the Constitution recommended by the House of Representatives to the states for adoption had not at this time been ratified. The ten later ratified comprising the specific Bill of Rights became part of the Constitution on December 15, 1791. The fifth amendment would provide that only by presentment or indictment by Grand Jury could a person be held to answer for a capital, 'or otherwise infamous' crime.

[6] An amendment to defeat the latter provision failed to pass. *Annals*, ii, 1572 (April 6, 1790). See report of debate on this issue in *Gazette of the United States* (Philadelphia) April 7, 10, and 14, 1790 and more substantially in Thomas Lloyd's notes on the debate. This manuscript is in the files of the Documentary History of the First Federal Congress, Ribbon Copy, Tingling Box 8, Washington, D. C. I am grateful to Charlene Bickford, the editor of these documents, for permitting me to use this material and other information about the bill in its passage through the Congress.

of Massachusetts that he was urging the completion of the Crimes bill (then pending before the Congress) 'without which I do not know in what predicament our Court will be as to carrying into Execution punishment for pyracies (sic) & felonies on the h. Seas & some other matters.'[7]

Examination of grand jury charges[8] during the first decade of the federal courts makes plain how infrequently the judges suggested indictments without statutory foundation. At the outset of the operation of the federal judicial system in 1790, Chief Justice John Jay had stated to the Grand Juries of the first circuit courts in the Eastern circuit that 'the objects of your inquiry are all offences committed against the laws of the United States' and reminded them that 'the laws of nations make part of the laws of this and every other civilized nation.'[9] James Wilson, far from referring to any non-statutory basis for grand jury action, discussed treason and the act to regulate collection of duties and told the jurors that Congress was expected to pass shortly a general law describing crimes and establishing punishments.[10] In 1791, following the bill's passage, Wilson went through the Crimes Act of 1790 section by section, explaining to the grand jurors that reference to the common law for the meaning of murder and manslaughter and other crimes was necessary since the crimes were not defined or described in the Act. There is, however, no mention of a jurisdiction over crimes apart from that provided by the statute.[11] In 1792, James Iredell referred to the criminal code as 'derived from the Legislature alone,' with crimes and punishments prescribed in Acts of Congress.[12] In charges to grand juries in 1793, when efforts to maintain neutrality became of paramount concern to the national government

---

7 William Cushing to John Lowell, April 4, 1790. Copy in files of Documentary History of the Supreme Court. I am grateful to Wythe Holt for calling this letter to my attention. The original is in the Free Library of Philadelphia.

8 The collection of charges at the Documentary History of the Supreme Court has been used here through the courtesy of Maeva Marcus, the editor of this project. I have referred to published charges where possible. Other references are to the charges in the files of the Documentary History.

9 April 4, 1790; Henry P. Johnston, ed., *The Correspondence and Public Papers of John Jay*, 4 vols. (New York, 1890–93) iii, 393 [hereinafter: Johnston, ed., *The Correspondence and Papers of Jay*]. The first of these charges were delivered prior to the passage of the Crimes Act of 1790. See Goebel, *History*, supra note 3 at 622. Jay noted that the penal statutes were few and related principally to the revenue.

10 April 12, 1790, at Philadelphia, published *Pennsylvania Gazette*, April 14, 1790.

11 February 21, 1791, at Philadelphia; May 23, 1791 at Richmond; Robert G. McCloskey, ed., *The Works of James Wilson*, 2 vols. (Cambridge, Mass., 1967) ii, 803–23.

12 October 12, 1792; Griffith J. McRee, ed., *The Life and Correspondence of James Iredell*, 2 vols (New York, 1949) ii, 369 [hereinafter: McRee, ed. *Life and Correspondence of Iredell*].

during the war between England and France, both Jay and James Wilson affirmed that the law of nations was part of the law of the United States although no act of Congress had so prescribed.[13] Iredell at this time noted 'some important differences of opinion' regarding the place of the law of nations within the laws of the United States.[14] By 1794, however, he had put aside his 'considerable doubts' and charged the grand jury that a right of prosecution existed for breaches of neutrality even where the legislature had made no provision.[15]

In 1796, he agreed that the law of nations was a part of the laws of the United States 'in the same manner and upon the same principle as any other offence committed against the common law.'[16] As national tension mounted stirred by criticism of the administration, Iredell in 1797 warned in his charges of the dangers of disunion from enemies foreign and domestic. 'The present situation of our country is such as to require the exertion of all good men to support and save it. I enter into no particulars, as the legislators of the United States are on the point of meeting, and for whose decision every worthy citizen must await with solicitude and respect.'[17] Although it is not clear when or whether a grand jury charge of William Paterson's was ever delivered prior to the passage of the Sedition Act of 1798, the judge's extensive warning about offenses 'of a treasonable and seditious nature' [which] 'have a tendency to deprive government of the confidence and affection of the people, to disturb our internal tranquility, and to break in upon and destroy the peace and good order of society'[18] rings of an invitation to indict at common law for these offenses in addition to those that violated the law of nations.

---

[13] Johnston, ed., *Correspondence and Papers of Jay*, supra note 9 at iii, 478–85; Francis Wharton, ed., *State Trials of the United States During the Administrations of Washington and Adams* (Philadelphia, 1849) 59–66 [hereinafter: Wharton, *State Trials*].

[14] May 7, 1793, Annapolis, McRee, ed., *Life and Correspondence of James Iredell*, supra note 12 at ii, 386–94.

[15] June 2, 1794, ibid. at ii, 423.

[16] April 12, 1796, ibid. at ii, 467–74.

[17] May 8, 1797, Annapolis; May 22, 1797, Richmond, ibid. at ii, 505–10. See also 511–13 for Iredell's denial that this charge to the Richmond Grand Jury had resulted in the presentment of Samuel Cabell for writing circular letters in which the Congressman had criticized the Adams administration. No action was taken by the federal district attorney.

[18] A copy of this undated charge, or perhaps a draft of a charge, is in the files of the Documentary History of the Supreme Court. The original is in the Paterson Papers at the Rutgers University Library. There is no reference in this document to legislation passed by Congress, which indicates that it would have been written prior to July 1798 when the Sedition Act passed. Other undated charges of Paterson's, obviously later, refer specifically to the Act, justify its passage, and uphold its constitutionality. Discussions with Wythe Holt and Stewart Jay about these charges have been particularly helpful.

In 1799, following the passage of the Alien and Sedition Act and the prosecutions of the Northampton insurgents for treason, Chief Justice Oliver Ellsworth charged a South Carolina Grand Jury in even broader terms. Offenses against the United States

> ... are chiefly defined in the statutes ... or they are acts manifestly subversive of the national government, or of some of its powers specified in the constitution. ... An offense consists in transgressing the sovereign will, whether that will be expressly or obviously implied. Conduct, therefore, clearly destructive of a government or its powers, which the people have ordained to *exist*, (italics in original) must be criminal. It is not necessary to particularize the acts falling within this description, because they are readily perceived, and are ascertained by known and established rules; I mean the maxims and principles of the common law of our land.

Ellsworth informed the grand jury that it should 'by the rules then, of a known law, matured by the reason of ages ... decide what acts are *misdemeanors*, (italics in original) on the *grounds of their opposing the existence of the national government, or the efficient exercise of its legitimate powers*'[19] (italics added).

So far as is known, only a very small number of cases before the federal circuit courts in the 1790s involved the issue of a federal common law of crimes: *Henfield* (1793),[20] tried before Supreme Court Justices Wilson and Iredell with District Judge Richard Peters; *Ravara* (1794)[21] before Chief Justice Jay and Peters; *Smith* (1797)[22] before Chief Justice Ellsworth and District Judge John Lowell; *Greenleaf* (1797)[23] before Ellsworth and Robert Troup; *Worrall* (1798)[24] before Justice Samuel Chase and District Judge Peters, followed by the initial proceedings at common law brought in 1798 on charges of seditious libel against Benjamin Bache before Judge Peters; those against John Daly Burk, Dr. James Smith, and William Durrell before District Judge John Sloss Hobart;[25] and the case of *Isaac*

---

[19] *Independent Chronicle* (Boston), June 10–13, 1799.

[20] U.S. v. Henfield, Wharton, *State Trials*, supra note 13 at 49; #6360, 11 Fed. Cas. (C.C. District of Pennsylvania, 1793) 1099.

[21] U.S. v. Ravara, 2 Dallas 299n; #16, 122 a, 27 Fed. Cas. (C.C. District of Pennsylvania, 1794) 714.

[22] U.S. v. Smith, 6 Dane Abr. 718; #16, 323, 27 Fed. Cas. (C.C. District of Massachusetts, 1797) 1147. The date 1792 given in Fed. Cas. is erroneous.

[23] U.S. v. Greenleaf, (C.C. District of New York, 1797) an unreported case that appears in a mss. volume of Court minutes for 1797, Harvard Law School. See the discussion of two indictments against Greenleaf in Goebel, *History*, supra note 3 at 629.

[24] U.S. v. Worrall, Wharton, *State Trials*, supra note 13 at 189; #16,766, 28 Fed. Cas. (C.C. District of Pennsylvania, 1798) 744.

[25] For discussion of the common law prosecutions for seditious libel, see James M. Smith, *Freedom's Fetters* (Ithaca, 1956) 200–02, 204–20, 385–90 [hereinafter: Smith, *Freedom's Fetters*].

Williams (1799)[26] tried before Chief Justice Ellsworth and District Judge Richard Law.

Some interesting facts issue from scrutiny of these familiar cases. *Henfield* and *Williams* involved violations of treaties and of the law of nations; neither in any way touched the questions of federal common law cognizance over domestic criminal acts. Greenleaf was indicted for libeling the British Consul General.[27] Jay and Peters agreed in *Ravara* that the offense (a consul from Genoa was accused of sending a threatening letter of extortion to the British minister) was indictable before the federal court, but as Julius Goebel has pointed out, the offense was clearly within section 27 of the Crimes Act of 1790.[28] In *Smith*, case after defendant was found guilty of counterfeiting bills of the Bank of the United States, a motion in arrest of judgment was made on the grounds that state courts had exclusive jurisdiction over common law crimes absent federal statute. Ellsworth and Lowell, acknowledging that the case could also have been prosecuted as a common law cheat in the state court, ruled however that the act establishing the Bank of the United States was constitutional, and that by the Constitution the federal judicial power extended to all cases arising under the laws of the United States. The Court carefully drew *Smith* case within the constitutional language on the ground that the bills of the Bank were made in pursuance of the statute that established the Bank. To counterfeit the bills therefore became a contempt of and a misdemeanor against the United States, punishable in the federal court notwithstanding the fact that no federal statute described or punished the counterfeiting of such bills. Nowhere in this opinion is there any indication that Ellsworth and Lowell believed that the federal courts were intended to exercise a jurisdiction over all crimes against the sovereignty that were known to the common law. Nor does it appear that they gave so broad a reading to the phrase 'laws of the United States' in Article III of the Constitution. The contrary is the case. The following year (1798), Congress enacted a statute punishing frauds committed on the Bank of the United States by counterfeiting,[29] and when another counterfeiting case, *U.S. v. Sylvester*, came in 1799 to the circuit court in Massachusetts, this

---

[26] U.S. v. Isaac Williams, Wharton, *State Trials*, 652; #17, 1708, 29 Fed. Cas. (C.C. District of Connecticut, 1799) 1330.

[27] A proposal made during the debate on the Crimes bill in the Senate making it 'highly criminal' to defame a foreign minister had been defeated. Maclay, *Sketches of Debate in the First Senate*, supra note 4 at 129.

[28] Goebel, *History*, supra note 3 at 627. Threatening personal violence to a public minister was made punishable.

[29] 2 Stat. 61 (June 27, 1798).

time before Justices Chase and Lowell, although the case has been mistaken for a common law case[30] it was more likely prosecuted under the statute. In *Worrall* case, an indictment for attempting to bribe the Commissioner of Revenue, Chase and Peters split dramatically on the common law issue. In 1798, critics of the Adams administration who were arrested on warrants issued by District Judges Peters and Hobart prior to the passage of the Sedition Act were bailed pending trial. It is possible that notes or drafts of an undated grand jury charge in the Paterson papers were prepared for use at the October term of court, 1798, when the New York cases were due to be tried before Paterson. The opportunity was there for another Supreme Court judge on circuit to counter Chase on the common law question, but the Sedition Act passed in July 1798, and for various reasons, none of the defendants indicted at common law was ever tried.

The evidence, then, is hardly conclusive for the position that there was a widely shared view among the early federal judges supportive of a federal common law of crimes. Twelve Supreme Court justices sat on the federal circuit bench during its first decade; only Wilson, Jay, Iredell, and Ellsworth are known to have held the view that the federal courts were vested with common law jurisdiction over crimes, and it is likely that Paterson shared this outlook by 1798.[31] Chase had vehemently opposed this doctrine, and of the views of others nothing is known. At the district court level, we know that Peters of Pennsylvania strongly supported the doctrine and that Hobart of New York and Lowell of Massachusetts had entertained initial common law criminal proceedings in their districts. Of the view of their colleagues, nothing is known. Perhaps it is more accurate, then, simply to note that there were differing views among some of the federal judges on the question of a federal common law of crimes, and that the opinions of most on the question remain unknown.[32]

[30] Leonard Levy, *Freedom of Speech and Press in Early American History: Legacy of Suppression*, supra note 3 at xvi; Leonard Levy, *Emergence of a Free Press*, supra note 3 at 278. Presser, 'Tale of Two Judges', supra note 3 at 69; Presser, 'Saving God's Republic', supra note 3 at 796, 146n. The case is unreported. See Final Record Book, Circuit Court, District of Massachusetts, Federal Records Center, Waltham, Mass.

[31] It is entirely possible that Bushrod Washington should be included with this group, although no direct evidence has come to light. In 1804, Washington directed an acquittal of a case argued on common law grounds; his language indicates that had the facts of the case been different, jurisdiction could have been accepted. U.S. v. Passmore, 4 Dallas 372; #16, 005, 27 Fed. Cas. (C.C. District of Pennsylvania, 1804) 458; Anonymous, 1 Washington C.C. 84; #475, 1 Fed. Cas. (C.C. District of Pennsylvania) 1032. See note 55 infra.

[32] I am in agreement with Julius Goebel that considerable uncertainty on the matter prevailed in the early years of the federal courts and that some of the judges do not seem

Furthermore, it is imperative to emphasize the distinction that even these judges themselves made about the common law with reference to federal jurisdiction. *The law of nations* as a part of the common law system of jurisprudence they did indeed appear to hold to be within the federal judicial power as among the 'laws of the United States' within the language of Article III of the Constitution.[33] There was no such agreement, however, with respect to common law jurisdiction over those crimes that were offenses within the domestic, not international, realm. *Worrall* (1798), where the court divided on the jurisdictional question, points up the conflicting views precisely. Here, Justice Chase vehemently held that the United States had no common law and that consequently no indictments for criminal offenses could be maintained merely at common law in the federal courts. It was, he said, the federal Constitution that was the sole source of all the jurisdiction of the national government, and no department of the government could ever assume any power that was not expressly granted by that instrument. It was as essential that Congress define crimes and punishments as that it should establish courts to try the criminal or pronounce sentence. The silence of the Constitution and federal statutes could not, in his view, be remedied by resorting to the common law for definition and punishment of crimes. District Judge Peters, was equally vehement, on the opposite position: 'Whenever a government has been established, I have always supposed, that a power to preserve itself was a necessary and inseparable concomitant.' The power to punish misdemeanors, a common law power, was one that Peters believed the United States constitutionally possessed, although from which part of the Constitution he does not say. 'It might have been exercised by congress (sic) in the form of a legislative act; but it may also, in my opinion, be enforced in a course of judicial proceeding. Whenever an offense aims at the subversion of any federal institution or at the corruption of its public

---

to have made up their minds on the point. Goebel, *History*, supra note 3 at 622. Kent Newmyer states that there were judges and lawyers of learning and ability on both sides. R. Kent Newmyer, *Supreme Court Justice Joseph Story: Statesman of the Old Republic* (Chapel Hill, 1985) 102.

[33] As did the first Attorneys-General in Edmund Randolph to William Rawle, March 12, 1793, Rawle Papers, III, Historical Society of Pennsylvania; William Bradford to Randolph, July 6, 1795, 'Opinions of the Attorney General', No. 123, 33; Charles Lee to Timothy Pickering, January 26, 1797, 'Opinions of the Attorney General', 26 Cong., 2 Sess., *House Executive Documents*, No. 123, 39–40. Notice also the earlier *Respublica v. DeLongchamps*, 1 Dallas 111 (Oyer and Terminer at Philadelphia, 1784) in which Chief Justice Thomas McKean had held that the law of nations 'in its full extent' was part of the municipal law of Pennsylvania. I am indebted to Sandra Van Burkleo for this reference.

officers, it is an offense against the well-being of the United States; *from its very nature* it is recognizable under their authority, and consequently, it is within the jurisdiction of this court by virtue of the 11th section of the judicial act' (italics added).[34] To be sure, here is a statement that was in essence declaratory of the broad reach of English common law criminal jurisprudence, and Chief Justice Ellsworth proceeded in similar vein in his 1799 grand jury charge when he declared that conduct destructive of a government ordained by the people must be criminal. Definition of such conduct, he asserted, was readily ascertainable by the principles of the common law, the law in every part of the Union at the time of the making of the Constitution and therefore attaching to the federal government 'for purposes of exposition and enforcement.'[35] But which position should we take as commonplace and which as exceptional?

Chase's role is important, for it is Chase's passionate denial of this doctrine in *Worrall* (1798) that provides the most substantial evidence of countervailing judicial opinion.[36] Given their differences over the

---

[34] U.S. v. Worrall, 2 Dallas (U.S.) 384 at 395, 400; The Judiciary Act of 1789, 1 Stat. 73, sec. 11. 'That the circuit courts . . . shall have exclusive cognizance of all crimes and offenses cognizable under the authority of the United States, except where this act otherwise provides. . . .'

[35] *Independent Chronicle* (Boston) June 10–13, 1799.

[36] In his argument to arrest judgment after the jury convicted Worrall, Alexander James Dallas declared that sec. 11 of the Judiciary Act did not confer jurisdiction on the court because that language referred only to express constitutional provisions or statutes passed by Congress. Worrall's crime, attempting to bribe a federal officer, and the place where the offense took place were not so specified. The nature of the federal government, he argued, was one of limited, enumerated, and delegated powers; these powers could not take effect until they were exercised through a statute. William Rawle, the prosecutor, followed a line of argument analogous to that which Judges Ellsworth and Lowell had taken in *Smith's Case* in Massachusetts on circuit in 1797 – that the office of Commissioner of Revenue had been established by act of Congress and that therefore an attempt to bribe him could be inferred to be an offense 'arising under a law of the United States.' However, it was when Rawle continued his argument to comment that federal cases could be brought at common law, that Chase cut him off, announced that the indictment could not be maintained, and then delivered from the bench a lengthy opinion on the subject. Wharton, *State Trials*, supra note 13 at 194ff. Presser suggests that the opinion seems to have been written anticipating Rawle's argument. Presser, 'Tale of Two Judges,' supra note 3 at 61. This is quite plausible. The year before, also in Philadelphia, Dallas, as counsel for a defendant convicted in a Pennsylvania court for forging names of soldiers to powers of attorney in order to receive military land warrants granted by acts of Congress, had stated that because the question of the common law jurisdiction of the federal courts, in criminal cases, had not been decided, it was his duty to bring it before the court. He moved to arrest judgment on the grounds that the offense arose under laws of the United States and was therefore exclusively cognizable in the federal court. The court overruled the motion upholding the

existence of a federal common law of crimes, Chase and Peters suggested that Worrall's counsel put the case in a form that would enable it to go to the Supreme Court for a definitive ruling. When counsel declined to do so, the judges 'after a short consultation' exercised the discretion of common law judges and sentenced Worrall to the traditional common law punishment, fine and imprisonment.[37] Sentence could not have been imposed unless agreed upon by both judges.

Much has been made of Chase's supposed 'change of mind' at this juncture on the question of a federal common law and the reach of federal judicial power, but this deserves another look. In a note on the case in his *State Trials* (1849), Francis Wharton suggested that Chase, after familiarizing himself with views of others on the Supreme Court, had altered his opinion about the jurisdiction to punish. Wharton's fictional

jurisdiction of the state court on the ground that section 11 of the Judiciary Act 'may be reasonably supposed not to have contemplated this case, which by no act of congress is designated as a crime, nor has it any appointed punishment.' Commonwealth v. Schaffer, Mayor's Court of Philadelphia, 4 Dallas Appendix xxvi (April, 1797). *Smith's Case* was also decided in 1797 in the federal circuit court in Massachusetts. The tempo of political partisanship increased markedly during 1797 and Federalists moved to silence attacks on the government. The first instance of this came when a federal grand jury in Richmond on May 22, 1797, presented as a real evil the circular letters of several members of Congress, particularly those of Samuel J. Cabell, for endeavoring 'at a time of real public danger to disseminate unfounded calumnies against the happy government of the United States.' Many assumed, although this was denied by jurors and judge, that the presentment was the result of Justice Iredell's charge, referred to at note 17 supra. Republican leaders were aroused by the presentment, and under the leadership of Vice-President Jefferson a petition he drafted was presented to the Virginia House of Delegates that adopted a resolution denouncing the presentment. Even though the presentment was not acted on and Cabell was never tried, Republicans were alarmed by the episode, while many Federalists applauded the action of the Richmond Grand Jury. Noble E. Cunningham, Jr. *Circular Letters of Congressmen to Their Constituents 1789–1829*, 3 vols. (Chapel Hill, 1978) xxxvi–xxxix, 67–78; Adrienne Koch and Henry Ammon, 'Madison's Defense of Civil Liberties', *William and Mary Quarterly*, 3d ser. v (1948) 152–53.

This sequence of episodes may be relevant to consideration of *Worrall*. Worrall was indicted on April 12, 1798. When he appeared on April 14 Dallas moved for further time to plead and it was granted. Trial and sentencing took place on April 26. Minutes of the United States Circuit Court for the District of Pennsylvania, April term, 1798. Prosecutor William Rawle, defense counsel Levy and Dallas and Judges Peters and Chase, after the twelve day interval, may all have come with parts prepared in advance. The eagerness of the prosecutor and the judges that the common law issue be settled is clear from their unsuccessful effort to have the case then framed for a definitive ruling from the Supreme Court. Wharton, *State Trials*, supra note 13 at 198–99. The hot debate on the recently introduced alien bill with that on the sedition bill soon to follow (and the outcome of each unclear) may also have contributed to their desire to have the high court determine the jurisdictional question as speedily as possible.

[37] 2 Dallas 384; Wharton, *State Trials*, supra note 13 at 199.

scenario in which Chase presumably underwent instant conversion from
an opinion expressed only minutes before has caused scholars – particularly Stephen Presser – untold difficulty, for such behavior does not square
with much of what we know about Chase. Accepting Wharton's account,
Presser has uncomfortably concluded that Chase's views on the law were
'malleable, if not a complete turnaround.'[38] There is, I believe, less here
than meets the eye, for Judge Peter's own account of the episode provides
a far simpler explanation, and one more plausible.

... As to the objection to Common Law Jurisdiction in Cases of nonenumerated
Crimes, it was first started by Chase in a Case of a Cheat & Misdemeanor
practiced on Tench Coxe in a Contract made by him for the U.S. Chase declared
it out of our Jurisdiction, as being a Case only at Common Law but he allowed the
Legislature ought to give Jurisdiction. I divided the Court; being of the opinion as I
am now, that we have Jurisdiction; tho' I am now controlled by the Opinion of the
Supreme Court. While he was pondering, after Conviction by the Jury, I practiced
a pious maneuver & he joined in pronouncing a very just, but mild Sentence. He
never cordially forgave me. The gentle Punishment I Professed, deluded him; and
he did not see, 'till too late, that he had pronounced Judgment with a divided
Court. I thought any punishment was better than none. I laughed him out of his
juridical Pet.[39]

---

[38] Presser, 'Two Judges', supra note 3 at 69. See also 'Saving God's Republic', supra
note 3 at 798–799. Presser's work gives us the most substantial analysis of Chase's
jurisprudence. For a different jurisprudential interpretation of the views of Peters and
Chase in this case see Morton Horwitz, *The Transformation of American Law*, supra
note 3 at 11–12.

[39] Peters to Timothy Pickering, March 30, 1816, Pickering Papers, 31: 89, Massachusetts
Historical Society, Boston. This letter is written shortly after the Supreme Court decision
in U.S. v. Coolidge, 1 Wheaton 415 (1816) in which the Court refused to overturn its
1812 opinion in U.S. v. Hudson and Goodwin, 7 Cranch 32 that there was no federal
common law of crimes. The language of the report 2 Dallas 384 at 393: 'The court being
divided in opinion, it became a doubt, whether sentence could be pronounced upon
the defendant; and a wish was expressed by the judges and the attorney of the district,
that the case might be put into such a form, as would admit of obtaining the ultimate
decision of the supreme court, upon the important principle of the discussion. But the
counsel for the prisoner did not think themselves authorized to enter into a compromise
of that nature. The court, after a short consultation, and declaring, that the sentence was
mitigated in consideration of the defendant's circumstances, proceeded to adjudge.'
    Worrall was sentenced to prison for three months, fined $200 and to be committed
until the fine was paid. It is Wharton who adds the speculation about the nature of the
'short consultation'; there is no evidence for this. I would speculate that it is equally
likely that the judges were consulting given counsel's unwillingness to enter into 'a
compromise', in order to send the case to the Supreme Court. (Imprisonment followed
by a petition for *habeas corpus* to the high court is the best guess of procedure available
at that time.) When Peters proposed his 'just, but mild' sentence for the convicted man
because 'any punishment was better than none' Chase agreed.

Presser observes that even if he did reverse himself on the question of a common law of crimes, Chase maintained until the end of his career that, English practice notwithstanding, it was the job of the judge to follow the directions of the legislature.[40] In my view, Chase did not change his mind on the common law question but remained opposed to the extensive power this sweeping doctrine would put into federal authority and the federal courts and into the hands of judges. Unless and until authority was bestowed by the sovereign will of the people through the legislative body, he would have none of it. Given authorization by the national legislature, no judge was readier than he to prosecute offenders against 'the national will,' whether they be libelers or counterfeiters.[41] As I have indicated, federal statute, not common law, provided jurisdiction to punish for *Sylvester's Case*. The Sedition Act would supply it for those who would criticize the Federalist administration.[42] It was not necessary, moreover, to be a committed member of the opposition Republican party to oppose a federal common law of crimes, as the debates over the passage of that legislation made plain. Even so stalwart a Federalist leader as Robert Goodloe Harper took the position that there was no common law jurisdiction with the federal courts and that a statute was necessary.[43]

Throughout the 1790s, the federal judiciary had become increasingly part of the political partisanship that divided Federalist from

[40] Presser, 'Saving God's Republic,' supra note 3 at 796 note 145, quoting Chase's 1804 opinion in *Penn's Lessees v. Pennington*. See also Chase's charge to grand juries in 1805 and 1806 at note 58 supra.

[41] For interesting parallel views expressed by Chase regarding civil litigation, see *Turner v. Bank of North America*, 4 Dallas, 8 (1799). For the continuing disagreement between Chase and Peters over a federal common law of crimes and Chase's refusal to punish absent statute, see Peters to Pickering Dec. 8, 1806, Pickering Papers, xxvii, Dec. 5, 1807, xxviii, 99, Massachusetts Historical Society.

[42] 1 Stat. 596 (July 14, 1798).

[43] *Annals*, 5 Cong., 2 sess., 2141. July 10, 1798. On the other hand, another leading Federalist, Harrison Gray Otis, insisted that federal judicial power and hence the jurisdiction of federal courts did extend to offenses at common law. Otis argued that within the language of Article III, the common law was incorporated in the phrase 'cases in law and equity arising under the Constitution' rather than in the phrase 'laws of the United States.' Ibid. at 2146–147. In Virginia in 1798, John Marshall, a Federalist candidate for the House of Representatives, in a public political statement said that he would have opposed passage of the Act had he been in Congress at the time. To a Freeholder, Sept. 20, 1798 in Herbert A. Johnson, et al., eds., *The Papers of John Marshall*, 4 vols. (Chapel Hill, 1970–1984) iii, 505. Marshall thought the Alien and Sedition Laws useless since each state had the authority to punish seditious libel and to regulate the activity of aliens. Ibid. at 496, 499 note 1.

Republicans on many issues.[44] By 1798, the division of the federal judges at the seat of the government in *Worrall* was followed by Peters's subsequent insistence (sitting alone and despite Chase's opinion in that case) on accepting a charge of seditious libel brought at common law against the editor of the *Aurora*, the opposition newspaper.[45] The Federalist Congress quickly clarified the jurisdiction as unmistakably as it had done with counterfeiting – by statute. The political context of the *timing* of *Worrall* gives it added significance, for the assertion of a federal common law jurisdiction over *domestic* offenses was a potent torch to toss onto an already flammable mix. Especially was this the case when Federalists in the Congress were determined to bring a halt to criticism of their administration of the national government. The inherited common law doctrine of seditious libel aimed at criticism of the administration struck at the heart of political opposition as counterfeiting did not. Moreover, it threatened more directly earlier understandings of the limited role the federal government was assumed to play in criminal matters. It seems clear that deliberate measures were being taken by Secretary of State Pickering to prosecute seditious libel at common law and by the judicial branch to determine the question of federal jurisdiction over this offense during 1798. The Federalist Congress would act as well. By July 14, 1798, the Sedition Act became law with the signature of President Adams.

After the passage of the Sedition Act, Republicans were powerless to halt vigorous prosecution under its authority, although Jefferson, Madison, and other Virginia Republicans explicitly denied 'that the common

---

[44] For a succinct summary, see Charles Warren, *The Supreme Court in United States History*, 3 vols., (Boston, 1924) i, 158–168.

[45] Smith, *Freedom's Fetters*, supra note 25 at 200–04; Goebel, *History*, supra note 3 at 632. Benjamin Franklin Bache was arrested on a warrant issued by Peters on June 26. Argument on the validity of the warrant and a federal common law jurisdiction was carried on again before Peters between Rawle, the District Attorney and Moses Levy, and Dallas, who now, in behalf of Bache, cited Chase's position in *Worrall*. Peters agreed to bail Bache after sureties were given and set trial for the October term of the circuit court. The Sedition Act became law on July 14 and Bache died of yellow fever in September before being tried. In New York, in July 1798, prior to the passage of the Act, John Daly Burk, editor of the Republican *Time Piece*, was brought before District Judge John Sloss Hobart by the federal attorney, Richard Harison, and charged with seditious libel. Burk was released on bail by Hobart pending his trial, similarly to be held in October before Supreme Court William Paterson sitting as circuit judge. This case never came to trial either. Smith, *Freedom's Fetters*, supra note 25 at 211–20.

See above at note 18 for Paterson's notes, perhaps planned to be used in this trial, on the question of federal common law jurisdiction over crimes.

or unwritten law made any part of the laws of the United States in their united and national capacities.'[46] So did Virginia Federalist John Marshall. In private correspondence late in 1800, Marshall denied that anyone before 1798–99 seriously maintained the proposition that the common law of England had been adopted as the common law of the United States by the Constitution. The 'strange and absurd doctrine,' he charged, was first attributed to the federal judiciary by 'some frothy newspaper publication in Richmond something more than twelve months past.'[47] Be that as it may, the passage in February, 1801, of a radical new Judiciary Act, with its extensive trial jurisdiction over federal question cases together with the appointment of the Federalist 'midnight judges,' fed further Republican antipathy toward the role of the federal judiciary.[48] By the time Jefferson was inaugurated as President, the broad question of federal common law rested unsettled at the level of the trial courts of the federal system.

Unsettled it remained. In the hope of laying to rest the question of a federal common law jurisdiction over crimes, the new President discontinued the prosecution against William Duane under the now expired Sedition Act and immediately directed a new prosecution against the editor under whatever law it could be rested. The federal grand jury, however, found no law against criticism of Congress and refused to return an indictment.[49]

[46] Madison's Report on the Virginia Resolutions, December 1799–January 1800, Gaillard Hunt, ed. *Writings of Madison*, 9 vols. (New York, 1900–1910) vi, 371–82. The Senators from that state were instructed by the legislature to oppose the passage of any law founded on or recognizing the principle 'lately advanced' that the common law of England was in force under the national government. James Madison, *Letters and Other Writings*, 4 vols. (Congress ed., Philadelphia, 1865) iv, 533–539. Not only the doctrine of a federal common law of crimes concerned the Republicans. Fears of the incorporation into federal jurisprudence of the common law in many civil causes were equally great. Jefferson to Pinkney, Oct. 29, 1799, Paul Leicester Ford, ed. *The Writings of Thomas Jefferson*, 10 vols. (New York, 1897) vii, 398 [hereinafter: Ford, ed., *Writings of Jefferson*]; to Granger, Aug. 13, 1800, vii, 450; to Randolph, Aug. 18, 1799, 383–84; 'Anas', March 5, 11, 12, 19, April 29, 1800, i, 285, 286, 288, 291.
[47] Marshall to St. George Tucker, November 27, 1800. Marshall Papers, Ac. 2354, Library of Congress. The Editors of *The Papers of John Marshall* identify the recipient, unnamed in the original manuscript, as St. George Tucker. I am grateful to Professor Wythe Holt for informing me of this.
[48] Kathryn Turner, 'Federalist Policy and the Judiciary Act of 1801,' *William and Mary Quarterly*, 3d ser., xxii (1965) 3–32. There is no clear evidence to indicate whether or not the specific inclusion of federal question jurisdiction in this legislation was related to the unsettled state of doctrine over a federal common law of crimes.
[49] Levi Lincoln to Alexander James Dallas, March 25, 1801, in Jefferson Papers, vol. cxi, Library of Congress; Jefferson to Albert Gallatin, November 12, 1801, in Ford, ed., *Writings of Jefferson*, supra note 46 at viii, 57n; Jefferson to Duane, May 23, 1801, to

Only months after Jefferson's inauguration, the Federalist judges of the
Circuit Court for the new District of Columbia instructed the Republican
District Attorney to institute a common law prosecution for libel against
the *National Intelligencer* for publishing an attack on the judiciary. The
Grand Jury returned a presentment but the district attorney refused to
act, and subsequently the jury refused to indict.⁵⁰ Perhaps Jefferson was
incensed by this reminder of earlier Federalist common law prosecutions,
but at the same time his own Attorney General, Levi Lincoln, ordered a
prosecution at common law in Kentucky in a case involving the murder
of Indians by white men and the rescue of one of the murderers by a
mob. This was ordered dropped after the District Attorney, a Federalist
who stated to the Court his own opinion of lack of jurisdiction, reminded
Secretary of War Dearborn 'of the public heat his party [Republicans]
had raised about the common law.'⁵¹

R.R. Livingston, May 31, 1801, to Edward Livingston, Nov. 1, 1801, ibid. 54–56, 55n–
57n, 57n–58n, U.S. v. Duane, Circuit Court, Eastern District of Pennsylvania, Criminal
Cases (Oct. 1801), Record Group 21, National Archives. The fullest account of the
complicated Duane litigation is in Smith, *Freedom's Fetters*, supra note 25 at 277–306.

⁵⁰ George L. Haskins and Herbert A. Johnson, *History of the Supreme Court of the United
States* Part I by Haskins; Part II by Johnson (New York and London, 1981), 161 [here-
inafter: Haskins and Johnson, *Supreme Court*]. Both Haskins and Charles Warren,
Supreme Court, i, 195, interpret this episode as the precipitant for Jefferson's policy
decision to attack the federal court system. Richard E. Ellis portrays the President as
more undecided at this juncture. Richard E. Ellis, *The Jeffersonian Crisis: Court and Politics in the Young Republic* (New York, 1971) 40–41 [hereinafter: Ellis, *The Jeffersonian
Crisis*].

⁵¹ Joseph H. Daviess, 'Sketch of the Political Profiles of Three Presidents,' in *A View of the
President's Conduct Concerning the Conspiracy of 1806* (Frankfort, Ky., 1807) 59n–
60n. On this matter, see the document by Jefferson discussing the relationship between
federal statute and state law, *Observations on the Force and Obligation of the Common
Law in the United States, on the Occasion of Hardin's Case, in Kentucky* Andrew
A. Lipscomb and Albert E. Bergh, eds. *The Writings of Thomas Jefferson*, 20 vols.
(Washington, 1903), xvii, 410–17. Although the document is dated November 11, 1812,
in this edition of Jefferson's writings, this may be owing to an error in transcription of the
original document, which has since been lost. Court records make clear that Hardin's
case (the rescue of one of the murderers by a mob led by Hardin) was in 1802. The
episode is discussed in Mary K. Bonsteel Tachau, *Federal Courts in the Early Republic
Kentucky 1789–1816* (Princeton, 1978) 128–33. In 1802, Lincoln, replying to an inquiry
regarding a riot in which the Spanish Ambassador had been insulted, stated that in such
a case the law of nations was part of the municipal law of the state, there being no
federal statute recognizing the offense. Levi Lincoln to Secretary of State [Madison],
May 12, 1802, 'Opinions of the Attorney General', 26 Cong., 2 sess., *House Executive
Documents* No. 123, 68–69. Compare this with *U.S. v. Greenleaf* (1797) cited above at
note 23 in which a conviction was obtained in federal court for a comparable offense.
Goebel, *History*, supra note 3 at 629.

Argument against such jurisdiction constitutes one of the many lines of debate over the repeal of the Judiciary Act of 1801 that dominated the Congress in the early months of 1802,[52] inaugurating a Republican policy to restrict the power of the federal judiciary. Republican prosecutions of Federalist editors for seditious libel were undertaken in the state courts in 1803, 1804, and 1806,[53] the president believing that the restraints of state law were sufficient if applied. Prosecution of seditious libel, whether at common law or under statute, was clearly perceived more as a matter of states rights than of federal jurisdiction.[54]

In the federal courts, in contrast, in cases less flamboyant politically than those invoking seditious libel, common law jurisdiction continued to be asserted by Republicans when convenient to do so. In 1804, Alexander Dallas, now the Jeffersonian District Attorney in Pennsylvania, attempted to support indictments for perjury on common law grounds, arguing that 'according to the opinions of some of the judges of the supreme court (sic),' the perjury charged was indictable at common law. Here, Justice Bushrod Washington directed an acquittal on other grounds, and the case seems to have drawn no public attention whatever.[55] Nor did judicial resort to common law procedures in federal criminal cases where

[52] The most extensive recent account of the repeal is Ellis, *The Jeffersonian Crisis*, supra note 50 at 36–52. See also Haskins and Johnson, *Supreme Court*, supra note 50 at 163–81.

[53] Federalists prosecuted included Harry Croswell of *The Wasp* of Hudson, N.Y. in 1803, Joseph Dennie of the *Port Folio* of Philadelphia in 1804, William Dickinson of the Lancaster, Pa. *Intelligencer and Weekly Advertiser* in 1806. See respectively Julius Goebel, *The Law Practice of Alexander Hamilton*, 2 vols. (New York, 1964–1969), i, 779 and 775–848 for extensive discussion and documents regarding the case from its inception through *People v. Croswell*, 3 Johnson (N.Y.) 337 (1807); Respublica v. Dennie, 4 Yeates (Pa.) 267 (1805); *Aurora* (Phila.) May 17, 1806.

[54] Jefferson to Thomas McKean, February 19, 1803, Ford, ed., *Writings of Jefferson*, supra note 46 at viii, 218; Jefferson's article signed 'Fair Play,' which he sent to Levi Lincoln in June 1803 with a view to publication, ibid., 238; to Abigail Adams, Sept. 11, 1804, ibid. 312n. See Leonard Levy, *Emergence of a Free Press*, supra note 3 at 307–08. In several states at this time, the general question of the common law within the state had become interwoven in local political conflicts. Ellis provides the best discussion. Ellis, *Jeffersonian Crisis*, supra note 50 at 129–30, 176–80, 189–91, 205–206.

[55] The indictment was for perjury under the repealed bankruptcy act of 1800. Washington directed an acquittal on the grounds that the repeal of the law barred criminal proceedings under the former statute. Because the common law definition of perjury did not cover the facts of the case, the common law could not, in any event, he said, here serve as the basis for the indictment. U.S. v. Passmore, 4 Dallas 372, #16,005, 27 Fed. Cas. (C.C. District of Pennsylvania, 1804) 458; Anonymous, 1 Washington C.C. 84, #475, 1 Fed. Cas. (C.C. District of Pennsylvania) 1032. These are clearly the same case. The report of Anonymous includes Washington's charge to the jury omitted in the report

Congress had made no substitute.[56] The disagreement between Chase
and Peters about punishing criminals by proceeding at common law had
erupted again because Chase was convinced that the federal courts had
no jurisdiction over assaults and batteries and many crimes at sea that
were not specifically designated in the Crimes Act. 'A most flagitious
culprit had escaped punishment entirely for the murder of his cabin boy,'
Peters wrote, because the blow was at sea and the death on land and
'Chase would not agree to punish him even for an Assault and Battery;
under a Whim that our Courts could not, *in criminal cases*, (italics in
original) proceed at Common Law.'[57] Chase continued to emphasize

of *U.S. v. Passmore*. Dallas in argument cited *Ravara, Williams*, and *Worrall*. Coun-
sel for defendant split on the common law issue, Dickerson denying its validity and
Rawle admitting it. Following this decision, two similar cases were nol pros'd by Dallas.
U.S. v. Howland, U.S. v. Litman, C.C. E. Dist. of Pa., Criminal Cases (1804), Record
Group 21, National Archives. At the same term, several indictments were returned for
assault on the high seas. Details regarding these assaults are not clear from the record.
Whether prosecutions of this sort represent instances in which Washington decided that
the federal courts had a common law jurisdiction is not possible to say. In 1806 in *U.S.
v. Magill*, 4 Dallas 426, Washington stated, 'There are, undoubtedly, in my opinion,
many crimes and offenses against the authority of the United States, which have not
been specifically defined by law; for, I have often decided, that the federal courts have a
common law jurisdiction in criminal cases;. . . .' Washington does not say in which cases
he did so and none is known. It is plausible that the lesser offenses committed by seamen
may be the answer. Difficulties in determining Washington's views are discussed above
at note 31.
56 U.S. v. Richard Johns, 4 Dallas 412, #15,481, 26 Fed. Cas. (C.C. District of Pennsylvania,
April, 1806), 616.
57 Richard Peters to Timothy Pickering, Dec. 8, 1806, Pickering Papers, 27:334, Massachusetts Historical Society. Pickering, who had been Secretary of State from 1795 to
1800, was at this time one of the Senators from Massachusetts. Identification of the unreported case to which Peters refers must remain uncertain. It should not be confused with
U.S. v. Magill, 4 Dallas 426 discussed above, supra note at 55. Peter's letter makes clear
that there are two different cases, one in which he sat with Chase and another (*Magill*)
with Washington. Chase and Peters sat together only twice, in the April term 1798 and
in the April term 1800. In the latter term (the one in which John Fries was being tried
for treason and William Duane indicted under the Sedition Act), the grand jury returned
a true bill against William Hampton for assault and battery; the record indicates that
Hampton defaulted, forfeited his bond, and did not come to trial. Nathaniel Calvert,
arraigned on the same charge, disappears from extant records. One of these may be
the case to which Peters here refers. Also at this term, three others were indicted for
murder and piracy, tried, and convicted. A motion made by Dallas to arrest judgment
was overruled and they were sentenced to hang. Chase would of course have had no
scruples over this punishment since jurisdiction of the offense on the high seas was clear.
U.S. v. Burger or Burroughs, U.S. v. Peterson or LaCroix, U.S. v. Baker or Boulanger,
Minutes of the United States Circuit Court, District of Pennsylvania, April 14, 15, 16,
21, 23, 24, 1800. The latter case is also referred to in Peters to Pickering, Dec. 5, 1807,
Pickering Papers, 28: 99, Massachusetts Historical Society.

the necessity for statutory authorization of federal jurisdiction,[58] and when another case came before Peters sitting with Bushrod Washington in 1806, with facts identical to the one in which Chase had refused to punish, both judges, employing the common law definition of murder on the high seas, agreed that both the stroke and the death must occur on the high seas and refused jurisdiction over the crime, which was unprovided for by statute. Washington held that neither could such prosecution be sustained within the constitutional grant of judicial power over 'all cases of admiralty and maritime jurisdiction' since the admiralty and maritime jurisprudence of England would not include such a case independent of acts of parliament. Congress, however, 'exercising the constitutional power to define felonies on the high seas, may certainly provide that a mortal stroke on the high seas, wherever the death may happen, shall be adjudged to be a felony.'[59] Writing Senator Timothy Pickering about the case, Peters advised, 'This ought to be put out of Doubt; tho' I do not like anything that shews the Common Law is not available.' Another major problem was federal jurisdiction over lesser offenses, which Peters believed was 'so very absurdly described' in the Judiciary Act of 1789 that he had not 'for years' taken cognizance of them or called a Grand Jury. He drafted remedial legislation to give the District courts jurisdiction over all crimes less than capital committed in Districts (at sea or in forts or places under federal authority) that, if committed in states, would be tried and punished in their inferior criminal courts. This would take care of assaults and batteries, forgeries, frauds, and thefts, he wrote Pickering, ironically adding, 'But whether you or I might not be whipped if some new or old political dogma should by a State be declared a Crime I have not calculated. On this view of the subject, it would perhaps be best to enumerate the Crimes.'[60]

---

[58] When discussing the jurisdiction of the federal courts in his instructions to the federal grand jury in 1805 (apparently used in June and October 1806 as well), Chase stated that by the Judiciary Act of 1789 'it is your Duty to enquire of *all* Breaches of any of the laws of the United States, committed within this District; Or within the jurisdiction of this court by any *Statutory* provision of which you shall have any knowledge, *or* shall receive information from witnesses *or* concerning which this Court shall direct you to make enquiry....' Instructions to Grand Jury, May 1, 1805, Samuel Chase Papers, Maryland Historical Society, Baltimore (italics in original).

[59] U.S. v. James Magill, 4 Dallas 426, #15,676, 26 Fed. Cas. 1088 (C.C. District of Pennsylvania, October, 1806). Both the Constitution and the Judiciary Act of 1789 gave admiralty jurisdiction to the federal courts but did not clarify what substantive law the federal courts were to apply.

[60] Peters to Pickering, Dec. 8, 1806, Pickering Papers 27:334–35, Enclosure, 335A, Massachusetts Historical Society. Pickering replied in favor of enumerating the crimes within

A year later, nothing having been accomplished, Peters complained again about defects in the federal criminal jurisdiction, which extended by statute only to crimes on the high seas, leaving those committed below low water mark outside federal jurisdiction and, since outside the body of any county, outside state jurisdiction as well. He himself had not awaited Congressional action.

> ...I who believe in the *Common Law*, have been willing to go farther to remedy the Evils, than comport with the Opinion of its Adversaries. When I meet with Occasions, *in my Place*, I always act as if no Dispute existed about that Matter; & am careless about Consequences, where my Mind is made up.... As to *Admiralty Jurisdiction* as to Place, & the *Common Law* Jurisdiction over Offences, I think more liberally (tho' not extravagantly) than some *tight laced* or time serving People. Yet there is no Man less remarkable for being hungry after *Jurisdiction*.... In Cases of the lower Offences–Assaults & Batteries etc. I take Jurisdiction & punish under Indictments at *Common Law*, if committed below Low Water Mark, & out of any State Jurisdiction.

All the Judges but Chase, who was 'particularly squeamish on such subjects,' Peters claimed to agree with him about this.[61]

Congress left the legal profession to its disputes and left district judges to grapple with their problems as best they could. Not until political combat merged with the legal issue would the question of a federal common law jurisdiction over crimes be resurrected again in the public life of the nation. It is hardly surprising that the issue of seditious libel brought it forward.

The background of *U.S. v. Hudson and Goodwin*, the case in which the Supreme Court in 1812 was to rule against the federal government's authority to punish acts made illegal merely by the common law, has been well told in much detail, and there is no need for me to repeat it here.[62] I do want to emphasize, however, the political antagonism that gave birth to this litigation. In Connecticut in 1806, where the Federalists controlled the state government, a prosecution for seditious libel was begun in the state court (under statutory authority) against the editor of the

---

the jurisdiction of the District Court in order to create uniformity throughout the federal system because of the great diversity in the offences cognizable by the inferior courts of the different states. Pickering to Peters, Dec. 30, 1806, Peters Papers, X, 114, Historical Society of Pennsylvania, Philadelphia.

[61] Peters to Pickering, December 5, 1807, Pickering Papers, 28:99, Massachusetts Historical Society.

[62] 7 Cranch (U.S.) 32 (1812). See William Winslow Crosskey, *Politics and the Constitution*, 3 vols. (Chicago, 1953) ii, 770–82, whose account is followed closely by Leonard Levy, *Jefferson and Civil Liberties: The Darker Side* (Cambridge, Mass., 1963) 61–67.

Jeffersonian Litchfield *Witness*.[63] Jefferson's newly appointed District Judge in Connecticut, Pierpont Edwards, retaliated by inviting the federal Grand Jury to return common law indictments for libels against the President. He reminded the Grand Jury that he delivered to them the sentiments of a majority of Supreme Court justices. 'Whatever may be my own opinion upon the question, are there any common law offenses recognizable by the courts of the United States? I deem it my duty to declare to you the law, as pronounced by those judges.'[64] The case against the defendants was continued; five years would elapse before it would be determined by the Supreme Court. There is no evidence that Jefferson himself initiated these prosecutions in the federal courts, nor did the President a few months later urge resort to a federal common law of crimes in his strenuous efforts to have Aaron Burr indicted for something.[65] Instead he sought from Congress (unsuccessfully, as it turned out) legislation that would have embraced English common-law doctrine by making conspiracy to commit insurrection, whether successful or not, a federal crime for which the degree of punishment (fine and imprisonment) was left to the discretion of the judge.[66]

[63] *Connecticut Courant* (Hartford), August 27, 1806.

[64] The *Witness* (Litchfield, Conn.), April 30, 1806.

[65] Precluded from prosecutions at common law by his earlier instructions from the administration, District Attorney Daviess sought an indictment of Burr in November 1806 under the Neutrality Act of 1794 but the Grand Jury refused to find a true bill and Burr went on from Kentucky to Nashville.

[66] John Dawson of Virginia introduced the bill, which also provided that when, in the opinion of the judge, any person *intended* to commit the prohibited offense, sureties for good behavior in an amount determined by the judge could be demanded. Imprisonment was provided in default of sureties. *Annals*, 9 Cong., 2 sess. 217–218. Pronounced unconstitutional and unprecedented and compared unfavorably with the Sedition Act, opposition from Jefferson's own party denounced punishment on mere suspicion and warned against the extensive powers given to the federal judges, who ultimately would give the definition of the offenses specified by the statute. Ibid. at 219, 261–64. The bill died. A few days later (January 23, 1807), Jefferson, having asserted that Burr was the prime mover in a Western conspiracy, requested authorization to suspend the writ of *habeas corpus*. This request was made just as Burr's alleged accomplices Bollman and Swartwout, arrived in Washington. Promptly passed by the Senate, this extraordinary bill was soundly defeated in the House. Unable to control his Congressional majority, the President's effort to prevent the judiciary from deciding whether Bollman and Swartwout were entitled to the writ had failed as well. In February 1807, they were released by the Supreme Court. Burr meanwhile had been captured, and on March 30, 1807, the famous trials began, to last until the end of the summer. This then is the larger historical context in which Jefferson first learned about the Connecticut cases. At the time he made no protest about them, nor did he make any effort to halt them. He did not then know that one of the cases (that against Azel Backus) involved allegations against his personal

As important to the administration as were questions of law enforcement and/or treason in the West, different problems became even more overwhelming as the Republicans faced a losing battle to make the unpopular embargo into effective national policy. Part of the problem to be sure was the result of inadequate administrative technique.[67] But more important, the Crimes Act did not touch embargo violators, and despite the desire of Attorney-General Rodney,[68] none of the four embargo acts (December 22, 1807, January 8, March 12, April 25, 1808) provided for criminal indictments for those who violated the statutes.[69] Jefferson's own appointees to the Supreme Court had rendered opinions on circuit that seriously hampered federal enforcement of the embargo,[70] and the frustrated Jefferson had written desperately to Secretary of the Treasury Gallatin, 'Congress must legalize *all means* which may be necessary to obtain its *end*' (italics in original).[71] But Congress was not in session and opposition to the embargo was mounting steadily within the President's own party. It is possible to imagine that desperation was driving the

morality in an early affair with the wife of a friend. Crosskey details the Connecticut cases in full. William Winslow Crosskey, *Politics and the Constitution*, supra note 62 at ii, 770–84.

   In the Burr trial, there is a colloquy between Luther Martin, Burr's defense counsel, and George Hay, the prosecuting attorney, on the question of federal common law jurisdiction over crimes. Martin, maintaining that no man can be guilty of an offense against the United States merely at common law, cites Chase's opinion in *Worrall*. He also mentions indictments in Connecticut and says that in a federal court, the offense could not be maintained. Hay seems to agree with him. David Robertson, *Reports of the Trials of Colonel Aaron Burr for Treason and for a Misdemeanor in the Circuit Court of the United States*, 2 vols. (Philadelphia, 1808), ii, 343. For analysis of Burr's trial, see Leonard Levy, *Jefferson and Civil Liberties*, supra note 62 at 70–92; George Haskins and Herbert A. Johnson, *Supreme Court*, supra note 3 at 246–291; Thomas P. Abernethy, *The Burr Conspiracy* (New York, 1954).

[67] Leonard White, *The Jeffersonians: A Study in Administrative History, 1801–1829*, (New York, 1951), 433–43, 453–60.

[68] Caesar A. Rodney to Jefferson, April 22, 1808, Jefferson Papers, vol. 177, Library of Congress.

[69] 2 Stat. 451 (December 22, 1807); 2 Stat. 453 (January 9, 1808); 2 Stat. 473 (March 12, 1808); 2 Stat. 499 (April 25, 1808). Forfeiture of ship and cargo was the penalty provided.

[70] Justice William Johnson held that the President's instructions to the customs collectors were illegal and void, unwarranted by statute. Gilchrist and Others v. The Collector of the Port of Charleston, #5, 420, 10 Fed. Cas. (C.C. District of South Carolina, 1808), 355. Justice Livingston demolished the administration's efforts to enforce the embargo by prosecution of offenders for treason in *U.S. v. Hoxie*, 26 Fed. Cas. (C.C. District of Vermont, 1808), 379. See the discussion of these and other embargo cases in George Haskins and Herbert A. Johnson, *Supreme Court*, supra note 3 at 298–08. Further detail will be found in Leonard Levy, *Jefferson and Civil Liberties*, supra note 62 at 121–41.

[71] Jefferson to Gallatin, August 11, 1808, Ford, ed., *Writings of Jefferson*, supra note 46 at ix, 202.

President himself to wish to utilize the very doctrine of federal judicial power that he had so execrated in 1798 at the time of the Federalist common law prosecutions. No evidence has been discovered to clarify this point.[72] However, the fact that Jefferson had not resorted to the common law to tag Burr for conspiracy may strengthen the probability that the District Attorney, in response to the local political situation, acted on his own. Late in 1808, Administration supporters in Virginia attacked Chief Justice Marshall (sitting as the circuit judge) and District Attorney George Hay for lacking determination to bring violators to justice.[73] Directly after a newspaper assault, the Richmond Grand Jury in December presented several persons for violation of the embargo law. Criminal indictments at common law were also brought against all of them in addition to the action for debt on a penalty as provided by the embargo statute.[74] The cases were set down for trial at the spring term, 1809. In Connecticut, meanwhile, following successive continuances, Judge Edwards and Justice Brockholst Livingston in September 1808 had divided on the jurisdictional question of a common law of crimes, and the Hudson-Goodwin case had been moved toward the Supreme Court.[75]

In Congress, Jefferson's urging that effective legislation be enacted received support when a newly arrived Congressman from Massachusetts, Joseph Story, introduced a resolution that a committee be established to consider whether amendments to the Crimes Act of 1790 were necessary. His object was 'to define certain crimes now loosely defined, and to provide a punishment for some crimes now committed with impunity.'[76]

---

[72] No instructions on the matter from the President or from either the Attorney General or the Secretary of State have been found.

[73] *The Enquirer* (Richmond), November 25, December 2, 1808; Philip Pope to Jefferson, January 5, 1809, Madison Papers, XXXVI, Library of Congress.

[74] *The Enquirer* (Richmond), December 17, December 22, 1808, June 2, 1809; U.S. Circuit Court, Dist. of Virginia, Richmond, Order Book No. 7, December 13, 1808, 206–207, Virginia State Library.

[75] U.S. v. Barzillai Hudson and George Goodwin, Records of the Supreme Court, Case Papers, Cases No. 395, National Archives. The certified circuit court record is dated Oct. 12, 1808, but the case was not actually filed before the Court until March 15, 1809. See William Winslow Crosskey, *Politics and the Constitution*, supra note 62 at ii, 781–82, for his argument that Jefferson deliberately delayed having the case presented to the Supreme Court until after a Jeffersonian majority was on the bench.

[76] *Annals*, 10th Congress, 2 session, 897, 909. Story arrived on Dec. 20, 1808 and presented the resolution on Dec. 26. In March 1809, he left the House and did not seek reelection. We do not know Story's entire mind here, but we do know of his support for the Embargo at this juncture even though he later favored its repeal. R. Kent Newmyer, *Story*, supra note 32 at 58–63, gives an excellent account of Story's relationship to Republican party and policy. It is possible that even at this time, Story hoped to have Congress enact legislation that would confer a jurisdiction broad enough to prosecute offenders against

Although a committee, including Story, was appointed, no report seems to have been made. Yet the enactment of the hotly debated Enforcement Act in January 1809, may have brought the remedy that Story, Jefferson, and others desired. The legislation provided that all penalties and forfeitures incurred by the Embargo Acts or the Enforcement Act could be prosecuted either by action of debt *or* 'by any indictment or information, any other usage or custom notwithstanding.'[77] The Crimes Act of 1790 had not empowered the federal government to proceed by information.

The momentum of this convergence of uncoordinated judicial and legislative activity gives the first of the Virginia common law cases, *U.S. v. William Smith*, a special interest. The unreported case came on for trial in June 1809 before Chief Justice Marshall sitting on circuit, and when federal attorney George Hay attempted to support the indictment at common law, more than a week of argument followed the motion by Smith's counsel to quash it. *The Richmond Enquirer* reported, 'A whole host of lawyers were enlisted on the side of this motion – the United States Attorney stood alone.'[78] Extensive search has failed to discover any information about this argument; even the names of the 'whole host of lawyers' remain unknown. But after hearing it 'fully argued' Marshall granted the motion to quash in a brief ruling:

… the court without deciding the question whether an indictment can be supported in this court on common law principles is of opinion that the offense charged in the indictment being reached by statute and a penalty being described for the commission of that act the penalty alone is recoverable and the act is not indictable.[79]

---

national policy. Newmyer speaks of Story's 'militant nationalism' as a clue to Story's final disillusion with party government. Story later claimed that he was never forgiven by Jefferson for his support of the repeal of the Embargo. William W. Story, ed., *Life and Letters of Joseph Story*, 2 vols. (Boston, 1851) i, 187 [hereinafter: W. W. Story: *Life and Letters*].

[77] 2 Stat. 506 (January 9, 1809), sec. 12. I read this to mean usage or custom in the various states. Gallatin had complained that every degree of opposition to the laws that fell short of treason was undefined and unprovided for by the laws of the United States. Such offenses went unpunished when state authorities did not intervene. Gallatin to Giles, November 24, 1808, Henry Adams, ed., *The Writings of Albert Gallatin*, 3 vols. (Philadelphia, 1879), i, 432, 434.

[78] U.S. v. William Smith, U.S. Circuit Court, Dist. of Virginia, Richmond, Order Book No. 7, June 2, 1809, 265. On May 25, the action of debt brought against Smith had by consent of both parties been removed from the district to the circuit court. Order Book No. 7, 235; *The Enquirer* (Richmond) June 2, 1809.

[79] U.S. Circuit Court, Dist. of Va., Richmond, Order Book No. 7, June 2, 1809, 265; *The Enquirer* (Richmond) June 6, 1809. The next day, eleven similar indictments were dismissed. Order Book No. 7, 267–68.

Absence of further information tantalizes. To what degree, if at all, did counsel's argument utilize Chase's opinion in *Worrall* or Madison's *Report on the Virginia Resolutions*? Were the Connecticut cases mentioned?[80] Who served as defendant's counsel, presumably organizing the 'whole host of lawyers'? How did George Hay, the libertarian author of *An Essay on the Liberty of the Press*[81] in 1799, present his argument for a non-statutory crime as federal prosecutor a decade later? Was it the strength of the 'Virginia theory' that overwhelmed the Republican efforts to enforce their policy?

It is important that Marshall was clearly unwilling to support a federal common law of crimes when so clear an opportunity to do so was presented. His ruling, on the contrary, seems entirely consistent with his opinions in *Ex Parte Bollman* (1807) that federal judicial power had to find its source in legislation[82] and with his denial in 1800 that anyone before 1799 had seriously maintained that the common law of England had been adopted as the common law of the United States by the Constitution.[83] Nor did Marshall divide the Circuit Court so that *U.S. v. William Smith* would go rapidly along to the Supreme bench, where *Hudson* was continued again and yet again.

Even lacking more detail about *U.S. v. William Smith*, the case gives us good grounds for presuming that John Marshall voted with the majority

[80] In the House of Representatives, John Randolph castigated his party for inattention to the Connecticut prosecutions, which threatened, he warned, to incorporate the entire system of British penal law within the federal judicial system, free from Constitutional restraints imposed on Congress by the First Amendment. 'Such is the difference between men in power and men out of power; such is the difference between profession and practice.' May 25, 1809, *Annals*, II Cong., 1 sess., 75–79.

[81] Leonard Levy, *Emergence of a Free Press*, supra note 30 at 311–15 for discussion of Hay. For a different view of Hay's concept of seditious libel, see Walter Berns, 'Freedom of the Press and the Alien and Sedition Laws: A Reappraisal', [1970] *The Supreme Court Review*, 141.

[82] '... This Court deem it proper to declare, that it disclaims all jurisdiction not given by the Constitution or by the laws of the United States.... Courts which originate in the Common Law possess a jurisdiction which must be regulated by the Common Law, until some statute shall change their established principles; but Courts which are created by written law, and whose jurisdiction is defined by written law, cannot transcend that jurisdiction. The reasoning from the Bar in relation to it may be answered by the single observation, that for the meaning of the term habeas corpus resort may unquestionably be had to the Common Law; but the power to award the writ by any of the Courts of the United States must be given by written law. 4 Cranch 75 (1807) at 93.'

[83] Marshall to [Tucker], November 27, 1800, Marshall Papers, Ac. 2354, Library of Congress. George Haskins and Herbert A. Johnson suggest in *Supreme Court*, supra note 3 at 309, 641, that the *Smith* decision may be evidence of a change of position on the part of Marshall. Their argument rests on the nature of Marshall's defense of the Sedition Act of 1798 and is not in my judgment entirely persuasive.

when *U.S. v. Hudson and Goodwin* was finally decided in March 1812
by a Supreme Court that had, for the first time, a Republican majority.
Gabriel Duvall and Joseph Story had been appointed by President Madison. Attorney General William Pinkney appears to have given the case
no attention; he did not appear to argue the long delayed cause.[84] No
counsel for defendants appeared. Nonetheless, the court proceeded to a
decision. Justice William Johnson, writing for the majority, declared that
the question of a federal common law of crimes 'had long since been
settled in the negative by public opinion and by legal men.' The judicial power of the United States was a constituent part of the concessions
granted by the several states, a power that could only be exercised by
courts brought into being by the legislative power of the union. Johnson
rejected the contention that judicial power over common law crimes was
an implied power derivative in some mystical fashion from the formation
of a political body and necessary to its preservation. If certain implied
powers resulted to the general government, it did not follow, in his view,
that the courts of that government were vested with an implied jurisdiction over offenses against the sovereignty. 'The legislative authority of
the Union must first make an act a crime, affix a punishment to it, and
declare the court that shall have jurisdiction of the offense.' Jurisdiction
of crimes against the state was no part of powers implied to the courts
from the nature of their institution.[85] We know that the opinion was not
unanimous, but which of the justices disagreed is unclear. I believe it most
likely that only Story and Washington dissented.[86] There was no written

[84] Pinkney apologized to Madison for spending his time practicing law in Baltimore, and
subsequently resigned after Congress passed a bill requiring the Attorney General to be
permanently in Washington. Pinkney to Madison, December 8, 1811, April 12, 1812,
January 25, 1814, all in *Madison Papers*, series 2, vol. 43, 47, 54, Library of Congress.

[85] U.S. v. Hudson and Goodwin, 7 Cranch (U.S.) 32.

[86] Johnson in an unreported circuit opinion in 1813 stated that the decision was 'almost
unanimous,' Bushrod Washington being the lone dissenter. [William Johnson], *Trial of
William Butler for Piracy* (1813) 12 [hereinafter: *Trial of Butler*]. Story, in a circuit
opinion also in 1813 stated that the decision was 'by a majority only.' U.S. v. Coolidge,
1 Gall. 488; #14,857, 25 Fed. Cas. 619 at 621 (C.C. District of Massachusetts, 1813).
Relying on Story's comment, William Winslow Crosskey, *Politics and the Constitution*,
supra note 62 at ii, 782, designates the Jeffersonians – Johnson, Livingston, Todd, and
Duval – as the majority, putting the Chief Justice with Washington and Story in dissent.
Leonard Levy, *Jefferson and Civil Liberties*, supra note 62 at 66, follows this design
as does Gerald T. Dunne, *Justice Joseph Story and the Rise of the Supreme Court*
(New York, 1970), 89. James McClellan, *Joseph Story and the American Constitution*
(Norman, 1971) 17 1n, believes Crosskey 'possibly correct.' To George Haskins and
Herbert A. Johnson, *Supreme Court*, supra note 3 at 645, Marshall's position is 'not
discernible.' R. Kent Newmyer, *Story*, supra note 32 at 101 puts Marshall with the

dissent. Court adjourned. Three months later, war was declared against Great Britain.

This war, which threatened the existence of his nation, together with the vehemence of New England's opposition to it combined to make an impact on Joseph Story hard to overestimate. New to the court in the context of war, he predicted 'excesses' which would require 'immediate reprehension' on the part of the national government. Immediately he suggested to Attorney General William Pinkney that Congress give to the federal courts a general common law jurisdiction over public crimes, with the authority to punish, at the discretion of the Court, all those acts done or not done that would at the common law be public offenses. Although Pinkney sent the letter on to President Madison, the President disregarded the suggestion.[87] Opposition to the war swiftly reached alarming proportions in New England; rumored threats of disunion circulated. Story carried his pleas to a friend in Congress. 'Pray induce Congress to give the Judicial Courts of the United States the power to punish all crimes and offenses against the Government, as at common law. Do not suffer conspiracies to destroy the union to be formed in the bosom of the country and yet no laws exist to punish crimes.'[88] It was his frustration with the failure of Congress to act that determined the young Justice on his deliberate course to overturn the *Hudson* doctrine, which deprived the federal judiciary of powers over non-statutory crimes against the nation.

Their decisions on circuit within a year after *Hudson* pointed up some of the practical consequences of the decision. These cases reveal sharp philosophical disagreement among the Supreme Court justices over federal authority to punish and over the scope of the English common law of crimes in federal jurisprudence. In 1813, five criminal suits in three circuit courts illustrate the widening dimensions of the problems.

majority, citing his circuit opinion in *Livingston v. Jefferson*, 1 Brockenbrough 211 (1811). Given Marshall's general position on the basis of Bollman and U.S. *v. Smith*, only awkward straining could have led him to dissent from Johnson's opinion in the Hudson case. I therefore include him with the majority. At the time of the decision itself, however, there is no direct evidence for the views of Marshall, Washington, or Story.
[87] Story to William Pinkney, June 26, 1812, enclosed in Pinkney to Madison, July 5, 1812, Madison Papers, series 2, vol. V, Library of Congress. Madison's disinclination to follow such a suggestion is clearly in line with his sentiments of 1799–1800. Kent Newmyer's biography is particularly good on the relationship between the war and Story's role on circuit. R. Kent Newmyer, *Story*, supra note 32 at 75, 83–92.
[88] Story to Nathaniel Williams, October 8, 1812, W. W. Story, *Life and Letters*, supra note 76 at i, 243.

Although the Constitution and the Judiciary Act of 1789 gave admiralty jurisdiction to the federal courts, neither spelled out what substantive maritime law these courts were to apply, and the first two of these cases arose from the piratical activities of the United States privateer *Revenge*. In April 1813, John Jones, first lieutenant of the *Revenge* and her second in command was tried before the Circuit Court in Philadelphia for piratically robbing a Portuguese brig.[89] In June 1813, the captain of the *Revenge*, William Butler, was indicted in the South Carolina Circuit Court for piracy in robbing a Spanish ship of a large sum of specie and bullion.[90] Both prosecutions were founded on section 8 of the Penal Act of 1790, which provided the death penalty for robbery on the high seas.[91] In each, the chief question made was whether the act of Congress reached these cases. And if not, was there no means of punishment for a crime that from time immemorial had been regarded as piracy?

In Jones's trial before Justice Bushrod Washington and District Judge Peters, Jared Ingersoll, counsel for the defense, argued that robbery was not piracy by the laws of the United States, since the offense of piratical robbery was not *defined* by statute. Relying specifically on the *Hudson* doctrine, he emphasized that the criminal common law of England was not the law of the United States and therefore no resort could be had to that code for the punishment of such an offense. Absent Congressional *definition* of this crime, the indictment could not be supported within the language of the Act of 1790.[92] His associate, William Rawle added: 'There

---

[89] *The Trial of John H. Jones, First Lieutenant of the Privateer Schooner Revenge, on a charge of Piracy, including the arguments of the counsel and the charge of Judge Washington. Reported by one of the counsel concerned in the cause* (Philadelphia, 1813) [hereinafter: *Trial of Jones*]; U.S. v. Jones, 3 Wash. C.C. 209, #15,494, 26 Fed. Cas. (C.C. District of Pennsylvania, April, 1813) 655. The latter report gives Washington's charge in full, but gives only a brief summary of the argument of counsel.

[90] *Trial of Butler,* supra note 86. Richard Rush's copy of this pamphlet consisting of Justice Johnson's opinion in this otherwise unreported case is in the Treasure Room at the Harvard Law School. The case is not mentioned in Donald Morgan's biography, *Justice William Johnson: The First Dissenter* (Columbia, S.C., 154), nor by the biographers of Story or by those of the Supreme Court.

[91] 1 Stat. 112 (April 30, 1790). The relevant part of sec. 8 was: 'That if any person or persons shall commit upon the high seas, or in any river, haven, basin or bay, out of the jurisdiction of any particular state, murder or robbery, or any other offence [sic] which if committed within the body of a county, would by the laws of the United States be punishable with death ... shall be deemed, taken and adjudged to be a pirate and felon and being thereof convicted, shall suffer death; the trial of crimes committed on the high seas, or in any place out of the jurisdiction of any particular state, shall be in the district where the offender is apprehended, or into which he first may be brought.'

[92] *Trial of Jones,* supra note 89 at 34–35. Ingersoll identified the Hudson case simply as one decided 'at their (Supreme Court) session before the last, in a case from the district

is no other source of authority, no other code of law, from which what is deficient or doubtful in the act of Congress can be supplied.'[93] Alexander Dallas, the prosecuting attorney, had no difficulty with the matter. The act of Congress, he asserted, specified the offenses to which federal criminal jurisdiction reached; the language employed by Congress to define a crime must be explained in doubtful cases by the source from which the language was derived. To fix the legal import of the word 'robbery,' therefore, it was necessary and appropriate to resort to the common law.[94] Justice Washington, charging the jury, made short shrift of the contention of defense counsel. It is true, he said, that unless the offense charged in the indictment be made punishable by some law of the United States, the prisoner must be acquitted. 'But nothing can be more clear than that robbing on the high seas, is declared to be felony and piracy by the 8th section of the act....'[95] Doubtless mindful of the punishment and very likely because of conflicting testimony of witnesses regarding the identity of the accused, the jury acquitted Lieutenant Jones.[96]

of Connecticut, of which not being reported, I am not apprised of the title.' According to Ingersoll, Jones's case was the first of its kind to be tried in America; for this reason, the decision of points of law was particularly important. A brief statement of the other points raised by counsel for the prisoner is set forth in 26 Fed. Cas. 655.

[93] *Trial of Jones*, supra note 89 at 42–43. Rawle stated that by the decision of the Supreme Court in *Williams*, an unreported case, he understood that the judicial power of the United States recognized no common law in criminal cases. Search of unpublished Supreme Court documents has failed to locate such a case. Perhaps Rawle had in mind *U.S. v. Hudson and Goodwin*, unreported at the time of his argument; perhaps he confused the name with *U.S. v. William Smith* tried in the Circuit Court of Virginia before Marshall in 1809, also unreported. His reference could hardly have been to *U.S. v. Issac Williams*, Wharton, *State Trials* (C.C. District of Connecticut, 1799), supra note 13 at 652; in that case (involving matters of international law), Ellsworth had enunciated the opposite doctrine on a point of law.

[94] *Trial of Jones*, supra note 89 at 51, 53.

[95] 'I understand the argument to be that as robbery on land is not declared by any act of congress [sic] to be a capital offense, it is not declared by this section to be piracy, if committed on the high seas. This is by no means the correct interpretation of the law. Murder and robbery committed on the high seas are declared to amount to piracy, and also any other offense, which would be punishable with death, had they been committed on land. It is clear that the words "which if committed within a body of a country" relate not to murder or robbery but to the words immediately preceding, "or any other offense."

All that remains then under this section is to ascertain the meaning of the word robbery, and it is admitted that the common law definition of the term may be resorted to. If a statute of the United States uses a technical term which is known, and its meaning fully ascertained by the common, or civil law from one or the other of which it is obvious borrowed, no doubt can exist that it is necessary to refer to the source from whence it is taken for its precise meaning.' Ibid. at 57.

[96] Ibid. at 63. In his opening statement, Dallas mentioned objections of jurors to convicting any persons when the punishment was death. Ibid. at 7. Later Judge Peters referred to

From Salem, Joseph Story was unsuccessfully continuing his efforts to persuade Congress to remedy the federal criminal code[97] when in June 1813 the second *Revenge* case came on for trial in Charleston before Justice William Johnson. Here, Captain Butler, the prisoner, went free when Johnson ordered the indictment against him dismissed. Johnson deliberately used the case to counter Washington's views in *Jones* and to impress on Congress the necessity of passing amendatory criminal legislation.[98] More importantly, he seized the opportunity not only to affirm elaborately his denial in *Hudson* of a federal common law power over crimes, but to extend that doctrine considerably into a new area, the criminal admiralty law.

To section 8 of the statute Johnson gave a construction completely opposed to that given by Washington. In order to construe robbery on the high seas as punishable under the statute, Johnson said, it was indispensably necessary that the same offense should have been made punishable if committed on land. Since robbery on land was not a crime punishable by federal statute, no punishment could be attached to the offense if committed on the high seas. He then considered whether the federal courts derived power over robbery on the high seas from any non-statutory source. As in *Hudson*, he attacked the proposition that the federal courts possessed any common law jurisdiction in criminal cases. Drawing upon Chase's argument in *Worrall* and from Marshall's statements in *Bollman*, Johnson asserted that claims to such common law jurisdiction had been made by only one judge of the Supreme Court and one district judge; the *Hudson* case had been decided 'almost unanimously' and had not even been argued because 'the universal conviction prevailing at the bar [was] that opinion had in every department [of the government] settled down against it.' Marshall's ruling in *Bollman*, he said, 'left no longer a doubt upon the mind of the Bar of what must be the decision of the Supreme Court on this subject, whenever it should be brought up distinctly for their determination.'[99] The *sole* authority for all the criminal powers that the federal government might exercise was to be found in

---

this case as 'one of the most infamous' in which he ever sat. Peters to Timothy Pickering, March 30, 1816, Pickering Papers, 31:69, Massachusetts Historical Society.

[97] Story to Nathaniel Williams, May 27, 1813, Story, *Life and Letters*, supra note 76 at i, 244–45.

[98] See the preface to the pamphlet that Johnson had published. *Trial of Butler* includes only the judge's opinion; argument of counsel is not given.

[99] *Trial of Butler*, supra note 86 at 12–13. Johnson quoted from *Bollman* the section set forth above in note 82.

four clauses of Article I of the Constitution and the treason clause of Article III. Article III otherwise contained nothing that added to federal judicial power. The sole object of Article III, in his view, was to establish a judiciary commensurate with the powers delegated to Congress 'to enforce the constitutional exercise of the powers of the United States on the one hand, and on the other, to protect the individual from the power of the general government, whenever the limits of constitutional power shall be transcended'... 'The pretensions of the prosecution officers of the United States, to implied Common Law jurisdiction over crimes, we consider an instance of this latter kind; and we maintain that the whole fabric of the Constitution is framed with sedulous care to preclude every department from the exercise of implied power.'[100]

Johnson solemnly warned against the potential evils of a judiciary whose power over crimes was unrestricted, and struck at those who argued that from the nature of sovereignty itself, a common law power resulted to the federal government and its courts. At the state level, by constitutional provision, by statute, or by continued practice, the reception of the common law had depended on the voluntary act of the legislative power.[101] By analogy, the national Congress under the 'necessary and proper' clause had the constitutional power to pass legislation even surpassing common law criminal provisions. Until it had acted, however, the courts had no authority in this area.[102] The Constitution alone gave no latitude for the exercise of power over crimes by the federal judiciary.[103] Nor, he continued, did section 11 of the Judiciary Act supply it. The phrasing 'cognizance over all crimes and offenses cognizable under the authority of the United States' could not be construed to mean jurisdiction over 'all crimes and offenses committed against the United States.' Even less could the language be interpreted as the equivalent of 'every individual act which if committed in Great Britain could be deemed an offense against the Crown.'[104] Johnson then examined the judicial power bestowed in Article III over all cases of admiralty and maritime jurisdiction, and in a sweeping conclusion denied that the circuit court had, under this clause, any jurisdiction over maritime offenses when Congress had provided no specific definition and punishment. Only in the statute books was jurisdiction to be found. Americans were not left dependent,

[100] Ibid. at 17.
[101] Ibid. at 20–24.
[102] Ibid. at 26–27.
[103] Ibid. at 30–31.
[104] Ibid. at 29.

he said, on decisions of the circuit courts from which there was no appeal nor did their lives rest on the ancient doctrine of the criminal admiralty law that well ought to pass, in his view, 'through a course of legislative filtration' before being incorporated into the federal jurisprudence. Should Congress vest the federal courts with jurisdiction over all cases to which the punishing power might by implication extend, then, and only then, would it rest with the courts to decide '(wild and devious as the track assigned then would be)' to what cases that jurisdiction would extend.[105] The Crimes Act of 1790 was in Johnson's view defective in its provisions for the punishment of robbery on the high seas. The prisoner's case was therefore unprovided for and the Court ordered Butler discharged.[106]

We do not know whether Story learned of the Butler case during the summer months of 1813, but it deserves emphasis that, at this juncture, both he and Johnson alike were convinced that remedy lay with the legislative branch of the national government. However, while Story continued to repeat his pleas that Congress give the federal courts a common law authority to punish crimes against the United States,[107] 'a disgraceful affair' in Boston, the rescue of a prize ship by the owners, provided a heaven-sent opportunity for him to turn directly to the federal judiciary in his quest for remedy of the problems of national law enforcement.

Briefly stated, the facts surrounding the important Coolidge case are these. Cornelius Coolidge and Francis Oliver, Boston owners of the brig *Despatch*, informed of their vessel's capture by two privateers at the

---

[105] *Trial of Butler*, supra note 86 at 32–35. To emphasize his point, Johnson mentioned a few of the hundreds of offenses known to the British admiralty law, e.g., combinations of ship carpenters to increase their wages, erecting water mills upon navigable streams, casting rubbish into navigable waters, employing foreign bottoms when there were enough domestic ones to be procured. On the question of whether Congress could punish before it defined offenses within the traditional range of the admiralty, Johnson thought that the word 'define' in that context meant only a designation that left no doubt of the identity of the crime. In a criminal case, no appeal lay from the circuit court to the Supreme Court until 1889.

[106] *Trial of Butler*, supra note 86 at 35. Had it prevailed, the significance of Johnson's interpretation of the admiralty clause of the Constitution to the development of federal admiralty jurisdiction goes without saying. For Johnson's conflicts with Story over the reach of federal jurisdiction in this sphere of American law, see Morgan, *Justice William Johnson*, 80–83; Gerald T. Dunne, *Justice Joseph Story*, supra note 86 at 168–70, 239–46, 263–66.

[107] '... the Government will be completely prostrated unless they give jurisdiction to their courts, and a common law authority to punish crimes against the United States.... What think you of a Government where public crimes on the seas, are, with very few exceptions, left wholly unpunished, and crimes on the land are suffered to remain without the least criminal action?' Story to Williams, August 3, 1813, W.W. Story, *Life and Letters*, supra note 76 at i, 246–47.

entrance to Boston Harbor, gathered friends in two rowboats, exchanged shots with the privateers, and then retook their brig. They were arrested on a complaint for piracy brought by the owner of one of the privateers, and in a separate action before the federal district court, lost their vessel and its cargo, which were condemned to the captors. The latter decision they appealed to the circuit court.[108] Simultaneously, Stephen Clark, master of one of the privateers, who had given evidence on the complaint for piracy, was arrested on a charge of perjury and bailed pending the October 1813 session of the circuit court. At that time, Story affirmed the decree of the district court condemning the ship, and Coolidge again appealed, this time to the Supreme Court.[109] In addition, the Grand Jury returned criminal indictments against Clark for perjury in the hearing before the district judge and against Coolidge and the others of his rescue party for their offense.[110] Although the Act of 1790 made perjury in suits before the federal courts a crime, no law declared the rescue of a prize ship to be a criminal act.

These two cases need to be read together in the light of Justice Story's frustration that Congress had not conferred upon the federal courts a general jurisdiction over common law crimes. His determination to compel

[108] Coolidge and Oliver, claimants in the action, claimed that their ship was on lawful voyage from Cadiz to Boston. Furthermore, they contested, the vessel was within one mile of the lighthouse at the time of capture, not on the high seas and thus not within the jurisdiction of the federal courts. At the hearing before Judge John Davis, completely contradictory testimony was given by witnesses regarding the precise place of capture. Davis, in his decree, simply stated that the capture 'appears to have been between one and five miles from Boston lighthouse' and set aside the plea to the jurisdiction. Judging the 'rescue' of the brig a forcible rescue from the possession of a lawful cruiser, Davis condemned the ship. See record of the proceedings, *The Brig Dispatch, Coolidge and others v. Clark and others, Privateer Castigator*, Case Papers, #645, Records of the Supreme Court, National Archives.

[109] The episode was a *cause celebre* locally. See *Independent Chronicle*, (Boston) August 5, 1813; *Columbian Centinel*, August 4, August 7, 1813. An account of the episode is also given in the record filed with the Supreme Court. In the docket of the Supreme Court, microfilm copy no. 216, case #645, the action is listed as *The Brig Dispatch, Cornelius Coolidge and others v. Stephen G. Clark and others. Privateer Castigator*. See also Case Papers, Case #645, Records of the Supreme Court, National Archives. The appeal was dismissed at the February term, 1815. Dispatch v. Castigator (Coolidge v. Clark), Supreme Court Records, Docket, microcopy no. 216. A complaint was also filed in the state court against Clark and the crew of the *Castigator* on a charge of assault with intent to kill those in the rowboats. *New England Palladium*, August 3, 6, 10, 1813.

[110] U.S. v. Stephen Clark; U.S. v. Cornelius Coolidge and others, C.C. District of Massachusetts, Docket 4 (1812–1821), Fed. Records Center, Waltham, Mass. All defendants entered pleas of not guilty. A copy of the indictment in *U.S. v. Coolidge* is in the Records of the Supreme Court, Appellate Case Files, Case No. 671, microcopy no. 214.

the Supreme Court to look again at the Hudson doctrine is unmistakable. When defense counsel in *U.S. v. Clark* moved to quash the indictment, arguing that the perjury alleged could not be grounded on the statute of 1790, Story not only granted the motion but suggested himself that the indictment might nevertheless be good at common law.

> ...We are however precluded from considering this question as at common law because the Supreme Court have held, that this Court has no common law juris-diction over offenses. I am bound to acquiesce in that decision; although I have never been able to satisfy my judgment of its accuracy. Had the point been fully argued, instead of passing *sub silentio*, I should have felt a greater satisfaction in the decision. It is, however, to be considered as settled, unless that high tribunal should hereafter choose, to review the question in a more deliberate argument. I should not regret it, however, if a division of the Court is made... because it will bring the questions solemnly before the Court of the last resort.

The amenable Judge John Davis thereupon dissented from Story's opinion and *U.S. v. Stephen Clark* was certified to the Supreme Court on a division of the judges.[111] When the District Attorney moved for trial in *U.S. v. Coolidge*, the same strategy was applied, the question of jurisdiction was again brought forward, the offense charged not being against a statute. This too was sent to the Supreme Court on a division.[112] A few months later, Story seized yet another case touching national policy in which the jurisdictional question could be made. This time, at issue was the rescue by local well wishers of British prisoners of war confined by the federal marshal in a state jail. Story and Davis again disagreed, and a third case, *U.S. v. Bigelow and Jenkins*, was sent to join the others before the Supreme Court.[113] Of the three, it was Story's elaborate circuit opinion

---

[111] The perjury alleged was at the hearing before the District Judge. Story, rejecting the prosecutor's contention that every proceeding held by the District Judge, in his official capacity, was an act of the District *Court*, held that the indictment was not supportable within the language of the statute. U.S. v. Stephen G. Clark, 1 Gall. (Massachusetts) 496 (1813) (italics added).

[112] Records of the Supreme Court, Appellate Case Files, Case no. 671, microcopy 214. No reference to argument of counsel appears in any source; very likely the question before the Court may have been put there by Justice Story himself. December 24, 1813, is the date of the division of the judges in both cases. C.C. Docket 4 (1812–1821). Both were filed at the Supreme Court in February 1814.

[113] *Boston Patriot*, January 14, May 18, 1814; *Massachusetts Spy* or *Worcester Gazette*, January 19, 1814; *U.S. v. Bigelow and Jenkins*, an unreported case. A copy of the indictment is included in the Supreme Court Records, Case No. 730, Appellate Case Files, microcopy no. 214. Docket Case no. 720, microcopy 216. District Attorney George Blake wrote Attorney General Richard Rush: 'As the case presents nothing more than the long agitated question of jurisdiction at common law in the courts of

in *Coolidge* that rather than overturning *Hudson* ironically enabled the Supreme Court to reconfirm it emphatically.

At the outset of his opinion in the Coolidge case, Story set aside the broad question of whether the United States as a sovereign power had entirely adopted the common law. He did, however, pose his question in broad terms: whether the circuit court had jurisdiction to punish offenses against the United States that had not been specifically defined, and a specific punishment attached, by federal statute. Echoing Marshall in *Bollman* he pushed beyond. 'I admit in the most explicit terms, that the courts of the United States are courts of limited jurisdiction, and cannot exercise any authorities, which are not confided to them by the constitution and laws made in pursuance thereof, but I do contend that when once an authority is lawfully given, the *nature* and *extent* (italics added) of that authority, and the mode in which it shall be exercised, must be regulated by the rules of the common law.' Both the Constitution and laws of the United States were predicated upon the existence of the common law; for explanation of the terms of the law and for the mode of conducting trials by jury, recourse must be had to the common law. The clause in Article III, 'the judicial power shall extend to all cases in law and equity arising under the constitution,' was otherwise inexplicable and the *extent* (italics added) of this power must be measured by the powers of courts of law and equity, as exercised and established by that system. The existence, therefore, of the common law was not only supposed by the Constitution, but must be appealed to for the construction and interpretation of its powers.

Under the Constitution, the Congress may confide to the circuit court jurisdiction of all offenses against the United States. And in the Judiciary Act of 1789 (sec. 11), the Congress, in Story's interpretation, unlike that of Johnson, had indeed done so. He read the clause giving the circuit court 'exclusive cognizance of all crimes and offenses cognizable under the authority of the United States . . .' not as a jurisdiction limited only to crimes created and defined by statute but one reaching all crimes to which, by the Constitution, the judicial power extended. For the definition of *this* power over crime, Story went to the common law: all offenses against the sovereignty, the public rights, the public justice, the public peace, the public trade, and the public police were crimes against the United States.

---

the U States (sic), it would be altogether useless for me to make any particular remarks respecting it.' February 1, 1815, Department of Justice, Record Group 60, Papers of the Attorney-General, Letters Received (Mass.) National Archives.

Whether or not specified by Constitution or statute, whether or not punishment had been fixed by the legislature, they were punishable by common law penalties in its courts. The ground for this, Story asserted, was that the legislature had in view the rules of the common law, and 'deemed their application *in casibus ommissis peremptory* (italics added) upon the courts.'

After a brief comment that the importance of the question that 'vitally affects the jurisdiction of the court of the United States' occasioned him to put the case before the Court notwithstanding the *Hudson* opinion, Story veered in his argument, since that case did not settle the question (presently before the Court in *Coolidge*) so far as it respected maritime offenses. Tacking in this direction, Story utilized the clause in Article III that included in the judicial power of the United States all cases of admiralty and maritime jurisdiction, reminding the Court that this jurisdiction comprehended criminal, as well as civil suits. As offenses of admiralty jurisdiction were exclusively within federal jurisdiction, it followed to Story that all such offenses were offenses against the United States, and in the absence of positive law were punishable by fine and imprisonment in the federal courts.[114]

The historical context helps explain the curiosity of this opinion, which in Kent Newmyer's apt description offered 'both a narrow and broad argument for the common law.'[115] Story was eager to make the case one of common law and chose not to rest his argument solely on the admiralty jurisdiction. Had he confined himself to the latter,[116] even had the court accepted his position (which it might well have done), the *Hudson* doctrine would have remained. That was his principal target. Indeed, the greater portion of the *Coolidge* opinion might well have served as Story's dissent in *Hudson* the year before, when he had sat silent in that case. His theory that the courts were competent, within the broad and inconclusive language of the Constitution and Judiciary Act, to try common law and admiralty crimes, offered a direct and immediate counterattack against the theory of statutory authorization that Johnson

---

[114] U.S. v. Coolidge et al, 1 Gall. 488; #14,857,25 Fed. Cas. (C.C. Dist. of Mass., October, 1813), 619.

[115] R. Kent Newmyer, *Story*, supra note 32 at 105, provides an admirable succinct analysis of the opinion.

[116] In 1824, Peter DuPonceau, commenting on Coolidge, stated that 'whatever else it might be, it was clearly not a case of common law.' Peter S. DuPonceau, *A Dissertation on the Nature and Extent of the Jurisdiction of the Courts of the United States* (Philadelphia, 1824) 9–10.

had more fully developed in his circuit opinion in *Butler* a few months earlier. It was Story, however, who held the loser's hand.

In his own circuit, the United States Attorney, George Blake, who in 1799 had repudiated the idea that the common law of seditious libel had been received by the Commonwealth of Massachusetts,[117] was understandably confused between the *Hudson* doctrine on the one hand and Justice Story's disregard of it on the other. He was also in the position of attempting to perform his duties. What about persons who went aboard enemy ships hovering off the Massachusetts coast? Was the bare act of going on board punishable under federal authority? In reply to Blake's query on these points, Richard Rush, the Attorney General, emphatically rejected the possibility of utilizing the common law to prosecute offenders, and reminded Blake of the *Hudson* decision. Only a statute could warrant prosecution.

I do not think that a federal Republic like ours, resting upon as its only pillars, the limited political concessions of distinct and independent sovereign States, drew to itself, by any just implication, at the moment of its circumscribed structure, the whole common law of England, with all or any portion of its dark catalogue of crimes and punishments; a code which the more liberal and humane wisdom of later days – the labors of the Romillys and the Benthams following the more ancient strictures of a Blackstone and a Hale – has been aiming ever since to free of its fierce and sanguinary features; . . . .'[118]

Rush was also hearing from Story, who wrote of the three indictments from his circuit pending before the Supreme Court; the Justice strenuously urged Rush to argue 'the great question of the common law' before that body. 'In my judgment,' he wrote, 'the decision will in effect decide whether the constitution of the U.S. can subsist – it is plain to me that congress (sic) never can enact a criminal code to meet the various frauds and subtleties of dishonorable men.'[119] But poor Rush was in the thick

[117] Leonard S. Levy, *Emergency of a Free Press*, supra note 3 at 217–19, 312.

[118] Rush to Blake, July 28, 1814, *Boston Patriot*, August 20, 1814. Rush advised that those suspected of acting against the public interest be arrested, with a view to laying the foundation of a charge in which the offender could be bound for good behavior by the court. He also told Blake that any boat without a flag of truce putting off from an enemy ship and heading toward shore could be considered fair game for American land or naval forces in the vicinity. Rush's letter was later printed in *Annals*, 13 Cong., 3 sess. (1823–26).

[119] Story to Richard Rush, August 20, 1814, Rush Papers, Box 7 Princeton University Library. Interesting also are Story's comments at this date regarding civil jurisdiction. 'Is it credible that the courts of the United States have no *general civil jurisdiction* in cases arising under the laws of the United States?' (italics in original).

of the farcical 'Battle of Bladensburg,' and owing to the burning of the
capitol by the British the Supreme Court did not hold its fall session in
1814. When the war ended in February 1815, Story wrote exuberantly,
'Let us extend the national authority over the whole extent of power
given by the Constitution. Let us have a national bank: a national system
of bankruptcy;.... Judicial courts which shall embrace the whole constitutional powers;....'[120] But Story's hopes for a Supreme Court reversal
of the limitations of federal judicial power imposed by *Hudson* were
thwarted once more when Rush became ill and was unable to appear
at the 1815 sessions of the court.[121] Story turned again to Congress for
remedy.

In November 1815, he sent Rush a revised judicial bill in which he had
fallen back a step from his 1812 views. 'I hope that the 11th section [of
the Judiciary Act of 1789] will be found to avoid your objections to the
common law jurisdiction, as it is merely a positive adoption of that law so
far as it applies to the *sovereignty of the U.S.* (italics in original).'[122] The
bill was intended for his friend, William Pinkney, now a member of the
House. Its overall object was to give the federal courts jurisdiction over

---

[120] Story to Nathaniel Williams, February 22, 1815, W. W. Story, *Life and Letters*, supra
note 76 at i, 254.

[121] John H. Powell, *Richard Rush* (Philadelphia, 1942), 52, 67. During his long conva-
lescence, Rush published anonymously *American Jurisprudence, written and published
at Washington, being a few reflections suggested on reading 'Wheaton on Captures'*
(Washington, D.C., 1815) [hereinafter: Rush, *American Jurisprudence*]. In his slight
reference to the question of whether the federal government had a general common law
authority over crimes, Rush stated that in his view, the substratum of common law in
the nation meant the common law as applied to the individual states. He also wrote:
'Notwithstanding the determination of the supreme court (sic) in the case of the United
States vs. Hudson and Goodwin, it is still by no means certain that that tribunal would
not sustain another and more full argument at this day on the question in its nature so
extensive and fundamental as whether or not the federal government draws to itself the
common law of England in criminal matters.' Ibid. at 15–16. Joseph Story was among
those in public life to whom Rush sent his pamphlet.

[122] Story to Rush, November 29, 1815, in Rush Papers, Princeton University Library.
For the provisions of the bill with accompanying commentary, see W. W. Story, *Life
and Letters*, supra note 76 at i, 293–301. Story's proposals also included the grant
of original federal question jurisdiction to the circuit courts. The editor states that
the bill was written in 1816, ibid. at 293, but internal evidence persuades me that
the manuscript printed in *Life and Letters* should be properly dated 1815 and is the
same bill to which Story refers in his letter of November 29 to Rush. The original of
the manuscript in the University of Texas Library, so the librarian has informed me,
shows the date 1816 as added at a different time, on different paper. In a letter to Rush
December 8, 1816, Story refers to the sketch of the judicial bill that he had sent to Rush
'last winter.' Rush Papers, Box 7, Princeton University Library.

all cases that Story deemed 'intended by the constitution to be confided to the judicial power of the United States where that jurisdiction has not already been delegated by law.' The courts should be given jurisdiction to punish wherever the authority of the United States was violated and should be empowered to settle on common law principles the specific instances of such violations. This was not, he claimed, assuming a general common law jurisdiction to federal power, but simply applying the common law definition of crimes to the limited powers delegated by the Constitution to the federal government. Story carefully steered wide of the question of whether the federal courts have from their very organization a general common law jurisdiction, or the federal government a general common law authority. On this, he himself had no doubts, he said, but he acknowledged the differences of opinion on the Bench. Since there was, however, no difference regarding the authority of Congress to invest the courts with the more limited jurisdiction so far as it applied to the national sovereignty only, Story claimed that this proposal had the support of all the Justices.[123]

All his maneuverings went for nothing if Story considered the message an opportunity to influence the argument of the Attorney General on the Coolidge case. On March 21, 1816, the day after Story delivered his ultranationalist opinion on federal judicial power, *Martin v. Hunter's Lessee*,[124] *U.S. v. Coolidge* was finally called for argument. Rush refused to argue the case for the United States, stating that he regarded the issue controlled by *Hudson*. Story angrily exclaimed that *he* did not. Johnson retorted that it was. Washington and Livingston expressed a willingness to hear argument. Marshall and Duvall apparently were silent. In a brief opinion by Johnson, the Court refused to review its former ruling or draw it into doubt.[125] In so anti-climactic a fashion did Story's 'great case' come to an end. His other two common law cases, *U.S. v. Clark* and *U.S. v. Bigelow and Jenkins*, were similarly struck off.[126]

---

[123] Story to Pinkney [or to Rush?] *Life and Letters*, supra note 76 at i, 297–300. Story said that Marshall and Washington revised his proposals and 'wholly approved'; Johnson expressed some doubts about sec. 11 on the ground of expediency, but raised no objection to the competence of Congress to enact it.

[124] 14 U.S. (1 Wheaton) 394 (1816). Among other things, Story insisted in this opinion that by Article III it was constitutionally mandatory upon Congress to establish a system of federal courts and to give them their full jurisdiction to limit of the Constitution.

[125] 14 U.S. (1 Wheaton) 415 (1816).

[126] Supreme Court Records, Docket, microcopy no. 216; Appellate Case Files, microcopy no. 214.

Story died hard on the issue.[127] Later in 1816, he wrote Rush that the question of common law jurisdiction in criminal cases continued to divide the court. 'Two judges are for it – three against it – and two will give no opinion until after argument – this is a most distressing state of Doubt.' The decision in *Coolidge*, Story insisted, was only *pro forma* until argument could be heard. Once more he exhorted Rush to work for revisions of the federal criminal code, particularly in the places where exclusive jurisdiction was given to the United States.[128] Once more he worked out a judicial bill in which statutory authorization was extended.[129] Once more he failed. The jurisdiction of the federal courts remained restricted regarding criminal matters; the federal criminal law remained restricted to positive law.

It had been the refusal of Congress to act that had prompted Story, in the area of common law crimes, to create for the judiciary the novel theoretical structure for the exercise of federal power to punish that emerged in his Coolidge opinion. That opinion should be seen as one part of Story's endeavors to increase federal jurisdiction and to develop a theory of federal judicial power stemming from the Constitution itself. Compelled, however, by the realities of adverse sentiment at the time in both court and Congress, he found it the better part of wisdom (in both his proposals to Congress and his opinion in *Coolidge*) to set aside his private conviction that the federal government did have from its very organization a general common law authority and its courts a general common law jurisdiction over crimes.[130] Rather, he sought to achieve

---

[127] After he learned of the decision in *Coolidge*, Peters wrote in dismay, '*I cannot carry on the Business of my District* (italics in original). It meets me in almost every criminal Case. Unless some legislative authority be given, to define Crimes, or Statutory Descriptions are established, the whole (or nearly) of our criminal Code may be expunged.... We are forbidden to resort to Common Law for Interpretation, & our Jurisdiction of Crimes punishable at Common Law, is excluded. I live in a District of mixed Population, as to Seamen particularly; & am subjected to constant Necessity of taking Cognizance of Crimes, great & Small, without a Guide to direct my Course. I had little Difficulty before the Decision alluded to [Coolidge]; but now my Hands are tied, & my Mind Padlocked....' Peters to Pickering, March 30, 1816, Pickering Papers, 31:89 Massachusetts Historical Society.

[128] Story to Rush, November 18, 1816, Rush Papers, supra note 122.

[129] Story to Rush, December 8, 27, 1816, Rush Papers, supra note 122. For discussion of the subject by Peters, see Peters to Pickering, April 10, 14, 16, 1816, Pickering Papers, 31:97, 100, 102 Massachusetts Historical Society.

[130] In this transcendant view of nationalism, as in new principles for admiralty law, Peters had anticipated Story. On Peters and admiralty, see Presser, 'Two Judges,' supra note 3, at 35–40.

this end by reaching from a base of broad statutory reference to crimes against the authority of the United States. The half a loaf was better than none, or so he hoped, to meet the problems of the maintenance of public order. But even here Story failed.

The ironies are many. Story was hoist by his own petard, his own overreaching. In *Coolidge*, he had utilized a case in which he attempted to extend principles of the criminal admiralty law to create a general common law criminal jurisdiction that he believed, as a matter of policy, the nation's courts had to have. In so doing, he got the common law issue before the Supreme Court once more, but the refusal of the Court to draw *Hudson* into doubt, in the absence of any argument, meant that the whole enterprise was lost. After *Coolidge*, the *Hudson* rule was applicable to *all* criminal prosecutions under federal authority, and the power of the federal courts – even over maritime crimes and torts – was the more restricted in criminal matters. Story's attack on the judicial reasoning of both Chase in *Worrall* and Johnson in *Butler* had utterly failed. Now, certain offenses committed within the admiralty and maritime jurisdiction but not within the territorial jurisdiction of any state, and those committed in federal enclaves such as forts and dockyards within the territorial boundaries of a state but over which the federal government had acquired exclusive jurisdiction, were left unprovided for. District Judge Peters in Philadelphia called the state of affairs following *Coolidge*, 'a perfect mockery and ridicule on public criminal law' and complained that he could not carry on the business of his district.[131] Gaps in the federal criminal law continued to be made apparent in later cases[132] and Story continued persistently his role as 'the unacknowledged legislator of his time.'[133] Through his friends in Congress, David Daggett in 1818 and then Daniel Webster in 1825, Story's Crimes Act of that year gave greater clarity to offenses against the United States, but his notion of a federal common law of crimes defined by the judiciary was dead forever.

---

[131] '...Whilst the opinion that we had no common law jurisdiction in criminal cases was held by some and denied by others, I thought myself justified in following my own views. But now I am bound by overruling decisions to avoid acting under my own sentiments...,' to Pickering, April 14, 1816, Pickering Papers, 31:100 Massachusetts Historical Society.

[132] E.g., U.S. v. Bevans, 3 Wheaton 336 (1818).

[133] The phrase is James McClellan's. *Joseph Story and the American Constitution*, (Norman, 1971), supra note 86 at 308. See also R. Kent Newmyer, 'A Note on the Whig Politics of Justice Joseph Story,' *Mississippi Valley Historical Review*, XLVIII (1961), 480–91.

By the 1825 legislation, crimes unprovided for even in federal enclaves were to be judged and punished not according to a general common law of crimes but according to the law of the state in which the crime took place.[134] This was a far cry from the enforcement of national sovereignty as Story had envisioned it.

A few observations of closure may be appropriate at this juncture, for the intricacies of the process by which the history of the federal criminal law merges with politics as well as reform of punishments and procedures cannot be detailed here in full. In the individual states, at different paces to be sure, statutes had replaced common law in efforts to render the criminal law more precise. The trend toward humanitarian doctrines was slowly replacing traditional systems of punishment, corporal as well as capital.[135] In addition, by 1825 certain states had amended their criminal laws and replaced the death penalty with imprisonment for many crimes hitherto capital.[136] Alexander Dallas's concern in *Jones's Case* that jurors would refuse to convict when the offense was robbery at sea and the punishment was death, and Attorney General Rush's contrast between the common law's 'dark catalogue' of crimes and punishments and 'the more liberal and humane wisdom of . . . the labors of the Romillys and the Benthams,' call our attention to the significance of jurisdiction over the punishment as well as over the crime. In 1818, when the Supreme Court in *U.S. v. Bevans* reiterated its rejection of Joseph Story's theories about a judicially declared jurisdiction over common law crimes, the tenacious Justice wrote that he had not changed his mind about the accuracy of his views but had yielded to his brethren only because the case was a capital offense.[137] Justice Johnson, dissenting the same year in *U.S. v. Palmer* when the majority of the court rejected the interpretation of the

---

[134] Act of March 3, 1825, 18th Congress, 2 Stat. 115. The resurrection of states' rights doctrine and concern over the potential collision between state and federal authorities had of course reached far more substantial proportions by 1825. This helps to explain the limited nature of the second federal crimes act.

[135] Myra C. Glenn, *Campaigns against Corporal Punishment, Prisoners, Sailors, Women and Children in Antebellum America* (Albany, 1984).

[136] David Brion Davis, 'The Movement to Abolish Capital Punishment in America, 1787–1861,' *American Historical Review*, LXIII (1957), 23–46; David Rothman, *The Discovery of the Asylum* (Boston, 1971), 59–62; Lawrence M. Friedman, *A History of American Law* (New York), 248–50.

[137] U.S. v. Bevans, 3 Wheaton 336 (1818). Story to Henry Wheaton, April 8, April 10, 1818, Story, *Life and Letters*, i, 303–05. Story wrote that he would have adhered to his views if the case had been of a different nature.

Crimes Act that he had earlier given on circuit in *Butler*, expressed in extraordinary language his refusal to support the conviction of any man whose life 'may depend upon a comma more or less.' 'Upon such a question . . . I will never consent to take the life of any man in obedience to any court; and if ever forced to choose between obeying this court, on such a point, or resigning my commission, I would not hesitate adopting the latter alternative.'[138] Such sentiments bespeak concerns shared by others at home and abroad, within legislatures and judiciaries of both the states and the nation.

Accompanying such humanitarian concerns, however, continued to be opposing ideas of the proper limits of national and state power within the federal system. There had been general and genuine difference of opinion over the place of the English common law in the new United States because the way in which the new government under the Constitution was actually going to function was *terra incognita*. What was the meaning of separation of powers at the national level? What of the relationship between the union and the states? What, in short, was limited government? This debate did not spring with a tremendous battle cry like Minerva from the head of Jupiter, fully dressed and armed as well. Its nature was in the process of being fashioned in the early republic, and there were competing versions of what federalism meant.

It is doubtful that there was any such thing as a settled 'original intention' on the part of the framers of Article III of the Constitution or of the Judiciary Act of 1789. Nor was there widespread agreement that federal judges should have the authority to decide rules of criminal law in the absence of federal statute. The evidence for this is not conclusive.[139] Contemporary judicial opinion (insofar as we can discover it) was by no means settled *in favor of* a federal common law of crimes; the picture is far more muddled. The pattern, if there is one, may be the reverse if we differentiate the cases in which the subject matter is purely domestic, unflavored in any way by general principles of the law of nations.

In the category of domestic offenses, very real problems confronted federal judges for which the familiar English tradition of judicial function

---

[138] U.S. v. Palmer, 3 Wheaton 610 (1818) at 636–637.

[139] Goebel, *History*, supra note 3 at 622. For a contrasting view, see Charles Warren, 'New Light on the History of the Federal Judiciary Act of 1789,' 37 *Harvard Law Review* 49, 73 (1923); Edwin L. Dickinson, 'The Law of Nations as a Part of the National Law of the United States', 101 *University of Pennsylvania Law Review* 26–56, 792–833 at 792–95 (1952).

230 *Kathryn Preyer*

supplied remedy, sensible and effective. Why should substantive common law powers *not* follow the creation of the national government that the people, as Richard Peters had argued, had ordained to exist, giving it the power to protect itself? The fact that during these early decades the common law issue at the federal level is primarily one of the *criminal law* is important, for the criminal side of the common law remained as powerful a weapon as ever it had been in early England.

At the disposal of those who ruled, whether in the name of the Crown or of the people, common law jurisdiction to punish was a doctrine to be feared. Its potential reach threatened the liberties of citizens and the polity of each and every state. Far better such matters be confined for determination principally within the individual states, to be settled as local battles between legislators and judges dictated. Here may be the greater measure of consensus within a post-Revolutionary generation. Even though opinions favoring or opposing a federal common law of crimes do not always coincide with lines of familiar political parties, radical differences emerge between the views of Chase, Jefferson,[140] Pendleton,[141] Johnson and Rush, and those of Peters, Ellsworth (after 1799), and Story. Definitions of what the 'national interest' or 'public order' were most frequently involved heated political controversy. These in turn involved fundamental questions of federal-state relations and widely accepted views that the federal legislature had a broad authority over the federal courts. Only with the political controversy prior to the passage of the Sedition Act does a doctrine of a federal common law of crimes manifest itself in issues other than those touching international matters. Even Story's fury that the nation could not maintain its authority led him to look first to Congress, the popular will, for remedy, not to the common law for whatever power might be teased out of it for the judiciary. Opinion had, as Johnson said in *Hudson*, 'settled down' against a doctrine of a federal common law of crimes. From the outset, the idea of a limited federal criminal law was paramount. Efforts to *expand* this by resort to common law doctrine were deliberate and owing to political controversies. Those regarding seditious libel or the embargo or the War of 1812 are illustrative.

---

[140] See note 51 supra.
[141] Edmund Pendleton's article, 'The Danger Not Over,' printed in the Richmond *Examiner* in 1801, advocated an amendment to the Constitution that would declare that the Common Law of England, 'or of any other foreign country' in criminal cases should not be considered as a law of the United States. David J. Mays, *Edmund Pendleton*, 2 vols. (Cambridge, 1952), ii, 335.

Is there a relationship between the federal common law of crimes and a general federal common law jurisdiction over non-criminal questions? Tony Freyer's *Harmony and Dissonance* asks how the decision in *Swift v. Tyson* could have been a unanimous one since the majority of the Court in 1842 was Jacksonian Democrats 'who shared the values and political persuasion of the Jeffersonian critics of a federal criminal common law.'[142] *Swift* dealt with commercial issues, and its assertion of a general law claimed an authority to ignore state jurisprudence similar to that which had been denied in *U.S. v. Hudson*. This is, however, the very point. A distinction can be made between criminal and civil questions, and ideas about the proper limits of federal authority may take different paths accordingly. I think it likely that they did. Accepted notions of potential jurisdiction over commercial law need not find a parallel in jurisdiction over criminal law. Freyer argues that in the minds of antebellum lawyers and judges, the idea of a general commercial law was held independent of and separate from notions of state sovereignty or jurisdictional authority.[143] Conversely, however, the idea of a general criminal law was held separate from the idea of a general commercial law, but it was never held separate from notions of state sovereignty or jurisdictional authority.

The serious political challenges of the 1820s to the role of the federal judiciary and the Supreme Court would engender speculation in the nationalist defenses of commentators such as Rawle, DuPonceau, and Sergeant about whether the question of a federal common law of crimes was definitively settled.[144] Intense national divisions over matters of slavery would see the revival of issues relating to this doctrine.[145] Toward the end of his life, in the same year as *Swift v. Tyson*, Justice Story once more prepared a Judiciary bill that would have given to the federal courts jurisdiction of all common law crimes committed within admiralty

---

[142] Tony Freyer, *Harmony & Dissonance: The Swift and Erie Cases in American Federalism* (New York and London, 1981), 3.

[143] Ibid. at 37.

[144] William Rawle, *A View of the Constitution of the United States of America* (Philadelphia, 1825); Peter Stephen DuPonceau, *A Dissertation on the Nature and Extent of the Jurisdiction of the Courts of the United States* supra note 116; Thomas Sergeant, *Constitutional Law. Being a collection of points arising upon the Constitution and Jurisprudence of the United States, which have been settled, by judicial decision and practise* (Philadelphia, 1822). In 1824, Pendleton's article of 1801, "The Danger Not Over,' was reprinted in Virginia as the proposed guide for Andrew Jackson. David J. Mays, *Edmund Pendleton*, supra note 141 at 334.

[145] U.S. v. Reuben Crandall, C.C.D.C. (1836), Fed. Cas. #14,885.

and maritime jurisdiction.[146] He was again unsuccessful. The reification of premonitory notions of an extensive national sovereignty that Story shared with Richard Peters would have to await a later day.

[146] Story to Richard Henry Dana, July 9, 1841, to John Berrien, Feb. 8, April 29, July 23, 1842. W.W. Story, *Life and Letters*, supra note 76 at ii, 372–73, 402–04, 405–06.

PART III

THE HISTORY OF THE BOOK AND TRANS-ATLANTIC CONNECTIONS

Introduction

Mary Sarah Bilder

In the 1990s, Kathryn Preyer greeted with enthusiasm a growing body of scholarship exploring the history of the book in early America.[1] She read the new scholarship and encouraged more junior scholars to explore its relevance to the field of early American legal history.[2] As these two final essays reveal, Preyer's scholarship in the 1980s already had turned toward the physical means by which ideas had been transmitted across the Atlantic. She wrote in her essay on Cesare Beccaria that she wanted to explore "the agencies of transmission of Beccarian doctrine, the scope of its transmission." For Preyer, reception and influence could not be separated from the question of transmission.

Preyer's interest in transmission may have arisen in part from her growing fascination with book collecting. One of the first books that she bought was the 1778 Philadelphia edition of Beccaria.[3] She eventually acquired three additional editions that testified to his popularity in England and Italy.[4] She similarly owned a copy of the central text of

[1] See *A History of the Book in America: The Colonial Book in the Atlantic World*, ed. Hugh Amory & David D. Hall (Cambridge: Cambridge University Press, 2000).

[2] See, e.g., Mary Sarah Bilder, "The Lost Lawyers: Early American Legal Literates and Transatlantic Legal Culture," *Yale Journal of Law & the Humanities*, 11 (1999), 47–118; Alfred L. Brophy, "The Law Book in Colonial America," *Buffalo Law Review*, 51 (2003), 1119–43.

[3] [Cesare Beccaria], *An Essay on Crimes and Punishments* (Philadelphia: R. Bell, [1778]); Kathryn Preyer in *Collectors on Collecting*, Catalog of the Daniel R. Coquillette Rare Book Room, Boston College Law School, (2002).

[4] *An Essay on Crimes and Punishments* (London: J. Almon, [1767]); *An Essay on Crimes and Punishments* (London: E. Newbery, [1785]); Dei *Delitti e delle Pene* (Parigi: Cazin, [1786]), Daniel R. Coquillette Rare Book Room, Boston College Law School.

the second essay, Peter Leopold's *Edict of the Grand Duke of Tuscany, For the Reform of Criminal Law in His Dominions* (1789), bound in the Italian marbled paper of which she was so fond.[5]

As important as Preyer considered the cataloguing of editions and publication dates, this information was only a starting point. As she wrote, "Does familiarity automatically imply influence?" She sought proof that the editions were read. As a collector, she liked volumes that demonstrated use. She treasured a small law grammar with "a homemade leather binding" and thought her books should be displayed open at the Grolier Club's exhibit "because their covers are simply old, very worn with use, truly ratty."[6] As a scholar, Preyer searched in sources such as Thomas Jefferson's commonplace book, John Adams's diary, James Wilson's lectures, and numerous pamphlets and tracts for evidence of Beccaria's influence. Concerning Virginia and Pennsylvania between the 1770s and 1790s, Preyer argued that criminal legislation revealed the influence of Beccaria.

Even as Preyer sought to trace that "alteration of sensibility" about criminal justice, she did not overstate her case for Beccaria's influence. Indeed, she carefully sought to delineate aspects of Virginian legislation that were *not* influenced by Beccaria. Similarly, she emphasized the interdependence of ideas and local conditions. She suggested that "Americans seeking to discover secular justification for social order and precedents for the penal codes towards which they were groping found validation of their goals in Beccaria's treatise." She then cautioned, "The success of legislation was everywhere contingent, however, on the texture of local political issues."

Two decades later, Preyer's work remains timely. In the early 1990s, the 250th anniversary of Beccaria's birth in 1738 produced new scholarship within Europe, although as Brendan Dooley noted, "a full assessment of the originality and influence of Cesare Beccaria's accomplishments may still be a long way off."[7] In the United States, Beccaria's influence on the

---

[5] *Edict of the Grand Duke of Tuscany, for the reform of criminal law in his dominions* (Warrington, [Eng.]: Printed by W. Eyres, [1789]), Daniel R. Coquillette Rare Book Room, Boston College Law School.

[6] Preyer to John Gordan and Preyer to Morris Cohen, quoted in *Kitty Preyer and her Books*, Catalog of the Daniel R. Coquillette Rare Book Room, Boston College Law School (2006).

[7] Brendan Dooley, Book Review (reviewing *Cesare Beccaria tra Milano e l'Europa: Convegno di studi per il 250° anniversario della nascita promosso dal Comune di Milano* (1990)), *The Journal of Modern History*, 66 (1994), 404–7.

right to bear arms has been debated.[8] His relationship to the rise of the penitentiary and the decline of capital punishment continues to be explored.[9] As the editor of a new translation writes, "The invitation to revisit Beccaria today would seem to require little justification either in academic or practical terms."[10] Beccaria was, as Preyer declared, the "vital precipitant" in "a transformation of policies and procedures which altered the fabric of the criminal law."

Preyer's focus on the relationship between American and Italian criminal reform demonstrated the breadth of her scholarly vision as an early American historian. The vast majority of trans-Atlantic scholarship has focused on intellectual influences among American, English, and French thinkers. Preyer was intrigued by the mutual interest in Beccaria in America and Italy. In this final essay, she built on her work on the Virginia criminal law code to compare the way Jefferson and Peter Leopold, Grand Duke of Tuscany, had responded to Beccaria. In so doing, she hinted at the possibility of a larger trans-Atlantic understanding of the rise of the modern state.

Preyer's sensitivity to questions of causation and difficulties of proof are evident in this essay. The Florentine merchant Philip Mazzei was friend to Jefferson and agent to Leopold. Although Mazzei left Virginia with Jefferson's *Bill for Proportioning Crimes and Punishments*, Preyer emphasized that Leopold likely never received a copy as a result of Mazzei's capture by the British. A lesser historian might have been tempted to imply a more direct causal connection between Jefferson and Leopold.

---

[8] See, e.g., Saul Cornell, *A Well Regulated Militia: The Founding Fathers and the Origins of Gun Control in America* (2006); David Thomas Konig, "Thomas Jefferson's Armed Citizenry and the Republican Militia," *Albany Government Law Review*, 1 (2008), 250–91; Saul Cornell, "A New Paradigm for the Second Amendment," *Law and History Review*, 22 (2004), 161–167; David Thomas Konig, "Influence and Emulation in the Constitutional Republic of Letters," *Law and History Review*, 22 (2004), 179–82.

[9] See, e.g., Matthew W. Meskell, "An American Revolution: The History of Prisons in the United States from 1777 to 1877," *Stanford Law Review*, 51 (1999), 839–65; Jim Rice, "'This Province, so Meanly and Thinly Inhabited': Punishing Maryland's Criminals, 1681–1850," *Journal of the Early Republic*, 19 (1999), 15–42; Markus Dirk Dubber, "The Right to be Punished: Autonomy and its Demise in Modern Penal Thought," *Law and History Review*, 16 (1998), 113–46; Michael Meranze, "The Denials of Justice," *Law and History Review*, 16 (1998), 153–57; Louis Masur, *Rites of Execution: Capital Punishment and the Transformation of American Culture, 1776–1865* (1989).

[10] Cesare Beccaria, *On Crimes and Punishments and Other Writings*, ed. Aaron Thomas, trans. Aaron Thomas and Jeremy Parzen (Toronto: University of Toronto Press, 2008), xxx.

The comparison between Jefferson and Leopold revealed Jefferson's distinct ideology and the disadvantages of "the popular sovereignty of a bicameral legislative filter." Preyer emphasized that, "unlike Jefferson, Leopold thoroughly shared Beccaria's views opposing capital punishment" and consequently abolished capital punishment and torture. Of equal importance, whereas Jefferson's bill gave discretion to the jury rather than the judge, Leopold "preserved a central role for the judge." Despite these differences, Preyer saw both Virginia and Tuscany as "early modern states moving toward a criminal justice system that was more rational and humane but one that also could afford more effective possibilities of social control."

In the years that followed these two essays, Preyer continued her support for scholars working in the field of the history of the book. She became increasingly interested in the precise manner in which ideas from England, France, Italy, and Europe literally moved into American hands and into books for the common reader.[11] In 2001, Preyer spoke at the Cambridge Project for the Book Trust Conference, "Publishing the Law." She chose as her topic the many editions of Giles Jacob, in particular, *Every Man His Own Lawyer.*

Preyer had hoped to write a scholarly article on what she described as "an appealing new genre in law publishing, the self-help manual." She described Jacob as a "prolific compiler of practical works for lay readers" who "saw his publications as a way to preserve English liberty through a common understanding." Preyer did not live to publish her article, but it is fitting to conclude with her paragraph on Jacob:

The first American edition of *Every Man His Own Lawyer* was not reprinted in the colonies until thirty years after the first English edition. Although the title page announces it to be from the seventh English edition, "corrected and improved," the seventh edition was not actually published in London until 1772. Gaine, the printer and bookseller, reprinted from the sixth edition and substituted his own title page after changing the edition and date, doubtless to present the volume to his customers as "brand new." I was happy to come upon this example of one of the tricks of the booksellers' trade in colonial America.[12]

---

[11] See James Raven, *London Booksellers and American Customers: Transatlantic Literary Community and the Charleston Library Society* (Columbia: University of South Carolina Press, 2002); see also James Raven, *The Business of Books: Booksellers and the English Book Trade* (New Haven: Yale University Press, 2007).
[12] Preyer in *Collectors on Collecting.*

8

Cesare Beccaria and the Founding Fathers

Kathryn Preyer

Change in systems of criminal justice was a cardinal ingredient of the social and institutional change taking place in all nations of the Western world during the eighteenth and nineteenth centuries. Changing conceptions regarding crime, the criminal, the nature and purpose of punishment, together with the transformation of both the substance and procedure of the criminal law itself, are common denominators that link very different national experiences. It is commonplace to emphasize the degree to which this widespread ferment was directed toward the abolition of torture and the reduction in the use of the death penalty, and their replacement with schemes in which punishment was made more proportional to particular offenses. Yet the simultaneous transnational attention to these matters and the networks among those engaged in efforts to reform criminal codes remain, like the abolition of slavery, one of the most absorbing phenomena of modern Western history. In this process, no name is more familiar than that of Cesare Beccaria.

Condemnations of excessive penal severity and pleas for a reduction in the number of crimes for which death was the penalty have, to be sure, a long history in human affairs, but this history comprises uneven attacks on disparate aspects of penal systems prior to the attention given in the eighteenth century to reformulating the nature and purpose of punishment. It was Beccaria who was the first to develop the fundamental principles of a

Kathryn Preyer, Wellesley College. Originally published as "Cesare Beccaria and the Founding Fathers," in *The American Constitution: Symbol and Reality for Italy* (Lewiston, New York: The Edward Mellen Press, 1989). Copyright © 1989 Emiliana P. Noether. Used with permission.

new system of criminal justice. In his *Essay on Crimes and Punishments*, published anonymously in Tuscany in 1764, Beccaria attacked the penal system of his day, its arbitrariness and secret examinations, its torture and mutilating punishments. He argued that the purpose of civil punishment was not the punishment of sin or revenge but deterrence; its only justification was to prevent the commission of offenses harmful to society. To achieve this goal, *certainty* of punishment was more important than severity. Cruel and barbarous punishments were unnecessary. The right to punish existed only when there was clear and convincing proof of guilt. Secret examination and torture were unjustifiable because they provided no reliable proof. The true measure of crime stemmed not from heresy or lese majesty but from actions that harmed the public security or injured the private security of citizens. There was to be a fixed proportion between crimes and punishments calibrated according to the extent of the injury done to society. Crimes and punishments were therefore to be written in a code that every person might know. The judge was merely to impose the specified penalty for the proven crime. Major penalties were fine and imprisonment, and Beccaria was the first to advocate the total abolition of capital punishment.[1]

Scholars of the Enlightenment, as well as historians of penal theory and the criminal law, invariably include Beccaria in their discussions of the eighteenth century.[2] Scholars of the American revolutionary era have also long been aware that some of the "the Founding Fathers" were familiar with Beccaria's work.[3] But what does such familiarity signify? Does familiarity automatically imply influence? Such relationships are notoriously difficult to determine, and pronouncement regarding the influence

---

[1] Cesare Beccaria, *An Essay on Crimes and Punishments, Translated from the Italian; with a Commentary Attributed to Mons. De Voltaire Translated from the French* (London: J. Almon, 1767).

[2] Franco Venturi, *Utopia and Reform in the Enlightenment* (Cambridge: Harvard University Press, 1971); *Italy and the Enlightenment: Studies in a Cosmopolitan Century*, trans. Susan Corsi (New York: New York University Press, 1972); Peter Gay, *The Enlightenment*, 2 vols. (New York: Alfred A. Knopf, 1969), II, pp. 437–45; Leon Radzinowicz, *A History of English Criminal Law and Its Administration*, 4 vols. (London: Stevens & Sons, 1948–68); Coleman Phillipson, *Three Criminal Law Reformers* (London: J. M. Dent, 1923); Marcello Maestro, *Voltaire and Beccaria as Reformers of Criminal Law* (New York: Columbia University Press, 1942); Marcello Maestro, *Cesare Beccaria and the Origins of Penal Reform* (Philadelphia: Temple University Press, 1973).

[3] Michael Kraus, *The Atlantic Civilization: Eighteenth Century Origins* (Ithaca: Cornell University Press, 1949); Henry F. May, *The Enlightenment in America* (New York: Oxford University Press, 1976); Paul M. Spurlin, "Beccaria's *Essay on Crimes and Punishments* in Eighteenth-Century America," *Studies in Voltaire and the Eighteenth Century*, 17 (1963), pp. 1489–1504.

of any single author on the Founding Fathers will be inevitably flawed. Perhaps the central problem may be better put in another way. Is an examination of the influence of Beccaria on the Founding Fathers tantamount to inquiring whether the same changes in the criminal law of the post-Revolutionary United States would have come about in virtually the same fashion at the same time had Beccaria never lived? It is the agencies of transmission of Beccarian doctrine, the scope of its transmission, and, most of all, the context within which the putative nature of Beccaria's influence took place that require more precise delineation before satisfactory linkage, if any at all, can be suggested between Beccaria's principles and the politics of enlightenment in the age of the Founding Fathers.

Such queries present intriguing problems when one remembers that few Americans, even of that small proportion of educated elite, knew the Italian language, and only a handful ever travelled to Italy. There were few Italians in the new republic. One investigation shows but twenty Italians listed in the city directory of New York in 1790 and only eight in the directory of Philadelphia, the seat of the new national government. Italian culture was not widely known. Even the masterpieces of Italian literature were seldom available in the original, and remained untranslated into English.[4] Yet we know that even before the Revolution, some Americans were reading Beccaria's *Essay on Crimes and Punishments*. After its translation into French in 1766, this brief work speedily spread its gospel throughout other countries.[5] The first English edition, including Voltaire's *Commentary* by an unknown translator, appeared in 1767 in London. That December, Beccaria's essay was quoted by the *Virginia Gazette* of Williamsburg on the best way to prevent the crime of duelling.[6] By 1769, George Washington was ordering the volume from London for his young stepson and ward.[7] Blackstone's references to Beccaria in his *Commentaries on the Laws of England*, published between 1765 and 1769 and widely available in the colonies,[8] may have communicated Beccaria's theories to a wider audience than read the original. However,

---

[4] Howard Marraro, "Italian Culture in Magazines," *Italica*, p. 22 (1945), 25.

[5] Maestro, *Beccaria*, pp. 34–45; Phillipson, *Reformers*, pp. 83–92.

[6] Spurlin, "Beccaria's *Essay*," *Studies in Voltaire*, 17 (1963), p. 1499.

[7] George Washington to Capel and Osgood Hanbury, July 25, 1769, *The Writings of George Washington*, ed. John C. Fitzpatrick, 30 vols. (Washington, D.C.: Government Printing Office, 1931–40), II, p. 516.

[8] By 1776, nearly 2,500 copies are thought to have been in use in the colonies. Julius S. Waterman, "Thomas Jefferson and Blackstone's *Commentaries*," *Illinois Law Review*, 27 (1933), pp. 629–59.

Blackstone's references to Beccarian doctrine are so oblique or so generalized that we cannot be confident that substantial knowledge about it derived form this source at that time.[9] In June 1770, John Adams copied a passage from Beccaria into his *Diary* and later used it to great effect in opening his defense of the British soldiers in the Boston Massacre Trials.[10] Booksellers in Boston and New York were advertising the volume in 1771, 1772, and 1773. A circulating library in Annapolis and the Harvard College library contained copies by the latter year. American editions of the *Essay* were published in 1773 in New York, in Charleston in 1777, and in Philadelphia in 1778 and 1793.[11] At some time between 1774 and 1776, Thomas Jefferson, using an Italian edition, copied lengthy extracts from the *Essay* into his *Commonplace Book*.[12] These extracts would clearly be reflected in Jefferson's attempt to revise the criminal law of Virginia once independence had been declared.

It is important, however, first to note certain features of the Constitutions, often with additional Declarations of Rights, that were adopted by the various states in the midst of the War of Independence. A few examples will suffice. The Virginia Declaration of Rights, adopted in 1776, prohibited, in accord with English antecedents, excessive bail or fines as well as the infliction of cruel and unusual punishments.[13] In Pennsylvania, sections 38 and 39 of the Constitution of 1776 provided that the penal laws be reformed by the legislature "as soon as may be" and punishments in general made more proportionate to the crime. Sanguinary punishments were to be limited and workhouses were to be established to punish by hard labor those who committed non-capital crimes.[14] In Vermont, the Constitution of 1777 and its Declaration of Rights would take these sections almost word for word from Pennsylvania; they would

[9] William Blackstone, *Commentaries on the Laws of England: A Facsimile of the First Edition of 1765–1769*, 4 vols. (Chicago: University of Chicago Press, 1979), IV, pp. 3, 14, 15, 17, 18.

[10] *The Life and Works of John Adams*, ed. Charles Francis Adams, 10 vols. (Boston: Little, Brown, 1850–1856), II, p. 238; *The Legal Papers of John Adams*, ed. Hiller Zobel and Kinvin Wroth, 3 vols. (Cambridge: Harvard University Press, 1965), III, p. 242.

[11] Spurlin, "Beccaria's *Essay*," *Studies in Voltaire* 17 (1963), p. 1494. I am indebted to David Lundberg of Tufts University for data from his yet unpublished investigation of American reading in the late eighteenth century.

[12] *The Commonplace Book of Thomas Jefferson*, ed. Gilbert Chinard (Baltimore: Johns Hopkins Press, 1926), pp. 298–316.

[13] *The Federal and State Constitutions: Colonial Charters and Other Organic Laws*, ed. Francis N. Thorpe, 7 vols. (Washington: Government Printing Office, 1909), VII, p. 3813.

[14] Thorpe, ed., *Constitutions*, V, p. 3090.

be repeated in the Vermont Constitution of 1786.[15] Implementation of such principles in these states as well as others would not be simple or instantaneous, however, because it was so closely intertwined with the process of clarifying which English laws were to continue and which were not, a process that could take several years.[16]

Consider Jefferson, whose Bill for Proportioning Crimes and Punishments in 1779 represents the first formal effort in a new American state to transform the English penal law. This bill was the work of men who were lawyers long experienced in the public life of Virginia, and it addressed what they perceived as current local problems. Although ultimately defeated by a single vote in 1786, the bill represents a striking departure from the English law applicable during the colonial period.[17] It was conceived as a practical program of change, appropriate to the requirements of a republican state. The doctrine of proportionality was foundational. Treason, narrowly defined, and murder were the only capital crimes.[18]

Particular categories of murder were given different punishments: for petit treason and parricide, the body was to be dissected after hanging. Murder by poison was punished with death by poison. The body of a convicted challenger in a duel was to be gibbeted after being hanged. Perfect symmetry was achieved for other crimes against the person. No longer capital, rape was punished by castration, maiming and disfiguring by retaliation in kind. Forfeited property of felons went not to the Commonwealth but to heirs of the felon and kin of the victim. For crimes against property, which hitherto had been capital, a precise scale of *mandatory* penalties was set combining labor in the public works with

[15] Thorpe, ed., *Constitutions*, VI, pp. 3747, 3760.

[16] See, for example, John Dickinson to Thomas McKean, Feb. 9, 1784, on the subject of *habeas corpus*. Thomas McKean Papers, II, p. 77, Historical Society of Pennsylvania, Philadelphia.

[17] The text, together with Jefferson's notes and comments, may be found in *The Papers of Thomas Jefferson*, ed. Julian P. Boyd, 20 vols. to date (Princeton: Princeton University Press, 1950 –), II, pp. 492–507. No action was taken until 1785. Jefferson was then in France as American Minister when he learned that the proposal had been rejected. James Madison to Thomas Jefferson, Dec. 4, 1786, Jefferson *Papers*, ed. Boyd, X, p. 575. For further detail, see Kathryn Preyer, "Crime, the Criminal Law and Reform in Post-Revolutionary Virginia," *Law and History Review*, (1983), pp. 70–73.

[18] Only levying war against the Commonwealth or adhering to its enemies, giving them aid or comfort, constituted treason. Jefferson, *Papers*, ed. Boyd, II, pp. 493–94. In addition to the preamble reflecting the ideas of Beccaria, see Jefferson's explicit citations to the *Essay* respecting certain categories of homicide, punishments, and forfeitures, II, pp. 496, 506n; on bestiality, II, p. 497; on promptness of punishment, II, p. 497.

multiple restitution to the victim. Slaves convicted of offenses punishable by labor in free persons were to be transported to be sold. Both benefit of clergy and pardons were completely abolished.[19] Deterrence would presumably be achieved through the *certainty* as well as the proportionality of precise mandatory punishment. Certainty was as crucial to Jefferson as it was to Beccaria. In Virginia, as in England, widespread use of benefit of clergy and pardon had mitigated the penalty of death for many a convicted felon.[20] Now these English modes of alleviation with their haphazard and uneven application were removed in favor of an inflexible scale of punishment established by the legislature that would eliminate the intervention of either judge or executive in the criminal process.

In accord with Beccarian precepts, Jefferson struck at pardons and at judicial authority. "Let mercy be the character of the lawgiver," he had written, "but let the judge be a mere machine."[21] Although Jefferson did not completely abolish the death penalty, his design of labor punishments represented an effort to organize convicts according to Beccaria's teachings to make them useful to society and to themselves. Neither Beccaria nor Jefferson mentioned reform of the criminal as a chief purpose of punishment, and by modern standards, Jefferson's retaliatory penalties appear retrogressive or excessive. From an eighteenth-century perspective, however, much in his proposal came to grips with the problem faced by any who would limit or abolish the death penalty, a scheme of punishments to put in its place.

Pennsylvania offers a second example of change. William Penn's initial plan to eliminate the death penalty for felonies other than murder, to abolish corporal punishment other than whipping, to implement reparations to victims of crime, and to use the workhouse as a penal institution had constituted a radical revision of the seventeenth-century English penal

---

[19] Jefferson, *Papers*, ed. Boyd, II, pp. 493–504. The English doctrine of benefit of clergy denoted a privilege of exemption from punishment of death. Originally a privilege of the clergy, it had been extended by innumerable statutes to those convicted of certain "clergyable" crimes. After conviction of a "clergyable" felony, the prisoner would "plead his clergy," be sentenced instead to be burned in the thumb, and then released. The practice was an important means of mitigating in practice the harshness of the criminal law in both England and the American colonies. George Dalzell, *Benefit of Clergy in America* (Winston-Salem, N.C.: John F. Blair, 1955).

[20] Arthur P. Scott, *Criminal Law in Colonial Virginia* (Chicago: University of Chicago Press, 1930), pp. 319–21; J. M. Beattie, *Crime and the Courts in England 1660–1800* (Princeton: Princeton University Press, 1986), pp. 140–48, pp. 430–49.

[21] Jefferson to Edmund Pendleton, Aug. 26, 1776, *Papers*, ed. Boyd, I, pp. 489–90; II, pp. 498–502. Beccaria, *Essay*, ch. XXVII, XLVI (London, 1767).

code, which was made possible by the independence of Penn's charter for his colony. In 1718, however, the criminal law of Pennsylvania was brought more into conformity with that of England[22] and subsequent statutes increased the severity of punishments during the years prior to independence.[23] Not only some familiarity in Philadelphia with Beccaria's *Essay* at this time but the drafting of sections 38 and 39 of the Pennsylvania Constitution of 1776 by democratic radicals on the drafting committee[24] may explain the resemblance between these sections and the principles of both Penn's Great Charter and Beccaria's *Essay*.

As in Virginia, the business of the war delayed action until 1785. Then, Benjamin Franklin, the President of Pennsylvania's Supreme Executive Council, urged the General Assembly to reform the criminal laws by substituting a system of labor punishments for fines then in use. Those who could not pay them, he stated, applied in increasing numbers to have the fines remitted. Punishment was thereby defeated and the expense of keeping persons idle in prison became a burden on the public.[25] Chief Justice Thomas McKean headed a petition signed by his fellow Supreme Court justices and grand jurors to press the Assembly to act on reforms.[26] McKean and Associate Justice George Bryan had been among the Pennsylvania radicals a decade earlier, and now Bryan reported the introduction of the ideas of "the great Becaria" [sic] to the Assembly.[27] William Bradford, also charged with administering the law as Attorney General of the Commonwealth, was equally active in pressing for its reform. Writing of the bill to Luigi Castiglioni in August 1785, he attributed this "revolution in the penal code," which reduced the death penalty and replaced corporal punishment with hard labor, specifically to Beccaria, whose work "well before the Revolution" was common knowledge among "lettered

---

[22] "An Act for the Advancement of Justice, and More Certain Administration Thereof...," May 31, 1718, *The Acts of Assembly of the Province of Pennsylvania*...(Philadelphia: Hall and Sellers, 1775), pp. 88–96.

[23] H. W. K. Fitzroy, "The Punishment of Crime in Provincial Pennsylvania," *Pennsylvania Magazine of History and Biography* 60 (1936), pp. 250–57, pp. 262–63.

[24] Especially Professor James Cannon and Quaker Timothy Matlack. Richard A. Ryerson, *The Revolution Is Now Begun, The Radical Committees of Philadelphia, 1765–1776* (Philadelphia: University of Pennsylvania Press, 1978), p. 241.

[25] Benjamin Franklin, Message from the President and Supreme Executive Council to the General Assembly, Nov. 11, 1785, *Minutes of the Supreme Executive Council of Pennsylvania...*, *Pennsylvania Colonial Records*, 16 vols. (Harrisburg: Theo. Fenn, 1853), XIV, pp. 575–76.

[26] G. S. Rowe, *Thomas McKean: The Shaping of an American Republicanism* (Boulder: Colorado Associate University Press, 1978), p. 234.

[27] George Bryan Papers. Historical Society of Pennsylvania.

persons." Since independence, he continued, "the name of Beccaria has become familiar in Pennsylvania, his authority has become great, and his principles have spread among all classes of persons and impressed themselves deeply in the hearts of our citizens."[28]

In September 1786, the new legislation, with its preamble drawn from Beccaria, emphasized that the ends of punishment would best be served by hard labor. The act abolished the death penalty for robbery, burglary, and sodomy, replacing it with forfeiture and imprisonment at hard labor in public for a period at the discretion of the court, but not more than ten years. Other non-capital offenses, then punished corporally, were at the discretion of the court to be punished by fines and hard labor for up to two years.[29]

In the same year that Jefferson's bill was defeated, the Pennsylvania system began. Public convict labor swiftly however began to produce the opposite effect of that intended. Scarcely a year later, Dr. Benjamin Rush, a Quaker signer of the Declaration of Independence, attacked the idea that public punishment of convicts was a means of reforming them, or of deterring others from crime. Quoting Beccaria and referring to European experiences with the abolition of the death penalty, Rush proposed its complete abolition and the creation of penitentiaries in which convicts would be disciplined by hard labor, cleanliness, simple fare, and religious counseling to effect their individual reformation.[30] By the time the delegates to the Constitutional Convention gathered in the city in 1787, the new criminal jurisprudence of Beccaria was more widely known and accepted among leading citizens and jurists. In 1790, public labor was abolished in Pennsylvania and a penitentiary system established.[31] Simultaneously, debate in the first national congress on the first federal criminal statute stressed the doctrine of proportionality.[32]

---

[28] Bradford to Castiglioni, Aug. 10, 1786, *Luigi Castiglioni's Viaggio*, tr. and ed. Antonio Pace (Syracuse: Syracuse University Press, 1983), pp. 313–14.

[29] "An Act for Amending the Penal Laws for this State," Sept. 15, 1786, *Pennsylvania Acts of Assembly, 1785–1790*, 1 vol. (Philadelphia, no date, copy at Harvard Law School Treasure Room), pp. 128–37. The broad discretionary powers drew considerable criticism especially from McKean's political enemies. Rowe, *McKean*, pp. 235–38.

[30] Benjamin Rush, *An Enquiry into the Effects of Public Punishments upon Criminals and upon Society* (Philadelphia, 1787). Reprint ed. (New York: Arno Press, 1972).

[31] "An Act to Reform the Penal Laws of this State," April 5, 1790, *Pennsylvania Acts of Assembly, 1785–1790*, 1 vol. (Philadelphia, no date, copy at Harvard Law School Treasure Room), pp. 293–306.

[32] *Annals of Congress*, II, p. 1573 (April 10, 1790). Treason, murder, robbery, piracy, mutiny, counterfeiting public securities, and accessories to these crimes were punished by death. Other offenses were punished by imprisonment and/or fine. Benefit of clergy was prohibited. *United States Statutes at Large*, I, p. 112 (April 30, 1790). Amendments

Beccaria's name had by then become more of a household word than most. Jefferson, advising a prospective law student in 1790, arranged a reading list of forty volumes for the young man. Of these, it is only Beccaria and Blackstone which are listed without title.[33] Jefferson clearly assumed that anyone who professed an interest in law would already know the name of Beccaria. James Wilson, Associate Justice of the Supreme Court of the United States, in his 1790 lectures on law to students in Philadelphia repeatedly quoted Beccaria on the need for reformation of the criminal law.[34] When John Breckinridge moved from Virginia to Kentucky in 1791, Beccaria accompanied him.[35] Harry Innes, later the first federal judge on that frontier, had owned Beccaria's *Essay* since 1785.[36] Another owner was St. George Tucker, the Virginia judge and law professor at William and Mary.[37] Examples can be multiplied. Beccaria was progressively becoming a staple in the libraries of respected lawyers and judges. In 1792, when Dr. Rush published another tract devoted solely to the abolition of the death penalty, his argument from Beccaria was even more extensive.[38] When Governor Thomas Mifflin requested William Bradford, now a judge of the Supreme Court of Pennsylvania, to draw up a proposal on the subject of capital punishment,[39] he found a seasoned spokesman in this cause. Bradford's own experience as a trial judge confirmed for him, so he wrote to his wife, that capital punishment was ineffective as a deterrent and drove jurors to acquit against clear evidence.[40] In his famous tract of 1793, Bradford advocated abolition of the death penalty for all felonies except premeditated murder. Quoting

to the Constitution, forced upon it by its critics, were also in the process of enactment but were not ratified until December 1791. A sufficient consensus of opinion in the states would guarantee by the eighth amendment that "Excessive bail shall not be required nor excessive fines imposed, nor cruel and unusual punishment inflicted."

[33] Jefferson to John Garland Jefferson, June 11, 1790, Jefferson, *Papers*, ed. Boyd, XVI, p. 481.

[34] *The Works of James Wilson*, ed. Robert G. McCloskey, 2 vols. (Cambridge: Harvard University Press, 1967), II, pp. 616–18, 495, 501, 535, 624, 634, 693, 694.

[35] Richard Beale Davis, *Intellectual Life in Jefferson's Virginia* (Cambridge: Harvard University Press, 1964), p. 82.

[36] Mary K. Bonsteel Tachau, *Federal Courts in the Early Republic–Kentucky, 1789–1816* (Princeton: Princeton University Press, 1978), p. 208.

[37] Davis, *Intellectual Life*, p. 94.

[38] Benjamin Rush, *Considerations on the Injustice and Impolicy of Punishing Murder by Death* (Philadelphia, 1792). Reprint ed. (New York: Arno Press, 1972).

[39] See Advertisement preceding the Introduction to William Bradford, *An Enquiry How Far the Punishment of Death is Necessary in Pennsylvania* (Philadelphia: 1793). Reprint ed. (New York: Arno Press, 1972).

[40] William Bradford to Susan Bradford, May 21, 1793, Bradford Papers, Wallace Collection, II, p. 76. Historical Society of Pennsylvania.

Beccaria, he argued not only from Beccaria's theoretical position but from the experience of Pennsylvania with its earlier reduction in the use of this punishment and that of certain European nations with its abolition.[41] In Vermont, where capital punishment had also been reduced, Bradford's counterpart, Justice Nathaniel Chipman of the Vermont Supreme Court, in 1793 also virtually copied the familiar words of Beccaria to authenticate his conviction that the prevention of crime was the sole purpose of punishment and that certainty, not severity, made punishment effective. For the inefficacy of the latter, Chipman too had his own experience as a judge on which to rely.[42]

In 1794, the reform legislation adopted in Pennsylvania inaugurated a new era in criminal jurisprudence in America, one grounded not on the idea of crime as sin but on the Beccarian prototype of the relations between the social order and the punishment of crime. Capital punishment remained only for premeditated murder. Those convicted of other crimes would undergo graduated punishments of hard labor with or without solitary confinement. The term of punishment remained discretionary with the judges under rubrics set by the legislature; retention of pardon also reduced the certainty for which Beccaria had called.[43]

In Virginia in 1796, the legislature passed a new proposal to proportion crimes and punishments. It abolished the death penalty for all crimes committed by free persons except for premeditated murder. Directing the governor to purchase land for a penitentiary, it inaugurated imprisonment for all crimes formerly capital, including treason. In place of the Beccarian mandatory sentences of Jefferson's proposal, minimum and maximum periods of confinement, according to the gravity of the offense, were established. The power to set the sentence within this range was, however, given to the *jury*, not, as in the Pennsylvania legislation, to the judge, preserving from the earlier bill restriction of judicial discretion over sentencing. Restitution of value to the owner was added to imprisonment for property crimes, and a $1000 fine, three-quarters of which was to go to

---

[41] Bradford, *An Enquiry*, pp. 9–10, 55–59.

[42] Nathaniel Chipman, *Sketches of the Principles of Government* (Rutland, Vermont, 1793), p. 200. There was great demand for this first American treatise on its subject. Chipman sent sixty copies to be bound for sale in Boston only two years after publication. Roy J. Honeywell, "Nathaniel Chipman, Political Philosopher and Jurist," *New England Quarterly*, 5 (1932), p. 568.

[43] "An Act for the Better Preventing of Crimes, and for Abolishing the Punishment of Death in Certain Cases," April 22, 1794, Alexander James Dallas, *Laws of the Commonwealth of Pennsylvania*, 3 vols. (Philadelphia: Hall and Sellers, 1795), III, pp. 599–606.

the party harmed, became the penalty for maiming or disfiguring. Benefit of clergy was abolished, but in opposition to Beccarian and Jeffersonian precepts, executive pardon was retained.[44] This bill's sponsor, George Keith Taylor, emphasized an element missing from the Jefferson bill and from Beccaria' *Essay*, the moral reform of the delinquent. Taylor pointed to Pennsylvania as the model to emulate because the penitentiary system was morally desirable and had there, he claimed, also resulted in a sharp *reduction* in crime. This was the successful deterrent to wrongdoing, not simply the means to a more effective mode of law enforcement.[45] Proportional punishments and solitary imprisonment were to serve a larger penitential goal. An institution of moral correction as a means of providing for effective secondary punishment was Virginia's inheritance from Pennsylvania, not from Beccaria.

How may we explain the fact that these changes in the criminal system were enacted not when independence severed the colonies from Britain but almost two decades later? What suggestions can be made about the influence of Beccaria on the generation of Founding Fathers?

We must first glance back to the colonial period. Formal institutional connections with the mother country were minimal. Uniformity did not exist among the separate legal systems of the thirteen colonies, and diversity of practice within the new states would persist after independence. American "cities" were few and their populations tiny in comparison to London, Paris, Amsterdam, or Florence. Poverty was less widespread than in England or on the Continent. There were no famines. Although there were wandering poor, there was not starvation for vast numbers. Colonial political culture had enabled Enlightenment ideology to be more manifest in America.[46] However, by mid-eighteenth century, physical and economic expansion and rapid population growth, increased by the transportation of English convicts and African slaves, were accompanied by assumptions of a rising rate of crime, whether accurate or not, particularly a rise in crimes against property. Capital punishment for these crimes existed, as it did in England, but an appreciable proportion of those convicted were never executed. Juries acquitted a considerable number,

---

[44] Samuel Shepherd, *Statutes at Large of Virginia, 1792–1806: Being a Continuation of Hening Statutes at Large*, 3 vols. (Richmond, 1835–1836), II, pp. 5–16 (December 15, 1796).

[45] George Keith Taylor, *Substance of a Speech . . . on the Bill to Amend the Penal Laws of this Commonwealth* (Richmond, 1796), 7, pp. 10–11.

[46] Bernard Bailyn, "Political Experience and Enlightenment Ideas in Eighteenth Century America," *American Historical Review*, 67 (1961–62), pp. 339–51.

benefit of clergy rescued some, pardons saved others. Both before and after independence, legislators passed more severe penal measures to small avail in their attempt to develop an effective mode of law enforcement.[47] These failing, it became easier for legislators to become convinced that harsh penalties deterred not crime but the conviction and punishment of wrongdoers, that the "bloody code" served no useful purpose. Neither certainty nor proportionality characterized American penal measures until the 1790s, even though independence came in 1783.

The seminal period for a new jurisprudence falls between 1764, the publication of Beccaria's *Essay*, and 1783, the conclusion of the war with England. Between 1700 and 1776, only the writings of Locke, Hume, Rollin, Montesquieu, and Addison circulated more widely in America than did Beccaria. Sentiments of moderation and proportion in punishments steadily became more commonplace. Statistical analysis of the reception in America of major authors of the Enlightenment demonstrates the quickening pace and the scope of transmission of Beccaria's *Essay*. The increase in its distribution between 1777 and 1790 and between 1791 and 1800[48] coincides precisely with the initial efforts to reform the criminal laws, and then with the fruition of such efforts in Pennsylvania, Virginia, and elsewhere.

Americans seeking to discover secular justification for social order and precedents for the penal codes towards which they were groping found validation of their goals in Beccaria's treatise. The success of legislation was everywhere contingent, however, on the texture of local political issues. Where, as in Pennsylvania, reform of the criminal law was sponsored by judges, lawyers, and major political leaders, it came more quickly. Yet as important a formative influence as were activities of leaders, it is equally appropriate to note that in the American context, there was not as sharp a differentiation between judges, lawyers, and other citizens as obtained in other eighteenth-century societies. Though members of bench and bar were generally drawn from better educated groups in American society, no university training was required for the legal profession. There was no exclusive cadre of "jurists" or "lawgivers" at this early time. Training consisted of an ad hoc apprenticeship system – reading law in the office of a senior practitioner for a few months – and was

---

[47] Kathryn Preyer, "Penal Measures in the American Colonies: An Overview," *American Journal of Legal History*, 26 (1982), pp. 326–53.

[48] David Lundberg and Henry F. May, "The Enlightened Reader in America," *American Quarterly*, 28 (1976), pp. 262–71.

more analogous to that of the shoemaker, or other skilled artisans, than to that of the Italian jurist or the English barrister. Furthermore, a society where no censorship obtained, where literacy rates were high, where social libraries, newspapers, and journals were abundant and eagerly sought after was a society in which new ideas reached wide audiences. Beccaria was an important agent for change in American society because his message reached a public wider than the men of law. Beccaria spoke to a broad general interest in the formation of a new social order in which many citizens believed that the United States was positioned to exemplify their conviction that a more rational criminal code was within the realm of human achievement.

Recent revisionist scholarship has tended to minimize the reformist impulse of the eighteenth century, attributing change instead to economic factors alone, or to the necessity for social control of the populace by ruling groups, or to the relationship between the origins of the modern prison and the formation of the modern state.[49] Such interpretations have offered healthy correctives to earlier models that explained change *solely* in terms of the ideas of humanitarian reformers divorced from the social context in which historical change inevitably takes place. Yet, does the social context have no room for the examination of changed modes of thinking, of perceiving reality? No room for examining the role of those who convey that alteration of sensibility that in itself becomes an historical artifact, even though less subject to empirical quantitative analysis than other data? This is where the familiarity with Beccaria and his influence intersect.

During the time of the Founding Fathers, a new era was exemplified by a transformation of policies and procedures that altered the fabric of the criminal law. The significance of Montesquieu, William Eden, and John Howard should not be ignored or denied, for the relationship between Enlightenment attitudes, both religious and secular, and moral and ethical concepts are all part of the complex ideologies of criminal justice. Yet to consider the role of any of these reformers will inevitably be to return to Beccaria's *Essay on Crimes and Punishments*, which is the vital precipitant.

---

[49] Joanna Innes and John Styles, "The Crime Wave: Recent Writings on Crime and Criminal Justice in Eighteenth-Century England," *Journal of British Studies*, 25 (1986), pp. 380–435.

9

Two Enlightened Reformers of the Criminal Law: Thomas Jefferson of Virginia and Peter Leopold, Grand Duke of Tuscany

Kathryn Preyer

In August 1783, a young Englishman only recently called to the bar, while travelling with a friend through Paris visited the aged Benjamin Franklin, then concluding his service as Minister to the Court of Louis XVI from the rebel government of the American colonies. In his *Memoirs*, Samuel Romilly reflected that of all the celebrated persons he had met in his life, Franklin seemed the most remarkable.

His venerable patriarchal appearance, the simplicity of his manner and language, and the novelty of his observations, at least the novelty of them at that time to me, impressed me with an opinion of him as one of the most extraordinary men that ever existed.[1]

Romilly recalled that Franklin read to his youthful visitors some passages from the recently published American Constitutions and expressed surprise that the French government had allowed their publication in Paris, where they had produced a great sensation.[2] His companion, John Baynes, recorded that Franklin had contrasted Pennsylvania and Pennsylvanians with England, where, in Franklin's view, the maxim of Lord North's administration was that all men were corrupt. "Such men," said Franklin of Lord North, "might hold such opinions with some degree of reason, judging from themselves and the persons they knew. A man who has seen nothing but hospitals must naturally have a poor opinion of the health of mankind." Franklin voiced his belief that

---

[1] *Memoirs of the Life of Sir Samuel Romilly*, ed. by his sons, 3 vols., 2nd ed. (London, 1840), I, 68–69.
[2] *Ibid.*

252

England could never be reformed because that nation was "simply too corrupt."[3]

Baynes mentioned to Franklin John Howard's book on prisons[4] as "one of our best-printed books" and offered to send the volume when Dr. Franklin said he had never seen it.[5] It is not clear whether Baynes ever sent Howard's work to Franklin or whether Franklin ever read *The State of the Prisons*, but Franklin was neither ignorant nor unconcerned about the state of the criminal law. Earlier in 1783, he had praised Filangieri for his attention to the necessity of its reform, writing to that ardent reformer that nothing was more necessary.

> They [the criminal laws] are everywhere in so great disorder and so much injustice is committed in the execution of them, that I have been some times inclined to imagine less would exist in the world if there were no such laws and the punishment of injuries were left to private resentment.[6]

Two years after Franklin met Romilly in Paris, he wrote a paper on criminal laws that first appeared anonymously in a small volume that Romilly published in 1786 entitled *Observations on Madan's Executive Justice*; it was printed as "a letter from a gentleman abroad to his friend in England."[7] And of course Franklin, long before he came to France, was an observer of English law as it obtained in his own colony of Pennsylvania. Let me briefly say a few words about English law in the American colonies before turning to reformers in the 1780s, the decade that

---

[3] Baynes's Journal, in *The Works of Benjamin Franklin*, ed. John Bigelow (New York and London, 1904, 12 vols.) X: 240–259 at 241, 252.

[4] JOHN HOWARD. *The State of the Prisons in England and Wales, with Preliminary Observations and an Account of Some Foreign Prisons* (1777); *State of Prisons* (1780).

[5] Baynes's Journal, Franklin, *Works* (Bigelow), X, 258.

[6] Franklin to Filangieri, January 11, 1783, Franklin, *Works* (Bigelow), X, 66. Gaetano Filangieri's great work, *La scienza della Legislazione* had substantial influence throughout Europe. Vols. 1 and 2 were published in 1780; vol. 3 in 1783; vols. 4–6 in 1785. The third volume relating to criminal jurisprudence was placed on the Index. Translated into most of the European languages, an English translation by R. Clayton, *The Science of Legislation*, appeared in 1806.

[7] Franklin to Benjamin Vaughan, March 14, 1785, Franklin, *Works* (Bigelow), XI, 11, 11 *n*, to M. Le Veillard, April 15, 1787, XI, 310. MARTIN MADAN'S *Thoughts on Executive Justice* was published in London in 1785; a second edition in the same year prompted the rejoinder published by Romilly. Madan was converted to Methodism by John Wesley, took holy orders, and was better known in his own day as the author of "Thelyphthora" (1780) in which he advocated polygamy as deriving from Mosaic law and in accord with Christianity properly understood. This set off a greater storm in England than did his thoughts on the criminal law, which advocated making the criminal law more stringent. See LEON RADZINOWICZ, *A History of English Criminal Law and its Administration*, 4 vols. (London, 1948), I, 239–248.

witnessed independence of the colonies from Great Britain and the establishment of the new United States of America, the promulgation of "La Leopoldina," and the beginnings of revolution in France.

To begin, the inhabitants of the English colonies were predominantly, but by no means exclusively, English in background. Increasing numbers of non-English, especially from Ireland, Scotland, and the German states, in addition to increasing numbers of blacks brought as slaves from Africa, characterized the eighteenth-century colonial population. The Atlantic ocean of course physically separated the colonies from the mother country, and formal institutional connections with England were minimal. The administrative bureaucracy of a colonial service characteristic of nineteenth century British and European colonialism was virtually non-existent. Despite the fact that each of the colonies by the provisions of its charter was required to establish laws "not contrary" to those of England, there is not an absolute uniformity among the separate legal systems of the thirteen colonies themselves, and diversity of practice within the new states would be a continuing feature after independence.

The establishment of the colonies in America took place over a century and a half: the first, Virginia, in 1607; the last, Georgia, in 1733. (After warfare, Dutch New Netherland had become English New York in the mid-seventeenth century.) The particular founding auspices of individual colonies – the greedy entrepreneurship of Virginia (1607), the Puritan origin of Massachusetts (1630), the Catholic institution of Maryland (1632), the Quaker beginning of Pennsylvania (1681) – all have bearing on the subsequent local cultures of each colony. The nature and pace of change within each colony requires emphasis as well, for these colonies, especially by the middle of the eighteenth century, although pre-industrial, are not static nor traditional societies. Geographical expansion, economic growth, substantial internal physical mobility, and rapid population increase marked by widespread religious, ethnic, and racial diversity characterize colonial development and identify societies quite different from those of the European world at this time. Profound decentralization of power characterized the institutional structure within each colony; the widespread dispersal of authority to local communities, towns or counties, was as much a response to colonial frontier realities as it was to the replication of familiar English models. Such widespread local authority, coupled with the absence of an effective national or "centralizing" presence, and local conditions themselves complicate the consideration of the actual operation of the disparate American systems of criminal justice.

The sense of scale is also important as we consider problems of reform of criminal justice in the colonies and in the new United States after the war for independence ended in 1783. Increasingly, complex capitalism, class stratification, and urbanization were dynamics of American society as they were elsewhere in the eighteenth century, yet each of these features is to be measured on a far smaller scale: poverty was less widespread and the degree of it less abject. American "cities" were few and their populations tiny in comparison to London, Paris, or Amsterdam.[8] In considering the ways in which local conditions vary, it is important to keep in mind that the size, complexity, and quality of European and English life have no American counterparts in the eighteenth century. Yet comparable questions arise: To what degree did criminal acts take place? To what degree were there significant groups of lawless persons? To what degree were different members of society reached differently by the punitve power of the law in practice? To what degree did the penal law *per se* permeate the society?[9] These questions are central to consideration of problems of changes in the criminal justice system in any society, needless to say, but the different local circumstances of eighteenth-century America provide a framework different from European societies, and needs to be mentioned.[10]

Although, as in England, capital punishment existed for a wide range of crimes against the person and against property,[11] the evidence we have indicates that an appreciable proportion of those convicted of serious crime were not executed. Many of those convicted and sentenced to the gallows received benefit of clergy[12] and were released; others were

---

[8] Philadelphia in 1775, the largest, had a population of little more than 23,000. Lester Cappon, et al., eds. *Atlas of Early American History* (Princeton, N.J.), 97.

[9] More extensive development of these matters may be found in Kathryn Preyer, "Penal Measures in the American Colonies: An Overview," *American Journal of Legal History*, XXVI, 326–353 (1982).

[10] See Franco Venturi, "The Chronology and Geography of the Enlightenment," in *Utopia and Reform in the Enlightenment* (Cambridge, 1971), 117–136; Venturi, "The European Enlightenment," in *Italy and the Enlightenment* (New York), 1972), 1–32.

[11] LAWRENCE M. FRIEDMAN, *A History of American Law*, 2nd ed. (New York, 1985) 68–75.

[12] The English doctrine of benefit of clergy, originally a privilege of the clergy, had been extended to free men from certain crimes punishable by death if they could read or recite a verse from the Bible. During the region of William and Mary, women were admitted by statute to clergy on an equal basis with men, and in 1707 (5 Anne, ch. 6) the reading test was abolished. In 1732, to clarify the operation of the English reform in the colony, Virginia statute abolished the reading test and extended the privilege to women, slaves, and Indians. After conviction of a "clergyable" felony, the prisoner would "plead his clergy," be sentenced instead to be burned in the thumb, and then released. The burning

pardoned.[13] A considerable number, impossible to determine precisely given the inadequacy of the records, were acquitted by juries of their peers. By the last quarter of the eighteenth century, the colonies had begun to confront more serious problems of effective punishment of crime. Assumptions of a rising rate of crime, whether accurate or not, particularly a rise in crimes against property, assumed a far greater role than had been the case in the seventeenth century.[14] Many of these perceptions are most prevalent in urban areas with larger concentration of population, a greater number of poor, and more varied economic activities that provided for crimes against property. In urban areas, legislators met and attempted to remedy many of the problems with severe penal legislation. But capital punishment, whipping, or burning the hand as a prelude to receiving benefit of clergy were ineffective solutions. Neither certainty nor proportionality characterized penal measures at this time in the eyes of those who made the laws and administered them.

Rebellion beginning in 1776 achieved independence from England in 1783 and permitted the new states to confront problems of criminal justice free from the superintendence of the mother country. The American political culture had enabled Enlightenment ideology to be more effective in America than in Europe throughout the colonial period.[15] Fuelled with

served as a punishment and as permanent evidence that the person had received his clergy, a privilege that could be claimed only once. The device is an extremely important means of mitigating in practice the use of the death penalty in both England and the American colonies. Since the common law earlier had developed the doctrine that all felonies should be clergyable for the first offense, it was necessary to take away by statute the benefit of clergy in such serious crimes as treason, murder, rape, arson, burglary, robbery. The long history of benefit of clergy shows innumerable statutes enacted that declared certain crimes to be clergyable or non-clergyable, and the status could change, depending on the degree to which legislative bodies perceived the need for a harsher or more lenient criminal code. In England during the seventeenth and eighteenth centuries, although the classes of persons who could claim the privilege was enlarged, the number of offenses for which it might be claimed was reduced. This would come to be the case in many of the colonies as well. The Virginia statute of 1732, for example, although it extended the privilege to women, slaves, and Indians, denied it to slaves and to Indians for manslaughter of a white person, breaking and entering a house in the night, and breaking and entering a house in daytime if more than 5s. was taken. For discussion of the subject in the colonies, see GEORGE DALZELL, *Benefit of Clergy in America* (Winston-Salem, N.C., 1955).

[13] The important subject of pardons or commutation has not been investigated. Governors did not have the power to pardon for treason or murder as they did for other crimes. They could recommend to the Crown pardons for these two most serious offenses.

[14] Preyer, "Penal Measures in the American Colonies," *AJLH*, XXVI, 352–353.

[15] Bernard Bailyn, "Political Experience and Enlightenment Ideas in Eighteenth-Century American," *American Historical Review* 67 (1961–62), 339–351. Daniel Boorstin has

a fervent republican ideology that would castigate English criminal law for its bloody code of harsh punishments, the new United States could join other nations in the conviction that a more rational criminal code that made punishment certain but humane was within the realm of human achievement. Reason and humanity, watchwords of the Enlightenment, were easily identified with the successful republicanism of the new nation, thereby becoming central components of early American nationalism.

The Western world did not, of course, have to await the latter eighteenth century for the appearance of voices that condemned excessive severity of punishments or urged the maintenance of a reasonable balance between crimes and punishments. Condemnations of excessive penal severity and pleas for a reduction in the number of crimes for which death was the penalty have a long history in human affairs. That history, however, has a relatively uneven quality to it before the eighteenth century, when a simultaneity of attention came to be paid to reformulating the nature and purpose of punishment. By that time, changing conceptions regarding crime, the criminal, the nature and purpose of punishment, and the criminal law (both its substance and its procedure) are common denominators of these different national developments.[16] The principles upon which penal laws ought to be founded were subjects for debate in many places; laws governing the administration of justice undergo change, variations in kind as well as pace dependent upon differing national legal cultures. The ferment is widespread. It is commonplace to emphasize the degree to which this attention is directed toward reduction in the use of the death penalty (and on the Continent, toward the abolition of torture as well) and its replacement with schemes in which punishment was made more proportional to particular crimes. Related to this and no less important were the developments of methods of secondary non-capital punishments to replace death penalties that could be imposed on those convicted of crimes. It is not the sudden appearance in the latter eighteenth century of the notable European and English reformers – Montesquieu, Beccaria, Eden, Howard, and Bentham – to which I allude, but rather to an even longer history of discussion within the political classes and among jurists of the cruel severity and the ineffectiveness of

argued that "the notion of an American Enlightenment may best be described as a set of highly sophisticated oversimplifications." "The Myth of an American Enlightenment," in *American and the Image of Europe, Reflections on American Thought* (New York, 1960). For the contrary position, see DONALD H. MEYER, *The Democratic Enlightenment* (New York, 1976) and HENRY F. MAY, *The Enlightenment in America* (New York, 1976).
[16] RADZINOWICZ, *History of English Criminal Law*, I, 268–300, 399–446.

criminal codes. These precede the more rapid pace and concerted change observable in the late eighteenth and early nineteenth centuries.

Central to the vigorous reformist sentiment that can be observed among enlightened men in Europe and America regarding the necessity of an amelioration in the criminal codes of their nations was the principle of proportionality, that every penalty be proportioned to the offense. In 1793, William Bradford, Attorney General of Pennsylvania, began his *Enquiry* opposing the death penalty with a statement that the principles upon which the penal laws ought to be founded appeared to be fully settled. "That the prevention of crimes is the sole end of punishment ... that every punishment which is not absolutely necessary for that purpose is a cruel and tyrannical act" were, for him, principles that had become axiomatic, no longer subject to doubt. To these axioms, Bradford added a third, "that every penalty should be proportioned to the offense."[17]

Although Bradford spoke as though this were a *fait accompli*, his words more accurately bespoke the change in sentiment that was still *in the process* of coming to pass in England, Europe, and in the United States. Recent revisionist scholarship has tended to minimize the reformist impulse of the eighteenth century, attributing change instead to economic factors alone, or to the necessity for social control of the populace by ruling groups, or to the relationship between the origins of the modern prison and the formation of the modern state.[18] Such interpretations have offered healthy correctives to earlier models, which explained change *solely* in terms of the ideas of humanitarian reformers, divorced from the social context in which historical change inevitably takes place. Yet, does the social context within which historical change takes place have no room for the examination of changed modes of perceiving reality?[19] No room

---

[17] WILLIAM BRADFORD, *An Enquiry How Far the Punishment of Death is Necessary in Pennsylvania* (Philadelphia, 1793), 3.

[18] Some examples: DAVID J. ROTHMAN, *The Discovery of the Asylum. Social-Order and Disorder in the New Republic* (Boston, 1971); MICHEL FOUCAULT, *Discipline and Punish: The Birth of the Prison* (American ed., New York, 1977); MICHAEL IGNATIEFF, *A Just Measure of Pain. The Penitentiary in the Industrial Revolution, 1750–1850* (New York, 1978); JOHN CONLEY, "Prisons, Production and Profit: Reconsidering the Importance of Prison Industries," *Journal of Social History* 14 (1981), 257–75; PIETER SPIERENBURG, *The Spectacle of Suffering: Executions and the Evolution of Repression* (Cambridge, 1984); SPIERENBURG, "From Amsterdam to Auburn, An Explanation for the Rise of the Prison in Seventeenth-Century Holland and Nineteenth-Century America," *Journal of Social History* 20 (1987), 439–461.

[19] For perceptive analysis of humanitarian rhetoric, RANDALL MCGOWEN, "The Image of Justice and Reform of the Criminal Law in Early Nineteenth-Century England," *University of Buffalo Law Review* 32 (1983), 89–125; "A Powerful Sympathy: Terror,

for examining those individuals in a social body who exercise power, have influence by virtue of their ideas as well as their position? Or for persons who are in a position to convey that alteration of sensibility that in itself becomes a historical artifact, even though less subject to empirical quantitative analysis than other data? The simultaneous transnational attention to the laws of crime and punishment and the networks among those engaged in efforts to reform criminal codes is – like the abolition of slavery – one of the most absorbing phenomena of modern Western history. It is to several aspects of this to which I now turn.

Let me begin with Cesare Beccaria, whose *Essay on Crimes and Punishments*, published in Tuscany in 1764, was translated into French in 1766, its gospel spreading speedily throughout other countries.[20] The first English edition, by an unknown translator, appeared in 1767 in London. Shortly after, Beccaria was being quoted in a colonial Virginia newspaper, and we know that by 1769, George Washington urged his nephew to read the *Essay*.[21] In 1770, John Adams and Josiah Quincy quoted Beccaria to good advantage in their defense of the British soldiers accused of murder in the "Boston Massacre" trials.[22] Beccaria's *Essay* with the commentary by Voltaire was known in America immediately after its first appearance in France; it became popular in lending libraries and as a quickly sold item in bookstores.[23] Blackstone's references to Beccaria's theories undoubtedly communicated them to a wider American audience than may have read the original.[24] American editions of the *Essay* were published in Charleston, South Carolina, in 1777, and in Philadelphia

the Prison, and Humanitarian Reform in Early Nineteenth-Century Britain," *Journal of British Studies* 25 (1986), 321–334.

[20] COLEMAN PHILLIPSON, *Three Criminal Law Reformers: Beccaria, Bentham, Romilly* (Montclair, N.J., 1975; orig. pub. 1923), 83–92; PETER GAY, *The Enlightenment: An Interpretation.* 2 vols. (New York, 1966, 1969), II, 445–447.

[21] PAUL SPURLIN, "Beccaria's *Essay on Crimes and Punishments* in Eighteenth-Century America," *Voltaire Studies,* XVIII (1963), 1489–1504.

[22] L. KINVIN WROTH and HILLER B. ZOBEL, eds., *Legal Papers of John Adams* (3 vols., Cambridge, MA, 1965) III, 16 *n*, 231–232, 242. As early as 28 June 1770, Adams had read and noted the passage, which he would use at the trial. *Diary and Autobiography of John Adams,* I, 352–353.

[23] MARY MARGARET BARR, *Voltaire in America, 1744–1800* (Baltimore, Md., 1941), 23, 119. By 1789, forty-eight libraries and booksellers in different American cities are known to have had copies. This was the first of Voltaire's works to be published in America.

[24] See, for example, the references to Beccaria in Chapter I ("Of the Nature of Crimes; and their Punishment") of Book IV *Of Public Wrongs,* the final volume of WILLIAM BLACKSTONE's *Commentaries on the Laws of England,* a Facsimile of the First Edition of 1765–1769 (Chicago, Illinois, 1979), 1–19.

in 1770 and 1793.[25] At some time between 1774 and 1776, Thomas
Jefferson, using an Italian edition, copied lengthy extracts from it into
his Commonplace Book,[26] apparently also then copying extracts from
the *Principles of Penal Law* by William Eden, which had been published
in London in 1771.[27] These, together with writings on the criminal law
by Lord Kames and Henry Dagge,[28] are clearly reflected in Jefferson's
attempt to revise the criminal law of Virginia once he had written the
Declaration of Independence and once independence had been declared
in 1776.[29]

It is useful to keep in mind that the Virginia Declaration of Rights had
been framed by a convention in Virginia, and adopted in June 1776. The
Declaration of Rights required trial by jury in all capital or criminal prosecutions, specified rights of the accused, and prohibited excessive bail or
fines as well as the infliction of cruel and unusual punishments.[30] Jefferson's efforts to implement the principles of the Declaration in his *Bill to
Proportion Crimes and Punishments* would not prove easy because these
were so closely intertwined with the larger subject of the degree to which
English law was to be retained in the new Commonwealth. The process
of defining the laws of Virginia and clarifying which English laws were
to continue and which were not would take several years, and entangled
with it was the subject of the penal law and the administration of criminal
justice. Jefferson's *Bill for Proportioning Crimes and Punishments*[31] was
presented to the Virginia legislature in 1779 during the war but was not
considered until 1785. By that time, the war had ended and Jefferson was
in France, having succeeded Franklin as Minister to the French court;

---

[25] SPURLIN, "Beccaria's *Essay . . . in America*," Voltaire Studies, XVIII, 1493.

[26] More precise dating of different parts of the manuscript is not possible. See discussion by
the editor, GILBERT CHINARD, *The Commonplace Book of Thomas Jefferson* (Baltimore,
Md., 1926) 12–14. Articles 806–831, at 298–316 are the specific extracts from Beccaria.

[27] CHINARD, ed., *The Commonplace Book of Thomas Jefferson*, Articles 838–845, at 322–
326.

[28] HENRY HOME, LORD KAMES. "History of the Criminal Law," *Historical Law Tracts*
(Edinburgh, 1758, 1761); HENRY DAGGE, *Considerations on the Criminal Law*, 2 vols.
(London, 1772).

[29] For the textual analysis of Jefferson's *Bill to Proportion Crimes and Punishments*,
together with Jefferson's notes and comments, see Julian Boyd, ed., *The Papers of
Thomas Jefferson*, 20 vols. to date (Princeton, N.J., 1950) II, 492–507. For an analysis
of the problems of reform in Virginia at this time, see Kathryn Preyer, "Crime, the
Criminal Law and Reform in Post-Revolutionary Virginia," *Law and History Review* I
(1983), 53–85.

[30] Sec. 8, 9. FRANCIS N. THORPE, *American Charters, Constitutions and Organic Laws*, 7
vols. (Washington, 1909), VII, 3813.

[31] JEFFERSON, *Papers* (Boyd), II, 321–322.

there in 1786 he learned from his friend James Madison that the proposal had been rejected by a single vote.[32] Nonetheless, the bill deserves our attention, for it is the first formal effort in a new American state to break with the past and alter the English law of crime and punishment. Furthermore, the bill was not the whimsy of theorists but the work of men who were lawyers long experienced in the public life of Virginia. It addressed what they perceived as current local problems.

Jefferson's bill represents a striking departure from colonial practice, when the criminal law in Virginia closely resembled that of the mother country. More illuminating, however, is its amalgam of notions of retributive justice, of deterrence achieved through the certainty of severe punishment, and of greater humanity in the abolition of the death penalty for many capital offenses. What is revealed by a closer examination of a bill conceived as a practical program of change, appropriate to the requirements of a republican state?

Most important, as the title indicates, the doctrine of proportionality was its foundation, Treason, narrowly defined,[33] and murder were specified as the only capital crimes. Particular categories of murder were given different punishments: for petit treason (the English doctrine of murder of master by servant or husband by wife) and parricide, the body was to be dissected after hanging. Murder by poison was punished with death by poison. The body of a convicted challenger in a duel which resulted in death was to be gibbeted after being hanged. The forfeited lands and goods of convicted murderers went not to the Commonwealth but were divided between the victim's kin and the heirs of the felon. Manslaughter was punishable by seven years of hard labor in "the public works"; a second offense was deemed murder and punished accordingly. Perfect symmetry was achieved for other crimes against the person. No longer capital, these were punished in kind or symbolic of the *lex talionis*. Castration for rape and for sodomy, if a man; sodomy, if a woman, by boring a hole in the nose; maiming and disfiguring was to be punished by retaliation in kind – literally an eye for an eye – with land and goods forfeited to the victim, not to the state. In all cases of forfeiture, the widow's dower was preserved, and gone was the English law that made concealment by

---

[32] James Madison to Thomas Jefferson, December 4, 1786, JEFFERSON, *Papers* (Boyd), X, 575.

[33] Only levying war against the Commonwealth or adhering to its enemies, giving them aid or comfort constituted treason. Conviction of "open deed" on the evidence of two witnesses or a voluntary confession were necessary to convict. JEFFERSON, *Papers* (Boyd), II, 493–494.

the mother of the death of her bastard child evidence of her having murdered it. For all crimes against property that hitherto had been capital, a precise scale of *mandatory* penalties was set; each combined labor in the public works with multiple restitution to the victim (arson, five years hard labor and triple restitution; robbery, four years hard labor and double reparation to the victim, for example, and so forth). The definition of grand larceny was raised from the common law's 12 pence to $5.00. (Its penalty, pillory for one half hour, hard labor for two years and reparation to the victim.) Slaves convicted of offenses punishable by labor in free persons were to be transported to the West Indies, South America, or Africa, to be sold. Aid of counsel was allowed defendants, and, extremely important, both benefit of clergy and pardons were completely abolished.

The degree to which the proposal altered the English system of criminal justice was dramatic. Capital punishment for only two crimes remained – those considered most harmful to the safety of the Commonwealth.[34] For property crimes, hard labor and restitution to the victim supplanted all those formerly capital. For atrocious wounding, short of death, revenge as well as deterrence would presumably be achieved through the *certainty* as well as the proportionality of precise mandatory retribution. Certainty is as crucial as proportionality in Jefferson's bill. In Virginia as in England, widespread use of benefit of clergy and pardon had mitigated the penalty of death for many a convicted felon. Now these English modes of mitigation, with their haphazard and uneven application, were removed in favor of an inflexible scale of punishment established by the legislature that would eliminate the intervention of either judge or executive in the criminal process.[35] Direct revenge and compensation to the victim (or his or her heirs) resurrected a principle long gone from English law as punishment for crime, and unlike in Massachusetts, restitution was a novelty in the laws of Virginia. The public interest was served by the labor sentences for crimes against property, and the terms were relatively short; there were no sentences for life. The retention of the crime of petit treason and the special severity of its punishment as well as that

---

[34] Jefferson saw capital punishment as one different in its very nature, not simply the most severe on a graduated scale. It was to be employed only as "the last melancholy resource against those whose existence is become inconsistent with the safety of their fellow citizens." These words, appearing in the bill's preamble, are a direct quote from Eden. JEFFERSON, *Papers* (Boyd), II, 492–493.

[35] Beccaria had advocated an end to pardons. *On Crimes and Punishments*, tr. Henry Paolucci (Indianapolis, 1963), ch. XX.

for murder by poison may well have been aimed specifically at slaves and/or servants. The design of uniformity, certainty, and proportionality was to achieve the goal of greater effectiveness in enforcement of the law. If punishments were proportioned to injury, "men would feel it their inclination as well as their duty to see the laws observed."[36] Available statistics for the colonial period in Virginia show that almost one third of those actually tried were acquitted; of those convicted, the number who received benefit of clergy or were pardoned was three times greater than those who were executed.[37] Legislators might easily attribute the difficulties of successful prosecution and conviction to the frequent allegation that the death penalty for nearly all offenses increased the likelihood of a failure to prosecute or a failure by juries to convict, and thus ultimately fail to deter. I know of no criminal code so proportional in its design. Jefferson's bill does differ, however, from other Beccarian precepts for it reduced but did not abolish capital punishment. Punishments of labor in the public works (in Virginia, this was generally the lead mines) represented an effort to organize convicts according to Beccaria's teachings to make them useful to society and to themselves. Jefferson also shared with Beccaria the goal of a balanced system of penalties proportionate to the crime, and also believed that crime would be more effectively deterred by moderate rather than by excessively severe penal laws. Like Beccaria, Jefferson eliminated pardons. The mandatory penalties reduced the power of judge and governor. Jefferson seldom mentions reform of the criminal as a chief purpose of punishment, and by modern standards, the retaliatory penalties for petit treason, parricide, murder by poison and duelling, as well as *membrum pro membro* for sodomy, maiming, and disfiguring, appear retrogressive or excessive. One wonders what relationship such penalties, in Jefferson's thinking, had to the prohibition in the Virginia Declaration of Rights against cruel and unusual punishments.[38]

---

[36] JEFFERSON, *Papers*, II, 492–493.

[37] ARTHUR P. SCOTT, *Criminal Law in Colonial Virginia* (Chicago, 1930), 319–321.

[38] More than thirty years later in his *Autobiography*, Jefferson attributed the bill's defeat to the legislature's rejection of the Beccarian principle of the inefficacy of the death penalty. He did not recall, he then wrote, how the "revolting principle" of the *lex talionis* had been approved by the revisors, "the modern mind having left it far in the rear of its advances." PAUL L. FORD, ed., *The Writings of Thomas Jefferson*, 12 vols. (New York and London, 1904–1905), I, 69. Jefferson's affection for the ancient common law of the Anglo-Saxons may explain some of this, for maiming and rape were capital felonies in these early codes. No evidence, however, exists that would shed light on Jefferson's thinking about this subject, although in Query XIV of his *Notes on Virginia* published in France in 1784–85, he described the revised code. *Writings* (Ford, ed.) III, 250–251.

From an eighteenth-century perspective, however, much in Jefferson's bill comes to grips with a basic problem faced by those who would limit or abolish capital punishment. What was to be put in its place? Jefferson's Italian friend Philip Mazzei[39] was carrying a copy of this bill with him to France and Tuscany when he left Virginia in 1779 as agent for the Commonwealth. The bills were apparently taken when Mazzei was captured en route and imprisoned by the British; they were never recovered.[40] Had they reached the Archduke Leopold, he would doubtless have found Jefferson's plan an interesting one.

From the time of his accession to the Duchy of Tuscany in 1765, Leopold had interested himself in reform of earlier criminal codes. As much a believer in personal autocracy as he was in reform, Leopold confronted the economic and social problems of his duchy with a vigor that reached broadly into every aspect of the administration of his state. An extraordinary man of vast learning, Leopold dominated reformism in

[39] Jefferson's activities at this time were as well known to his friend and neighbor, the Florentine merchant Philip Mazzei, as they were to Virginians. Mazzei arrived in Virginia in 1773 from London, where he had lived for nearly twenty years, meeting there in 1767 Benjamin Franklin, Thomas Adams of Virginia, and other Americans. At their suggestion, he decided to move to Virginia, intending to plant Italian grapes. He took ten winegrowers with him and was given by Jefferson two thousand acres of land adjacent to Monticello on which Jefferson's slaves built his estate, Colle, while Mazzei stayed at Jefferson's home. Arriving at a time of great tension between the colonies and Great Britain, Mazzei became keenly interested in politics and gave speeches, wrote for the press, and participated in the local political scene on behalf of the colonial cause. He translated the Declaration of Independence into Italian and sent a copy to Grand Duke Leopold of Tuscany. In 1779, Mazzei took the oath of allegiance to Virginia and was appointed as an agent to Leopold to obtain aid for Virginia. Arriving in Florence in October 1780, he wrote to Leopold explaining "the causes and ideals of the Revolution" and the advantages that Tuscany might derive by aiding the colonies toward independence from Great Britain. Mazzei flattered the Grand Duke that in Virginia his name was "eagerly and widely mentioned with every sign of respect and gratitude" and that through Jefferson and Franklin (and indirectly, by implication, through his own good offices) he, the Grand Duke, "soon became known, beloved and esteemed everywhere in the States." Philip Mazzei to Grand Duke Leopold, May, 1781, Howard B. Marraro, "Mazzei's Correspondence with the Grand Duke of Tuscany during his American Mission," *William and Mary Quarterly*, ser. 2, 22: 277–280. There is no indication in either Mazzei's letters or his *Memoirs* that he and the Grand Duke ever actually spoke about the criminal law of Virginia or Tuscany.

[40] It is possible that Jefferson had the Bill printed in 1779, for Mazzei asserted that five of Jefferson's proposals to the legislature were seized. Mazzei to Jefferson, March 19, 1780, JEFFERSON, *Papers* (Boyd), III, 319. Elsewhere, Mazzei wrote that the papers also included the bill on liberty of religion, one on the qualifications for citizenship, and two on public establishments for education. Mazzei to Sir George Collier, May 9, 1783. PHILIP MAZZEI, *Memoirs of the Life and Peregrinations of the Florentine Philip Mazzei 1730–1816*, transl. Howard R. Marraro (New York, 1942), 229–230.

Tuscany. The reconstruction of local administration, the modification of the vestiges of feudalism, reform of taxation, the customs system and economic policies, the abolition of guilds and religious policy are of a piece with his efforts to reform the criminal law. All are consonant with the pervading concern for public good and for moral improvement. All the new policies had strongly humanitarian goals. Indeed, the centralization of the state by administrative rationalization was intended as a means to achieve the greater well-being of the people of Tuscany as well as a greater measure of social order.[41] No head of state identified more fully with the goals of the Enlightenment philosophes than Leopold. In this great creative period of history, he stands out as one of the most notable of lumières and must be counted among others whose work in jurisprudence, penology, and economics was immediately effective. Although only Beccaria attained such widespread and lasting international fame, the impact in some of the Italian states of Palmieri, Filangieri, and Verri, as well as Beccaria, was substantial. In Tuscany, Leopold himself was the leader of reform. Beccaria had been encouraged by Pietro Verri and instructed by Alessandro Verri, whose office in Lombardy as "Protector of Prisoners" enabled him to know first hand the system of criminal justice. Beccaria was neither ignorant of nor unrealistically utopian about the value of reform in the laws of crime and punishment.[42] As the leading scholar of the Italian Enlightenment has written, "Logical strictness and eighteenth-century philanthropy, utilitarianism and sensitivity, combined to give us *On Crimes and Punishments.*"[43]

Leopold, impressed by the writings of Beccaria and aware himself of the chaotic administration as well as the disproportionate and cruel punishments of the criminal law, began to experiment with a number of reforms through ordinances and instructions. Unlike Jefferson in Virginia, Leopold's experiments would not have to pass through the popular sovereignty of a bicameral legislative filter before they could take effect. By 1786, the year that Jefferson's proposal was defeated by the Virginia legislature, the Archduke was sufficiently convinced of the efficacy of his endeavors to promulgate a remarkable new criminal code for Tuscany.[44]

---

[41] STUART WOOLF, *A History of Italy 1700–1860: The Social Constraints of Political Change* (London, 1979), 104–107.

[42] PHILLIPSON, *Three Criminal Law Reformers,* 6–9.

[43] FRANCO VENTURI, "Cesare Beccaria and Legal Reform," in *Italy and the Enlightenment,* 154–164.

[44] *Edict of the Grand Duke of Tuscany, for the Reform of Criminal Law in His Dominions.* Warrington, 1789. The English translation of *Riforma della Legislazione Criminale*

Leopold's preface to the code enunciated Beccarian principles clearly.

With the utmost satisfaction to our paternal feelings, we have at length perceived, that the mitigation of punishments, joined to a most scrupulous attention to prevent crimes, and also a great dispatch in the trials, together with a certainty and suddenness of punishment to real delinquents, has, instead of increasing the number of crimes, considerably diminished that of the smaller ones, and rendered those of an atrocious nature very rare: we have therefore come to a determination, not to defer any longer the reform of the said criminal laws ...[45]

Milder penalties, certainty of punishments, speed of trial, so Leopold claimed, had actually reduced the number of crimes in Tuscany, a region known hitherto as much for its murders and violent robberies as for the rigors of its criminal code with the rack, wheel, and gallows.[46]

The most striking innovation was the complete abolition of torture and capital punishment "as useless things which do not fulfill the object society aims at."[47] Unlike Jefferson, Leopold throughly shared Beccaria's views opposing capital punishment.[48] Leopold's code, however, did not appear to question the right of the state to impose that penalty, but rather sought a rationalized system of non-capital punishments in the interest of more effective criminal justice, diminishing crime, and improving social control. Leopold's code, like Jefferson's proposal, is particularly interesting in the answers it supplied for the major question left unanswered by Beccaria: what form of punishment for crime was to replace capital punishment? Like Jefferson's proposal, the foundation of Leopold's code was the doctrine of proportionality.

As important as the abolition of torture and of capital punishment[49] was the code's abolition of *lèse majesté* and all the crimes entitled *lèse majesté* "as having their principal source in the despotism of the Roman empire, and as not being admissible in any well regulated society."[50]

Toscana, November 30, 1786, was edited by John Howard, the English reformer and author of *The State of the Prisons*. The copy of the English translation of Leopold's *Edict* in the Houghton Library at Harvard University contains in a contemporary hand these words: "Reader! this pen shall inform thee that the Philanth[ropist?] Howard caused to be translated, printed and distributed this pamphlet, which like its editor breathes the sentiments of justice and benevolence!" Citations below to the *Edict* are taken from this English translation.

[45] *Edict*, 2.
[46] PHILLIPSON, *Three Criminal Law Reformers*, 95–96.
[47] *Edict*, 2.
[48] The only other ruler to do so was Leopold's brother, Joseph II of Austria.
[49] *Edict*, ch. XXXIII, LI.
[50] *Edict*, ch. LXII.

Such acts – robbery, for example – were henceforth to be regarded as ordinary transgressions and punished as such without the pretext of *lèse majesté* or high treason, which had formerly been annexed by the law and warranted the most severe of penalties. Henceforth all transgressions against the security, liberty, and tranquillity of the government without exception were to be classed as "public violences" and liable for a degree of punishment that would accord with the greater or lesser degree of the offense. Sweeping away the wide range of offenses that had constituted *lèse majesté*, and making the penalty proportional to the gravity of the offense, would presumably spare some Tuscans the horrors of the past. In the code, public labor for life replaced capital punishment for capital crimes. These felons were to wear an iron ring on the foot as well as a double chain, to be barefooted and employed in "the most difficult and fatiguing occupations." They were also to wear clothes of distinctive color and shape bearing a label indentifying their crime together with the words "the last punishment."[51]

Punishments for crimes less serious in nature included pecuniary fines, lashes administered in private, banishment from the jurisdiction or from the duchy, and "for vagabonds, quacks, begging foreigners, foreigners who transgress and calumniators," the pillory, public flogging, or public flogging on an ass. Between the penalties for minor offenses and the penalty of public labor for life for capital crimes were public labor punishments for various terms of years scaled to the nature of the offense. For men, these terms were for 3, 5, 7, 10, 15, 20 years, with a label identifying the crime to be worn on their clothing. Those who escaped received ten years additional labor. Women were sent to the Bridewell, or house of correction, to have their hair cut and to labor for terms ranging from one year to life imprisonment. Women who were condemned for life were to be clothed differently from the others and to have a label sewed to their clothes on which was written "the last punishment."[52] The former custom of allowing persons condemned for life to petition for their liberty after thirty years "as if they became entitled to it" was abolished.[53]

New protections for those accused of crime were introduced. Nonappearance was no longer construed as confession of guilt; confiscation of property was curtailed; the obligation upon Tuscans to kill without trial persons accused of murder was abolished; the use of secret evidence

---

[51] *Edict*, ch. LII, LV.
[52] *Edict*, ch. LV.
[53] *Edict*, ch. LIII.

was forbidden. A lawyer was to be appointed on behalf of accused persons too poor to have one, and the lawyer was given the right to speak with the defendant. The prisoner was empowered to confront witnesses against him and to question them in the presence of the judge.[54]

Although punishments involving mutilation of limbs had not been employed in Tuscany, according to the language of the code, "for many years," they remained legally available in different statutes of the duchy. These statutes were abolished by Leopold's code, and judges and tribunals were forbidden to brand prisoners with a red-hot iron or to employ the *strappado* either as punishment or in police procedures. They were ordered to destroy the gallows and the pullies and cords used for the *strappado*.[55] Though torture was abolished, the code simply provided that truth was to be gained "in the readiest manner" without specifying what that manner was to be.[56]

Perhaps gentler interrogation by the judge or tribunal coupled with the end of torture and the death penalty were expected to induce confessions more readily, or the giving of evidence by witnesses. Such a supposition directs our attention to one of the chief differences between Leopold's *Edict* and Jefferson's *Bill for Proportioning Crimes and Punishments*. This is the role of the judge.

Jefferson's proposal had confined the judicial role in a fashion totally at variance with English criminal law and Virignia practice during the colonial period. After a defendant had been tried and convicted by a jury, it was the judge who pronounced the punishment he would receive. Through Jefferson's scheme of mandatory penalties prescribed by the legislature, the judge no longer was to have such authority.[57] "Let mercy be the character of the lawgiver," Jefferson had written, "but let the judge be a mere machine."[58] Where discretion was permitted by the legislature, it was to the jury not the judge that it was given. In the event that the punishments by retaliation for maiming or disfiguring ("by cutting out

---

[54] *Edict*, ch. XXXVIII, LII, XLIX, L.

[55] *Edict*, ch. LIV.

[56] *Edict*, ch. XXXII.

[57] In English law, punishment for certain crimes was defined by statute, with the discretion of the judge to impose sentence within a particular range. Other crimes known to the traditional common law carried penalties, which had traditionally been employed. Here, too, judicial discretion played an important role, ordering, for example, the number of lashes a person was to be whipped or the amount of a fine, or allowing benefit of clergy in felonies where this was permitted (but not required) by statute.

[58] Jefferson to Edmund Pendleton, August 26, 1776, JEFFERSON, *Papers*, II (Boyd), 489–90, 505.

or disabling the tongue, slitting or cutting off a nose, lip or ear, branding or otherwise") could not be carried out because that same part was already missing, Jefferson gave to the jury not the judge the power to decide which other part of the felon's body would be of equal value. Similarly, Jefferson's statute punished witchcraft by ducking, and gave to the jury but not the judge the discretion to add a whipping not to exceed 15 stripes.[59]

Leopold's code, on the other hand, preserved a central role for the judge even though it was somewhat curtailed. Leopold concluded his *Edict* with the statement that although he had established "the most general rules for the punishment of each crime, adapting and proportioning the same to different cases," the implementation had been left to the discretion of the judges. They were to act within his classification of offenses and scale of punishments. Notice the degree to which it was the judge who held the sole power to readjust according to the circumstances of the case: it was he who determined the magnitude of the particular offense and determined what number of years would be "proportionate" to the crime. For example, coiners of false money were now to be charged with grand larceny, not high treason, now abolished. A short labor term was specified in the *Edict* for coining a "small amount" of value. However, if the magnitude and importance "appear to the judge to be considerable enough to deserve it," punishment of labor for life could be awarded.[60] Similarly, for violent rape, the *Edict* specified public labor for a term of years or for life "according to the quality of the case to be determined by the judge."[61] Even though the rapist would not be executed, from the perspective of the condemned this discretionary gap between one year public labor and a life sentence doubtless loomed large.

Another reform of the *Edict* left considerable control within the discretion of the judge. In Tuscany, there was no precise equivalent to the English and American writ of *habeas corpus*, a writ to determine whether a prisoner is lawfully held. *Habeas corpus* served to restrain arbitrary arrests and to move the criminal process toward trial rather than toward excessively protracted pre-trial imprisonment.[62] Leopold's

---

[59] JEFFERSON, *Papers* (Boyd), II, 498–98, 502–504.
[60] *Edict*, ch. XCIV.
[61] *Edict*, ch. XCIX.
[62] Enacted by Parliament in 1679 to confirm common law rights, the statute, adopted also in America, provided a prompt remedy in many cases of illegal imprisonment and was regarded as the great guarantee of personal liberty. A person imprisoned was entitled to the writ directed to the keeper of the prison, commanding him to bring the prisoner to the

Edict addressed these problems in its provision that all crimes should
be tried, condemned, and punished within ten years of the time of the
commission of the offense; for misdemeanors, within five years.[63] How
closely does this comport with Beccaria's emphasis on the certainty of
the law and infallibility of prompt enforcement, rather than harshness of
punishment? The process would be judicially controlled. Technically not
a punishment, lengthy imprisonment *before* judgment even within the
limit imposed by the code would leave open the way for judicial abuse
of the discretion the judges were permitted by the Grand Duke. Aware
of this possibility, and in order that they not avail themselves of their
discretionary power "without the excuse of a solid and well-founded reason," the *Edict* required the judges to give reasons for their determination
of the specific punishment selected.[64] Judges of the Supreme Tribunal of
Justice in Florence and of the Fiscal Auditory of Siena were empowered
to alter decisions of the lower judicial hierarchy, and the former powers of the Council of State of Florence and of the Lieutenant-General at
Siena to do so were revoked.[65] Nonetheless, built into this new criminal
justice system was the role that would be played by the judges. Except
for the choice of torture and capital punishment, their discretion would
govern the system and could defeat any Beccarian notion of certainty and
uniformity.

What happened next to the plans of these two reformers of the criminal law? Leopold's efforts were directed toward a total transformation of
his state. Basic to all else was economic reform. The increase of production and a rationalized administrative structure was aimed to bring about
greater prosperity and public good, not simply the good of the wealthy
landowners and merchants. Famine and popular agitation led to divisions
about policies over the export of grain regardless of internal shortage. Disputes arose over the creation of small landholdings and improvement of
agrarian labor contracts to provide minimum subsistance levels. The need
to coordinate reforms resulted in new administrative arrangements, and
local autonomies were attacked by changes of communal and provincial administrations. Violent reactions in Florence followed the abolition
of the guilds. Leopold's audacious efforts to achieve religious reform
of the Church in Tuscany divided his supporters among the clergy. His

court with the cause of his detention in order that the court might judge its sufficiency,
and either remand the prisoner, admit him to bail, or discharge him, according to the
nature of the charge.
[63] *Edict*, ch. CXIV.
[64] *Edict*, ch. CXVI.
[65] *Edict*, ch. CXVII, CXIX.

consideration of a constitution that would allow election of deputies with legislative powers came to naught. In many respects, Leopold's reforms had results very different from his hopes or his expectations. In his Tuscan laboratory of Enlightened reform, the promulgation of his new criminal code in 1786 may have been his greatest success, although a detailed empirical analysis of the actual effects of the code is wanting. How many persons received sentences of public labor in chains for life? For which crimes? Did the formal abolition of the imprecision of *lèse majesté* simply transfer all matters of public order into equally indeterminate charges against any opposition to the authority of the state? To what degree did procedures actually change, if at all? Much praise was lavished by contemporaries on Leopold's *Edict*. But how is its success best measured? By 1790, Leopold had gone to Austria to succeed his brother as Emperor. Twenty years later, the introduction of the French penal code restored the death penalty in Tuscany.[66]

How far the various new states of the United States underwent "revolutions" following independence from Great Britain has long been a debated question among scholars. In Jefferson's view, however, there were no doubts. Independence was necessary in order that other changes might follow – "the pulse of reformation," he called it. The *Bill to Proportion Crimes and Punishments* is only one of the bills that he presented to the Virginia legislature in his effort, like Leopold, to transform the polity of the Commonwealth.

This bill, as well as his bill to provide a free educational system in his state, were unsuccessful, and they are less well known than Jefferson's *Bill for Establishing Religious Freedom* (1786) or others that abolished primogeniture and abolished land-holding in fee-tail.[67] All should be seen as part of a single broad and energetic program of reform. After Jefferson arrived in France, he learned of a "highly recommended" prison design by an architect in Lyon, and inspired by its design for labor in solitary confinement, sent a copy to Richmond in January 1786.[68] The legislature had already killed his reform bill by a single vote; the rage against horse

---

[66] A convenient summary is WOOLF, *A History of Italy*, 104–107, 130–132.

[67] Jefferson scholars have customarily given brief attention to this bill in comparison to that accorded other Jeffersonian legislative reforms, perhaps owing to the paucity of materials regarding it, perhaps because it failed to pass, or perhaps because it does not completely accord with modern humanitarian standards.

[68] Jefferson to James Buchanan and William Hay, August 13, 1785, *Papers* (Boyd), VIII, 366–368; to Buchanan and Hay, January 26, 1786, *Papers* (Boyd), IX, 220–222. HOWARD C. RICE, JR., "A French Source of Jefferson's Plan for the Prison at Richmond," *Journal of the Society of Architectural Historians*, XII (1953), 28–30.

stealers, according to Madison, had influenced the outcome.[69] Each innovation of the bill may, however, have met serious opposition: the limitation of the death penalty, the principle of retaliation, multiple restitution from felons who were invariably from the poor and lowly, mandatory sentences, transportation of slaves, and an absence of pardoning power as well as benefit of clergy. Lacking records of debate, we cannot know.[70]

We do know that of felonies prosecuted in Virginia in the late eighteenth century, about one-third were acquitted by juries; a larger proportion were convicted, then clergied or escaped or were dismissed before trial. Proportionately few were sentenced to hang. The number of felonies is small in light of the total free population (crimes committed by slaves are not included here; they were tried by justices of the peace and not juries). Almost half the total was prosecuted in the court of the most disorderly part of the state; prosecutions for murder were about half of the number prosecuted for larceny, an extraordinary proportion. Despite the attention legislators in Richmond gave to increasing punishments, in 1792 successful prosecutions were no greater.[71]

Primitive techniques of law enforcement may have resulted in few felonies ever reaching the trial court and the court records. Its population settlements more widely scattered than in New England, Virginia lacked an urban center larger than 3,000 people, lacked adequate roads, lacked any semblance of a police force and had no prisons, only insubstantial jails for those awaiting trial. Felonies deemed less serious (for example, thefts of a few dollars value) may have been summarily punished with whippings or fines by local magistrates with or without statutory authorization. In Richmond, there was an increase in crime during the disorderly years of the Revolution and the 1780s, followed by decreases after that time.[72]

[69] Madison to Jefferson, December 24, 1786, WILLIAM T. HUTCHINSON, ed. *The Papers of James Madison*, IX, 225. Madison to Jefferson, February 15, 1787, JEFFERSON, *Papers* (Boyd), XI, 152. Jefferson later wrote that the general ideas of the country had "not yet advanced" to an acceptance of Beccaria's suggestions. *Autobiography*, 71–72.

[70] Legislative records for the period do not report debates. Newspapers that have been examined make no mention of the subject. Searches in unpublished letters of members of the assembly have produced nothing legislative, and executive materials, both printed and unpublished, have shed no light on this bill.

[71] For more detailed analysis based on the court records for the period in the Virginia State Library, Richmond, Virginia, see Preyer, "Crime, the Criminal Law and Reform in Post-Revolutionary Virginia," *Law and History Review*, I, 70–73.

[72] ROBERT M. SAUNDERS, "Crime and Punishment in Early National America," Richmond, Virginia 1784–1820," *Virginia Magazine of History and Biography*, lxxxvi (1978), 33–38; HARRY M. WARD and HAROLD E. GREER, JR., *Richmond During the Revolution, 1775–1783* (Charlottesville, 1977), 109–25.

Richmond was where the legislators were. If harsher penalties of 1792 had failed to improve the effectiveness of law enforcement, legislators by 1796 may have become convinced that harsh penalties deterred prosecution and conviction but not crime. Legislation to make criminal justice more effective by providing milder punishment became plausible. It is possible that there may have been relatively little serious crime actually being committed in Virginia, and it was therefore easy for Virginians to see the bloody code as an anomaly that served no purpose. The harsh and oppressive criminal code of eighteenth-century England, after all, developed out of the efforts to control or intimidate a large landless and unemployed population with an enormous concentration in London. There the thrust of the capital code was centered with increasing severity on crimes against property. This was very different in Virginia. Even though depressed economic conditions following the war may have produced an increase in wandering poor, marginality was not tantamount to starvation for vast numbers of human beings.[73] There were no famines. Theft and robbery may have been committed with less frequency and therefore be even less regarded as deserving the same punishment as murder or rape. A high degree of aggression did, however, characterize Virginia society. Jefferson's efforts to cope with this by the most severe of physical punishments coupled with forfeiture of property to victims can be seen in this light.

In 1796, the Virginia legislature passed a different bill to proportion crimes and punishments. This bill abolished the death penalty for all crimes committed by free persons except for murder in the first degree, defined as murder by poison and other premeditated killings. Directing the governor to purchase land for a penitentiary, the legislature inaugurated imprisonment as the punishment for all crimes formerly capital, including treason. In place of mandatory sentences, minimum and maximum periods of confinement, according to the gravity of the offense, were established.[74] The power to set the sentence within this range, however,

---

[73] The subject of the poor in Virginia badly needs study. Vagrancy measures of the later eighteenth century demonstrate legislative fears, but these may have exaggerated the dangers. One examination of Augusta and York County Courts reveals that neither heard any prosecutions for vagrancy. Nor was there a workhouse for the poor. JAMES W. ELY, JR., "Poor Laws of the Post-Revolutionary South, 1776–1800," *University of Tulsa Law Journal* 21 (Fall, 1985), 20–22.

[74] SAMUEL SHEPHERD, *Statutes at Large of Virginia, 1792–1806: Being a Continuation of Hening*...(Richmond, 1835–36), II (December 15, 1796), 5–16. *Virginia Argus* (Richmond) Friday, December 9, 1796. Penalties ranged from 6 to 12 years at hard labor or in solitude for high treason to restitution of full value, and 6 months to 1 year for petty larceny, under $4.00 in value. Details about the evolution and passage of

was given to the *jury*, not the judge, continuing from the earlier plan the restriction of judicial discretion over sentencing. Restitution of value to the owner was added to imprisonment for property crimes, and a $1000 fine, 3/4 of which was to go to the party harmed, was made the penalty for malicious maiming or disfiguring. Benefit of clergy was abolished, but executive pardon was retained. The legislature appropriated $30,000 to construct a prison large enough to hold two hundred convicts.

How can the changed reaction within the decade be explained? In 1785, at a time when massive waves of change such as new attacks on the established Anglican church, a law encouraging the manumission of slaves, and even petitions for the abolition of slavery were sweeping the Virginia legislature,[75] it is probably too much to expect that a proposal to end capital punishment by substituting imprisonment in a non-existent prison could pass. A decade later, after the reorganization of the courts was accomplished and the revisal of the laws completed, it may have been easier to muster support for an overall revision of the punishment of crime. Much else had changed as well. Economic depression had ended; greater fiscal stability might make feasible the appropriation of public monies for an adequate prison. In 1795, the legislature appointed a committee to amend the penal laws and, interestingly enough, to establish the first district poor houses and houses of correction as well. In 1796, the successful reform bill followed.

The eloquence of its sponsor, George Keith Taylor, included a new emphasis on the moral reform of the delinquent, totally missing from the Jefferson bill. His bill, Taylor argued, "is founded on principles of humanity; it professes to substitute a system of clemency and mercy for a code of carnage and horror; and it endeavors at once to correct, to amend, to save the Citizen." Stating that the time was an era of liberality in moral and political opinions, Taylor identified reason and humanity of the proposal with the successful republicanism of the new nation and

this legislation are as elusive as for Jefferson's proposal almost 20 years before. No debate is reported in the Journal of the House of Delegates and none has been located elsewhere.

75 See ALLAN NEVINS, *The American States during and after the Revolution 1775–1789* (New York), 1924), 194. More recent works such as WILLI PAUL ADAMS, *The First American Constitutions, Republican Ideology and the Making of the State Constitutions in the Revolutionary Era* (Chapel Hill, 1980), JACKSON T. MAIN, *Political Parties before the Constitution* (Chapel Hill, 1973), and GORDON WOOD, *The Creation of the America Republic, 1776–1787* (Chapel Hill, 1969) do not deal with these subjects, although Wood at 121–122 alludes to the extent of reforms that Jefferson planned for the new republic.

urged revision of the criminal law "to comport with the principles of our government."[76] Taylor pointed to Pennsylvania as the model for Virginia to emulate, not only for its humanitarian qualities but also because the penitentiary system there had resulted in a sharp *reduction* in crime. Introducing statistics from Philadelphia, he praised the convict labor system as morally and fiancially desirable. Here was the success-ful deterrent to the commission of crime, not simply the means to a more effective mode of law enforcement. Proportional punishments and imprisonment were to serve a larger penitential goal for wrongdoers. Immediately after passage of the bill, the Governor of Virginia wrote to Dr. Caspar Wistar of Philadelphia requesting information about Pennsyl-vania's experience as well as a copy of the plan of that penitentiary.[77]

It is not suprising that the model of Pennyslvania came into the argu-ment, for by 1796 the reformative incarceration instituted there had be-come well known in both America and in Europe. In an effort to make punishment more proportionate to the crime, the Pennsylvania legisla-ture in 1786 (the year Jefferson's bill was defeated and Leopold's *Edict* promulgated) substituted imprisonment at public hard labor for several crimes formerly capital. The plan was remarkably like that of the Grand Duke's. Wearing prison uniforms, bearing symbols of their crimes and fettered, these gangs of "wheelbarrowmen" were put to work in the streets of Philadelphia. Protests were not long in coming, especially from prominent Quakers and others motivated by Enlightenment rationalism or Christian piety or distaste for public spectacles. Influenced chiefly by John Howard, the English reformer, these groups pressed for a penal system that would bring about moral reform of the convict. By 1794, the death penalty was eliminated for all crimes except for premeditated murder; felons were to be punished by imprisonment in solitary cells for at least part of their sentence.[78]

---

[76] GEORGE KEITH TAYLOR, *Substance of a Speech . . . on the Bill to Amend the Penal Laws of this Commonwealth* (Richmond, 1796) 7, 10–11. Taylor listed as the objects of punishment: 1. Amendment to delinquent; 2. Example to others; 3. Retribution to the injured party; 4. Retribution to the public.

[77] "I have been induced to take the liberty from an anxious desire that no time should be lost in bringing this humane law into operation, and which is not to be in force until the necessary Buildings are completed." Wood to Wistar, January 6, 1797. Virginia State Library, Executive Letterbooks. Reel #5.

[78] An excellent recent analysis is MICHAEL MERANZE, "The Penitential Ideal in Late Eighteenth-Century Philadelphia," *Pennsylvania Magazine of History and Biography* CVIII (1984), 419–450. Also PAUL TAKAGI, "The Walnut Street Jail: A Penal Reform to Centralize the Powers of the State," *Federal Probation* XXXIX (1975), 18–26; THORSTEN

This would set a pattern for the future. The scheme and design of the Pennsylvania prison became models for many to visit, among them Benjamin Henry Latrobe, the architect of the new prison in Virginia. Old attitudes were being undermined, and in the next generation the criminal justice system in both Europe and America would become more consciously woven into the *process* of building the infrastructure of the modern state. In Virginia and in Tuscany, the earlier age of enlightenment and experiment had begun under the leadership of Jefferson and Leopold in a context prior to the establishment of genuine nation-states in either Italy or the United States. During their time, a new era had been exemplified by transformation of policies and procedures that altered the fabric of the criminal law. Both Virginia and Tuscany were early modern states moving toward a criminal justice system that was more rational and humane but one that also could afford more effective possibilities of social control. When young Samuel Romilly talked with Benjamin Franklin in Paris in 1786, he could add indirect experience of events in America to the activities of Howard and Bentham in his own country as he began his long and most arduous struggle to reform the criminal law of England in the next generation. The relationship between Enlightenment theories of moral sentiments, both religious and secular, and ethical concepts, particularly the idea of compassion, play very much into future ideologies of criminal justice. Understanding this, as well as the politics of enlightenment and mapping the spread of the zeitgeist from its cosmopolitan networks of reformers to the larger social body, becomes the continuing task of the scholar.[79]

SELLIN, "Philadelphia Prisons of the Eighteenth Century," American Philosophical Society, *Transactions*, New Series 43, Part I (1953), 326–330; NEGLEY K. TEETERS, *The Cradle of the Penitentiary, the Walnut Street Jail at Philadelphia* (Philadelphia, 1955); MICHAEL KRAUS, *The Atlantic Civilization, 18th Century Origins* (Ithaca, New York, 1949), 127–132.

[79] LESTER G. CROCKER, "Interpreting the Enlightenment: A Political Approach," *Journal of the History of Ideas*, XLVI (1985), 211–230.

Index

CPSIA information can be obtained at www.ICGtesting.com
Printed in the USA
BVOW05s1906010814

361308BV00003B/62/P